RISING ELEPHANT

The Growing Clash with India Over White-Collar Jobs and its Meaning for America and the World

Ashutosh Sheshabalaya

Common Courage Press   Monroe, Maine

Library of Congress Cataloging-in-Publication Data is available
from the publisher on request.

ISBN 1-56751-295-X cloth

Common Courage Press
Box 702
Monroe, ME 04951

(207) 525-0900; fax: (207) 525-3068
orders-info@commoncouragepress.com

See our website for e-versions of this book.
www.commoncouragepress.com

First Printing

Printed in Canada

There is nothing in a caterpillar that tells you it's going to be a butterfly.

—Richard Buckminster Fuller (1895-1983)

The Blind Men and the Elephant:
An Ancient Indian Fable*

It was six men of Indostan
To learning much inclined,
Who went to see the Elephant
(Though all of them were blind),
That each by observation
Might satisfy his mind.

The First approached the Elephant,
And happening to fall
Against his broad and sturdy side,
At once began to bawl:
"God bless me! But the Elephant
Is very like a wall!"

The Second, feeling of the tusk
Cried, "Ho! What have we here,
So very round and smooth and sharp?
To me `tis mighty clear
This wonder of an Elephant
Is very like a spear!"

The Third approached the animal,
And happening to take
The squirming trunk within his hands,
Thus boldly up he spake:
"I see," quoth he, "the Elephant
Is very like a snake!"

The Fourth reached out an eager hand,
And felt about the knee:
"What most this wondrous beast is like
Is mighty plain," quoth he;
"'Tis clear enough the Elephant
Is very like a tree!"

The Fifth, who chanced to touch the ear,
Said: "E'en the blindest man
Can tell what this resembles most;
Deny the fact who can,
This marvel of an Elephant
Is very like a fan!"

The Sixth no sooner had begun
About the beast to grope,
Than, seizing on the swinging tail
That fell within his scope.
"I see," quoth he, "the Elephant
Is very like a rope!"

And so these men of Indostan
Disputed loud and long,
Each in his own opinion
Exceeding stiff and strong,
Though each was partly in the right,
And all were in the wrong!

*John Godfrey Saxe, *The Blind Men and the Elephant*, Whittlesey House, New York, 1963.

This book is written in memory of my grandfathers, Rai Bahadur D.C. Das and Professor R.K. Das.

It is dedicated to my parents, P.N. Das and B. Das, who left Minnesota, Harvard, Columbia and Oxford, and returned to awaken the Elephant.

CONTENTS

CHAPTER IV: ... 134
The 'Definite Smell' of Curry—
How India Spiced Up America's Hot Industry

CHAPTER V: ... 148
The Elephant's Mounting Weight

Author's Note

Like almost everyone, this writer was surprised by the governing BJP coalition's defeat in India's May 2004 polls—while 'Rising Elephant' was already at press. Nevertheless, as would be borne out by its sixth chapter, behind the 'surprise', such electoral upheavals are to be expected, and only underwrite the stability of this complex country. For the world outside, they also provide a working answer to the what-after—that perennially uneasy question with respect to the other emerging giant, China.

As far as India's pull on white-collar jobs is concerned, the what-after is clear: more of the same. Exports of software, growing four times faster than gross domestic product, are clearly driving the Indian economy. While the BJP's defeat will result in some fine-tuning of policy, the new Congress-led coalition will have to deliver. Otherwise, its promise to tackle poverty more aggressively will turn out to be empty, its days will be numbered, and the door opened for a return of the BJP—but with the same mandate. More than Hindutva, or the Anglophone cosmopolitanism of New Delhi's salons, India's voters—rich, poor and middle-class, urban and rural—clearly want (the benefits of) more economic growth, not less.

Stability and its political twins, early warning and correction, are indeed intrinsic to India; so too is continuity. Lest one forget, a previous Congress government was routed by the BJP in 1998, notwithstanding its 'Dream Budget', atop an early 1990s economic reform program which laid the foundations for India's software boom. The BJP, for its part, implemented most of the goals in the Congress party's very same Dream Budget, as borne out by its (now-unsuccessful) 'India Shining' campaign.

Behind the Dream and Shine, and after the May 2004 Surprise, the Elephant's rise will continue. As the New York Times noted shortly after the election, even India's (elected) communists—now its third largest party in parliament—agree that "outsourcing is a must in this era of globalization."[1] Readers of this book would note that India's communists have in fact already implemented some of the country's most relocation-friendly policies.

Like this author, most Western technology employers may have been surprised by the BJP's defeat; few seem concerned about its impact on jobs relocation. At the sidelines of an analyst meeting in New York, Intel Corp. Chief Executive Craig Barrett observed, "I think if you look at the trajectory of the Indian economy, it has been unbroken by changes in government.... It just continues to march forward."[2]

'Rising Elephant' was both inspired and helped by friends and colleagues.

Michael de Toro, an American lawyer and conflict-resolution expert, first suggested that I write the book and worked with me in shaping it. Michael is providing advice on ways to make my own offshore IT services company, Allilon, not only efficient for our customers, but palatable to its place of business too.

I have been a personal witness to the white-collar relocation process since 1997, when my 250-page report on Indian information technology, then the first of its kind, was published by Find-SVP in New York, and forecast the shape of things to come. However, the effort on this book itself coincided closely with the emergence and intensification of the relocation debate in America at the middle of 2003.

Much of the book's content is an outcome of continuing discussions with another colleague, Guido Doucet. As a senior European IT consultant (previously with PriceWaterhouse and PA Consulting), Guido has been closely involved with the business and technology settings of white-collar jobs relocation to India.

Several friends have also helped my effort. In particular, I would like to thank Rob, Jyotsna, Johan, Sophie, David, Pramod, Yiannis, and Quentin, as well as inspirations from another era—Kamakhya and Souren—for offering a variety of sounding boards about the implications of relocation.

I began writing in August 2003 during a motorcycle trip across Europe to celebrate my recovery from an accident 11 months previously. In this context, I would like to reconfirm my gratitude to fellow motorcyclist George, Genevieve, and the rest of the Wannabecq Gang, who, in several senses, provided a soft landing for my own relocation effort, onwards from early 2003.

Thanks, above all, to my wife Ilse, for her patience and immense support, in spite of several round-the-clock days and nights of writing, and the usual inability to talk about anything else.

Bassilly, Belgium
July 2004

Leviathan's Veil

Eight Myths Which Conceal The Rising Elephant

India accounts for 60 percent of the offshore white-collar jobs market. Its presence in the growing pool of high-value jobs leaving America—and, crucially, not being created there—seems set to accelerate.

In spite of some obvious differences in this exodus compared to its more familiar blue-collar counterpart, two facts demand especially close examination. Though masked by the frenzy of the dotcom boom, white-collar jobs have been relocating to India for well over a decade, and today's strong pull from there is both follow-up and consolidation. Secondly, such jobs do not simply concern call centers; in India, in particular, they have ended up, as we shall see, with Indians designing integrated circuits, wireless solutions, composite materials, genetic engineering tools, luxury cars, jet engines and complex econometric models; others are now probing still-newer areas such as filing tax-returns, interpreting MRI scans and researching Wall Street firms.

Several such jobs will not return because fewer Americans are being hired for them, and fewer still will choose to study in these areas in the future. In addition, the Indian challenge to technology jobs has deep roots. The incentives for such a shift are not going to disappear, with or without Western economic recovery, or a few upticks in hiring; instead, they are likely to strengthen with time.

As a result, entire chunks of the Western economic system may be eroding at a faster pace than few believed possible only a few years ago.

In brief, this is the unexpected, flip side of 'globalization.' It is no more just Nike shoes and Disney toys being made in Mexico or Southeast Asia. It is also high-value, technology jobs—both current and future—moving out in droves, and doing so to giants like India and China, who not only 'pull' Western jobs from much stronger foundations than before, but are building up systemic dependencies on continuing to do so.

Even as the story of white-collar job losses rages across headlines in the U.S. and elsewhere, what is missed may be more than half the story: India, whose content-oriented culture stands in sharp contrast to the West's obsession with form, has been quietly leveraging its fast-emerging strengths to position itself on the road to world power status—economically, technologically, militarily. Few have cared to look behind the trees of the globalizing forest at the awakening Elephant, or heard it stir. Revealing the details of this story drives the theme of this book.

The key question now is what it will take to bring Americans up to speed on a problem that threatens their livelihoods and, in the longer term, America's predominant position in the world? The answers are neither easy nor straightforward. Instead, they are enmeshed in a complex set of new equations focused on India and China, but especially India. Understanding the Indian specificities central to white-collar job relocation is a categorical imperative to cope with its challenges.

It should by now be clear why India scrupulously ignored self-serving Little Brother platitudes from a galaxy of Western pundits in the 1980s and 1990s, to follow faithfully in the footsteps of southeast Asia's now-faded economic darlings. Instead, rather like Wal-Mart, it contributed a wholly unique combination of volume and value, skills and scale, to commodify the New Economy. Accompanied by an equally systematic and strengthening assault on its higher-skill frontiers, India is showing that the broader Western advantage may not last forever.

Although hardly a Big Bang, only the naive would believe that India will not acquire a much bigger slice out of the next New Economy, whatever be its shape, as indicated by the mass of examples discussed in this book. Whether it takes one, three or five decades to become manifest, India's rise will erode the foundations of Western supremacy.

And yet, by no means should India's ascension entail an inevitable hard landing for everyone in the West hit by the process. The impact of relocation will be less than pessimists fear, but more than Western optimists hope. The final chapter offers some clues to solutions for victims of such a historical tide. Before this, however, much needs to be understood.

So far, eight myths stand in the way of Americans' (and Europeans') ability to grasp what is happening to them—and what to do about it. Each is in turn examined in detail in the book.

Myth I

This new sucking sound is an echo of the previous round.
Americans have to somehow ride it out.

Fact: Several New Economy jobs seemed to be in massively short supply as recently as mid-2000. As examples in this book establish, no one knows what may replace them and in what numbers, within a still-hypothetical New, New Economy. More worrying is the apprehension that there is almost no ceiling to the kind (or number) of Western jobs which can eventually be done offshore, at lower cost, even in the next New Economy.

Myth II

Relocation of white-collar jobs began
after the dotcom bust and downturn.

Fact: Relocation began in a significant way in the early 1990s, although it was masked by both the frenzy of the Silicon Valley boom and the intangibility of technology services. Few Americans, for example, know that their Saturday morning cartoons are developed by animators in India, or that the 'hidden hands' of Indians execute their Amazon.com book orders and lie embedded in the brain of their mobile telephones and X-Ray machines, and within the algorithms of their hi-fi sound systems. Unlike bathtub toys, shoes and made-in-China washing machines, India's colonizing of 'cyberspace' and seepage into Silicon Valley's 'marrow,' to quote *BusinessWeek*, are hardly visible on an everyday basis.

Myth III

America's white-collar jobs will go to many places,
and it does not really matter where.

Fact: In reality, it is India (a billion-strong, stable and demo-cratic country with a mature free market and 2 million university graduates a year) which is due to gain most—according to one wide-ly-quoted forecast, equivalent to 800 American jobs every day until 2015; technology employment in the southern Indian city of Bangalore has already overtaken Silicon Valley. The process, as this book establishes, is connected intimately, and often invisibly, to the huge role Indians have long played within the heart of the American technology community, from the 'Father of the Pentium' to IBM's 'Patent King' and beyond.

Software exports alone account for over 3 percent of the Indian economy and are growing four times faster than gross domestic prod-uct. As India attains critical mass in offshore services, Western tech-nology companies have become heavily dependent on the country. Meanwhile, the Indian IT industry's globalization is illustrated by a growing pace of acquisitions, large and small, in both the U.S. and Europe. Extrication from such a complex process of mutual lock-in will require much more than wishful thinking.

Singapore's Prime Minister Goh Chok Tong explains it simply: "China has become the world's factory floor, while India has become its IT and back office."

Myth IV

India is home to a low-end software coding industry.

Fact: As discussed later, core software R&D in India by U.S. technology titans such as Hughes, Honeywell, Motorola, GE and Texas Instruments, began in some cases as far back as the 1980s, picking up massively onwards from the mid-1990s. In just two years since the process formally took shape, Indian R&D centers of American tech firms were filing more patents than Bell Labs. Both Indian IT companies and universities are investing massive sums of money to retain their intellectual property, and close last-mile gaps with the richer Western world. Since the mid-1990s, India also boasts a much-larger number of software facilities certified to the "gold standard" of the U.S. Defense Department-inspired CMM Capability Maturity Model, than America, Europe and the rest of the world combined.

Myth V

India's success is easy to duplicate in other developing countries.

Fact: By the year 2008, Indian software revenues are forecast to be larger than the entire economies of Chile, Nigeria or Pakistan. Such success in software is intimately coupled to very specifically-Indian contexts. No developing countries have either India's first-mover advantage in offshore services delivery, the advantages of a billion-strong population or its world-class educational and high-technology support infrastructure. Accounting for these is imperative to understand the meaning of relocation, anticipate its impact and find ways around. In a different direction, given some of the breakthrough social-technology paradigms being set there, India, as explained later, may very well be paving the way for a New, New Third World Thing.

Myth VI

*India is like Japan—high impact on
a few sectors but slight overall.*

Fact: As much as call-center jobs, high-value technology skills are also at risk. India's sweep of competencies has not only made relocation irreversible, but will result in its steady rise as a high-tech competitor to the U.S. Unlike Japan, or now, China, India's focus is a full sweep of high-value white-collar services rather than blue-collar manufacturing. On average, services account for four or more times the share of manufacturing in Western economies.

In addition, the debate will be complicated by India's status as a poor, but nonetheless democratic country, with one of the world's fastest growing economies, a clear resolve to return to the ranks of great powers, and its own homegrown but world-class multinational manufacturing firms (in areas such as steel, automobiles, energy and consumer goods); such companies, as we will see, have also begun rapidly emerging on both Western markets and elsewhere.

On another note, scholars such as American management guru
Peter Drucker, have begun pointing to India's many intrinsic advan-
tages vis-a-vis China, among them its high-technology lead, a superior
higher education system and potentially word-class private sector.
Others have raised disturbing questions about parallels between the
Chinese economic miracle and 1990s Southeast Asia.

Myth VII

*Pressure on India to stem the jobs drain would be
straightforward, given it is poor and a geopolitical lightweight.*
Fact: India has the resolve, and is rapidly acquiring the capacity,
to emerge as a major power. Its economy, in purchasing power terms,
is already two and a half times the size of Russia, and almost as large
as France or the U.K. and Brazil combined. As borne out in reports by
leading American think-tanks discussed in this book, from teraflop
supercomputers and fast-breeder nuclear reactors to a fifth-generation
combat jet, stealth warships, state-of-the-art remote-sensing satellites
and two plus-tonne space launchers, India has some key qualitative
superiorities in military high-technology compared to China, and is
10-15 years ahead of an otherwise-'similar' country like Brazil. Even as
Western reliance on India's technology industry becomes critical,
influential American commentators have urged the U.S. to actively
support India's drive for world power status, arguing for example, for
Indian permanent membership of the UN Security Council, in certain cases to replace old powers such as France.

Myth VIII

*Such a seismic shift in power has no precedents,
and may therefore be unsustainable.*
Fact: In contrast to America's relatively brief history, India and
China go back many millennia, and their people think in long-term
contexts. Many Indians, as shown in the book, see the country's leap
to the frontlines of the Knowledge Economy vindicating its status in
the 19th century as one of the world's richest countries, the source
of mathematics and many sciences apparently only 'rediscovered' by
the Europeans, but in the failed search for whose treasures,
Columbus discovered America.

CHAPTER I

Heralding
the New, New Economy

Another Giant Sucking Sound

The relocation of white-collar technology jobs out of the West is a powerful undercurrent in today's globalizing world economy.

One study by American consulting firm, Forrester Research, estimates that such a process could send "3.3 million American jobs overseas by 2015."[1] Another, by Deloitte Consulting, predicted in 2003 that Western financial companies alone would move a total of 2 million jobs "over the next five years."[2]

These concerns mounted further when respected technology consultant, The Gartner Group, warned that one in 10 U.S. technology jobs might be moved out, already by the end of 2004.[3] It followed this up with a forecast that the accelerated pace of job losses is expected to last through 2005,[4] by when of course, entire swathes of technology skills may have vanished from America.

In the U.K., the Mitial Research consultancy predicts one-third of the country's larger call centers would shut down by 2005 with the loss of 90,000 jobs.[5] The ongoing acceleration in the relocation process is evident in figures from Britain's Communication Workers Union, which say 50,000 jobs were shifted overseas by end of 2003; as recently as mid-2002, consultants Accenture had forecast 65,000 jobs would move, but only by 2010.

Symbolizing the inexorability of the relocation tide was the announcement of plans by U.S. information technology firm Perot Systems in February 2004 to further boost its 6,000-strong Indian facility, from where it targets a 40 percent rate of annual growth;[6] the bulk of this growth will be out of America. The company was founded by American billionaire Ross Perot, whose 1992 presidential campaign saw him coin the phrase 'giant sucking sound' to describe the loss of jobs to Mexico caused by the North American Free Trade Agreement (NAFTA).

Table I: Number of U.S. jobs moving offshore				
Job category	2000	2005	2010	2015
Management	0	37,477	117,835	288,281
Business	10,787	61,252	161,722	348,028
Computer	27,171	108,991	276,954	472,632
Architecture	3,498	32,302	83,237	184,347
Life sciences	0	3,677	14,478	36,770
Legal	1,793	14,220	34,673	74,642
Art, design	818	5,576	13,846	29,639
Sales	4,619	29,064	97,321	226,564
Office	53,987	295,034	791,034	1,659,310
Total:	102,674	587,592	1,591,101	3,320,213

Source: U.S. Department of Labor and Forrester Research, Inc. All numbers are rounded

A Job Lost By Any Other Name...

Throughout this book, the term 'relocation' covers both off-shore outsourcing and contracting with foreign—rather than Western-owned companies, both directly and via their sub-contracts with Western IT service firms. It not only refers to direct transfer of skilled, knowledge-intensive jobs by employers in the West to low-cost countries, but also to employment of personnel from the latter in the West, and most significantly, to the creation of new white-collar jobs in such countries.

Though there are differences between each of the above, their aggregated impact—for the purposes of this book—is the same, namely a loss of jobs and employment opportunities for local-born staff in Western countries. In the longer-term, such processes may be paving the way for de-skilling the U.S. and other Western countries, with an impact across-the-board—economic, social and political, as well as in the military and geopolitical sphere.

Given the reasoning and arguments in later chapters of this book, it is also important to underline that relocation is part and parcel of the wider and better-known process of 'globalization.'

The Hard Choice: Outsource Or Die

According to American IT consulting firm META Group Inc., an average of 41 percent of new development activity is now out-sourced. "'Going offshore and using the economics of offshore outsourcing have been the only competitive options left for larger companies since all the IT budget decreases of 2000, 2001, 2002, and even 2003,'" says its executive vice president Dr. Howard Rubin.[7] Economic recovery or not, such a trend is unlikely to reverse, because there would be few reasons to. Consultants IDC predict that the offshore component in the delivery of IT services in the U.S. may grow to as much as 23 percent by 2007, up from its 2003 level of 5 percent.[8]

For business, offshore outsourcing is not really a choice. With time, it is likely to become even less so. Technology portal TechWeb observes:

> What about a company that needs a whole new set of applications written? They may have a few coders on staff to do things such as daily/weekly maintenance of a Web site or database, but a major project would be beyond staff capacity. The obvious thing to do is to contract the majority of the work out, and let the regular employees put in any finishing touches.
>
> After accepting bids for the job, it boils down to two feasible candidates: One contractor will bring the job home for $15,000; another will do it for $3,500.
>
> Looking at the backgrounds of the two contractors, the company finds a rough similarity in the quality of previous work done, the reliability of delivering by deadline, and everything else. The only discernible difference between the two contractors is the price—and their countries of origin. The higher price comes from a home-grown, domestic crew; the lower is from India.
>
> Put yourself in that company's place right now. Either the cash saved allows the company to do something else needed, as well as stay within budget (perhaps even to include a good chunk of a possible new hire's salary), or it actually makes the difference between doable and not.[9]

'Real Weapon of Mass Destruction'

For Western industrialized economies, their business leaders, and eventually, their political leadership, the consequences of the relocation process remain unfathomable. Intel's Chairman Andy Grove warns that India "could surpass the United States in software and tech-service jobs by 2010."[10] A feature in leading American business journal *Fortune* comments that, unlike other wannabes across the world, Bangalore's claim of being a new Silicon Valley had "an eerie ring of truth."[11] More now than a ring; a *BusinessWeek* cover story at the end of 2003 stated that Bangalore had surpassed Silicon Valley in high-tech employment; it also reported that Indians were taking the lead in "colonizing cyberspace."[12]

The process has long moved beyond Silicon Valley to Anywhere, USA. Travelocity's shift to India, for instance, entails 250 job losses in Dickenson County, Virginia, "a serious setback for the area, which has persistent double-digit unemployment rates."[13] It includes not only technology giants but thousands of smaller companies too—specialized in fields ranging from chip design and wireless applications to computer animation and hi-fi codecs. Among them are typical American firms such as a business process software company called Approva, 41 of whose 67 staff are based in India.[14]

Unlike previous waves of relocation, which involved the transfer of blue-collar manufacturing jobs, the shift now clearly concerns the higher ends of the skills spectrum—exactly where (new) employment previously (more-than) compensated for the relocation of other, lower skilled jobs. Notes the *Free Press Detroit*: "Some things never change, like big U.S. companies with high-cost labor at home seeking to buy labor-intensive parts or products from the lowest-cost third-world producer that can do the job: China, Vietnam, the Philippines, Morocco, you name it. We may not like that idea, but we've accepted it. What's new about the emerging trade brouhaha is that higher-end jobs in engineering, value-added manufacturing and information technology are migrating to China, India and elsewhere by the thousands."[15] Unlike the past, this migration is not merely pushed by America. An across-the-board economic boom in India is pulling the process too.

The exodus of technology jobs has made its impact felt across swathes of the U.S. economy. "'When jobs disappear, industrial, retail and office buildings go dark,' says Dr. Mark Dotzour, chief economist for the Real Estate Center at Texas A&M University.... Not only are computer science and software design industries flourishing in Bangalore, all sorts of businesses are sending their paperwork and accounting jobs...to India."[16]

Writing in October 2003, a columnist in the *Washington Times* takes a fashionable concern further: "If you want to see a real weapon of mass destruction, try a $1,000 computer in Bombay. High-tech jobs in the computer industry are bailing out of the United States. Fast."[17]

The grimness of this outlook is confirmed by employment trends. The American Electronics Association found U.S. high-technology industries lost 540,000 jobs in 2002 and total technology employment fell to 6 million from 6.5 million in 2001.[18] In spite of an uptick in the economy in mid-2004, new hiring levels, crucially remained at one-third of those at a similar stage in previous economic cycles. The Information Technology Association of America[19] says U.S. hiring managers will see only 493,431 jobs created from May 2003 to May 2004, three times lower than the 1.6 million IT workers hired in the U.S. in 2000.

The downturn has hit computer programmers especially hard. According to the U.S. Bureau of Labor Statistics, unemployment among programmers has quadrupled in just two years, from 1.6 percent in 2001 to 7.1 percent in the first nine months of 2003.[20] For technology jobs in particular, the kind of economic recovery seen in early 2004 may do very little to address the huge backlog. Worse, it may be years before the underlying composition and trend of new job creation becomes clear. As we shall see later, fears about a deskilling of America are both widespread and real.

Crucially, the (white-collar) service sector accounts for a much larger share of Western economies than manufacturing. In the U.S., for example, services make up 60 percent of the economy, compared to manufacturing's 14 percent. In France, services account for nearly three out of four jobs.[21] In other words, the ceiling for potential damage to Western economies through white-collar job relocation is three to four times higher than it has been with manufacturing jobs. Such a difference will become even more obvious in the years ahead.

An *Associated Press* report warns: College seniors "are finding that a high-tech degree isn't the job guarantee that many thought it would be.... 'The entry-level positions just aren't out there now'."[22] Elsewhere, in Australia, a survey of information technology managers claimed outsourcing could well "sound the death knell" for the country's technology industry; the survey also found more than 90 percent of managers saying they would not recommend information technology to students as a viable career path.[23]

Coupled to the looming build-up by India of its software and broader technological capabilities, this trend may point to the long-term de-skilling of the West—an erosion of capacities in today's leading-edge technologies, before anything realistic replaces the latter.

Demographics add another dimension to the challenge. Aside from an impending end to the West's Baby Boom population cohort discussed below, these issues also relate to competition from India and China, not only from their thriving technology and new manufacturing sectors, and their growing determination to play a major role in the world, but also their far-younger populations.

Subsequent chapters establish such trends. Consultants McKinsey, for example, forecast Indian IT exports at $50 billion by 2008, most of which will go to the U.S. and Europe. Given that average Indian wages are accepted to be a fifth those in the West, the value of what this figure represents (and substitutes) would be five times more, or worth $250 billion. Even should there be an increase of one-third in average Indian IT wages over the period, the export equivalence would still represent about $165 billion, and at the upper rate of $75,000 per average Western IT job, equate to more than two million information technology jobs—lost, transferred or simply created elsewhere.

Other findings also attest to the growing strength of such a tide, and its often-multiplied correspondence vis-a-vis job losses in the West. A widely quoted calculation by the University of California at Berkeley, for example, shows U.S. firms shipping as many as 30,000 new service-sector jobs to India in just the month of July 2003 "while eliminating some 226,000."[24]

Complacent arguments about the larger pool of American jobs vis-a-vis India's, therefore, miss the threat, possibly dangerously. One good example of this is *Business 2.0*, whose September 2003 issue states that the (Indian) subcontinent's "150,000 tech workers represent less than 2 percent of America's domestic IT labor force, barely enough to make a ripple in the looming job shortage."[25] The writer, Paul Kaihla, makes serious errors at both ends of the equation. Firstly, according to researchers IDC, America's software development community reached 2.35 million in 2003. India's software development community was estimated at 813,500 in February 2004, up sharply from 650,000 at the end of 2002.

The impact of this unremitting acceleration is already recognized. According to the *New York Times*, although America has more than four times as many software developers as India, and nearly seven times as many as China "what is more important is the fact that the recent growth rate (of software developers), and projected growth, is far higher in those well-educated, developing nations."[26]

Reshaping the World: Another Great Displacement

Complicating the relocation debate are essentially three factors: the absence of precedents for white-collar job shifts, the continuing (and now possibly strengthening) transfer of traditional manufacturing jobs, and finally, the fact that white-collar jobs have, in reality, begun being transferred since a decade or more and already involve powerful (but rarely informed or mutually aware) interest groups.

In spite of the inherent inability to benchmark such trends against previous experience, it is amply clear that the impact of the relocation process will be momentous.

In the longer term, its implications may be staggering. For Roger Bootle, economic adviser to consultants Deloitte, the rise of India and China "will radically reshape the location of economic activity across the world." According to him, this is "the Great Displacement. It is the modern equivalent of the development of North America in the 19th century—only bigger."[27] A more stark, endgame view was expressed by columnist Paul Craig Roberts in the *Washington Times*: As "China and India become fully employed first world economies...the United States might be a third world country."[28]

Europe too is concerned, at the highest levels. After seemingly abandoning plans to overtake the U.S. economy by 2010, a strongly worded critique by the European Commission "blames low overall European productivity on a lack of investment and poor use of information technology, and warns that China and India are becoming key competitors."[29] For French Prime Minister Jean-Pierre Raffarin, Europe faces 'deindustrialization' as a result of this challenge.[30]

Alarm bells are ringing elsewhere too. Canada's Prime Minister Paul Martin noted at the 2004 World Economic Forum in Davos, Switzerland, that "superpowers like China and India are emerging to rival the economic might of the United States."[31]

Such concerns go beyond economics. British daily *The Guardian* echoes Deloitte's Roger Bootle: "New superpowers (like India and China) will arise to challenge America's supremacy, just as imperial Germany and the U.S. itself were challenging Britain's by the end of the 19th century."[32]

Experts At a Loss for Words: Something Will Turn Up, In Some Form

There are, quite simply, no precedents for today's form of relocation. Well-meaning but misleading attempts to soothe the anxiety, such as that by *Business 2.0*'s Paul Kaihla, hardly help.

An equally ill-considered effort is an American newspaper article, "Putting job flight in perspective," which claims that a closer look at the Forrester relocation numbers "finds them less frightening than at first glance." Half of those (3.3 million) jobs "are in traditional office services, like bill processing, order handling and the like. Only 14 percent of the total is in computer services."[33] Such a breakdown is neither reassuring for those currently employed in the so-called 'traditional' services, or those in 'computer services' who really do take a closer look: 14 percent of 3.3 million amounts to over 450,000 jobs.

In contrast, Diane Morello, Vice President of The Gartner Group, is a straight-shooter: "Suddenly we have a profession—computer programming—that has to wake up and consider what value it really has to offer."[34] Indeed, Gartner estimates that through 2005, less than 4 out of 10 information technology workers whose jobs go overseas will be redeployed by their own companies.[35]

The difference between blue-collar job shifts and the current trend is also reflected in the 'virtuality' of the New Economy, in the inability to explain matters adequately or react against an identifiable (and tangible) target. For example, while in the late 1970s, it was possible for Detroit workers to expend their frustrations by queuing up to kick a Japanese-made Toyota automobile, it is difficult to see how similar catharsis can be achieved with Adobe's Pagemaker 7.0.

Other significant differences in the current process, compared to relocation of manufacturing jobs, include not only new geopolitical realities but massive changes in other enablers of relocation. The medium of the Internet permits transfer offshore of a very extensive range of white-collar jobs, providing stark evidence of the theory of capitalism's unremitting process of 'creative destruction' expounded by American economist Joseph Schumpeter.

Most experts overlook these differences.

Drawing parallels with the previous blue-collar job exodus, Eduardo Porter notes in the *New York Times*: "From 1999 to 2003, as the economy peaked and went bust, 1.3 million nonfarm jobs vanished. Manufacturing lost 2.8 million jobs; 800,000 management positions disappeared—including CEOs and other executive jobs that are not easily outsourced to Bangladesh."[36]

Another example is Professor J. David Richardson of Syracuse University, who is confident that "jobs that will stay and proliferate in the United States in fields such as global coordination, sophisticated design, customization and consulting."[37] However, he does not attempt to answer how many new, higher-end jobs should, or can be, realistically created, to match the millions forecast for overseas relocation. Neither does he seem aware (as discussed below) about India's inexorable, but still-enduringly cost-effective levitation up the white-collar value chain, its hugely-advantageous demographics, or the corresponding evidence about a potential long-term de-skilling of America, given that entry-level technology jobs are drying up, fast.

The essential dilemma here can be expressed in four questions:

- What can replace the so-called New Economy jobs, including those which were supposed to be in short supply through the dotcom boom, barely a few years ago?
- Can this be done in adequate numbers, since classically, higher-value economic segments require less employment than those they displace? Crucially, previous rounds of relocation involved jobs pushed out by Western economies. The Indian economy in particular, with its accelerating high-value focus, is now also pulling relocation.
- As a result, will the relocation trend strengthen even further

after the beginnings of economic recovery? In other words, will there be enough new, high-end jobs left behind for those who emerge in 5-10 years from even a reinvigorated American schooling system?

• Finally, is relocation open-ended? In other words, is there a ceiling to the kind of Western jobs which can be done off-shore?

Answers to these questions, however, are hardly reassuring. The best illustration of this was Chairman of the U.S. Federal Reserve Alan Greenspan, when he faced a Congressional Committee studying the white-collar job exodus. As a newspaper reported, the usually eloquent Greenspan could do no more than, in essence, say "I don't know, but something will turn up. It always does in this country, with its adaptable labor market and availability of finance and what might be generally catalogued as creative juices."[38] Robert Reich, Secretary of Labor in the Clinton Administration, is similarly optimistic. The U.S. economy, he is sure, will fully bounce back from recession by mid-2005, and that a 'large portion' of high-tech jobs lost after 2000 will, in fact, come back, albeit 'in some form.'[39] For British Deputy High Commissioner in India, Stuart Innes: "In the search for competitiveness, our workforce will keep scaling up and finding new skills to replace the old ones."[41]

Devoid of concrete answers, some free market advocates have become simply assertive. Economics professor Robert Feenstra of the University of California at Davis says that outsourcing is the only way to "maintain profitability of the activities you're still doing in the U.S., and in fact you enhance their profitability. "...It's just got to be done," he says. Prof. Feenstra makes no attempt to connect higher profitability with re-investment on local jobs.

Private corporations have not escaped the vagueness bug. A good example is James Magee, director of the ITD Group, which sponsored the 2003 Outsource World conference in New York. Outsourcing "allows U.S. companies to focus on innovation and creativity, which is always their strength anyway," he proclaims. "I think you're going to see high school, college students shift away from studying data programming to coming up with ideas."[42]

In spite of India's growing presence at still-unexhausted frontiers of high-tech (for example, chip design, 3D animation and wireless applications), gurus of the technology media too have been infected by the amoeba of unfocused optimism. "Send the maintenance to India and, even after costs, 20 percent of the budget is freed up to come up with the next breakthrough app," writes Chris Anderson, Editor-in-Chief of *Wired* magazine. The result, according to him: "more workers focused on real innovation. What comes after services? Creativity."[43]

Indeed, unlike previous downturns—where signs of the next New Thing were already tangibly on the horizon (semiconductors, personal computers, the Internet, mobile telephony)—no one, for example, can define the promise of nanotechnology leading to a hydrogen-powered New NanoEconomy, complete with its own Nano Valley. The U.S. Congress has authorized $3.7 billion spending over four years on this technology, but according to most scientific accounts, "the nanotech future may be 10 to 20 years off"[44]—time enough of course, for India and China to have caught up; as discussed elsewhere, Indian firms are now offering doctorate programs in nanotechnology in Russia.

In Europe, too, leading executives of technology companies remain bewilderingly obtuse about the profound, structural and long-term impact of relocation. At the Cisco Connection 2004 conference, Caspar Rorsted, HP's Managing Director for Europe, the Middle East and Africa, said "fears that Europe is pricing itself out of the IT sector are probably misplaced. 'We have 30 years of experience optimizing IT into business process.'" Rorsted acknowledged "that many IT-based jobs are moving from Western Europe" and named countries "such as Bulgaria, Russia and Romania."[45] As following chapters explain, such places not only have relatively small populations, but their IT industry is miniscule, compared to India. Equally puzzling is the lack of attempts by Rorsted to address any of the following factors, discussed later in the book:

- HP's only Capability Maturity Model Level 5 software facilities (certified to the highest standards of the U.S. Defense Department) are in India.
- HP's R&D facility in Bangalore has been scaled up from 2 in 2002 to 20 in 2003 and will be doubled in 2004. It is wholly dedicated to "high-level research on futuristic technologies."
- HP has started a new support center for its North American

operations in India, which will add further to similar work already outsourced to about 1,000 staff at Indian IT firms.[46]

- HP is moving software development work for two key products called OpenView and OpenCall (its next-generation telecoms software platform[47]) to India from the U.S. and Europe. Meanwhile, OpenView's General Manager has resigned and joined an Indian start-up.

- HP plans to center its Microsoft .Net strategy in India and hopes to move even consulting operations there. According to Jurgen Rottler, its Vice President of marketing, strategy and alliances, "In an ideal world, you'd migrate as much as you possibly could to India."[48]

The onus on straight talk has been left to politicians like Donald Manzullo, an Illinois Republican and Chairman of the House Small Business Committee. "The assumption was that while lower-skilled jobs would be done elsewhere, it would allow Americans to focus on higher-skilled, higher-paying opportunities."But what, he asks, "do you tell the Ph.D., or professional engineer, or architect, or accountant, or computer scientist to do next? Where do you tell them to go?"[49]

Consultants McKinsey & Co. can only identify "jobs in services such as retail, restaurants and hotels" which would not be exportable, and although "services that are necessarily produced and consumed locally" account for 70 percent of economies like the U.S., this still leaves a substantial chunk of the economy under threat.

In Britain, Rebecca Harding, chief economist at the Work Foundation, estimates that "Up to one-third of British jobs could feasibly be carried out abroad".... According to the *Financial Times*, "It is a sobering thought for the country's workers" that 10 million jobs "might just as easily be held by people in another part of the globe."[50]

The high priest and priestess of the IT industry use a blunderbuss. "There is no job that is America's God-given right anymore," asserts Carly Fiorina, Chief Executive of Hewlett-Packard. For Intel's Chief Executive Craig Barrett, "Unless you are a plumber, or perhaps a newspaper reporter, or one of these jobs which is geographically situated, you can be anywhere in the world and do just about any job."[51] One such category, in fact, seemed to also be buckling to the Elephant's charm, after David Schlesinger, the global managing director of Reuters news agency, said he would be hiring journalists in India to do some 'basic financial reporting' on American companies[52]—propelling the news agency further into the maw of India after a decision in summer 2003 to shift 'much of the core' of its technology operation there.

The sky-is-the-limit threat of relocation was parodied by Russ Winter, in a letter to the *Washington Post* protesting a pro-offshore editorial. "I can assure your paper's publisher," writes Winter, "that he can save hundreds of thousands of dollars annually by finding talented, underpaid Indian scribes to put together your editorial page-unless, of course, he's already doing that and this editorial was written by one."[53] Going higher was a retort to HP's Fiorina and Intel's Barrett by Jesse Kornbluth, previously editorial director of AOL (which set up Indian operations in 2001). In a *Los Angeles Times* column titled "We Import Cars and Stereos, So Why Not CEOs," he notes: "My bet is that Indian or Chinese executives would happily become American CEOs for salaries of $250,000", without sweeteners and golden handshakes.[54]

Some trades-unionists, too, seem reconciled to the inevitable. Brendan Barber, secretary-general of Britain's Trade Union Congress, echoes this with an estimate that "only 1 percent to 5 percent of the 200 million service sector jobs must be tied to a particular geographical location."[55]

Quite simply, there are no comforting answers to such questions, not least because their wider context (both historical and futuristic) remain unclear. Whether or not there is a recovery in the Western jobs market, it is impossible to know if another phase of relocation will not return yet again, or whether there are going to be huge structural gaps in the Western skills ladder, given the sharp decline in entry-level IT jobs. Both quality and quantity are indeed the Elephant's winning argument.

In a feature mainly devoted to the escalating Indian presence in information technology, the *Los Angeles Times* observes: With the U.S. "once again gripped by the fear that it's losing its economic essentials, what is today's comforting story? Answer: There is none."[56]

No Let Up To the Older Sucking Sound

Another key factor in today's white-collar relocation debate is that the longer-running trend to shift manufacturing jobs continues in parallel. For the *Associated Press*: "there is a fundamental restructuring going on, with employers shifting manufacturing jobs to China and software jobs to India, rather than hiring in the United States."[57] Another news report expresses the risks of this dual-edged process as "the equivalent of exporting not just the automobile industry's assembly line jobs—but the core engineering and car design jobs, too."[58]

As shown by examples in Chapters II and V, Indian auto firms are indeed vigorously globalizing and moving up this industry's value chain. One result will be to shake up complacent observers, who rest secure in the view that "China has begun making cars but isn't designing or manufacturing quality auto parts," but its growing car market "will inevitably create design and organizational and many other judgment jobs in the United States." The news article, from the *Los Angeles Times*, is (as it happens, appropriately) titled "To Ease Fears About Jobs, Put Imagination to Work."[59]

A synergy of sorts between India and China has now become an accelerator for the larger-scale relocation of more traditional industrial sectors. For those whose 'imagination' still soothes, it would be salutary to take a look at a recent A.T Kearney report. This found that while China would become a key locale for low-cost manufacturing operations over the next decade, "India is playing an increasingly integral role in the rapid globalization of the business with its excellent capability to provide a full range of business processes (engineering, accounting, R&D, customer service, data processing, etc.) for vehicle suppliers."[60]

India's eventual pull on the auto sector is best illustrated by another A.T Kearney survey of American auto executives, who ranked the country "as the top outsourcing destination with 24 percent of the respondents giving it the thumbs up", compared to just 15 percent for China. India also comfortably outranked other well-known contenders in Latin America, Asia and Eastern Europe: Mexico (13 percent), Brazil (10 percent), Canada (7 percent), Hungary (6 percent). Asia's erstwhile 'miracle' Thailand secured a mere 2 percent, while Australia had 1 percent.[61]

Process Hardly 'New', Although Scale Is

The third complicating issue for the relocation debate is that, although few have been aware of it, the process has been under way for quite some time. One exception is Jim Rogers, co-founder (with billionaire George Soros) of the Quantum Fund. In 1997, he warned, "your accountant will be a person on a computer, someone that you won't even know, and may very well be an Indian."[62] However, the time frame he proposed was less than urgent. Such a process, he said, might unfold in "10 or 20 or 30 years." As the white-collar job exodus accelerates, even this comfort, of a long-drawn process, is turning into an illusion.

As a result, the relocation process now already involves entrenched interest groups (State-level, sub-national and international, from governments, Big Business and the seamless global financial community), and has acquired it its own autonomous momentum and dynamics. The complex implications and interplay of such factors is illustrated in the remaining chapters of this book.

Five years ago, in an interview with a European business monthly, this author explained the essence of the difference: "One has been used to shoes, clothes, even machinery. Never before in history has a high tech, knowledge-intensive sector relocated overseas because of comparative advantage."[63] Such a view was echoed more recently by the *Christian Science Monitor*: "No longer," it said, "is it just Disney toys and Nike shoes made in Haiti and Indonesia."[64]

Opportunity or Peril:
The Limitations to Cost Cutting

Within the West, the relocation of white-collar jobs broadly pits the interests of local communities and trade unions against shareholders and management. Political, government and consumer interests oscillate, often uncomfortably, between the two.

The core challenge is to reconcile social and political concerns, on the one hand, and the need for business to make profits and economies to grow, on the other.

Dave Cooper, former Chief Information Officer of Lawrence Livermore National Laboratory, believes that "the social costs of off-shore development will exceed the corporate bottom-line benefits."[65] Circumstances are, however, hardly this straightforward, and, as a news item notes, in spite of its inherent and powerful contentiousness, "no definite statistics or research have swayed the (relocation) debate either way."[66]

Proponents of relocation have drawn up compelling, but complex, arguments, in support of their case. McKinsey Global Institute claims that "of the full $1.45 to $1.47 of value created globally from offshore outsourcing $1 of the U.S. labour cost, the U.S. captures $1.12 to $1.14 while the receiving country captures, on average, just 33 cents."[67] However, as expected, McKinsey notes that "at least theoretically," displaced workers "will find new jobs in more dynamic industries"[68]—without explaining this further.

The most powerful supporters of relocation include Western corporations who need to access 'cost-effective' skills for competitive success. The largest U.S. IT companies, among them IBM, Hewlett-Packard, Intel, Dell, EMC, Motorola, NCR and Unisys, have "come out in the open" to lobby "against any government moves that may curb outsourcing, especially in the backdrop of upcoming elections in the U.S."[69] Highlighting the strategic importance of outsourcing, they have set up an organization chaired by Intel's Chief Executive Craig Barrett, and called 'The Computer Systems Policy Project' (CSPP), which is comprised exclusively of their top executives.

Indeed, it is naive to expect anything else. For example, a British newspaper reports that Citigroup's Indian operations directly "helped the group become the world's most profitable financial services firm."[70] It notes that numerous other large British employers are now seeking to emulate Citi, among them the HSBC and Standard Chartered banking groups, telecoms giant BT, insurance firms Prudential and Aviva as well as the Powergen utility. Probably the best example of the offshore relevance for Western firms is U.S. industrial giant GE, whose huge, "mission-critical"[71] Indian operations (discussed in more detail in Chapter II) span practically every skill-set from airplane engine design to clerical back-office functions. GE, the archetype of America Inc., is also a breeding ground for future Chief Executives of scores of other large corporations[72]; this has obviously produced a willing constituency for serial emulators of its own success in India, which is now host to IT operations of 250-300 Fortune 500 firms. One example of the GE Ripple Effect is Stefan Spohr, a principal in A.T Kearney's financial services division: "If GE can do the advanced research over there (in India) on its next generation of jet engines, then there's no reason why that can't be the same case for financial institutions." Spohr's statement also brings into question the argument that America can afford to lose software jobs and replace them with "ideas," especially for larger companies whose raison d'etre is the business of ideas.

The irony—and an illustration of the Elephant's omnipresence—is that for many smaller technology firms, India-related survival issues now explicitly protect existing jobs. Thus, Jennifer Cotteleer, Vice President of Phase Forward, a Massachusetts company designing software for drug companies, used offshore Indian employees to customize applications, and then, to develop "highly-customized" programming. Not only did this help the company grow rapidly. "'What I've been able to do in very tough economic times is manage very directly to my margins,'" she told *Time* magazine. "I'm providing job security for the workers I do have."[73]

The Demographic Pitfall

Even as the jobs drift continues, the demographic overhang of the West's aging population is another perplexing but ticking time bomb.

Projections by the U.S. Bureau of Labor Statistics "indicate a dramatic shrinkage in the numbers of what is called the 'prime-age work pool' (people between the ages of 25 and 54) that are properly trained and educated to address the growing demand for IT professionals.... Anthony Carnevale, a former chairman of President Clinton's National Commission for Employment Policy, stated that we'll start to see labor shortages all over the place by 2005."[74] This will occur, he adds, "without any heroic growth rates or bubblelike economic anomalies; all it will take is a return to the economy's long-term growth rate of 3 to 3.5 percent a year."

Such concerns, according to *Business 2.0*, are shared by former treasury secretary and current Harvard University president Larry Summers, former Deputy Secretary of Labor Edward Montgomery and Sigurd Nilsen, the director of education, workforce, and income security in the General Accounting Office.

As *Business 2.0* urges its readers, "To see the demographic time bomb in microcosm, just count the gray heads around your own office. At Sprint, for example, half of the 6,000 field and network technicians are over 50. At Cigna Systems, about a quarter of the 3,400 IT workers will pass 55 this decade. And at Cary, N.C., software maker SAS, more than a quarter of the staff will be eligible to retire by this decade's end."[75] The magazine observes that the shortage "will be most acute among two key groups: managers, who tend to be older and closer to retirement, and skilled workers in high-demand, high-tech jobs," and wryly comments that "the long-term tragedy of offshore outsourcing isn't that it's snatching away skilled American jobs. It's that it can't possibly snatch enough of them."

The Indian IT industry lobby group Nasscom has quickly seized upon such apprehensions for its cause. A study sponsored by Nasccom argues that offshore outsourcing will be the only way for the U.S. to address a shortfall estimated at 5.6 million workers by 2010, and one which could cost the American economy as much as $2 trillion, if measures such as offshore outsourcing were not (already) encouraged.[76]

Another explosive consequence of Western demographics is the financial shakiness of pension and social insurance programs—also a direct result of an aging population. At the 2004 World Economic Forum in Switzerland, a report found that in "Italy, where the total national debt is already more than 105 percent of GDP, retirees will outnumber active workers by 2030." According to the report, "Europe will have 24 million fewer workers and Japan 14 million fewer than they have today." In fact, "Japan would have to increase immigration elevenfold from its current level to make up for the nation's low fertility rate and rapid decline in its working population."[77]

Unlike his endeavors to define the New, New Economy, Fed Chairman Alan Greenspan has the data to support his warning about this issue. America, he warns, cannot afford "the retirement benefits promised to baby boomers and urged Congress to trim them." He said "projections show the country will go from having just over three workers supporting each retiree to 2.25 workers for every retiree by 2025" and that "at some point the country needed to face the fact that the government has promised more in entitle-ment benefits than it can afford to pay."[78]

Proposals to increase immigration of course have their own critics, especially in mono-cultural Japan and Europe. Resistance to immigration extends beyond the traditional right wing, sometimes in a perverse way. Britain's leftist daily the *Guardian*, for example, covered a speech on immigration to the European Parliament by UN Secretary General Kofi Annan, almost wholly in terms of its 'humanitarian' elements and as a plea "for a warmer welcome"[79] to immigrants, rather than its more significant context—Europe's imploding demographics and its looming shortage of workers, topics highlighted by the *Associated Press* just one day before.[80]

In contrast to Europe and Japan, the demographics report at the World Economic Forum expects the U.S. to fare better, but only "because the American workforce is expected to increase by 31 mil-lion workers by 2030," largely due to its traditional receptiveness to immigration. Nevertheless, anti-immigration pressures are also ris-ing in the U.S. Part of this involves the "war on terrorism," which has led to the deportation of hundreds of immigrants, as well as tighter rules and a generally more restrictive environment (e.g. on H-1B and L-1 visas, as explained below), which will discourage oth-ers from moving there.

Expanding offshore operations and investing in demographical-ly-younger markets may therefore be the best way to revitalize the creaking pension system of the aging West. In the words of John Haley, Chief Executive of Watson Wyatt: "exporting capital to more dynamic parts of the world could generate more money for the developed world's pension coffers."[81]

Here too, numbers favor India. India will add more people to its workforce in the next 30 years—335 million—than the total work-ing-age populations of the EU and U.S. combined. In addition, as the *Financial Times* noted, India also "has one of the youngest demo-graphic profiles in the world, with 68 percent of its 1.05bn people under the age of 35."[82]

Permanent Changes in the U.S. Economy, Departed Jobs Not Coming Back

In spite of such population trends, there are few signs that Americans are being groomed to address the possibility of a future 'jobs shortfall.' In fact, the reverse appears to be the case, even as the American economy shows the first signs of emerging from recession. As businesses seek to attain previous rates of growth, there will inevitably be renewed pressure to maximize operational efficiencies, accompanied by the possibility of further acceleration in the relocation of jobs.

The difficulty, as summarized succinctly by the *New York Times*, is that employers have a choice that was not as available in the last downturn 12 years ago. "Rather than halt production at home, they shift it abroad to cut costs, particularly labor costs. They feel compelled to do this. If they did not, their competitors would upstage them with their own lower-cost, overseas production that takes away sales back home."[83]

To sum up, no one precisely knows either what is happening now ('jobless' recovery?) or whether it would be 'natural' for the impending domestic jobs shortfall to be addressed (eventually) by local—as opposed to overseas—job creation. As the *New York Times* noted in early October 2003, in spite of the heated pre-election debate on employment, "an essential statistic is missing: the number of jobs that would exist in the United States today if so many had not escaped abroad. The Labor Department, in its numerous surveys of employers and employees, has never tried to calculate this trade-off."[84] Thus more than solace, there is reason for fear in the news that "most jobs going to India are in the high-technology and professional-services sector. Data released by the U.S. Bureau of Labor Statistics show, however, that U.S. job losses are taking place mainly in manufacturing and retail services."[85]

A Federal Reserve Bank of New York study echoes such apprehensions. "The vast majority of the 2.7 million job losses since the 2001 recession began were the result of 'permanent changes in the U.S. economy and are not coming back,' it said, underscoring the challenge for governments "scrambling to reverse the longest hiring downturn since the Depression."[86]

Furthermore, millions of Americans have also "become discouraged and left the labor market."[87] One consequence of this is forced under-employment. In October 2003, the Bureau of Labor Statistics found that the number of those involuntarily working part time—either because they could not find full-time jobs or because their employers had put them on part-time schedules—rose to 4.8 million, from 4.3 million a year earlier.

Compared to the official jobless rate of 5.9 percent at end 2003, the addition of involuntary under-employed as well as those no longer actively seeking work would take the unemployment rate to 9.7 percent of the labor force.[88] This is almost on par with Europe's worst performing economies, but devoid of their social welfare net.

The above factors underscore the prognosis by the *International Herald Tribune* that, even if jobs were to be filled after an eventual economic recovery, "the economic pain for those who have been unemployed for a substantial period will be severe and lasting. Widespread and prolonged unemployment has produced such significant financial problems for so many people that it may well represent a drag on the economy for years to come."[89]

Not Since Herbert Hoover...

The underlying political ramifications of such issues (especially on the threshold of U.S. elections in 2004) are evident from the observation that President Bush would be "the first occupant of the White House since Herbert Hoover to end a term with fewer jobs available than when he started"[90] and that his "biggest obstacle" to re-election is "his track record on jobs."[91] *New York Times* columnist Paul Krugman put it bluntly: "if jobs are scarce and wages are flat, who's benefiting from the economy's expansion? The direct gains are going largely to corporate profits, which rose at an annual rate of more than 40 percent in the third quarter."[92]

For trade unions, this is the most inflammatory aspect of relocation—what the U.S. Labor Department terms "a surge in corporate productivity" accompanying the one-way freefall in jobs. This is not just an American phenomenon. In France, too, leading daily *Le Monde* discussed the same 'paradox,' by which corporate recovery has made no impact on employment.[93]

Another red flag is the bulging cash reserves of large corporations highlighted for example by Intel's $13.5 billion[94] or Microsoft's $51.6 billion,[95] and fuelled by one focus of Senator John Edwards presidential campaign on the "avarice of multinational corporations."[96] Once again, this is not only an American phenomenon. In Britain, Dave Fleming, national secretary of the Amicus union's finance department, noted that insurance giant Aviva (one of the largest relocators to India) "is making extraordinary profits while at the same time sacking thousands of workers."[97]

The jobs issue, and the wider political implications of globalization quickly became central to the campaign of the Democratic Party's presidential candidates in the U.S. According to the *New York Times*, "challenging the wisdom of free trade agreements has become a blood sport" in presidential primaries.[98] Senator John Kerry seized the jobs bull by the horn with a statement that President Bush has "failed to deliver on a promise to create 250,000 jobs last month when only 1,000 new jobs were recorded."[99] On the other hand, Kerry also has an exposed flank for attacks by Republicans, who accuse him of being "elitist and offensive,"[100] since he opposes white-collar relocation far more vigorously than he did with its blue-collar counterpart, having voted for NAFTA.

The domestic political temperature in America about offshore outsourcing is clearly rising. In the *Washington Post* of January 14, 2004, columnist Harold Myerson observed: "Outsourcing has turned the phrase 'investment-led growth' into the grimmest of oxymorons. It means that Bush's tax policy subsidizes job growth in India and China rather than the United States." The undercurrents of such a statement become truly explosive, given that these two countries could very well emerge as global economic and political rivals to the U.S.

Fred Bergsten, director of the Institute for International Economics and a former Treasury official in the Carter administration puts such a challenge in context: The next president will "confront the great changes that are occurring in a world in which China and perhaps India will come to dominate global manufacturing.... Globalization—more than terrorism, the end of the Cold War or any other phenomenon—represents the dominant change in world affairs."[101]

Evidence of American strategic concerns about the white-collar job exodus came in the form of a keynote address in July by former U.S. Secretary of State Henry Kissinger to the CA World 2003 Conference, an annual jamboree sponsored by Computer Associates. In response to a question by Sanjay Kumar, the Indian-origin Chairman and Chief Executive of the U.S. IT services giant, Dr. Kissinger said that "the United States needed to develop incentives to prevent increasing outsourcing" and added that "if the outsourcing would continue to a point of stripping the U.S. of its industrial base and of the act of getting out its own technology, I think this requires some really careful thought and national policy probably can create incentives to prevent that from happening.'"[102]

Seizing such apprehensions, some U.S. opponents of relocation have begun associating with the 'Buy America' movement (which mainly concerns manufactured goods, above all with strategic-military implications). In October 2003, at a hearing on outsourcing of high-technology jobs, Don Manzullo, the straight-talking Republican Chair of the U.S. House Committee on Small Business, advocated a more U.S.-centered purchasing plan for the Department of Defense stating that it was "imperative that Congress strengthen and fight for stronger 'Buy America' legislation.'"[103] *Tech Republic* notes that there are "plenty of people" who would call a company outsourcing to India "'unpatriotic' (or worse—if in fact there IS a worse insult, these days!)."[104] Issues of security (and privacy) are expected to acquire center-stage status in the relocation debate in the years ahead, although as explained, India is already preparing itself to robustly counter such concerns.

If You Can't Beat Them, Ban Them

In late 2002, New Jersey—followed by three other American states (Maryland, Connecticut and Washington)—tabled legislation to stop offshore outsourcing of IT work involving public funds; another four states quickly joined.[105] As explained later, Indiana actively blocked a relocation contract to India in a high-profile case in late 2003.

Such efforts moved upwards to Congress at the end of January 2004, when the U.S. Senate approved a bill to ban American companies from outsourcing parts of federally awarded contracts. The restriction formed one clause within a $328 billion spending Bill, and was co-sponsored by two Republican senators, Craig Thomas and George Voinovich. It will remain in effect till September,[106] two months before the U.S. elections.

For the Indian IT industry, at whom the measure is largely directed, the impact will be largely symbolic;[107] American officials acknowledged to the *New York Times* that its effect "was likely to be minimal."[108] It is confined to certain kinds of federal contracts where few Indian companies have yet ventured, and does not apply to their mainstay private-sector clientele. Nevertheless, India is apprehensive that the Senate move sets precedents for other similar bills, as well as more moves by U.S. states. Above all, such trends, India fears, may sour its wider agenda for offshore business, even in the private sector. In alliance with powerful proponents of relocation in the U.S. and overseas, India has fired the opening shots in what will almost surely be a complex series of trade-offs over the next few years, involving the wider international trade and geopolitical agenda. Such a counter-campaign is expected to be low key in the run-up to the U.S. elections in November 2004, in order to avoid further provoking relocation opponents and raise the likelihood of more anti-offshore outsourcing measures.

Meanwhile, the first signs of a renewed bid by the states to tighten restrictions on offshore outsourcing did appear in early 2004, and the National Foundation for American Policy, a research group, said that a total of 30 bills were pending in 20 states to curb offshore outsourcing in state and local government contracts.

More moves are likely at Congress, too. In February 2004, Democratic Senator Christopher Dodd of Connecticut introduced the U.S. Workers Protection Act, seeking to ban offshore outsourcing in three areas of government work: "privatizing of federal work, federal purchase of goods and services, and state government procurements using federal funds."[109] Senate Minority Leader Tom Daschle's 'Jobs for America Act' will require corporations that send jobs overseas to report how many are being sent out, where and why. In addition, companies that lay-off 15 or more workers and send the jobs overseas must provide at least three months notice.[110]

While attention remains focused on pure offshore outsourcing, other elements of relocation remain in play. These include H-1B and L-1 visas, which permit foreign staff to come and work in the

U.S. Other than anti-offshore outsourcing efforts by states, such questions too will further complicate the scenario in the years ahead.

In the U.S. Congress, House Resolution 2688, a bill proposed by Colorado's Republican Congressman Tom Tancredo, claims that H1-B high-tech visas are a source of 'cheap labor' and has sought to abolish the program altogether[111]; onwards from October 2003, the number of H1-B visas annually issued has been allowed to lapse from a level of 195,000 to the pre-Silicon Valley boom level of 65,000.[112]

Others have turned their sights to L-1 or temporary visas, intended to allow companies to transfer employees from a foreign branch or subsidiary to the U.S. These, say some critics, are being misused (among other things, as an alternative to the H-1B). Crucially, there is no legal ceiling for L-1 visas, and their number rose nearly 40 percent to 57,700 in 2002 from 41,739 in 1999.[113] The principal culprits, says the *New York Times*, consist of India-based companies using the visas to bring in IT workers from India, and then contracting them out to American companies, sometimes on wages as little as "one-third to one-fifth of what their American counterparts earn."[114]

Florida Republican John Mica's bill (HR 2154) seeks to prevent employers from contracting out L-1 visa holding employees to other firms once they arrive in the U.S. Congresswoman Rosa DeLauro, a Connecticut Democrat, has called for a cap of 35,000 in the number of L-1 visas. Meanwhile, the USA Jobs Protection Act of 2003, co-sponsored by Connecticut Republican Congresswoman Nancy Johnson and Democratic Senator Christopher Dodd (also the architect of the U.S Workers Protection Act), sought to limit L-1 visas to companies that "did not displace U.S. workers for 180 days before or after the filing of the L-1 petition. Companies would also be required to prove that they had "taken good faith steps to recruit U.S. workers for the position." In addition, it would compel employers to pay L-1 employees "wages that are the greater of the actual wage or the prevailing wage."

Nevertheless, as discussed in subsequent chapters, establishing definitions of misuse of a visa like the L-1 is an extraordinarily difficult task, given the ingrained complexities of any cross-border service business as well as India's already massive interlocking with the Western IT services industry. Another source of confusion: unlike

H-1B visas, where Indians were by far the largest national group, they are by no means the 'principal culprits' in L-1; out of 313,699 L-1 visa holders in 2002, according to Department of Homeland Security Figures, only 20,413 were from India, while Europeans counted for the bulk, with 146,546.

In the medium-term, there will also be an uneasy trade-off between preventing foreigners traveling to work in the West on H-1B and L-1 visas, and such work being simply moved offshore. This is a straightforward prospect, given the increasing sophistication in delivery of offshore IT services, and one with arguably worse impact on U.S. jobs. A study by the American Immigration Law Foundation echoes this. Controlling inflows of skilled foreign professionals into the U.S., it warns, "would encourage increased efforts to outsource and place overseas high technology jobs and centers for research and development."[115] The political context here was also emphasized in late 2003 after the normally-reserved Indian Prime Minister concluded, "If people cannot go to where the business is, business will eventually come to where the people are."[116]

Even as the prospect of a future jobs crunch hangs in the air, views like these—encouraged from India—have found resonance. According to the *Wall Street Journal*, a group of influential U.S. Senators, led by Judiciary Committee Chairman Orin Hatch, have been "pushing a plan to circumvent the 65,000 cap on H-1B temporary worker visas...by expanding exemptions."[117]

Give or Take a Million: Two Billion Consumers in the World's Fastest Growth Markets

Politically, relocation will inevitably be encouraged and 'pulled' by governments of giant countries like India and China, which are recipients of the relocated jobs, and with who Western governments have their own increasingly complex set of dependencies. This is especially true in today's uncertain geopolitical environment. Indeed, as discussed later, India has already fired several warning shots to indicate that restrictions on offshore outsourcing will be met with forceful responses, with a potentially major impact on the wider international political and trade agenda.

Such logic has resonated powerfully with Western multinationals, for whom free trade means access to the huge Chinese and Indian markets, respectively the world's fastest and second-fastest growing, and the possibility of selling just about everything from consumer goods to infrastructure and high-technology products. As discussed later, Coca-Cola's sales in India and China in 2003 rose by 22 percent and 16 percent, compared to a global average of just 4 percent.

Business Roundtable, an association of Chief Executives of some of the U.S.' biggest firms, has sought to persuade the Bush administration "not to be swayed by the public furore over the loss of American jobs overseas and not to espouse policies that would prevent American firms from getting jobs done cost-effectively, including outsourcing and subcontracting to countries like India, China or Russia."[118]

On the other hand, it would also surely require extraordinary dexterity from Western governments, who have long lectured counterparts in developing countries on the virtues of free markets and trade, to oppose its workings once this has begun to benefit the latter.

For Azim Premji, Chairman of Indian IT giant Wipro, the anti-offshore outsourcing bill by the U.S. Senate in early 2004 was "unforgivable"—an "extreme demonstration of double standards." He pointed out that, responding to American requests, the Indian government had reduced import duties on software and information technology imports "from 200 percent to about 5 percent in the last two years"[119]—thus providing huge opportunities in India for American businesses.

India will no doubt also point out that it is playing by the rules of the free-market game. Examples include a major order for 800,000 telephone lines to China's Huawei from State-owned telecoms company MTNL, overturning a bid by another Indian State-owned firm, ITI.[120] Such market access, however, not only concerns hardware. In spite of the huge presence of its homegrown software industry, India's (federal) Reserve Bank awarded a key IT contract to Europe's LogicaCMG, while its income tax department has done the same with American firms. In February 2004, Indian mobile phone operator Bharti TeleVentures' awarded an outsourcing contract to Sweden's Ericsson; the $400 million Bharti order was twice the size of India's own largest outsourcing order until that date.[121] Such examples stretch to high-end niches. An animated epic (on the Indian god Krishna) by India's JadooWorks has been outsourced to Emmy Award-winning American animation writer, Jeffrey Scott; voices belong to American actors in Los Angeles, and the music is being written in London.

Zero Sum, Or Worse: The Indians and Indiana

In contrast with such interlocked, two-way complexities, the Western world's trade conflicts with India or China on items like steel, shrimps and bed linen will remain sideshows. Their scale of impact is relatively limited, for example in the U.S., seldom concerning more than a handful of swing states, allowing for effective counter-maneuvering of interest groups, and relatively straightforward measurement of damages and punitive tariffs.

This is clearly not the case with white-collar jobs and the seamless world of cross-border IT services. Other than the sheer scale of relocation, or the trade-off between preventing foreigners traveling to the West and such work being simply moved offshore, yet another kind of zero-sum challenge central to the relocation debate riveted Americans (and Indians) in the fall of 2003.

The State of Indiana had outsourced a project to upgrade its jobless claims system to India's TCS, which triggered a furor over having an American unemployment office employing Indians rather than Americans. Unlike California, some of whose welfare benefits are managed by Citicorp Electronic Financial Services from Bangalore and Pune,[122] Indiana rescinded the contract, as part of an initiative to review the state's IT procurement process and offer greater opportunities to local companies.

But there is more beneath the surface than meets the eye. Indiana's move is expected to "appease voters, media and unions in the short term, but it will probably force the state to spend more taxpayers' dollars on revamping the benefit claims system than it had planned."[123] TCS' $15.4 million bid was as much as $8.1 million lower than those of its rivals, and its withdrawal provides a lease of life to only 65 local staff (whose Indian substitutes TCS would have brought in to work alongside 18 Americans) for the contract's duration: just four months.

In other words, 65 Indiana jobs were extended for four months at a cost of just over $8 million. There is therefore some irony in the statement by Marcus Courtney, organizer of the anti-offshore Washington Alliance of Technology Workers, about the cost of awarding the contract to TCS. It could put "state residents out of work. Free trade is not free."[124] In fact, if the above example is a typical trade-off, it is worse, and such profligacy could even turn into a campaign issue during the next U.S. elections in 2008.

But Indiana is by no means the only State impaled on the horns of these dilemmas. New Jersey now spends 28 percent more supporting a welfare claims processing system, after compelling contractor eFunds International Corp. (which has most of its staff in India), to hire 12 U.S. residents for the order.[125]

Fencing the Internet?

Indiana's effort to 'territorially' stem the relocation tide will eventually mean little due to another reason. This one, integral to the very essence of the information technology miracle, concerns Internet technologies which permit complex IT services to be both virtual and collaborative. Indeed, IT services are today not only defined as much in terms of physical jobs as procedures, alongside an intricate system of structured support inputs. IT services are also deployed effortlessly across several locations, often spanning international borders—a fact central to the 'global delivery' model of the larger firms. Complex links with India for delivering IT services are in fact already commonplace, sometimes for decades.

Before the outcry over relocation, such connections were widely advertised. For example, in a press release on a $137 million contract with National Life Group in January 2003 (which involved acquiring 158 employees from the latter), American IT services firm Keane states that the engagement will be supported both on-site at National Life's Vermont-based headquarters as well as by its Advanced Development Center in India.[126] In two job advertisements on the online recruitment portal Monster Board in mid-2003, Cap Gemini Ernst & Young explicitly notes that project support for a New Jersey-based pharmaceutical clinical trials order would be provided out of its facilities in Mumbai, India.

Such interlocking but virtual arrangements also bear upon the anti-offshore outsourcing debate. Thus, in Indiana, aside from TCS, the only other contenders for the contract, Accenture and Deloitte Consulting, already have sizable Indian operations, and plan huge expansions in the near term. Accenture, for example, plans to double its Indian staff to 10,000 by the end of 2004[127]; it is unlikely to be using them exclusively for servicing local customers in India.

Similar reasoning may apply too to Sprint Corp's shutting out of India's Wipro and Infosys from a five-year software applications contract, which was eventually awarded to IBM and EDS. Dan Zadorozny, an EDS vice president, said his company was chosen, in part, because workers 'are U.S. citizens paying U.S. taxes.' Although "Sprint gets to wave the U.S. flag", it has, he warned, also "got to get the cost of systems down."[128] Like Accenture and Deloitte, EDS and IBM too have huge Indian operations, and India would be an obvious means to 'get the cost down,' surely over five years.

More crucially, Indian inputs need not even be announced, and will be impossible to track or quantify, given the ingrained complexities of large IT services contracts, above all those with multi-year lifetimes. In fact, there already is substantial evidence about difficulties in determining how global IT firms structure (and price) such kinds of large bids. In early 2004, the U.S. General Accounting Office was reported to uphold a protest by Lockheed Martin against an $860 million contract won by EDS from the Department of Housing and Urban Development, on just such grounds.[129]

Complicating matters still more is the lack of choice. In January 2004, IBM moved part of a contract with Australia's telecoms carrier Telstra to India, for 'competitive' reasons. The price: 450 Australian IT jobs, and although unions estimate that the figure could grow to 1,500, there was little they could do. A Telstra spokesman "said the contract with IBM covered the delivery of services, but not who was employed or where."[130] One month later, the embattled Australians saw Telstra seeking to renegotiate another $300 million five-year contract with global consulting group Deloitte, "which has substantial information technology operations in India.... Close to 800 Telstra jobs related to IT may have moved to India in the recent past," said an Indian newspaper.[131]

The political response in Australia has sought to address the who-and-where, but returns directly to the parameters (and limitations) of the Indiana case. An opposition spokesman urged the Government to review Telstra's eligibility for future federal contracts "if it continued to export jobs." This is of course hardly feasible given that few other contenders are likely to replace either Australia's largest telecommunications carrier, IT services companies like IBM and Deloitte, or for that matter EDS and Accenture; only such firms (alongside their large Indian competitors) have the capacity for global delivery—buttressed, in turn, by fast-growing Indian operations; as explained below, Telstra also awarded substantial contracts in September 2003 to India's Infosys and Satyam.

Arguments would also apply to the above anti-offshore outsourcing initiative in Colorado where Senate Bill 169 is directed against companies which relocate 100 jobs or more outside the U.S.; finding an American IT services company which has adequate skills, but has yet to relocate just 100 jobs, is going to be difficult indeed.[132]

Such structural factors (directly related to the longer-running rise of India) will eventually also undermine efforts like Senator Dodd's U.S. Workers Protection Act, under which state governments would be eligible for federal funds only after they "certify" that the money will not go offshore. Efforts like this will at best serve to only prevent Indian IT firms becoming principal contractors, not from subcontracting with 'American' firms; neither would they wholly rule out contributions by the latter's growing staff in India.

Meanwhile, government contracts will remain impossible to police—in the event that anti-offshore laws do (even temporarily) take hold. Who, for example, will (or can) determine whether or not American IT services firm Covansys, whose clients include the National Flood Insurance Program and the Washington State Department of Health, but which has "52% of total headcount"[133] in India, has used no IT-procedural 'Indian' inputs for such contracts, or if it has, extricate them after passage of such a law? More important, who would bear the extra costs of determining and enforcing territorial compliance? IT services firms, for one, are unlikely to volunteer.

As BearingPoint (formerly KPMG LLP) became the latest global player (in February 2004) to join the India bandwagon, it will

become an increasingly-tough call to find territorially-pure alternatives, unless of course governments sets up their own IT companies.

A Nation of Fat Cats and Hair Dressers?

In the face of such complex (and sometimes inexorable) factors, the challenges of relocation are regularly reflected in doomsday
headlines in a suddenly-awakened mass media, and in increasingly-
bitter protests by white-collar trade unions, from California to
Australia. Rumblings of discontent are found too in the 'anti-globalization' movement, which, as Chapter VII explains, has yet to
grasp the fact that more than a third of the world's population in its
two largest countries, China and India, seem on their way to becoming clear winners from globalization.[134]

The media has naturally leaped into this kind of fray, and news-
paper headlines covering the issue of white-collar relocation have
screamed: 'Despair of the Jobless,' 'Outsourcing to Usurp More U.S.
Jobs,' 'Outspoken, Outgunned, Outsourced,' 'New Epic War Over
U.S. Jobs,' 'Outsourcing Tsunami Gets Stronger,' 'British Union
Warns of Indian Jobs Decimation,' 'Visa Program Robs U.S.
Technology Workers of Jobs, Dignity,' or 'Indian Call Center Move
Idiotic.' Nor, amidst a recession, would many U.S. white-collar
workers have been encouraged by a report that the 'Collection
Bureau of America Pledges to Keep Investing in American Labor.'[135]

Even respected magazines have used personal names, selective-
ly picking 'human-interest' angles for their stories, and trivializing
the complexities of the issue. For example, *BusinessWeek* highlighted the case of Toshiba America adding "insult to injury" by compelling an American software professional to train his (future)
replacement from India.[136] Once again, using a single example, the
Associated Press called such training a "humiliating assignment,"
which Americans are forced to accept "unwittingly or reluctant-
ly."[137] Another report quoted Evie Barber, 54, an American microbi-
ologist who stated: "I know people with advanced degrees going into
pet-sitting, or dog-grooming."[138] Raising the temperature further,
TechWeb mentioned a Bank of America programmer who apparently committed suicide when his job was moved to India.[139]

In Britain, white-collar science and engineering union Amicus urged the government in June 2003 "to tackle an alleged social and industrial 'earthquake' caused by the export of information technology jobs to India." Amicus advised ministers to set up an independent commission to investigate the issue, warning that "Britain will turn into a nation of 'fat cats and hairdressers'" unless action was taken.[140]

Another proposal was a consumer boycott of companies who relocate. According to a study conducted for Amicus, "British consumers would 'punish' companies that transfer call centre and other jobs to India."[141] Near the end of 2003, Amicus released the results of a survey, which endorsed its views.[142] One out of three respondents were highly concerned about employment trends as well as the seeming absence of corporate responsibility or government action to stem the tide (especially in light of the collapse of manufacturing industry in the 1980s). A larger share, one of two, thought it important to know the geographical location of a call-center, while a clear majority thought British consumers should support British jobs. Most pertinently, a majority also said that service by U.K.-based call-centers was "highly satisfactory or excellent." In contrast, only 17 percent believed cost savings from offshore outsourcing were passed on to consumers.

Nevertheless, the limits to the usefulness of the government's 'independent' commission were quickly evident. As mentioned later, powerful Indian business interests forced their way into the government commission. Also indicative of the shape of things to come was a report by the *Guardian* in February 2004 that after a "government-inspired 'round table' of opposing sides" in the relocation debate, "delegates were banned from revealing the content of discussions, which were held in secret."[143]

As for the boycott, it remains to be seen if tactics developed for manufacturing companies could be applied to the far-more concentrated services sector. In general, only a handful of service firms provide access to necessities such as telecoms, healthcare and insurance. Thus, substitution is not only impossible, but given today's highly competitive climate, relocation to India by one company is almost always, quickly followed by others. On the other hand, as discussed later, Indian IT firms have recently begun stepping up recruitment of Western nationals, both for their home operations and in the West; at Belfast, India's HCL Technologies, for example, already employs 861 staff, an increase of 30 percent in 2003 alone.

Given such ingrained complexities in the relocation tide, opponents have sometimes simply resorted to shooting obvious blanks.
For example, reflecting little awareness of the scope of sophisticated
geographical information systems (GIS) in use today—both in India
and elsewhere—Caroline Jones of the Rail Passengers Council crit-
icized British Rail plans to move part of its passenger inquiry services to India: "Our main concern would be a lack of knowledge about
the rail network in the U.K. If you call up asking about trains from
Peterborough to King's Cross, there's no way they're going to know
every stop en route."[143]

As 2003 turned, in spite of British unions' Pink Elephant campaigns to alert the public about the drift of white-collar jobs to India,
the real Elephant continued to rise. So too did temperatures, among
the victims of relocation.

Raising the Temperature:
Gut Reactions and Short-Term Feelgood

In Australia, massive trade union protests accompanied the
announcement in September 2003 that India's Infosys Technologies
had won a bellwether $75 million order from telecoms carrier
Telstra. The situation was further aggravated by the revelation that
the Australian firm had also set up an offshore unit in Bangalore
with yet another Indian IT firm, Satyam.[145] In response, critics of the
unionists' ire, "focused mainly against Indian IT companies with significant presence in Australia, have been terming their protest as
'racist.'"[146] No one, of course, minded when non-Australian
American firms such as IBM or EDS were winning similar orders, or
anticipated that such orders might later be farmed out to their fast-
growing operations in India (which as described earlier, is exactly
what IBM and Deloitte have since done).

Reactions by victims of relocation have been sharper than
trade unions. One good example is the widespread kind of statement
that American programmers are forced by employers "to teach a
bunch of Indians your job"[147]—not 'group' or 'team,' but 'bunch,'
like fruit, implicitly suggested to be doing the job of one American.

Like trade unions, such reactions are, however, to be expected.
After all, Indian farmers have done worse, more recently, by seeking

to set American chemicals giant Monsanto's offices on fire. Large sections of the Arab world too do not agree with what Americans are doing to their countries. But these kinds of reactions are largely reflexes, and can be explained.

What cannot are provocative but reasoned actions by governments of 'civilized' States. In March 2003, the Netherlands demonstrated an extraordinary sense of irresponsibility by pushing for the jailing in Britain of the local Chief Executive of Indian software company i-Flex.[148] The reason: procedural violations, by some of his staff, of 'business' visas. As obvious to everyone involved in information technology consulting, it is extraordinarily difficult to determine when 'business' ends and 'work' begins—including those Europeans and Americans who visit India for business/work.

Such a scenario has yet to be played out in the U.S.,[149] but could be a consequence of the ongoing review of L-1 visas in that country. Once again, this would be due to unpredictabilities in cross-border business procedures, by which, for example, an Indian firm contracting for the supply of IT services to an American customer, may require the 'transfer' of manpower from its Indian operations to the U.S. for a period of time; neither the level of manpower nor the duration of transfer can be established upfront. However, such imprecision may be no more than a technical issue, rather than binding proof of 'illegitimate' intentions.

i-Flex, now the world's largest banking software company, was an Indian spin-off from Citigroup, the American financial services giant, and is due to list in the U.S. stock market in 2005. Many in India wondered whether a white American Chief Executive from Citi would have met the same fate in the Netherlands. Others speculated about the sequence of events if the reverse had occurred. What if India had jailed a top European executive on similar regulatory gray-area grounds? The outcry would no doubt have been different.

Fortunately, India's response was merely diplomatic, if still forceful. As shown later, one of the Indian government's priorities in Europe seeks to ensure that new rules will clear such confusion over visas held by Indian professionals.

But such barely-concealed racism is not only about IT. American Congressman Billy Tauzin casually describes Indian generic drugs as "nothing but pond water."[150]

Both the i-Flex and Tauzin cases illustrate the absence of recognition in the West about the rapid scale of change underway in India (especially over the past decade) and the fact that many traditional assumptions about the country mean little any more.

i-Flex is hardly a backwater supplier of cheap labor. As Britain's *Economist* belatedly recognized two months after the arrest of its Chief Executive, i-Flex is the developer of Flexcube, "the world's best-selling banking-software product," with "more than 120 customers in over 50 countries," including blue-chip Western banks and the IMF.[151]

Likewise with Congressman Tauzin, who is clearly unaware that India is one of the world's largest exporters of generics and bulk drugs, with 60 FDA (Food and Drug Administration) certified manufacturing plants (the highest number outside America), and already the top foreign supplier of antibiotics to the U.S. As Chapter II shows, Indian firms could soon be selling low-cost generic versions of nine of the top 20 drugs in the U.S., propelled by the inevitable pull from Americans to contain soaring costs of prescription medicines. Indeed, if Congressman Tauzin ever has need of a pain-killer, an antibiotic or a hypertensive, there is a one-in-four chance that he is already using Indian-made medicines.

Such jaundiced and anachronistic associations of India are stronger in Europe. While *Computer Business Review* proclaims that "high-end technology consulting, back-office and call center work is expected to keep 813,500 IT workers **off the streets** in India,"[152] Germany's respected *Frankfurter Allgemeine Zeitung* newspaper is a little subtler in its resistance to accepting a poor and 'dirty' Third World country probing the upper ends of its country's clean, high-tech competencies. In its search for foreign software professionals, and in spite of a language providing enormous room for subtlety, Germany, after all, continues to label some of the world's most-talented people 'Gastarbeiter' (guest laborers).

Thus, the revelation (in a summer 2001 speech by U.S. President George Bush) that India was among a select group of countries in the field of advanced stem-cell research was described by the German daily as 'grotesque.'[153] Needless to say, it has yet to report on something described in the next chapter—German drugs giant Bayer's purchase of pathbreaking, once-a-day antibiotic drugs delivery technology from India's Ranbaxy (a means to control an enduring problem associated with antibiotics, namely compliance)—a task in which Bayer itself had failed.

Hiding the Elephant's Hide

As the report by *The Frankfurter Algemeine Zeitung* shows, the gap between fast-changing global realities, and complacent, sometimes racist, prejudices, on the part of the Western media, is growing. This is particularly damaging for one reason. Unlike the Chief Executives of corporations, whose job it is to make profits, the media's role is to inform, and where possible, explain. Given the tectonic shifts underway in the world order, as much as being wrongly opinionated, a lack of basic research and follow-up of facts by journalists, especially pertaining to the eight myths listed in the beginning of the book, is foolish.

For readers, above all victims of relocation (present and future), such rehashing of clichés simply misleads their attempt to understand events, and the context of faraway developments impacting, often massively, upon their lives.

While ample examples of the media's propensity for temporarily-comforting myths about relocation (and India itself) are provided through the book, an especially damaging instance, however, is the trend, especially since end 2003, to overplay the smallest signs of reversal in relocation. Such a habit is expected to strengthen in the years ahead, as powerful forces associated with relocation increasingly manipulate gullible journalists.

Thus, the months of November and December 2003 saw a veritable blizzard of news articles, which grossly exaggerated routine and relatively-small adjustments by two American giants, Dell and Lehman Bros., with respect to their Indian operations.

On November 25, an *Associated Press* headline proclaimed "Dell Returns Corporate Tech Support to the U.S.," following an alleged "onslaught of complaints." This was quickly picked up by the international media and widely reported, although *Reuters*, the Associated Press' rival, quickly changed its tack later in the day with a "CORRECTED—Dell says some calls to India being rerouted," advising editors to note that only "some," "not all" calls were at issue.

But the damage had been done. The next day *Computer Business Review*, in an article titled 'Dell Calls Switched Away from India," claimed Dell was "re-routing customer calls away from India, following complaints over the company's level of technical support." Even the authoritative *Financial Times* could not resist the headline 'Dell cuts back India customer service venture,' although it pointed out that, rather than 'technical support,' what prompted the move was 'complaints about the Indian accent'[154] of some of its staff.

In early December 2003, a Dell spokesman clarified the picture, saying that the re-routing was just a shuffle and the company "would not be sending fewer calls over all" to its Indian operation. "'We just flipped a switch,' he said, explaining that some consumer calls that had been handled by domestic call-centers would now be sent to India."[155]

A Dell-type scenario was again replayed, when Lehman Bros. decided to return a small 26-person help-desk from India back to the U.S. *BBC News* claimed that the move "bucks a trend that has seen Indian companies attract an increasing number of U.S. and European clients,"[156] while *Computer Business Review* (once again playing up to its mainly European readership) proclaimed "Offshore Backlash Grows as Lehman Pulls Out," citing "poor quality of service"[157] as a principal reason for the decision.

Clarification came later in the month from the *Financial Times*. The pull-back concerned "a small information technology help desk...leaving most of its Indian outsourcing unchanged." It also noted that such a move was not unusual in a young industry, especially given the "breakneck" 60 percent annual growth rate of Indian revenues. The more relevant information, completely absent from *Computer Business Review* and many other media reports (and never clarified): "Charlie Cortese, Lehman's IT chief, was quoted as saying that despite moving the 26 help desk jobs back to the U.S., by 2005 Lehman may double to 900 the number of people working on its software design and support projects at its Indian IT partners, Wipro and Tata Consultancy Services."[158]

Indeed, as discussed below, while large IT firms have capped back-office exposure, much of the wider Indian industry is aware of the serious correction overdue, and the risk of reaching out too far and fast to low-end contact centers targeted at the general Western public.

It is easy to see the forces of racism and fear working in such examples. But more important is the media conjuring up consolation by suggesting that outsourcing was being stemmed after an outcry over call centers. As will be shown, call centers are not only a very small part of relocation, but the far-more significant issue about relocation of higher-value information technology jobs was buried as a result, within the falsely-comforting whiteout of half-truths. Such a higher-value exodus is in fact strengthening.

The Unstoppable Storm

In late 2003, a jobs plan from IBM (known as 'Global Sourcing') reported that: "We expect our hiring next year in the U.S. to equal or increase over 2003 levels. In fact, on a percentage basis, our forecast is for hiring across the Americas to outpace the hiring in the rest of the world." However, according to data from the *Wall Street Journal*, IBM's only job creation by the end of the year was in India. In addition, observed the *Journal*, about 947 people in IBM's key Application Management Services Division would be told in the first half of 2004 that their jobs would be handled overseas; another 3,700 jobs would move later but the timing was uncertain.[159]

Even as giants like IBM (and, as described later, Microsoft and Sun Microsystems, Oracle and Cisco, Yahoo and Google, EDS, Accenture and BearingPoint) continue a seemingly-ravenous pace of expansion in India, Wall Street too seems to have succumbed to the Go-India trend. New entrants include J.P. Morgan Chase, Morgan Stanley, Deutsche Bank, Bank of America and Bank of New York, following the likes of GE, McKinsey & Co. and A.T Kearney, which already have huge, and in several cases, 'mission-critical' operations in India.

In Britain, where "some 30 companies have shifted 50,000 jobs" to India in 2001 and 2002,[160] the relocation process gathered near-breakneck momentum in late 2003. In the month of October alone, banking giant HSBC said it would shut five processing centers in Britain and move 4,000 jobs to India, Malaysia and China,[161] while Lloyds TSB announced it would close its call center in Newcastle (the second to be shut down after another operation at Gateshead) and transfer about 1,000 jobs to its new center at Hyderabad, India.[162] Also in October, the Barclays banking group announced it was conducting a 'feasibility study' on an Indian operation and was looking at outsourcing some of its 350 positions abroad,[163] while high street bank Abbey National confirmed that 100 jobs would be filled in Bangalore by the end of 2003 (in January 2004, Abbey moved 400 Scottish jobs[164] as well as another 200 from its Derby call center[165] to India). British Rail, too, joined the bandwagon, announcing in November that it was planning to move its National Rail Enquiries service to India;[166] soon after, the country's largest insurer Aviva (accounting for one-fifth of Britain's home and motor car policies) announced it would move 2,350 call-center, information technology and office jobs to India.[167] In December, another insurance giant, Prudential, said it planned to increase employment in India to 850 people by mid-2004, as well as delegate more complex work to its Indian center,[168] while BT (British Telecom) announced that 2,200 back-office jobs would be created in India.

Marking the comprehensive pull by India in early 2004, both Aviva and BT also announced major software technology deals in early 2004 with Indian IT firms. Aviva selected Wipro as "a strategic partner" to provide "a range of IT services covering application development and maintenance, package implementation and testing,"[169] while BT assigned Infosys an "advanced development deal" to provide an automated resource management system,[170] alongside continuing telecoms software work with its longstanding joint venture partner Mahindra.

Alex Taylor, head of BT's technical services arm Exact, does not conceal the fact that the company is considering outsourcing the entire lifecycle of IT processes from start to finish, largely due to "the maturity of many of India's outsourcing suppliers." While in 1999 he had returned from India wondering what the company could outsource, he now asks himself "'What should we keep onshore?' because they can do everything there now."[171]

Offshore Stuffed Back in the Closet

One consequence of the rising political temperature accompanying the relocation debate is an 'undergrounding' of offshore outsourcing, the undesirability of this fact made even more so because of the gullibility of much of the business media.

Though long practiced in Europe, where companies were loath to release details of their Indian activities, mainly for a profound fear of being seen as 'exploiting' 'cheap' workers, this trend is also strengthening elsewhere.

According to news reports in the Indian media, many American firms too have suddenly begun turning cold "to the idea of announcing expansion plans in Asian countries, due to the fact that it may cause ripples and repercussions back home."[172] Confirming such a trend was a *Reuters* news item at the end of 2003, which quickly changed its title "US Companies Moving More Jobs Overseas" to "CORRECTED: U.S. Companies Quietly Moving More Jobs Overseas."

The *Reuters* report stated that the U.S. sales director of "one of India's top computer services providers said his company has won business from customers such as Walt Disney Co., Time Warner Inc.'s CNN and the Fox division of News Corp.—none of which want public disclosure." In India, the report added, some U.S. technology companies "have recently adopted lower profiles. Microsoft Corp. has been removing its name from minibuses used to ferry engineers on overnight shifts."[173] In the politically-charged call-center business, "suddenly" Indian reps "weren't eager to divulge where they were from. 'Oh, we're not allowed to disclose location,' said one nervous voice. It was very cloak and dagger."[174]

On their part, Indian companies also face an additional worry. "Clients are said to be very particular about the non-disclosure agreement and very stringent about it."[175] Such secrecy even extends to U.S.-listed Indian IT firms such as Wipro and Infosys Technologies ("which used to come out with names of 'marquee' clients during their quarterly results," but "hardly announced any names during the June (2003) quarter results"[176]).

Two unfortunately-timed developments in the U.S. in July 2003 added significant fuel to the belief that large corporations had already developed an ingrained habit of furtively making major relocation decisions. On July 3, the WashTech affiliate of the Communication Workers of America union reported software giant Microsoft's "secret plan to lay off at least 800 tech support employees as it shifts the work to India and Nova Scotia."[177] The report was based on workers who "overheard managers discussing the planned layoffs and office closings." More damagingly, it said the relocation plan "calls for quietly and steadily laying off groups of workers over the next several months so that the magnitude of the firings doesn't make headlines." On her part, a Microsoft spokeswoman, echoing the practice of intelligence agencies, "declined to either confirm or deny the report but did acknowledge that the company had a new 'pilot program' for call-center work underway in India."

More damaging was a conversation recorded by an employee at another U.S. technology giant, IBM, and provided through a white-collar union to the *New York Times* later in the month. During a conference call with colleagues around the world, "two senior IBM officials" said the company needed to "accelerate" its efforts to move "white-collar, often high-paying, jobs overseas even though that might create a backlash among politicians and its own employees."[178]

Pressures for secrecy will inevitably be limited in time, given the already major role of offshore outsourcing in many Western corporations, and the fact that its share is expected to grow in the years ahead. In other words, the numbers involved will soon be simply too big (if they already are not) to avoid making relocation central to discussions on strategy, not just between top management (as in the case of IBM) but with shareholders and market analysts too.

Nevertheless, such 'undergrounding' remains highly undesirable for now, given the growing need for hard and verifiable information as well as proactiveness and transparency, in order to responsibly engage in the debate and manage the relocation process itself.

There are however exceptions, such as Kyocera Wireless Corp., a leading U.S. wireless handset manufacturer. Its Vice-President for Software Engineering Refael Bar said simply "We are looking at shifting software jobs from our San Diego center" to a new facility in India. He added that "nearly one-third of the total number of software engineers employed with Kyocera Wireless will be based out of the Bangalore center" by the end of 2003 and was "looking at the possibility of stopping further recruitments in the U.S. while beefing up the team in Bangalore."[179]

A Job Created by Any Other Name

As previously discussed, there are real concerns about whether 'departed' American jobs, especially those being created overseas rather than in the U.S., have left the country for good.

The first signs of U.S. economic recovery in early 2004 reinforced the prevailing pessimism, especially about the higher-value technology jobs segment. The American Electronics Association warned that the information technology sector would lose about 234,000 jobs in 2004, most of them earlier in the year, compared with 540,000 job losses the year before. U.S. commentators were quick to point out that "what qualifies as good news in the technology industry is not so much evidence of overall job gains, but signs that job losses have slowed considerably."[180]

In February, a veritable volcano of protests accompanied comments by the Chairman of the President's Council of Economic Advisers, N. Gregory Mankiw, who said that 'outsourcing' was "just a new way of doing international trade"[181] and "was good for the U.S. economy in the long run."[182] Mankiw, who later apologized and said he had been misunderstood, was merely echoing both the hands-off policy of the Bush Administration and (in spite of what Senate Democrat Tom Daschle called 'Alice In Wonderland' economics[183]) also some compelling new facts of life in the changing world order. However, like Gen. Wesley Clark's own goal over relocation discussed in Chapter IV, he was merely victim to the old adage about the bearer of bad news....

There thus remains a strong risk of false consolation, should there be on-off hiring blips in the months and years ahead, even if this does not serve to make up for a good part of the backlog, let alone structurally reverse relocation, especially with respect to high-technology jobs. Indeed, as mentioned previously, there are strong signs that American companies are simply moving higher-value jobs offshore, and that this is a long-term structural shift, accompanied domestically by unreported self-employment, and lower-skill, lower-wage—and often-temporary—jobs.

Such perspectives are endorsed by the Economic Policy Institute in Washington, for who growth in U.S. employment is largely driven by "low-skilled service jobs" in "lower-paying sectors such as retail sales and tourism." Notes the *Los Angeles Times*: "Fully two-thirds of American jobs are (already) in occupations that do not require a college degree. Of the 25 occupations projected to add the most positions between 2000 and 2010, more than two-thirds can be learned in a few days of on-the-job training. And almost half pay wages near the poverty line."[184]

The implications require little imagination. According to Christopher Jencks' new book *Low Wage America*,[185] more than 27 million working Americans (or about a fifth of the workforce), already earn wages below the poverty level.

For Jack Kyser, chief economist for the Los Angeles County Economic Development Corp., the long-term implications of such developments are "really scary", because of the cumulative and cascading impact across the wider American economic system. An economy increasingly dependent on lower-wage jobs, he says, "will have a smaller tax base and see less consumer spending, checking economic growth and reducing the quality of public services and infrastructure", he added.[186]

To sum up, other than the critical 'missing statistic' referred to previously—in terms of the correspondence between relocated jobs, and those not created at home in the U.S.—it may also be years before the underlying composition of reversals in the previous freefall can be really understood. Indeed, it is likely that a wave of political consolation conjured by new employment in the U.S. will mask the kind of jobs being created. Only out-of-work technology workers would know the real difference.

To History's Exit Ramp?

Elsewhere too in the West, the outlook remains mixed. The U.K. is forecast to see a rise of 190,000 jobs in 2004, although the Confederation of British Industry warns that two-thirds of these jobs are paid for by the taxpayer, and such growth is therefore untenable in the long term.

Continental Europe, on the other hand, remains mired in a near-recession. Two of its largest economies remain in the doldrums, with France growing just 0.3 percent in the third quarter of 2003,[187] while Germany shrank by 0.1 percent for the year.[188] For the EU as a whole, the European Central Bank forecasts economic growth of only 1.7 per cent in 2004.[189] Europe's short-term outlook is not helped by the strength of the Euro, while its navel-gazing approach to engagement with the changing world order is hardly encouraging.

Indeed, entire swathes of the New Economy have vanished from Europe without a trace. The key reason: the lack of effort by many of its firms (relatively small by international standards) to build up a serious offshore presence. Instead, like numerous other European IT companies, they sought protection solely through their 'local' credentials and generous government handouts. Meanwhile, devoid of any connection with fast-changing global realities, the decisions of a cozy cabal of intriguing backroom old-boys, Napoleonic-era Viscounts and free-lunch journalists quickly felled the likes of Holland's Baan[190] and Belgium's speech recognition specialist Lernout & Hauspie (L&H), once they stepped into the big world outside.[191]

One illustration of such time-warped perceptions is the investigation by a leading Belgian Flemish daily *De Standaard*, which concluded that L&H's collapse was engineered by foreign intelligence agencies; in the careful reasoning of the newspaper's Wim De Preter, the Belgian speech-recognition firm was developing competencies in commercially obscure languages such as Hindi, which could be of interest only to spies;[192] as Chapters V and VI indicate, India's massive e-government projects (potentially the world's largest), have made Hindi-language versions of their software central to the strategies of Microsoft, Oracle, Adobe and others. De Preter might also be puzzled by the announcement at Jerusalem in early 2004 that IBM's India labs were becoming the hub of its global R&D effort in three areas, among them "its specialization in speech recognition"— alongside "grid computing and bioinformatics."[193]

Such structural and perception fault-lines are not limited to the Benelux. Even France faces a series of Hobson's choices. While continuing to invest hundreds of millions of Euros to bail out a terminally-ill behemoth like computer manufacturer Bull,[194] 15,000 workers are due for lay-offs from France Telecom,[195] one of Bull's principal shareholders.

Businesses in Europe are evidently apprehensive of the longer-term political contexts which are rapidly emerging. According to Ruth Lea, formerly Head of Policy at the British Institute of Directors, "India and China are re-establishing themselves as major economic heavyweights," and whether or not we complain, "this seismic shift is occurring and we cannot ignore it." Though she is more optimistic about the U.S., "with its 'can-do' entrepreneurial attitudes," she quotes Paris-based Institut Francais des Relations Internationales, which states that "unless the EU changed its policies, its movement on to 'history's exit ramp' is foreseeable."[196]

Whether in America or Europe, solutions to such a morass of perplexing challenges—political, social, economic, demographic, and in the final stage, personal—are clearly not going to be straightforward. The threat is nevertheless ample and clear, above all because of its seeming unexpectedness. Even as some still seek consolation in the easily patronized parody of accent-neutralized Punjabis playing John and Jill at foreign call centers, it may be a good idea to look at the other side, the destination of the departing jobs, and the real shape in which they are emerging.

CHAPTER II

From Backoffice to Biotech

How the Elephant is Playing to Win

Though recipients of the Western white-collar job exodus range from China and Russia to the Philippines and Mexico, it is clearly one country, India, which stands out. While drawing out Western jobs in exchange for its high-quality, low-cost offerings, India has leveraged the English language and its huge lead in software services to keep well ahead of large competitors like China and Russia. On the other hand, India's massive population advantage will continue to prove a competitive handicap for smaller rivals such as the Philippines, Mexico and many others.

As the *New York Times* observed in May 2003,[1] "with its large pool of English-speakers and more than two million college graduates every year, (India) is expected to get 70 percent" of the shift of 3.3 million jobs from the U.S. forecast by Forrester Research—in other words, equivalent to almost 800 jobs, every working day. However, it is by no means only the U.S. Europe and Japan too are expected to bleed jobs. A Deloitte Research study "estimates that 2 million jobs will move to India—850,000 from the U.S., 730,000 from Europe, and 400,000 from elsewhere in Asia," and that this will happen within 5 years.[2]

Meanwhile, there remains plenty of room for growth, still untapped or coming on-stream in India. Its graduates are expected to double in number by 2010, while engineering colleges are slated to increase 50 percent in number to nearly 1,600, in four years.[3] For business guru Peter Drucker, India's higher education system is its biggest strength, and a crucial advantage against China, whose "greatest weakness" is its "incredibly small proportion of educated people."[4] Indeed, as discussed later, India produces six times more engineering graduates a year than China.

Evidence of the growing strength of the relocation process to India is perceptible. As discussed elsewhere, hardly a day now passes by without media announcements on relocation to India by large Western employers. Meanwhile, India's traditional allure for Western information technology giants such as Microsoft and Sun Microsystems, Oracle and Cisco, EDS, IBM and Accenture, also continues to strengthen, as it does for thousands of smaller software firms, most of who do not figure in national job trend samples.

Hidden Hands Everywhere

India's success in software has clearly played a decisive role in cementing its presence as a global powerhouse for skilled (and highly-skilled) manpower. "What started out with the outsourcing of application related information technology services to India has increased in scope to include the entire gamut of business processes," according to Sujay Chohan, Research Vice President of the Gartner Group.[5]

However, India's growing significance now clearly extends further than software, and involves world-class offshore services in sectors ranging from chemicals and pharmaceuticals to automotive and aerospace design, financial services research and beyond, to tax filings, book publishing and mortgage operations. The prestigious American Mayo Clinic "e-mails X rays and MRIs to radiologists in India"[6] as does Massachusetts General Hospital.[7] American mortgage lender Countywide Financial says it plans to open a 250-person call center in India by the end of 2005,[8] while, backed by an Indian production facility, publishers GGS Information offer "a complete 'One-Stop Shop' for content development, artwork and design, XML/SGML development, and prepress work."[9] Media giants Time Warner, Disney and Bertelsmann, are also reported to be "considering outsourcing parts of their information technology and back-office operations to India."[10]

BusinessWeek explained it succinctly:

> The hidden hands of skilled Indians are present in the interactive Web sites of companies such as Lehman Brothers

and Boeing, display ads in your Yellow Pages, and the electronic circuitry powering your Apple Computer iPod. While Wall
Street sleeps, Indian analysts digest the latest financial disclosures of U.S. companies and file reports in time for the next
trading day. Indian staff troll the private medical and financial
records of U.S. consumers to help determine if they are good
risks for insurance policies, mortgages, or credit cards from
American Express Co. and J.P. Morgan Chase & Co.[11]

Trolling and digesting aside, India has also rapidly climbed the
intellectual creativity chain to host top-end R&D laboratories for
some of the best known global businesses. Already, for example, the
Indian lab of Unilever, one of the world's top consumer-goods companies, has become the country's largest single private R&D facility,[12] while British foods group Cadbury is setting up a global
Innovation Center in India.[13] Both MIT's Media Lab and Bell
Labs,[14] the world's largest research lab, have opened Indian R&D
operations.

Monsanto's massive R&D facility within the Indian Institute of
Science has worked, among other things, on the 'Terminator' gene,[15]
while Strand Genomics, a U.S. venture capital-backed spin-off from
the Institute, has—in quick succession—launched three bioinformatics software products; these have been sold, among others, to the
likes of Eli Lilly, Sequoia and Abgenics. Already, in the late 1990s,
Indian biotech firm Shanta Biotechnics stunned the scientific community with the first recombinant DNA-based vaccine to emerge
from a developing country, and, as described elsewhere, others are
rapidly following. While Indian government scientists are expected
to win the race to be the world's first to develop a 'functional' genet-
ically modified food[16] using proprietary and "patented tools developed for gene prediction and functional analysis,"[17] New Delhi-
based Institute of Genomics and Integrative Biology (IGIB)
announced discovery of three new genes of the SARS virus—a step
that should help speed up development of drugs or a vaccine against
the disease.

As India revs up to also emerge as an automotive hotspot (see
Chapter V), the U.S. auto-engineering industry is busy leveraging
the country's huge range of skills. Delphi's Indian facilities, for
example, are now "an integral part of its worldwide engineering and
technical footprint."[18] In November 2003, Delphi's erstwhile parent

GM announced the opening of a software R&D center in Bangalore, its first outside the U.S., which would take up responsibility for 30 projects already underway in the country.[19] GM's Indian effort not only involves top universities such as the Indian Institute of Science but large Indian IT firms like Wipro; in late 2003, Wipro joined the handful of global IT firms claiming 'master service agreement' status with GM; the U.S. giant already contracts an estimated $400 million to Indian IT companies.[20]

For engine manufacturer Cummins, its new Indian R&D center at Pune is developing computer models needed to electronically design prototypes and upgrades; as a result, Cummins will "be able to introduce five or six new engines a year instead of two," on the same $250 million R&D budget it spent previously.[21] Also in Pune, Ferit Boysan, president and chief operating officer of American computational fluid dynamics (CFD) heavyweight Fluent, announced plans at the end of 2003 to "make India our second major hub next to our headquarters in New Hampshire in the U.S."[22]

Smaller software firms too have begun making a mark. For Quantech Global (a supplier of engineering services to GM, Ford, DaimlerChrysler, Honda and Toyota), the even distribution of jobs between 200 engineers in Bangalore and 200 in the U.S. will shift after it adds another 200 in Hyderabad.[23] Accompanying such firms are a savvy new breed of Indian niche players, such as Soliton Automation, the only winner from outside the U.S. and Europe of Advanced Imaging's Solution of the Year Award; its contribution: "a fully automated brake drum assembly inspection system for the automotive industry."[24] Elsewhere, Indian electric car manufacturer Reva is launching a Microsoft-compatible software for Palm Pilots, to enable drivers to view and record the car's energy-management, control systems and other activities.[25]

And yet, India's auto industry value-climb does not end with just information technology. Mumbai-based DC Design has successfully unveiled the prototype of the new Aston Martin AMV8 Vantage luxury sports car. DC Design aims high, and is now "seeking to take on world-leaders, (Italy's) Pininfarina and Bertone"[26] by designing and building other concept cars and prototypes.

India has now developed its competencies to the point where it has fostered another industry: teaching advanced science skills to others. India's I2IT has begun offering Masters and Doctorate programs at Moscow's Russian-Indian Centre for Advanced Computing Research (RICCR), not only in IT, but also in "emerging technologies such as biotechnology and nanotechnology,"[27] according to O.M. Belotserkovsky, the President of RICCR, which is due to be equipped in 2004 with the Indian Param Padma supercomputer.[28] Such factors, again, underscore something else: as with hydrogen power,[29] even a future NanoEconomy may have to contend with competition from an ever-advancing India.

The mindboggling emergence of India is probably most impressive at industrial giant GE, where Indians supply a near-full range of white-collar skills. At the company's Bangalore-based R&D center, according to *BusinessWeek*:

> 1,800 engineers—a quarter with PhDs—are engaged in fundamental research for most of GE's 13 divisions. In one lab, they tweak the aerodynamic designs of turbine-engine blades. In another, they're scrutinizing the molecular structure of materials to be used in DVDs for short-term use in which the movie is automatically erased after a few days. In another, technicians have rigged up a working model of a GE plastics plant in Spain and devised a way to boost output there by 20 percent. Patents? Engineers here have filed for 95 in the U.S. since the center opened in 2000.[30]

Meanwhile, at another GE facility in Bangalore:

> Gauri Puri, a 28-year-old dentist, is studying an insurance claim for a root-canal operation to see if it's covered in a certain U.S. patient's dental plan. Two floors above, members of a 550-strong analytics team are immersed in spreadsheets filled with a boggling array of data as they devise statistical models to help GE sales staff understand the needs, strengths, and weaknesses of customers and rivals. Other staff prepare data for GE annual reports, write enterprise resource-planning software, and process $35 billion worth of global invoices. Says GE Capital India President Pramod Bhasin: 'We are mission-critical to GE.' The 700 business processes done in India save the company $340 million a year, he says.[31]

It is therefore clearly no longer a question of IT services, or low-cost coding. India not only has matured as an offshore supplier of skills; these skills now encompass a huge, growing and near-comprehensive sweep of white-collar competencies and jobs. In turn, the massive response by Western businesses to the Indian advantage clearly underscore the limits to even defining what 'buy American' might mean. India is no longer just enmeshed in the marrow of Silicon Valley. The Elephant has become part of the marrow of the American, and indeed, the entire white-collar world economy, and beyond.

More Than Just A Back Office: How Business, Management Skills, Add To India's Pull

Acquisition of top-end technical skills alone would not have ensured the kind of success now being enjoyed by India. The country's free markets ensured that local IT companies quickly saw the limits to purely techno-demographic opportunities such as the Year 2000 coding boom. Instead, they realized that long-term value (and profits) required investing (sometimes heavily) in the creation of adequate professional skills at the techno-managerial middle level, an area where a potential competitor like China is simply outclassed.

The impact is dramatic, as India not only does what Japan did with the motor car, but goes beyond. "The Japanese pioneered the introduction of efficiencies within a single organization," says Arvind Thakur, head of the software-services division of Indian IT firm NIIT. "But we are introducing efficiencies through the whole chain from supplier to customer through the application of IT."[32]

Other than their armies of software programmers at home, one reason why Indian software firms like Infosys Technologies and Wipro are now ranked on par with the likes of EDS and Computer Sciences Corp. in U.S. market capitalization is that they are winning orders for end-to-end business solutions, rather than simply programming skills. Similar market capitalization scenarios are also expected from India's largest software exporter, privately-held TCS, whose IPO in 2005 is expected to raise $6-7 billion.[33] All three firms, TCS, Infosys and Wipro, are set to pass the billion-dollar revenue mark for the year 2003.[34]

Atul Vashistha, Chief Executive of U.S.-based IT advisory firm neoIT, underscores this crucial Indian advantage vis-a-vis China, which faces a huge "shortage of (a) middle management workforce."[35] This may explain the massive preference for India vis-a-vis

China as an offshore destination, in spite of relatively higher costs. For example, consulting giant Accenture predicts that 70,000 British insurance jobs will have moved to India by the turn of the decade,[36] in spite of only very small savings in cost per life assurance policy ("above £20" in the U.K., compared "to under £15" in India, but as little as "under £5" in China).[37]

A very similar process of internal reshaping of Indian corporations—to enable them to compete globally within the next decade—has also been underway in sectors other than IT. This is especially true for pharmaceuticals and biotechnology where "India could become as prominent"..."as it is in information technology,"[38] according to the *Los Angeles Times*. A key factor for such success lies beyond India's R&D skills alone, extending to its steadily-nurtured management expertise.

BusinessWeek concludes simply: Unlike China, "India's significant cheap labor isn't a big pool of factory workers but a huge crop of scientists."[39] Singapore's Prime Minister Goh Chok Tong goes further: "China has become the world's factory floor, while India has become its IT and back office."[40]

Show Me the Money:
India Moves in on Financial Services

Indian software firm MphasiS processed tax returns of 20,000 Americans in 2003; analysts predict that 100,000[41] to 200,000[42] will be processed in India in 2004, in what the *New York Times* describes as "one of the best-kept secrets among tax preparers."[43] News and financial information giant Reuters, heavily dependent on Indian-American founded IT firm Tibco for its online technology, is shifting "much of the core" of its operation to India,[44] while according to the BBC, "lawyers in England and Wales are moving legal document production overseas in the latest transfer of skilled jobs to India."[45]

In 2003, Wall Street began to succumb to the Go-India trend. J.P. Morgan Chase said it plans to outsource stock-market research and analysis to India.[46] Morgan Stanley and Deutsche Bank are also considering such a move, taking the cue from firms such as McKinsey & Co. and A.T. Kearney Inc., which have already "shifted the bulk of their research divisions to India."[47] Bank of New York says it expects to shift 250 jobs to its India operations, increasing staff to almost 1,000.[48] After working for a decade with Indian IT firms, Bank of America plans to set up its own Indian 1,000-staff subsidiary[49] and move "more jobs offshore"[50]; this decision is the outcome of a high-level visit by its executives to India as long ago as 2001.

More than economics drives such decisions, in certain cases. A survey by headhunters Russell Reynolds found that "Wall Street is (also) outsourcing white-collar research positions to India as a reaction to the independence issues that have plagued the sell side"[51]—namely the series of scandals which erupted in 2002 and 2003, concerning conflicts of interest within the U.S. financial services industry.

The sums associated with such moves will be staggering. The Deloitte Research study referred to earlier estimates that "$356 billion worth of global financial services will relocate to India in the next five years, producing a cost saving of $138 billion for the top 100 financial service firms."[52]

From Six Sigma Management Down to the Call Center: How India Hangs Up on its Competition

In effect, drawing on its strengths in information technology, India is steadily accruing advantage in the wider white-collar services sector, especially what has come to be known as back-office services. These are formally labeled as business process outsourcing (BPO) services, or more tellingly, information technology-enabled services (ITES). BPO ranges from data entry and data processing through accounting, customer service and call-centers, market research and engineering support to R&D—across a panoply of economic and business sectors.

India's unusually broad range of industrial and service, as well as technical and managerial, competencies, provide critical mass in its back-office offering. Compared to rivals "like China, East Europe, South Africa and Philippines," India's advantage lies in the fact that it can offer the "entire range of BPO services," according to U.S.-based Evalueserve.[53] Even at the lowest end of BPO, the humble call-center, India is targeted to have 158,000 seats by 2004, or 60 percent more than its next two competitors, China and the Philippines, put together (with 53,500 and 40,000 respectively).[54] Indeed, the serious competition for Indian back office firms comes from their Indian rivals, not those overseas.[55]

Like software, there is also a concerted effort by Indian companies to systematically move up the BPO value chain.[56] Following up their massive global lead in Capability Maturity CMM certifications from the U.S. Software Engineering Institute (see Chapter III), larger Indian IT firms have also begun concerted COPC (Customer Operations Performance Center) and Six Sigma initiatives for their dedicated BPO facilities (e.g. Wipro's Spectramind, Satyam's Nipuna and Infosys' Progeon). Alongside, equally important too are moves by Indian IT firms to limit exposure, especially at the volatile, politically-charged, lower-end call-center business. Infosys, for example, has opted to cap its overall exposure to BPO at 30 percent of income.[57] Wipro's Spectramind plans to grow its non-voice, higher-value BPO business even faster than before; last year, the share of this already leaped dramatically, from 5 percent to 14 percent.[58] For large Indian firms, BPO exposure in sectors like financials and telecoms also lends a key strategic ingredient to their IT services expertise—vertical industry competency—as they steadily move up the value chain and lock horns with their international rivals.

Small, specialized and highly-competitive Indian start-ups have entered the BPO fray—directly at the top of the value chain. One good example is marketRx, which employs just 25 people, a majority with degrees from India's elite, world-ranked Indian Institutes of Technology and Indian Institutes of Management. Funded by U.S. venture capital firm Westbridge Capital, marketRx focuses on KPO (or knowledge process outsourcing) for the sales force of pharmaceutical firms in the U.S. Its clients include Bristol Myers Squibb, Johnson & Johnson, GlaxoSmithKline and Eli Lilly, and its per-head billings are at least 10 times an average Indian BPO firm.

Like marketRx, the high-value (and in the West, increasingly cost-sensitive) healthcare business is seen as a priority opportunity by Indian back-office firms. According to some estimates, Indian BPO services in healthcare alone will bring in revenues of about $5 billion by 2008.[59]

Such factors drive home why India is leaving potential rivals behind, above all in the higher-value segments of the BPO business.[60] Indo-British firm Xansa, for example (which won the first bellwether, large-scale British offshore BPO orders from two giant firms, BT and Thames Water), began cutting back staff from Malaysia and Singapore in 2003, while ramping up its Indian staff from 1,200 at present to a targeted 7,000 within three years,[61] by when India would count for 50 per cent of the company's global operations.[62] Meanwhile, India's giant Hinduja group (transport, media, banking, chemicals and trading) plans to buy low-end capacity through acquisition of BPO firms in Southeast Asia.[63] Using a $20 million investment from U.S.-based General Atlantic, leading Indian BPO operator Daksh (whose customers include Amazon.com), has also begun rolling out a 1,000-person facility in the Philippines; other Indian firms with longer-established centers in southeast Asia include FirstRing.[64] However, such moves are not limited to Southeast Asia. In North America, Indian engineering services firm Infotech Enterprises has established a BPO center in Puerto Rico,[65] MphasiS BFL has set up a Spanish-language facility in Mexico[66] and Datamatics is scouring for opportunities in Canada.[67] Europe, too, is facing the onslaught, which began after HCL Technologies, India's fifth largest IT exporter, acquired a 90 percent stake in British Telecom's call center in Northern Ireland in October 2001[68]; more recently, Infosys started up new operations in the Czech Republic.[69]

Moving in the opposite direction towards higher-value positioning, BPO companies from the Philippines such as SPI Tech have begun entering India, to "scale up" their operations.[70] The lure of the Indian BPO dream has also not been lost on American firms. In October, Keane Inc. of Boston acquired a 60 percent stake in Indian BPO services provider Worldzen Holdings Ltd. The acquisition marked Keane's first foray into business process outsourcing" and highlighted the growing overlap between IT and BPO services, centered in India.[71] One month previously, the Indian subsidiary of Anglo-Dutch Unilever, one of the world's largest consumer goods companies, set up Indigo, a wholly owned BPO subsidiary in India, for its internal customer service and logistics support. Indigo has two divisions—one focused on the domestic Indian market, and the second on international markets.[72] Others are expected to follow suit, among them IBM and Accenture.

Neither is the BPO opportunity being ignored by India's multi-billion dollar private business houses. Aside from the Hinduja group mentioned above, other giant conglomerates, such as Essar (steel, oil, power, construction, shipping and telecoms), Godrej (personal care, food, home appliances and materials handling), Mahindra (automotive, real estate, IT), Hero (the world's "biggest bicycle manufacturer")[73] have also made acquisitions overseas to kickstart their BPO operations at the higher-value, customer-facing end; this is discussed in the next chapter. Some have acquired at home, such as the Aditya Birla Group (activities ranging from cements, metals and chemicals to energy and telecoms), which bought venture cap-ital-funded Transworks and plans massive capacity expansions in the near future.[74]

The above examples, a small sample among many, are an illus-tration of why India is indisputably becoming the world's back-office.

The Cutting Edge: Heart Surgery, Anyone?

One example of India's leveraging of its techno-process deliv-ery strengths into yet another frontier is medical care. While Indian surgeons and physicians are a common sight at hospitals in the U.S. and Britain, India-based physicians have also begun to attain grow-ing prominence. So too has Indian medical education; in January 2004, American management guru Peter Drucker noted that the "medical school in New Delhi is now perhaps the best in the world."[75]

Though little noticed outside the country, Indian doctors in mid-2003 successfully performed a highly complex open heart-surgery pro-cedure on a Pakistani baby girl. Doctors in Pakistan had advised the girl's parents to take her to Bangalore for the complicated surgery "because of the superior facilities there."[76] This followed another heart surgery on an Afghan child the previous year at a hospital in Chennai.[77] Both operations were paid for by the Indian public.

In 2003, for the first time ever, Europe's EuroPCR conference invited an Asian country to demonstrate cutting-edge medical expertise. At this event, more than "2,000 interventional cardiolo-gy professionals from all over the world" watched Indian surgeons simultaneously perform two complex procedures at Chennai's Apollo Hospitals, using the "latest-generation sirolimus-eluting stent."[78]

Indian hospitals already treat over 150,000 foreign patients a year and news agency *United Press International (UPI)* notes that India is fast emerging as one of the most sought after medical destinations in Asia for offshore patients. *UPI* gives the example of India's 30 hospital-strong Apollo group, which has already treated over 60,000 foreign patients from 34 countries in the last decade. It explains the reason behind the sudden rush—not only cost savings of "between 200 percent and 800 percent," but also "an abundant supply of brains."[79]

Such advantages have also begun encouraging patients from Britain and North America. According to Naresh Trehan, Chief Executive of Escorts Hospital, "foreigners are arriving in hordes for quality medical care at low cost," especially for "angiography and angioplasty;"[80] Escorts Hospital counted more than 100 patients from the U.S. and Britain in 2003 alone. In April that year, in a widely publicized report, Chennai's Madras Medical Mission "successfully conducted a complex heart operation on an 87-year-old American at a reported cost of $8,000," inclusive of airfare and a month's stay in hospital; the patient claimed that a less complex operation in America had earlier cost him $40,000.[81] More publicity was given to a double knee-replacement operation in October, on a Scotsman who sought to avoid a prolonged (two-year) wait for treatment on the NHS, Britain's creaking, State-funded healthcare system, and instead took his chances at what he called a "top class" facility in Ahmedabad.[82]

The *BBC* explained this in more detail. While open-heart surgery in the U.K. "can cost more than $20,000 and double that in the United States," India's leading "hospitals can perform that surgery for less than $5,000. And the costs can also be covered by most major insurance policies,"[83] both in Europe and North America. Priority areas identified by Indian hospitals include "cardiology, oncology, minimal invasive surgery and joint replacement."[84]

Many such efforts will derive additional synergy from India's high-tech but highly cost-effective national telemedicine network, leveraging which, the country's private hospital groups, as discussed later, are already probing opportunities overseas.

Indian pharmaceutical firms are also extending their involvement into the hospital sector. For example, U.S. private health insurers Blue Cross and Blue Shield insure patients treated at hospitals set up by Indian pharmaceutical company Wockhardt, as does British (private) health insurer Bupa. Wockhardt is now also in talks "with Britain's National Health Service about outsourcing the treatment of British patients to India."[85]

Outsourcing healthcare is a high priority for Indian pharmaceuticals giant Ranbaxy, which has a $200 million expansion plan targeted at building up a network of pathology labs across India, the Middle East and Asia, along with an Indian hospital network consisting of five hubs and 100-125 spokes. Anchoring the process will be alliances with large hospital systems in the U.K. and West Asia. Also planned is a U.S. venture. According to the company, "It's a matter of two-three years before we reach U.S. shores and play a major role in outsourcing."[86]

Consultants McKinsey & Co. forecast that by 2012, India will earn over $2 billion a year from "healthcare tourism."[87] Given the $5,000 fees charged even for operations like open-heart surgery, this translates into no fewer than 400,000 surgical procedures. In turn, the equivalent 'loss' to the Western health care system, given an average cost of $30,000 (halfway between what *BBC News* estimated for open-heart surgery in Britain and the U.S.) would correspond to $12 billion a year. Given overstretched health care budgets in the West, the question remains: will this be seen as another cost-containment boon or yet another source for white-collar job losses?

The Drug War:
India Carves Up a New White-Collar Frontier

The challenge from India is clearly more than software or backoffices. India has positioned its skills offering across a sweeping range of white-collar sectors. However, like IT, these skills are not only directed at servicing Western employers, but also steadily building up the country's own high-technology industrial base. One of the best examples of this, and the sector most likely to have an IT-like impact on Western jobs over the next decade, is pharmaceuticals.

In February 2003, *BusinessWeek* commented, "After IT, pharmaceuticals. Faced with a glut at home, (India's) drugmakers are looking overseas for growth, and the effect could be like China's impact on electronics prices."[88] India is already "the largest exporter of antibiotics" to the U.S.[89] Its drug exports grew sharply from $1.8 billion to $2.5 billion in the year to March 2002, according to the Organization of Pharmaceutical Producers of India, and McKinsey & Co. forecasts that Indian drugs output could soar to $25 billion by 2010.[90] In turn, this growing boom "has enabled Indian drugmakers to pour money into their manufacturing facilities. They now have 60 plants approved by the Food and Drug Administration, the highest number outside the United States."[91] Today, India "ranks second only to the U.S. in the number of global Drug Master Filings every year," according to Kotak Securities; India's share has risen from 2.4 percent in 1991 to 19 percent in 2003.[92]

In essence, the relocation process in pharmaceuticals (and increasingly, biotechnology) too will be driven by factors similar to those which have made India a software powerhouse, albeit with a separation of about a decade.

Indeed, the IT-pharma interplay has itself become explicit within India. The use of Indian software strengths to leverage advantage in the pharmaceuticals sector (in fields such as in-silico modeling, clinical data management, and collaborative R&D) is now integral to India's billion-dollar pharmaceutical firm, Ranbaxy Labs, in its drive to become a global drugs industry player.[93] As mentioned earlier, Strand Genomics, a spin-off from Bangalore's Indian Institute of Science, has launched three futuristic bioinformatics products: Spathika (image analysis), Avadid (data mining) and Acuris (workflow); its clients already include Eli Lilly, Sequoia and Abgenics. According to Westbridge Capital Partners of the U.S., one of Strand's venture capital backers: "These guys are among the very best in the world in areas such as image processing, pattern recognition, visualization, and complex systems modelling."[94]

While pharma companies from India such as Dr. Reddy's, Ranbaxy, Cipla and scores of smaller ones, notch growing successes in the U.S. and Europe, in cutting-edge fields such as recombinant DNA vaccines or R&D in stem cells,[95] India is already far ahead of other developing countries, China included, and in several instances, on par with the West.[96]

For pharmaceuticals R&D, according to Peter Pfeiffer of McKinsey: "The overall cost advantage in bringing a drug to market by leveraging India aggressively could be as high as $200 million. India clearly provides an opportunity for Western pharmaceutical companies because of the availability of large patient populations, access to highly educated talent and a lower cost of operations."[97] This opportunity has already begun to be grabbed by giant international drug companies,[98] and on February 19, 2004, the *Wall Street Journal* published a feature dedicated to India's emergence as a "proving ground for new drugs." The relevance of this is compelling, given the shrinking number of drugs in the R&D pipelines of global pharmaceutical firms and the large number of drugs going off patent in the next five years—ironically, opening the door for competition from Indian generic equivalents. More important than the moral debate about Indian drug firms playing 'unfair' with 'copycat' products, the fact is that the Elephant is eroding yet another key Western high-tech frontier, pulling the global pharmaceutical industry at both ends of the value chain—from high-value R&D skills to low-end bulk drugs and generics, where India already has one-fourth of the world market.

Indian drug firms are also playing high-stakes politics on the world stage. In November 2003, former U.S. President Bill Clinton made a public appearance at an Indian pharmaceutical plant "to back the production of low-cost, lifesaving medicines" for 2 million AIDS patients in Africa and the Caribbean.[99] The deal, brokered by the Clinton Foundation, will see four Indian drug companies, Ranbaxy, Matrix, Cipla and Hetero Drugs, supply low-cost drugs to Africa.

The size of the Indian pharmaceutical industry is a key factor behind its capabilities in the AIDS battleground. Another large developing country, Brazil, lacks the capacity to treat its own AIDS patients, let alone export drugs, according to Eric Noehrenberg of the International Federation of Pharmaceutical Manufacturers' Association.[100] Indeed, India's Dr. Reddy's and Ranbaxy set up joint ventures in Brazil in 1998; other Indian firms, including Torrent, followed them after a visit to India by Brazilian Minister of Health Jose Serra in July 2000.[101] Elsewhere, Russia—once again, a large developing country—is one of Dr. Reddy's fastest growing markets, with exports rising at 40 percent,[102] and in early February 2004, Ranbaxy set up a Russian subsidiary, staffed with 120, but due to expand "substantially" in the near future.[103]

For some of the world's most powerful firms, who bitterly resisted, but failed in blocking the Indian AIDS drugs-for-Africa deal, India's combination of size and quality resources simply means little choice. As with IT, India's huge, skilled and cost-effective work force provides compulsive opportunities for pharmaceutical R&D, which simply do not exist elsewhere. Thus more than irony, there is an element of competitive necessity for Anglo-American drugs giant GlaxoSmithKline (GSK), which has signed an R&D agreement with Ranbaxy, assigning the Indian firm to "identify promising potential drugs and perform early clinical trials in India, while GSK takes care of the later-stage development."[104] GSK, meanwhile, remains locked in legal conflict with Ranbaxy over a variety of generics drugs, which GSK says infringe its patents, such as its second best-selling drug, the antibiotic Augmentin—for which Ranbaxy acquired U.S. marketing authorization in December 2003.[105]

The AIDS drugs-for-Africa deal marks the success of a sophisticated campaign by the charismatic Chief Executive of India's Cipla in the UN, conducted in association with high-profile non-governmental organizations such as Oxfam and Doctors Without Borders.[106] For international firms, a key worry lies in terms of the precedents this deal may set. Vaccines companies, largely dependent not only on Western healthcare budgets, but also international public tenders from the likes of the World Health Organization, may have special cause for apprehension. Unlike generic drugs, India's 21st century-oriented vaccines industry does not carry any generics baggage.

India's Shanta Biotechnics, as noted previously, stunned the scientific community in the 1990s with the first recombinant DNA-based vaccine to emerge from a developing country. Another firm, Bharat Biotech, is developing a third-generation hepatitis-B vaccine in collaboration with the Indian Institute of Science. This is part of a rollout of ten vaccines targeted mainly at the developing world, including one against malaria (for which Bharat is involved in a joint R&D effort with the U.S. Centers for Disease Control as well as the New-Delhi based International Centre for Genetic Engineering and Biotechnology).[107]

Such cutting-edge efforts are also apparent in fields beyond vaccines. In August 2003, Indian pharma firm Wockhardt launched its own recombinant human insulin, using a state-of-the-art drug-delivery system acquired as part of a buy-out of Britain's CP Pharma.[108]

As with IT, international venture capital funds are clearly aware of the huge opportunity offered by Indian pharma. In the third-quarter of 2003, venture capital funding in India reached $304 million; of this, three fourths went into pharmaceuticals. Reflecting the growing number of Indian drug industry players, VC recipients included the relatively unknown Aurobindo Pharma (which raised over $70 million).[109]

For international pharmaceutical companies, perhaps the most ominous long-term development is the growing (and potentially sophisticated) assault by Indian drug firms on Western markets. After the success of the AIDS drugs-for-Africa campaign, few doubt any longer that Indian firms have the political savvy for playing hardball. In America, for instance, it cannot be ruled out that Indian drug firms leverage their low-cost advantage to address a growing concern, namely the escalating costs of health care. As the *New York Times* noted in January 2004, drugs account "for 23 percent of what Americans spent on health care out of their own pockets, and 51 percent of the increase in such out-of-pocket spending from 2001 to 2002."[110] One month later, GlaxoSmithKline agreed to pay out $175 million to settle a lawsuit by American consumers, health plans and pharmacies, who alleged that it had violated antitrust law by blocking cheaper generic forms of its Relafen anti-arthritis drug.[111]

By the end of 2003, according to the *Financial Times*, Indian firms had filed applications "to sell generic versions of nine of the top 20 medicines in the U.S.—which have combined annual sales of about $29 billion."[112] They have obtained authorization for generic versions of several blockbusters, including Augmentin and another antibiotic, Ceftin, the anti-depressant Prozac, anti-acne drug Accutane and anti-AIDS Ganciclovir capsules. Dr. Reddy's generics product pipeline in the U.S. comprises 27 abbreviated new drug applications (ANDAs) and 44 drug master files (DMFs). In 2004, it expects to file another 15-18 ANDAs and 15 DMFs.[113]

The Indian generic threat, meanwhile, is also appearing in Europe. In September 2003, France's Sanofi-Synthelabo faced massive investor jitters over generic threats to its top-selling blood thinner, Plavix, from Dr. Reddy's (as well as Canada's Apotex).[114] In January 2004, Deutsche Bank downgraded stocks in Belgium's UCB to 'sell' after two Indian firms, Dr. Reddy's and emerging peptides powerhouse Divi's Laboratories, submitted Drug Master Files to the U.S. Food and Drugs Administration for generic equivalents to the anti-epileptic Keppra, one of UCB's two biggest products. Although UCB spokesman Arnaud Denis stated that this was a "nonevent for us,"[115] an indication of the shape of things on the horizon is the announcement by Ranbaxy about an agreement to acquire French drugs giant Aventis' entire generics division, RPG Aventis SA, in a bid to expand its business in Europe.[116]

However, as with IT (once again), the Indian challenge in pharmaceuticals will hardly be limited to low-value generics, and the signs of this are already emerging. Dr. Reddy's, for example, has filed two NDAs (new drug applications) in the U.S.; additional NDAs are due in 2004. It also has three molecules in clinical development (licensed to Novartis of Switzerland and Novo Nordisk of Denmark), five in pre-clinical development and has received 38 patents from the United States Patent and Trademark Office.[117] On its part, Ranbaxy has already revealed its fast-emerging higher-end capabilities by selling German drugs giant Bayer its novel, once-a-day antibiotic drugs delivery technology—for $65 million.[118]

The Speed of the BPO Revolution

Having outlined the massive sweep of industries targeted by India, the key question is: how rapid is its impact going to be. This topic is addressed more thoroughly in the next chapter, but a taste of the issue is worth sampling here. As it happens, the speed could not be swifter.

The Gartner Group estimates India had a 60 percent share of the offshore BPO (or back-office) market in 2003,[119] and by 2007, Indian BPO revenues are forecast to grow 11-fold to $13.8 billion.[120]

It is important to keep in mind the fact that Gartner's figures exclude revenues from 'captive' outsourcing centers set up in India

by individual Western corporations, such as the massive BPO operations of GE or HSBC. Excluded too are pure software service
exports out of India; this would amount to another $35 billion by
2008, according to estimates by consultants McKinsey.

Also to be accounted for are the impressive sums mentioned in
the Deloitte Research study on financial services outsourcing—
"$356 billion worth," discussed previously.

India's drive for offshore BPO dominance will be supported by its
other assets. Unique among developing countries, the country's technical communications infrastructure (from fiber-optic land and undersea cables through to communication satellites) is mainly local-built
or-owned and rupee-zone costed. Such an infrastructure provides
ample autonomy to retain cost advantages vis-a-vis new competitors.
For Delta Airlines, India's "robust communications infrastructure" was
a key component behind its decision to outsource call-center support
to Mumbai.[121]

Room at the Top, Space Below Too

Due to a variety of reasons, India clearly can deliver white-collar skills, and on the scale required. In other words, one cannot
speak of the current pace of relocation to, say, Indonesia or Nigeria
on the one hand (also large and low-cost, but lacking India's tech-
no-market and educational support structures), or to Sri Lanka,
Romania and the Philippines (far smaller countries, and thus lacking India's demographic advantage). Even a 'giant' like Indonesia (in
the 1990s held up as a high-technology competitor to India), has
had to turn to Indians for maintaining its warships, training its space
scientists and establishing telemetry, tracking and command stations.[122]

Crucially, in spite of the impressive pace of development over
the past two decades, India remains a poor country with a billion
people and massive room for retaining its cost advantages.[123] Not
only are there huge population groups but entire provinces within
the country, which have yet to access the benefits from relocation,
but who, because of India's federal democracy, can still influence
policy and throw out governments—both state and national. In
other words, there is little likelihood that rising standards of living

in India will place any significant upward pressure on wages, and force a search for 'cheaper' alternatives, at least for the foreseeable future.

Meanwhile, in spite of the huge growth in Indian software revenues, India has so far not faced any significant squeeze on supplying an adequate number of IT professionals. With the exception of certain niche techno-managerial skillsets, this is also unlikely to change for at least a decade.

India's 290,000-strong annual output of engineering graduates in 2004 could be morphed, if required, into IT. Software giant Wipro's Chairman Azim Premji pointed this out to business weekly *Talouselama* of Finland (a country whose flagship company Nokia depends heavily on Wipro, as discussed later). If those studying IT run out, "we can choose from others who study sciences. They have a strong mathematical background, which we can use to train them as software people."[124]

But neither has India sought a Chinese—or Malaysian—style government program to mass-produce software graduates.[125] Closely tuned to evolving market requirements and armed with three-year rolling plans on changing skills requirements, Indian private-sector IT training companies like NIIT, Aptech and SSI, have adequately managed to calibrate supply to demand. In an indication of India's demographics, and the capability of such companies, NIIT is "often dubbed the McDonald's of software education because of its reach."[126]

Plugging the Faucet. Diverting the Flood?

At the time of writing, it is still premature to confidently assess job-exodus forecasts by the likes of Forrester Research. Though previous reports about the 'return from India' by Dell and Lehman Bros. were grossly exaggerated, there were signs in early 2004 of the beginnings of some correction in the rampant excesses of offshore outsourcing. This was true, above all, at customer-contact call-centers, especially in Britain.

Such a development might justify British Trade and Industry Secretary Patricia Hewitt, who in December 2003 said Britain's call-center business "was prospering, despite the number of companies outsourcing work to India."[127]

Although Ms. Hewitt's statement was attacked by "businesses and unions alike," on January 11, 2004, the respected *Financial Times* predicted a decline in what it noted was a current "fashion for exporting customer service jobs." This followed a report by a firm called Contactbabel, which investigated service quality issues at Indian call centers.

Contactbabel pointed a finger at the high level of Indian staff attrition in such jobs, a natural-enough process at the low-end, given the sheer pace of the boom and the upward mobility of the Indian middle classes, as explained later. It may have also been useful had Contactbabel also sought to explain why, almost three years previously, the *Financial Times* itself complained that British call centers faced "one of the highest staff turnover rates in the country."[128]

There are, however, more damaging information gaps, which bear on relocation. No serious attention has been given, for example, to some (small but possibly significant) signs of an ebb in the tide, for example, a decision in October 2003 by Scottish telecoms firm Thus to create 250 call center jobs in Glasgow, "putting an end to speculation that it would outsource the operation to India,"[129] or a move in early 2004, by Leeds-based Shop Direct (formerly Kays), to shut down a Bangalore call center begun in March 2002, and return 250 jobs to Britain.[130] Even some large British financial service firms, among them Legal & General, the Alliance and Leicester and the Co-op have "decided it made business sense not to move parts of their operations abroad."[131] Understanding the motives for these moves may become crucial in the years ahead.

Such a correction is also likely to extend to the U.S., with or without the American government's intervention. In Virginia, according to the state Employment Commission, telemarketers in some districts "make an average of $9.43 an hour"[132]—not much more than their counterparts in India (especially given added costs of offshore operations in the first years).

In spite of these signs of a damming of the tide, it is worthwhile to note that the Indian IT industry itself has been aware of such an inevitability. At a conference in Hyderabad on January 13, 2004, McKinsey & Co. Partner Ajay Dhankar and Malcolm Wagget, Chief Operating Officer of HSBC Electronic Data Processing, explained why: Indian IT not only continues to rapidly move up the 'value chain' but has now also acquired 'critical mass' for its upward drive.[133]

Call centers, the subject of the Contactbabel study, are not only at the back-end of this value chain, but also account for a very small drop in the Indian IT exports basket. In 2002, direct customer-interaction services constituted just 25 percent of business process outsourcing (BPO) exports (or barely 5% of overall Indian IT services), according to figures from India's software federation Nasscom. The far larger share consisted of higher-value back-office services, where there is very little attrition, and which do not involve any contact with the general public (or problems with accents); these will continue to grow as before, relentlessly.

This is precisely where care must be taken, before jumping to comforting conclusions, and imagining that the relocation tide has turned. A slowdown in India's suction of low-end, high-volume white-collar jobs will be meaningful only to those in the West, whose jobs have otherwise already been marked for the axe. Given its spare demographic capacity, India will not lose these jobs to another contender (especially if economic recovery in the West sets off another round of low-end offshore outsourcing). Indeed, issues of job drift are already being pre-emptively addressed by an Indian BPO industry-wide code of conduct.[134]

In the near term, even should the call-center offshore outsourcing slowdown cut out as much as half of the 295,034 'Office' category jobs forecast by Forrester Research for relocation by 2005 (see Chapter I), thereby returning some sense to Western firms (and hope to Western economies), India's projected 70 percent share of the halved figure would still be about 100,000 jobs—possibly more, given its maturity over other BPO contenders. In addition, as explained later, thanks to India's seamless social paradigms for creating support jobs, this would still provide enough momentum for its continuing emergence.

Such a scenario remains very likely, since the deceleration is likely to be far less in other job categories, above all the core field of computer technology. Remarkably, even now, the media fails to differentiate call-center services from higher-end IT efforts. Thus, the *Washington Post* confuses TCS' (now annulled) contract in Indiana to upgrade the State's unemployment claims software system—with the administration of "unemployment services from a call center in India."[135]

This kind of oversight will, in fact, continue to keep the decks clear for India's quiet rise at the higher-end of the white-collar jobs spectrum.

The Strength of the Elephant

As discussed in subsequent chapters, the resilient glue of India's democracy and mature federal system, as well as other inbuilt 'systemic' advantages (including its free markets), will keep the Indian locomotive on track to continue acquiring competencies in a whole range of white-collar skills. Party politics, inter-regional competition, and above all, state and national elections will provide open, corrective checks and balances, and prevent the Indian system from being derailed by its own success. Unlike much of Asia or the developing world in general (above all, China), India's emergence may be accompanied by the odd hiccup—but never with a sudden unpleasant end-of-the-road shock.

Such India-specific factors are barely understood today. For example, in an otherwise-commendable effort to explain the relocation process, two respected American technology consultants not only confused India with Southeast Asia, but went on to claim that while America's "competency in Internet commercialization has been superseded by Southeast Asia's (sic) process-heavy competence in programming and development, the latter competency will be superseded by other regions' competencies in, for example, biotechnology, integrated consumer-business services, or life sciences."[136] India has in fact already begun to develop synergies to draw in the entire gamut of such competencies towards itself, at the higher-end. Given the vastly different levels of development coexisting inside this huge country, such a form of future competitive specialization will almost surely be carried out by different regions within India.

More than technology consultants or the journalist at the *Washington Post* who muddled up a call-center job with an IT systems upgrade, it would be useful for opinion leaders and policy makers in the West to begin understanding the context within which the relocation process is anchored in India—strategic and geopolitical, commercial and industrial, social and cultural. This is especially true given the enormous changes underway in India since it opened up its economy in 1991 and demonstrated a new assertiveness on the world stage after it tore down its 24-year moratorium on nuclear testing in 1998.

The need for this might become critical, not least because of the widespread refusal to accept or comprehend the Indian challenge, both in the U.S., but even more so in continental Europe. Even today, in spite of the potential tsunami headed towards Western white-collar jobs, the image of a poor, lumbering India, persist in the media and public opinion, as well as among decision-makers in both business and government. As recently as June 2003, one of Belgium's largest newspapers, *De Standaard*, recommended to its readers that good candidates for outsourcing included India and Cambodia—a country whose entire economy is smaller than India's information technology revenues in 2002.[137]

More significant than this kind of muddle-headedness is the frequently active sense of denial. In the middle of February 2004, for example, back-to-back announcements by two leading European technology firms, Germany's Siemens conglomerate and chip-maker STMicro, to massively boost their Indian operations (already the largest outside Europe) went largely unreported in either the business or technology media.

Indeed, the massive rise of the Elephant is clearly not a conjurer's illusion. But just how did India get there, while the Western world's Rip Van Winkles, its governments, pundits and media, were seemingly in collective repose?

The roots of India's ascendancy in software may reveal just how the country is, and has been, playing its hand.

CHAPTER III

A Rising
Software Titan

'Only A Matter of Time'
Before America and Europe Wane

In the global software stakes, India has rapidly gained near-overwhelming critical mass. Coupled to developments in China in hardware, The Fletcher Forum at Tufts University argues that "it is only a matter of time before American and European dominance in this sector begins to wane."[1]

Indian software revenues reached $12 billion in 2003 and will cross $15 billion in 2004.[2] By 2008, the figure is forecast by consultants McKinsey & Co. at $87 billion,[3] of which exports alone would be worth about $50 billion. For an industry which has, since 1990, consistently overshot its own forecasts, such projections are not shots in the dark. Business research firm Cris Infac calculates that compared to India's near-$10 billion in software exports in 2003, there is a 'goldmine' of $44 billion in opportunities still to be tapped; Indian companies, it says, can increase their market share of global IT offshore services five-fold.[4] Indeed, figures in March 2004 showed that, in spite of the hue and cry in the West over offshore outsourcing, growth in Indian software exports had accelerated, to 30 percent.[5]

At the end of 2003, palpable attention to the rise of Indian IT began emerging in a succession of lead stories, both in top business journals and the general media. In November, *Fortune* provided a feature on India titled 'Where Your Job is Going.' The story noted that the fact that "India may turn out to be one of the winners of the digital, global, interconnected economy has of course come as a surprise to many people" and underlined India's lead over other contenders. "Ah, the Valley," it exclaimed. "The world is lousy with places claiming to be another Silicon Valley. But in Bangalore the claims have an eerie ring of truth."[6]

In December 2003, *BusinessWeek* followed with a four-part cover story titled 'The Rise of India.' It began with a quote from renowned technology trends forecaster Paul Saffo of the Institute for the Future, who stated: "Indians are taking the lead in colonizing cyberspace." While one entire section was titled 'India and Silicon Valley: Now the R&D Flows Both Ways,' *BusinessWeek* also observed that the city of Bangalore had overtaken Silicon Valley in technology employment.

Nevertheless, attention to the Elephant's emergence is not just confined to the U.S. In early December 2003, France's leading daily *Le Monde* referred to the country's annual output of 260,000 "high-level" engineers and noted that, unlike China, India's strength does not lie in natural resources or low-wage labour but in its "brainpower."[7] Less than two weeks later, *Le Monde* again returned to the subject. In a commentary titled the 'Economic News of the Year',[8] the influential French daily observed that while China's manufacturing focus has allowed the West to remain complacent about its edge in services and the generally higher-end service focus of Western economies, India was seriously shaking up such a view. *Le Monde* too observed that Bangalore had more high-technology personnel than did Silicon Valley.[9]

Such reports nevertheless only signify culmination of a longer trend. However, as noted earlier, awareness about the rising tide has been handicapped by Western media (and consequently, public) perceptions of India, usually patronizing, sometimes racist.

At a conference in 2002, the Chief Executive of a now-faltering Belgian IT firm explained that he had no plans for India given that 'everyone (there) was running around looking for drinking water.' Another example of such thinking is a Raj-nostalgic British daily, the *Independent*, which acknowledges (indeed lauds) the connection between the IT boom in the Indian state of Andhra Pradesh and a reduction in poverty to "one of the lowest" in the country. Nevertheless, its correspondent, Katherine Griffiths, cannot still help feeling (as discussed in Chapter VI, in spite of overwhelmingly opposite information from the World Bank) that "the contrast between those sections of the economy and community swept up in the swift advance of technology and those who remain outside it is still immense."[10]

As future chapters establish, not only are these highly-subjective views; the eventual impact of the trickle-down benefits of India's high-value adding IT boom will clearly be without parallel in any other country, possibly at any time in history.

One key factor here is the massive upward social mobility of Indian IT engineers (many of whom come from the middle- and lower-middle classes). Secondly, Indian wages are themselves rising at record levels. As noted later, human resources firm Hewitt Associates reports that the average salary increase of 14 percent in 2003 in India was twice that of second-placed Philippines.

Shorn of patronizing blinkers, it is in fact possible to be both subjective and correct. An 'emerging' city like Bangalore now not only has far less beggars than ten years ago, but also fewer than in London or New York (Griffiths of the *Independent* may do well to go and count). One may even use other such yardsticks: refugee figures out of India compared to those from Latin America, central Asia or Africa, or migrant workers into India from many of its neighbors.. Given that poverty in a still-poor country will visibly consist of some very-poor people (in the eyes of Western visitors at least)—short of a magical redistribution in global inter-country income, India's systematic turnaround may be the only way to durably reverse underdevelopment (more on this in Chapter VI).

Nevertheless, it is just such resistance—to adapt perceptions to India's steady but otherwise-subtle rise—which explains the bewilderment about its 'sudden' emergence as a global force in IT, and in high technology in general.

Its roots actually go back a decade, and more.

One misperception in this context was the belief, in many cases a 'feeling,' that India was only a place for drudge work and low-end coding, strongly reinforced by the erroneous but widespread assumption that India was just one in a list of candidates for U.S. H-1B visas.[11] In reality, a total of about 400,000 IT engineers from India accounted for 45 percent of all H-1B visas issued.[12] In the words of both John Chambers, Chief Executive of Cisco[13] and Microsoft Chairman Bill Gates,[14] Indians accounted for 20-25 percent of the workforce of most Silicon Valley firms; a very large chunk of these obviously consisted of H-1B visa holders. The strength of the Indian presence has also been remarkable in Britain. In 2002, "78 percent of the computer programmer applications" granted by the U.K. came from India.[15]

Another related (and still widely-believed myth) is that H-1B visa-holders are/were low-paid and 'exploited'[16] (or worse, 'cyber-coolies'[17]). The truth is rather different, as a September 2003 report from the U.S. General Accounting Office reveals. H-1B visa holders in IT and engineering below the age of 30 earned more than Americans with a similar degree, while those between 30 and 50 have roughly equivalent wages; only the above-50s earned less, and not significantly so.[18]

There are other good examples of this kind of wanton (but ultimately delusional) misperception. For instance, in spite of clear evidence to the contrary, 'authoritative' sources (paying little heed to Mark Twain's warning about "greatly exaggerated" reports of his death) have been serially sure of the Indian software industry's demise, following the resolution of the Year 2000 bug,[19] the dotcom collapse in 2001,[20] and then after the September 11, 2001 terror attacks in the U.S.[21] In the more-recent call-center business, where the Indian juggernaut began sweeping across Britain in 2003, the Chief Executive of British company Vertex (part of United Utilities, whose in-house operations it runs since 1996) went on the record in 2001 to say that that its high-tech, 'third-generation' call-center would provide it with "levels of skills and efficiency" which the Indians "will struggle to emulate."[22] Hardly a struggle as it turns out.

Some Numbers: Elephants Do Gallop

Yet another misleading, but sometimes still pervasive, myth, as exemplified by the *De Standaard* conclusions on India and Cambodia, is that India is just one among many places for offshore software.

For the sake of scale, it might be pertinent to note that the tenth largest Indian software company exported more than the entire country of China in 2002.[23] Wired.com reports that China hopes to achieve "$1.5 billion in software exports in 2005."[24] Even if one accepts a sudden leap in Chinese software exports, already in 2003, to "about US$1 billion"[25] according to a Chinese newspaper, or the even more dramatic and unattributed "$1.8 billion, four and a half times those of the previous year,"[26] according to a European publication, this is still 15 percent of the Indian figure, estimated by India's far-sounder statistical data collection procedures.[27]

Other facts and figures also attest to the strength of India's lead vis-a-vis China. China's (civilian) engineering graduates number just 50,000 a year, compared to India's 290,000[28]—a crucial Chinese handicap, for American business guru Peter Drucker. Oracle's employees in India at the end of 2003 are estimated at 6,000[29]; for the sake of comparison, apart from "100 engineers in Shenzhen," Oracle has approximately "300 workers handling day-to-day operations, sales and support in China."[30]

Meanwhile, for the other giant, Russia: Russian software exports were $300 million in 2002, on par with India's sixth or seventh largest information technology firm (and less than what U.S. automotive giant GM alone now outsources to Indian IT firms); using another measure, Russia's annual software exports are equivalent to two weeks of India's.[31] Furthermore, Russian software exports' annual growth rate also lags that of India. In December 2002, Russia's Industry Minister Ilya Klebanov acknowledged this unwinnable lead and said his country would "never catch up...(with India) or repeat the Asian giant's explosion in high-tech expertise."[32]

The truth of the matter is that India has long won the offshore race, but for various reasons, this fact has for long been overlooked. Worse, in spite of India's galloping ahead, such oversight continues, especially in Europe. For example, a one-year scan of the trickle of reports covering Indian software in Belgium's leading IT publication *Datanews* finds almost every article playing Cupid by compulsively coupling the Elephant with China[33, 34], with "China and the other tigers of the Far East",[35] or with "Poland and the Philippines."[36]

While one might excuse such cases of systemic confusion in small and relatively obscure journals such as *Datanews*, their impact is much stronger, especially in terms of confusing victims of relocation (both past and future), when it involves respected international newspapers.

Take, for example, this reference by the *Financial Times*[37] to a project by courier giant DHL in Prague: "Whereas previously service

projects went to cheaper destinations such as India and the
Philippines, Western companies now see central Europe as a viable
alternative because it is closer in culture and time zone to companies' headquarters and it has a better qualified workforce." The article claimed that Prague was fast becoming an outsourcing 'magnet.'
It made no reference to DHL's huge IT services business with India's
Infosys, which is expected to rise sharply by March 2004 from its
current $35 million to $54 million[38]—on its own, either figure
would account for much, if not all, of, the Czech Republic's entire
software exports.

Even *BusinessWeek* could not resist a headline: 'Outsourcing:
Make Way for China,'[39] which then rolled out to clarify that "Indian
computer-training companies are teaching 20,000 students in more
than 100 centers across China," and that "Indian firms will eventually control 40 percent of China's IT services exports." Sheepishly
(given its headline), the article concludes, "No big Chinese rivals
for the multinational outsourcing firms have yet emerged." With
"training and experience," continued the writer, "such obstacles are
surmountable." One of the major sources for such training is in fact
India's NIIT; by 2002, it already had a partnership with "six universities and three software technology parks" in China, and plans to
grow this network to 500 centers by 2007.[40]

For those still on the fence, The Gartner Group drove home
India's huge lead on China in software, identifying nothing smaller
than a $11 billion opportunity for Indian software exporters, in
China.[41]

The Chinese themselves are all too aware of such facts, especially given the kind of blue-chip customers brought to their country by Indian IT giant TCS' Hangzhou center.[42] In November 2003,
at the Bangalore IT.com tech fair, the Hong Kong government
"wooed Indian firms by pitching its proximity to Chinese markets
and dangling a zero-tariff pact with Beijing which comes into force
next year...." Not to be outdone, Hao Kangli, vice mayor of the
southwestern Chinese city of Chengdu, stated, "'India is leading in
software skills in Asia and we want to learn that. China is also looking for Indian talent in the software education sector.'"[43] In February
2004, Bangalore hosted yet another 14-member Chinese delegation
scouting for Indian IT expertise—and investment, this time from

the northeastern province of Dalian, and led by its vice-mayor Dai Yulin.[44] During that month, Cognizant, another Indian IT firm, hinted it might follow TCS by setting up a development center in China;[45] so did several smaller Indian firms, such as Infinite Solutions, which confirmed it was going beyond its current Hong Kong office by mandating Ernst & Young to identify a Chinese IT company for acquisition.[46]

The best example of such confusion, however, is a news report on a study by one Pierre Audoin Consultants (PAC) headlined 'India's new outsourcing rival—Romania.' The report, quickly picked up by the European technology media, claimed that "Romanian IT workers have fewer cultural differences than India, which makes Romania the first choice for outsourcing."[47] Other than the intriguing concept of 'cultural differences' mattering in what has for long been the world's most global business, the PAC report also estimates Romanian software exports at $124.2 million in 2003. However, it does not measure this: barely two days worth or 1 percent of India's software output the previous year. Nor does it underscore the implications in terms of availability of structured skills and expertise, manpower and technical infrastructure—above all, what would happen to local IT wages if half a dozen employers suddenly chose to simultaneously ramp up their staff by a few thousands, in Romania. Indeed, during a visit to India in January 2004, Romanian Prime Minister Ion Iliescu urged Indian companies "to invest aggressively" in his country and build "technological parks."[48] (Iliescu is no doubt aware of India's growing clout after Romania's largest steel company was acquired by the Indian Mittal group—as discussed elsewhere). India's TCS, for one, may be the first to move out to Romania from its current Hungarian outpost (where it launched a 100-strong GE-certified center in summer 2001, bringing to eastern Europe its first exposure to top-end U.S. Defense Department-compliant CMM practices—see next chapter[49]); others are expected to follow.

Another curious example is a recent preference for political correctness by the British media in reporting relocation to 'South Asia' or 'the Indian subcontinent.'[50] Other than Pakistan's and Sri Lanka's very-fledgling presence in offshore services, it is puzzling to explain what exactly companies still grappling with the implications of commencing operations in India also plan to do in Nepal, Bangladesh and Bhutan. But such insights have also appeared elsewhere. For example, Colorado Senator Phillips' anti-offshore outsourcing bill (Senate Bill 169) was inspired by news reports that EDS, which has a Colorado state contract, was "shifting technical support jobs to India and Pakistan."[51] As a little spot of homework on the Internet would have established, EDS has no operations in India's frequently-twinned 'arch-rival,' Pakistan.

Britain's Datamonitor consulting firm takes a uniquely original route. A *Reuters* news report on its study 'Global Offshore Call Center Outsourcing: Who will be the next India' confusingly plugs together India and the Philippines. What finally emerges is the statement: "Mexico, South Africa and Malaysia are becoming popular offshore locations. They are growing in stature at the expense of India and the Philippines whose share of the offshore market will drop to 64 percent in 2007 compared with 70 percent in 2002."[52] However relevant be the sum of the two countries together (one could, for instance also think of coupling the U.S. and Canada), the crucial factor (for understanding where BPO jobs are headed to) is India's huge lead over the Philippines, as explained previously.

Unlike the media, technology workers, in America at least, know the truth: "We are not condoning or encouraging hatred against anyone. India was chosen for the title because it is currently responsible for approximately 80 per cent of offshore technology outsourcing," says the Web site, yourjobisgoingindia.com.

In brief, other countries can only seek to imitate India's success, and it is likely that they will learn this from Indian IT companies. Inserting their very-different agendas into the debate only muddles the picture.

India's lead is also hardly recent. In 1998, this author explained India's equation vis-a-vis the Philippines (the perceived competitor of that time for IT services), in an interview with a Belgian monthly:

> Most crucially,...(the Philippines) has a far smaller population and therefore skills base (than India). Though in the late 1980s and early 90s it figured in the competitive scenario, one has to only look at the success of Indian companies in the wider Far East. NIIT, for example, has been accorded Multimedia Super Corridor Status in Malaysia for the MSC's Smart School flagship application. Indian companies have already been man-

aging training at Malaysia's Asia Pacific Institute for Information Technology and at the R&D Center at Singapore Science Park. These are all jewels in the Southeast Asian crown. Where are the Filipino companies here?[53]

New Kid On The Block—Hardly So: Indian IT In The Eighties

As far back as 1986, leading American business magazine *Forbes* referred to chip giant Texas Instruments' spanking new R&D operation in India and said, "The country boasts 148 universities, 1,600 colleges, 5 technology institutes and over 900 laboratories. India graduates 160,000 scientists and technical personnel annually. For most of these graduates English is a second—and sometimes a first-language...." "India's knowledge of software," it prophesied nearly two decades ago, "may help make it a world power in all facets of the computer."[54]

Like Texas Instruments, Computervision too was an early India hand. Within less than a decade of its opening in the mid-1980s, its Indian operation at Pune had already played a key role in developing the MEDUSA product suite and was readying itself for design of the next generation of Computervision's flagship automation products (EDM and CADDS 5); by 1995, India had become the company's largest operational base worldwide, contributing almost 50 percent of its parent's global R&D requirements.[55]

Cadence Design Systems, which started Indian operations in 1985, was another pioneer. By the mid-1990s, Cadence's Tick-IT certified India lab had grown steadily to a 100-strong team, making it the company's largest R&D facility outside the U.S. Cadence's Indian unit developed flagship products like Checkplus and Vital, and collaborated extensively with the Indian Institutes of Technology on VLSI (very large scale integration) chip design.

Nevertheless, such examples were rare in pre-reform socialist-inspired India, a country which barely a decade previously had thrown out IBM and Coca-Cola, after they refused to allow domestic investors to acquire majority stakes in their listed Indian operations.

The Nineties: Quietly, The Boom Unfolds

India's presence as a force in world software strengthened quickly after its economic liberalization in the 1990s, when Fortune 500 companies began to invest heavily in Indian back-offices. Although the Silicon Valley boom years distracted attention from the process, it was soon to become a tough call to ignore evidence that India was involved in far more than a grinding, low-end contribution to the efforts of international companies.

The mid-1990s saw a flood of new entrants arrive in India, ranging from giant technology firms and industrial conglomerates to hotel chains, such as Holiday Inn and Carlson (owner of Radisson and Regent)—which developed its central reservations system at Bangalore, and then used the facility thereafter for global support. In 1996, *Foreign Policy* noted, "Citibank, American Express, General Electric, IBM, Reebok, Texas Instruments, Hewlett-Packard, and Compaq Computer are but a few of the many companies that depend on computer software developed and tailored to their needs in Bangalore and other Indian cities." By this time, American companies like SMART Modular Technologies were designing cutting-edge products in India; already indicating a reversal in classic flows of industrialization, SMART was manufacturing its Indian-designed products in Scotland.

While Year 2000 work laid the foundations for Indian IT, both international and Indian firms had begun looking beyond this date, well in advance. In 1997, *Forbes* (once again) discerned this still-subtle shift, with a report that "India has been exporting computer software for years, but what's new is the extent to which American businesses have begun entrusting critical, leading-edge software development to Indian programmers.... GE divisions, such as aircraft engines, are doing development work in India so proprietary that GE refuses to talk about it."[56] Another early indicator of India's emergence in the global IT stakes: by the late 1990s, Texas Instruments had begun to release new products directly from India (some with Hindi names).

Through the 1990s, several Indian software firms began an intensive, systematic effort to move up the value chain, not least to derive competitive advantage against other Indian competitors. Some plunged into innovative niches. In 1991, *Time* magazine referred to Statart Software's MyScript, by virtue of which computers were taught to "provide the personal touch of a handwritten note by imitating a person's script."[57]

The best-known example from the early 1990s, however, was the Distributor Management Application Package (DMAP) from India's Infosys, implemented at Reebok International. Another high-profile success was achieved in 1993 by TCS, when it rolled out a complex, multi-platform settlement system in Switzerland known as SECOM; this provided an online, real-time linkage of the Swiss stock exchange, the country's national payments system and the central securities depository, as well as custodians and 500 participant banks. The SECOM order, won by TCS against American giant Arthur Andersen, obtained the Smithsonian Award "for innovative use of technology and project administration." TCS quickly went on to more successes in Switzerland, developing a cargo-handling system and then the passenger reservation systems for Swissair.

Other Indian firms too were furiously globalizing, and in several cases, striking gold. By 1995, India's IIS had developed a works management system for North West Water, a giant British utility, while NIIT had set up both the global messaging system and a computer-based training product for the World Bank. In 1996, NIIT launched a futuristic dial-up interactive TV system, using existing telephone lines and eliminating the need for what then still were expensive set-top boxes[58]; it also designed a state-of-the-art satellite-based fleet management system for Singapore's Citycab taxi company. M2P2, a multimedia Internet-enabled payphone system (with electronic firewalls, a WebLink server and a BankMonitor server) was developed for use in Canada by India's Amsoft Systems (a company which had previously won the contract for the TV graphics system at the Barcelona Olympics in 1992).

On their part, international customers also seemed happy, and occasionally surprised. In 1995, the high-profile British investment fund 3i found that an Indian firm "had a better understanding of our needs" than any U.K.-based rivals. The assignment concerned a "very-advanced windows-based client-server system, at the leading edge of the technology."[59]

By the middle of the 1990s, there were also no fewer than 200 different Indian software packages, aimed at the country's local market specificities and selling almost wholly on price; with tariffs on imported packages still touching the ceiling, this was a compelling argument. By now, Indian firms were clearly proficient students of Adrian Slywotzky, the guru of competitive advantage through value migration.[60] What such efforts led to was continual self-improvement and skills enablement at progressively higher ends, if not yet the cutting edge, of the emerging New Economy; that was to come later, but still underwritten by this thrust for value, explains India's eventual across-the-board threat to Western technology jobs.

Large Indian IT companies such as TCS and Infosys led the way in developing their own branded solutions, mainly focused on financial services (e.g. TCS' EX and Infosys' Bancs 2000). Tata Infotech's AirportVision, an automated decentralized check-in system and departure control system, was quickly snapped up by Air India. For these fast-growing companies, even otherwise unsuccessful efforts at product development were not wasted efforts. TCS, for example, used RTwo, a less-than-successful database analysis system launched in 1995, to develop its current datawarehousing offerings, where it has a roster of blue-chip customers.

However, smaller rivals too were in the race, and in a sign of things to come, were surviving, innovating and adding value, in spite of the massive pressures on finding (and keeping) local talent, given the huge exodus of Indians on H-1B visas to the U.S. Peutronics, by a clear margin, was market leader in the accounting software segment with a product known as 'Tally,' while Bangalore-based Cranes Software had an impressive presence with a suite for scientific applications. Punjab Communications counted Siemens, Proctor & Gamble, Pepsi, Coca-Cola and American Express among its customers for a product known as Wizdom Workhorse.

Such a process continued through the second half of the 1990s, with products from once-obscure firms such as Softek (wordprocessors, databases and spreadsheet clones), Sofstar (whose Customizer-2000 was focused on the Oracle environment) and Vedika (a package called TakeOff, targeted at travel agents).

Some small firms also ventured overseas with their own packages in the mid-1990s. Coromandel Software tied up with Borland for 4 GL tools and VDB offerings, while India's Softplus Computer, which was selling about 300 copies a month of its Personal

Information Manager—Executive Desk, developed a German version for the European market.[61] Sankhya Infotech, one of the first companies outside the U.S. and Europe to focus on the aviation market (its IRMAO integrated resource manager for airline operations was sold in India and southeast Asia) pioneered Computer Based Training (CBT) facilities for airline cockpit crews on the Internet; the achievement won it laurels from the U.S. Federal Aviation Administration. Elsewhere, Newgen (which struck gold by selling top-of-the-line image-compression technology to Japan's Canon) rolled out a series of packages: Omni, Gold Reports, Clippings, SignBank, FotoID and ImageEnable; other than Canon, its customers included Enron, Hoechst Marion Roussel and Jardine Fleming.

By this time, Indian firms were also becoming more ambitious, venturing into complex fields like systems integration and software engineering tools. Development tool solutions from Indian firms in the mid-1990s included Tata Infotech's CLASIK (for client server applications), DARTS (for on-line tuning of databases), ASSURE (for automated system and application software testing) and LITMUS (for automated testing on Unix). Infosys' inlegoe was an architectural toolkit to develop and deploy distributed, multi-tier, heterogeneous services based on client-server applications.

A major milestone concerned an Indian-branded ERP (enterprise resource planning) package called Marshall, which was endorsed by Microsoft's Bill Gates in March 1997 and bested giants like SAP and PeopleSoft to win orders from Switzerland's Swatch as well as Sunkist, Hoosier Energy, Bemis Company and Columbia Helicopters in the U.S. Soon after, another Indian firm, Maars Software, launched its own suite of ERP modules called Maarsman, proceeding in 2000 to develop an ASP version and a 'plug-and-play' compact version for small-scale users.[62]

In 1998, this author summed up the emerging state of play in British business magazine *Business Eye*. By this time, he noted, not only was Canon purchasing color compression technology "more advanced than its own" from India's Newgen, but "HCL was licensing its ASIC (application specific integrated circuit) technology to Samsung of Korea, and Geometric Software had sold its feature recognition algorithms to a dozen of the world's leading machine tools manufacturers;"[63] as it happens, France's Dassault is now one of the companies which openly seeks mileage from the fact that it counts on Geometric's world-class algorithms in its flagship CATIA computer-aided manufacturing solution,[64] used in designing one out of two cars and seven out of 10 aircraft.[65]

Once again, when coupled to the fast-growing Indian presence in the heart of the U.S. software industry and the role of international IT firms in India, it was clear that India and its feverishly-ambitious software companies were already sowing the seeds for the country's emergence as a software superpower.

Not many, however, understood the scale, pace and eventual impact of the process. In December 1995, the *Financial Times* reported that India could attain $5 billion in software revenues by the end of the decade[66]; the real figure, as forecast by the author,[67] was to be almost twice this amount. Worse, in September 1997, the newspaper's coverage of the IT industry's globalization strategies failed to mention India, even once.[68]

Quiet Opportunists Or Too Busy to Notice: International IT Firms in India in the 1990s

As the examples above establish, Indian software was hardly wholly low-end, especially onwards from the mid-1990s after international IT firms began sweeping into the country. By the end of the decade, an estimated 180 Fortune 500 companies were also outsourcing to India, providing much needed revenues to the industry.[69] Currently, the number is estimated by *CIO* magazine at "one-half to two-thirds of all Fortune 500 companies."[70]

Several such facilities were quickly immersed in making major contributions to their parents. "AT&T's computer unit, NCR," said *Foreign Policy* in 1996, "has established a facility in Bangalore that develops software for NCR's global customers."[71] Likewise with Citicorp, whose Indian unit developed the banking package Microbanker, and by the mid-1990s, had sold it to 80 banks in over 40 countries around the world. For Honeywell, its India operation "became the highest-rated software organization in the company"[72] and was soon to be immersed in designing avionics systems for Boeing.

In 1992, Motorola set up an R&D unit at Bangalore to develop software for key projects, including paging and cellular systems, development tools and the Iridium global satellite communications network. Within two years, Motorola's Indian facility became only the second in the world to achieve the U.S. Defense Department-inspired Capability Maturity Model (CMM) Level 5 rating, paving the way for the CMM league table to become a Who's Who of Indian IT. Motorola's bets on India were best illustrated by its Bangalore office, which employed 250 in 1995, but had space for 750.

Telecom giant Sprint's Indian operation was set up in 1994 in a joint venture with India's RPG Group and soon became its largest development unit; key contributions included the rollout of SprintNet. During the same year, the world's largest business information vendor Dun & Bradstreet signed a strategic alliance with India's Satyam to provide software services for its global operations, including maintenance of its mainframes and Very Large Database Management.

Oracle too opened an Indian development center in 1994, to develop modules for Oracle 8 along with platform-specific Oracle products. Such efforts from India brought in revenues of $110 million for the company already in 1995 (excluding internal transfer-pricing systems, the figure is estimated to be several times higher). In 1996, Oracle's Indian R&D manpower had risen to 140 (from four in 1994), and was slated to grow to 240 in 1997. One feather in Oracle's Indian cap: successful development of its Network Computer (NC) in a 'who's faster' race against the company's U.S.-based team, prior to the NC's unveiling by its Chief Executive Larry Ellison in Japan.

1995 saw the arrival in India of Informix, Novell and Digital Equipment. Informix's $25 million development center at Bombay was, from its launch, slated to quickly become its second largest R&D facility outside the U.S., with 150 staff; its earliest Indian projects included design and implementation of class libraries for Windows-based NewEra application tools, followed by contributions to its mainstay database products. As Table II shows, Novell's new Indian operations too shortly went on to launch a slew of solutions.

Digital Equipment opened its first Unix development center in

Bangalore, alongside sponsoring basic research at the Indian Institute of Science (joining other program sponsors such as IBM, Texas Instruments and Intel). The Indian operation quickly took responsibility for several third-party assignments, such as StreetWorks, a public works information system for the U.K. government, and in 1997, Digital announced that it would increase employment at its Indian center from 100 to 350 within the year.

In September 1995,payments specialist Verifone (founded by an Indian-American) began an expansion of its Bangalore-based R&D center to allow employment to increase from 140 to 200 the next year and 300 in 1997. The Indian team made a major contribution to the design of Verifone's Gemstone transaction automation system; soon after, it also conceived and developed 'Omnihost,' targeted at transaction automation networks.

By the mid-1990s, another major player in India was American electronics giant Hughes. In October 1995, its Indian unit, Hughes Software Systems, opened a new corporate complex at Gurgaon, near New Delhi, and in 1998 expanded to Bangalore. Hughes Software specializes in development of real-time embedded software for voice, data and video communications and networking products, and has rapidly become India's largest exporter of communications software. Products from Hughes Software's stable by 1997 included communication stacks, state-of-the-art technologies like CDPD (cellular digital packet data) to allow wireless data transmission by cellular networks, as well as Expoze, a software productivity tool, targeted at the testing and analysis markets; it also continued to develop software for its parent company's satellite communications network. As discussed later, Hughes' Indian operation has since 1996 been directly marketing its own software products in Europe, Latin America and the Far East (rather than supplying them through its U.S. parent) alongside establishing joint operations with other international telecom firms, especially in Europe.

In 1996, component and supplier management (CSM) company Aspect Development (also founded by an Indian-American) began to shift development work to India; almost 50 percent development on its flagship Explore had already been undertaken in Bangalore. Soon after, American open client-server systems giant Sequent launched an India-based 'Worldwide Information Systems Support Centre,' to supplement the efforts of Indian partners Wipro and TCS, respectively undertaking quality assurance/testing and systems integration.[73] During that year, computer display systems giant S3 too opened an India design center, with a team of 10 engineers rising in strength to 50 within 18 months, focused on VLSI (very large scale integration) design and the development of software for ASICs (application specific integrated circuits) on 0.25 and 0.35 micron technology.

Electronic design automation firm Duet Technologies (like Aspect and Verifone, founded by Indian-Americans) was also an early entrant to India, setting up two development facilities in the early 1990s, at Hyderabad and New Delhi. By the end of 1996, with Indian employment strength at 250, it had begun to double space at its New Delhi facility to 55,000 sq. ft. Duet also acquired CrossCheck India, a Hyderabad-based firm active in a similar field, which became its subsidiary.

1997 saw the launch of Cisco Systems' largest development center outside the U.S. in Chennai, staffed with 75 software engineers from India's HCL and dedicated to developing software for testing and maintaining networks. One of the biggest developments that year, however, was IBM's announcement that it would invest $25 million to establish a Solutions Research Center at Delhi, to focus on exploratory technologies in areas such as electronic commerce, supply-chain management and distribution, cellular and mobile telephony systems as well as distance learning and weather forecasting. IBM also mandated the Center to foster joint research projects with India's top universities.

In 1998, the Indian R&D unit of Texas Instruments' competitor Analog Devices designed "a 32-bit digital signal processor, ADP-21065L, codenamed Shark, which Analog said was 'the world's highest performance 32-bit general purpose DSP.'"[74] Gerald McGuire, product line manager of Analog Devices, underlined the Indian IT advantage: "Never before has the highest performance available been offered at a mass market price." Before this, Analog collaborated with India's Accord Software to develop the basic chipboard for GPS (global positioning system) receivers.

As with Sequent and Cisco, most international IT firms initially worked exclusively with Indian partners, among them India's largest companies TCS, Infosys, Wipro, HCL and Satyam. For some,

Indian capacity was already a winning argument. In 1995, Telogy, then the world's fastest-growing supplier of test equipment, rental and leasing services), mandated HCL to move from a centralized system to a three-tier client/server architecture.[75] In 1997, Microsoft appointed Bangalore-based Aditi Technologies as a Recommended Support Point, while Computer Associates set up a Global Unicenter Competence Center with Wipro,[76] following this by joint ventures with Satyam, TCG, Pentafour and Escosoft.[77] Partnerships were also formed due to perceptibly world-class technical competencies of some Indian IT firms. Tata Elxsi, for instance, was awarded a project in 1997 on Silicon Graphics' Irix operating system, the first time such a sensitive project was assigned outside the U.S.

Companies like Nortel made a political choice to stick with development partners, rather than seek to navigate the complex business environment of a country like India. By 1997, Nortel was outsourcing software development to about 1,000 software engineers at Wipro (R&D), Infosys (product competency centers) as well as HCL, Tata Infotech and Tata Elxsi, and had announced a decision to spend $70 million on R&D in India—targeted at more-effective routers as well as IP software for embedding directly into servers, processors and consumer devices such as refrigerators and heaters.

However, the Indian firms in such alliances were by no means passive. Since the two set out together in 1988, Mahindra, for example, not only rapidly became one of the largest external providers of software services to its joint venture partner British Telecom (BT), but seven years later drew up a 'Vision 2000' plan to shift focus from services to projects, and sharply grow its offshore component from its then-10 percent level, creating a telecoms consulting and systems integration arm along with full-life cycle capability. Also in its sights was a diversification of its customer base (that is, away from BT). By the end of 1998, both goals were met; more pointedly, Mahindra had also begun developing its own intellectual property portfolio of reusable components.

BT's solutions from its Indian partnership with Mahindra include location-based WAP (wireless application protocol) services and WAP banking solutions, including a crucial transaction product called Solutions Studio. By 2000, these were already being widely implemented in Britain and continental Europe.[78] As mentioned previously, BT now plans to outsource the entire lifecycle of IT processes to Indian firms.

Other firms from Europe have also been immersed in harnessing the Indian software advantage for more than a decade. One of the earliest entrants from Europe was enterprise software vendor Baan. In 1995, the Dutch firm decided to establish a development center in Hyderabad (its second worldwide after Amsterdam). The next year it announced $17 million in investments by 1999 to make Hyderabad its largest product development center worldwide. Employment quickly tripled to 300, and in July 1997, Baan said it would invest an additional $11 million in India operations, and make Hyderabad larger than head office in the Netherlands, with 1,000 developers.

Like Baan, Germany's ERP giant SAP also set up a development center in India in 1995, at Bangalore. In August 1996, SAP said it would invest $7 million over a period of three years to enhance its Indian operations. During 1997, following a visit to India by Les Hayman, the company's Asia operations Chief Executive, SAP shifted parts of its core product testing and development for its R/3 flagship to Bangalore, from Germany. The shift was already billed as part of SAP's plans to make India its main operations base in Asia by 1998 and the largest worldwide by the year 2005 (SAP boosted its commitment massively in early 2001, when Board member Dieter Matheis announced a $125 million investment, to be made within just two years).

Dutch electronics giant Philips, too, set up a Bangalore operation in 1995, its first global unit for multi-divisional software, to cater exclusively to the company's worldwide operations and design software for support of its next-generation products. One of Philips' first contributions from India was a new series of software-driven health care products launched in 1997, including a radiology information system and software-based radiology equipment, as well as a diagnostic help-center for use in high-end Philips TV sets. Indian software engineers were also used by Philips for contracts in Europe, at the European Parliament and with the Belgian underground metro system. According to Dr. Bob Hoekstra of Philips, every product having software in it "has a contribution from the Bangalore campus."

As illustrated by Texas Instruments and Motorola, India was playing a growing role in core chip design, and such efforts were not ignored by Europeans, among them SGS Thomson of France. In 1997, an Indian joint venture by Britain's GEC Plessey too began 0.25 micron library development and embedded software development for DSP (digital signal processor) and RISC (reduced-instruction set computing) processor-based systems.

A sweeping commitment to India was also demonstrated by German technology conglomerate Siemens, which had established two software development operations by the early 1990s. In 1997 alone, Indian contributions to Siemens included its Access integrator, the ADMOSS Advanced Multifunctional Operator Service System and the BCT Basic Craft Terminal; a year later, this was followed by a telemedicine system named MagicView.[79] Siemens' JPEG-2000 Toolkit, which is used for image compression, was also developed in India. In a then-rare instance of an international firm quantifying its contribution from India, Franz Beinvogl, the Director of the software unit of Siemens Communications, acknowledged that BCT "has been jointly undertaken with Siemens Austria, has been built by a team of 40 Indian engineers in 18 months time with 80 percent of the work" contributed by Bangalore. Indian inputs to Siemens continued to strengthen, and by the turn of the decade, Siemens India released a new Internet-enabled version of the Multifunctional Switch Board (MSB) console used by call centers. Together with ADMOSS, these form Siemens' integrated solution for call centers; by the end of 2000, ADMOSS was installed in 25 countries with over 5,500 operators.[80]

Emperor's New Clothes: The Great Refusal to See

As firms ranging from Kanbay, Keane and Xansa, LG and Samsung, Yahoo and Google, to HP, IBM, Microsoft, Oracle, EDS, Accenture and Computer Sciences Corp. begin boosting their Indian staff literally by the tens of thousands, the systematically accumulated strengths in the 1990s referred to above anchor India's emergence as a vacuum cleaner for Western technology jobs. On the other hand it was not just large Western firms, but hundreds of smaller, specialized firms too. Their presence in India too counts for a significant part of the country's continuing pull on Western jobs.

Observers of today's relocation process (and its victims) ought not to be really surprised at India's ascension; it is hardly sudden. As examples in the above section establish, strong roots for technology job relocation to India date back to the 1990s, and before. But, in the U.S., the dotcom frenzy shielded any comprehension that a serious structural shift was under way—in spite of the presence of no fewer than 400,000 highly qualified software professionals from India on American H-1B visas, including many behind some of the bellwethers of the New Economy, as discussed later.

In Europe, the 'Old' Continent too preferred to ignore growing evidence of this process. Even the technical media refused to leave behind complacent prejudices that a Third World country might be directly attacking the foundations of their high-tech Fortress, frequently resorting to near-racist comments, for example, about 'tandoori software' and high-tech 'guest laborers.'

More than two years after the veritable flood of software products from Siemens' Indian lab discussed in the previous section, widespread skepticism greeted a proposal at the company's Belgian affiliate ATEA to transfer engineers from Siemens' Indian operations, already by then certified to the U.S. Software Engineering Institute's CMM Level 4 (it is now Level 5), and thus way ahead of ATEA's software quality processes in Europe.

Sadly (for those at the receiving end of the relocation tide), such blinkers persist. In the middle of February 2004, announcements by two European technology majors to ramp up their Indian operations (and inevitably, cut down employment in Europe) went unreported in the business and technology media. On February 19, the president of European chip giant STMicro, Pasquale Pistorio, announced that it would "invest $100 million in its Indian R&D unit," which, he noted, "helped us in no small measure to shape our world-leading portfolio of products and technologies."[81] STMicro's 14-year old Indian center employs 1,400 and is already its "single largest design facility outside Europe," but it has also trawled for the Indian advantage elsewhere: India's Wipro, for example, has "licensed its multi-mode 802.11 MAC and BB IP" to the European firm, to accelerate its time-to-market advantage in the fast-growing wireless Internet access segment.[82]

Three days before STMicro's announcement, the *Associated Press* reported[83] that Siemens "will move most of the 15,000 software programming jobs from its offices in the United States and Western Europe," and explicitly noted that about "3,000 of the 30,000 software programmers that Siemens employs worldwide are already in India." Crucially, it quoted Siemens spokesman J. Schubert, about the impact of this. "It is a problem. They could lose their jobs," he said. One of the first casualties of this move will be increasingly-peripheral units like Belgium's ATEA.

1998-2001: Stage Set for Future Tidal Wave

Except for the wantonly ostrich-like, the irreversibility of India's rise in the global software league should have at least become evident by the late 1990s, after the arrival of three bulwarks of American IT—Intel, Sun and Microsoft—as well as numerous others who had so far stayed away. Table II provides examples.

In 1998, Indian American-founded i2 (the world's largest vendor of supply chain management solution) established an Indian center with 20 people; since then, this has been rapidly scaled up to 1,000 and now drives nearly 60 percent of the company's global development. In early 2000, office networking leader 3Com too decided to set up six centers in India for technical support and followed this up with a lab focused on "enhanced Internet Protocol (IP) and data services."[84]

Other significant developments at the turn of the decade include Computer Associates' announcement of an increase in its proposed Indian investments from $100 million to $130 million,[85] Chicago-based Kanbay's opening of three operations at its Pune-based global design and development center (one for Morgan Stanley and two others focused on IBM WebSphere and on e-solutions consulting),[86] a decision by Ford Motors to set up Ford Information Technology Services Enterprise (FITSE) in the southern Indian city of Chennai, close to its car manufacturing facilities[87] as well as AOL's establishment of an India operation.[88] India's already-looming strengths in the core sector of chip design were highlighted in 1999 by broadband pioneer Broadcom's $67 million purchase of Armedia, a fabless multimedia IC supplier whose R&D was based almost wholly in India.[89]

Meanwhile, prior entrants into the country too continued to steadily ramp up their Indian commitments. Adobe Systems' President Bruce Chizen visited in January 2001 and announced plans to "invest up to $50 million in research and development,"[90] dramatically raising employment from 90 to 500; given that the Indian facility already accounted for "nine per cent of the total R&D in Adobe", the impact of such an expansion on its intellectual property output was clearly significant. Chizen's visit followed that of Cisco's Chief Executive John Chambers, during which he announced $50 million in fresh investments—part of plans to increase its staff in a country he was already then describing "as a potential world number one in software."

By this time, for Cisco as with several other global IT firms—large and small—their Indian operations were already the biggest outside their countries of origin, and, as shown in Table II, focused on core (and in some cases, futuristic) technologies. In August 2002, the *New York Times* noted that "the brain chip for every Nokia cellphone is designed in Bangalore."[91]

The Finnish cellphone giant's center in Hyderabad dates to February 2001, and is focused on Network Internet Communications products and solutions; the growing convergence of international operations in India was illustrated by its immediate assimilation of U.S.-based Ramp Networks' Hyderabad security solutions R&D hub, following Nokia's acquisition of Ramp a month earlier.[92] Within two weeks of the Nokia move, a leading player in Internet security software, Rainbow Tech of the U.S., announced it was buying out India's Viman Software, also active in the security solutions market.[93]

During 2000-2001, many of the larger IT companies also began to get locked into the wider Indian system. Some sought partnerships with India's top technical universities. In late 2000, (following in the footsteps of IBM and Digital), Sun Microsystems signed agreements with three Indian Institutes of Technology (IITs) for joint research into programming theory, software languages and tools. The aim: to "enable the creation of technologies to improve the quality and power of network computing." Sun also agreed to share its source code with the IITs, as well as patents. "It (the program) can have an enormous impact on Sun's product line," said Jeff Rulifson, director of Sun Microsystems Laboratories in Europe.[94] By the end of 2000, Sun was also drawing heavily from Indian IT firms such as Goldstone Tech (which designed the middleware for applications from Siebel Systems) and PSI Data (which built its interface for the SWIFT global banking transfer system).

Others sought alliances, including strategic investments in Indian IT companies. By 2003, for example, Intel had already invested $100 million in 30 Indian firms, including chip-design high-flyer Sasken as well as R Systems—which has set up four competency centers for the company's 64-bit Itanium chip. Microsoft, too, continued strengthening tie-ups with leading Indian IT firms. In June 2000, its key Federal Consulting Services unit entered into a strategic alliance with Satyam to provide Web and enterprise integration application development solutions using Windows DNA 2000 technology. Six months later, Microsoft appointed Wipro as a global partner for outsourcing software development and testing, focused on enhancing the capabilities around Microsoft's Windows 2000, Windows CE and Internet applications.

Swedish telecoms giant Ericsson too mandated Wipro to set up and operate a major R&D lab (which the Indian firm has subsequently acquired). Other than the Ericsson effort, Wipro's huge clout in telecoms software was illustrated when it was selected in 2000 by the Euro-Japanese Symbian mobile telephony consortium (Ericsson, Nokia, Panasonic, Psion, Samsung Electronics, Siemens and Sony Ericsson, set up as a counterweight to Microsoft) to develop a full suite of telephony, messaging and Internet applications as well as middleware, porting, system integration and testing.[95] In February 2004, Wipro set up a Global Competence Center to provide smartphone development and integration for another Symbian member, Nokia.[96] Wipro's close ties with Nokia may explain the Finnish firm's confidence in seeking to double its Symbian holding to 63 percent by buying out Psion.

Today, as the shift into India acquires additional, and more public, momentum, what is possibly a key implication for relocation is not only moves by the large firms, but, as before, those by several hundreds (now possibly thousands) of specialized, lesser-known firms too. In fact, given the obvious pace of growth, there is very good reason to doubt whether the media's serially repeated statement "Bangalore, India's technology capital, houses software centres for about 1,200 companies"[97] has not been already left far behind by reality.

Table II: Examples of R&D Activities by International IT Firms in India[98]

HP

- Bangalore R&D Center established in 2002 with just two people, and has since been scaled up to 40. It is totally dedicated to high-level research on futuristic technologies.
- HP has started a new support center for its North American operations in India, which will add further to similar work already outsourced to about 1,000 staff at Indian IT firms.
- HP affiliate Digital GlobalSoft targets 10,000 to 12,000 employees by 2007, up from 2,500 in March 2003.
- HP plans to center its Microsoft DotNet strategy in India and move consulting operations. According to Jurgen Rottler, its Vice President of marketing, strategy and alliances, "In an ideal world, you'd migrate as much as you possibly could to India." The company has already moved software development work for two key products, OpenView and OpenCall (its next generation telecom software platform), from the U.S. and Europe to India.

i2 Technologies

- Established in 1988 with 20 people, i2's India development operation is 1,000 strong today, and based at centers in Bangalore and Mumbai. India drives nearly 60 percent of the company's global development delivery.
- The Indian centers have developed a strategic sourcing solution for i2, besides delivering eight manufacturer-industry templates and retail solutions.

IBM

- IBM's total employment in India was 4,000 in mid-2003 and is rising fast.
- A development center was established in 2001 to work on all IBM software—WebSphere, DB2, Lotus, Tivoli and

Rational, as well as business intelligence tools. Newer areas include "networking protocol products, high-end graphics and multimedia, database and compilers and high-end applications in manufacturing, banking, telecom and media" as well as a dedicated Linux Lab. Like Sun (see below), IBM also selected India for unveiling its new Linux desktop computer.

- In May 2003, IBM opened a new Technology Center to provide "design services for advanced chips and hardware boards." IBM also inaugurated its Center for Advanced Studies (CAS) at Bangalore, one of just eight worldwide and Asia's first. In June 2003, IBM was reported to be considering a new 1,000-strong call-center in Bangalore.

- IBM's India labs are expected to generate over $1 billion worth of innovations over the next three years.

Intel

- The India center is already Intel's largest R&D operation outside the U.S., and soon after its opening in 1999, Vice President David Perlmutter announced scale up plans. Staff numbers were 1,500 in 2003 and will rise to 3,000, according to Intel President Paul Otellini, as part of a $41 million investment.

- The India R&D center is focused on core design and development of the high-end 32-bit computing Xeon chip processor as well as enhancements on next generation Intel Centrino mobile technology; another priority is wireless technologies.

Microsoft

- Microsoft's India Development Center was opened in 1999 at Hyderabad. It employed 50 in June 1999, but by this time, was targeting 200 by mid-2001. By end-2003, it employed 970 staff in India, three-fourths in software development and support.

- The first focus areas for the India center consisted of Unix interoperability, COM+, distributed enterprise management and Office components.

- In April 2000, Microsoft announced launch of the first product to be wholly designed and developed in India: Windows

SFU, for interoperability between the Windows 2000 and Unix operating systems. In 2001, the Indian lab released a key product in Microsoft's battle with Sun, for migration from Java to the .NET platform; this has since been branded Banjara after a community in the state of Andhra Pradesh where the R&D operation is located.

- Other releases included platform components for COM+, Visual J#.Net, Windows Distributed Enterprise Management and a Dot Net e-commerce platform. By early 2004, Microsoft had begun building a 42.5 acre campus in Hyderabad which could accommodate 'several thousand.'

Novell

- Set up in 1995, the Indian lab developed Novell Directory Services (NDS) on Unix, later used by a majority of Internet Service Providers. This was followed up with NDS for the Solaris and Linux operating systems, as well as ZEN works (zero effect networks for users), a directory services-based desktop management tool.
- Novell India also played a key role in the development of Super NOS (to integrate UnixWare with NetWare), SNMP agents for emerging LAN standards such as FDDI, multi-threaded TCP/IP stacks and Windows-based network management, NetWare directory services, LAN protocols (X.25, frame relay, TCP/IP, IPX/SPX, AppleTalk), GroupWise Gateways for MS Exchange, storage management services and products for Unix-based cross-platform services.
- By 1997, the India facility had become Novell's largest R&D operation outside the U.S., and was focused on high-end activities related to network protocols, including enablement of higher performance on multi-processor machines.

Oracle

- Oracle's Bangalore center was established in 1994; a Hyderabad center followed in 1999. As Oracle's largest development facilities outside the U.S., India accounted for 2,500 staff by end 2002, when it was referred to by *Reuters* as "the hub of its global research and development operations." In July 2003, Oracle Chief Executive Larry Ellison said he planned to double Indian staff numbers to 6,000 "in the near-

term." Staff reached 4,000 by the end of 2003.
- The India labs have worked on Oracle's database products, applications, business intelligence products and application development tools, and driven its network computing initiative. Their current focus is grid computing, Linux porting and Sun's Itanium initiative.

Philips
- Established in 1996 with 10 people, strength reached 1,000 in 2003, and will be doubled by 2005. It is the largest software center for Philips outside Holland, and in a sign of the times has been rechristened as an Innovation Campus. Almost every Philips product having software in it has a contribution from the Bangalore campus, says Dr. Bob Hoekstra, the Chief Executive of Philips.
- In 1998, Philips' IT services affiliate Origin (now Atos Origin) inaugurated its second office in India, at Mumbai, to work in two areas, Year 2000 remediation as well as SAP Advanced Business Applications Programmes (ABAP). Along with Siemens, it is one of the only CMM certified centers of a European IT firm.

SAP
- SAP established an India development center in November 1998 with 100 researchers. The German company quickly shifted development work on its flagship R/3 suite to India, and boosted its commitment massively in early 2001, when Board member Dieter Matheis announced a $125 million investment, to be made within just two years.
- SAP's India facility is its largest single-location R&D lab outside Walldorf, Germany. R&D staff in India touched 750 in September 2003. In June 2003, SAP's chief executive Henning Kagermann announced plans to increase its Indian headcount to 2,000.
- Products include SAP's Channel Management Solution; Dealer Portal for the automotive industry; mobile laptop solutions and oil and gas upstream solutions. The Indian labs are also working on key solutions for Mobility and Value Added Tax (VAT). Another focus is Business Intelligence Solutions, according to Chris Neuman, SAP Labs Joint

Managing Director.

Siemens

• Siemens established two software development operations in the early 1990s in India. In 1997 alone, Indian contributions to Siemens included its Access integrator, the ADMOSS Advanced Multifunctional Operator Service System and the BCT Basic Craft Terminal; a year later, this was followed by a telemedicine system named 'MagicView.' Siemens' JPEG-2000 Toolkit, which is used for image compression, was also developed in India. Siemens set up a Scientific Applications Center (SAC) at Pune in 1998 in order to "establish new algorithms for its security solutions," among them an Intelligent Digital Passport, which uses three biometric scans (speech, face, fingerprint) for card-holder verification, the BioLock biometrics-based door lock system, and BioLogon, a biometrics-based computer log-on system. Siemens also has released a new Internet-enabled version of the Multifunctional Switch Board (MSB) console used by call centers. Together with the Indian-developed Advanced Multifunctional Operator Service System (ADMOSS), these formed Siemens integrated solution for call centers; by the end of 2000, Siemens said ADMOSS was installed in 25 countries with over 5,500 operators.

Sun Microsystems

• Established in mid-1999 with 20 staff, Sun rapidly scaled up its India R&D operation to 500 by June 2001 and 1,000 by June 2002. The Indian lab works mainly on Solaris and Sun One, and accounts for an estimated 50% development effort on Sun's Application Server. India was chosen by Sun for launch of its Java desktop in September 2003.

• Products from the India center include Sun's Portal server, Web server, Identity server and Meta directory. Sun One Application Server Enterprise Edition is also being developed in India.

• In late 2000, led by one of its founders, Indian-born Vinod Khosla, Sun signed agreements with three Indian Institutes of Technology (IITs) for joint research into programming theory, software languages and tools "that would enable the creation of technologies to improve the quality and power of network computing." Sun agreed to share its source code with the IITs as well as patents. "It (the programme) can have an enormous impact on Sun's product line," said Jeff Rulifson, director of Sun Microsystems Laboratories in Europe.

- Sun's recent partners in India include Orbitech and i-Flex (for banking solutions), HCL and Ramco (business solutions), MindTree (Web solutions), Hughes (communications products on the Sun Chorus operating system).

Texas Instruments

- TI was an early bird, establishing its Indian lab in 1984, even before other pioneers such as GE, Motorola, Honeywell and Hughes. The Indian center started with 20 engineers. In 2003, it had 900 people working on VLSI and embedded software, with a new focus on 3G technologies. TI's India operations accounted for 225 U.S. patents by the end of the year.
- Products developed: Ankur Digital Signal Processor; Sangam, a bridge router for the DSL; Zeno, which runs multimedia applications, and at least 17 other products.

A New Bell Labs, In Just Two Years

In December 2003, the *New York Times* noted that the Indian operations of U.S. firms had already filed "more than 1,000 U.S. patent applications."[99] More importantly, although some dated to the early 1990s, "most applications from India," it said, "have been filed in the last two years." This rate, of nearly two every working day, is already equivalent to Bell Labs,[100] the world's largest R&D facility; it is, moreover, almost certain to accelerate further, given the increasing focus in India on high-end work.

The newspaper quoted Sammy Sana, managing director of Motorola India Electronics, who estimates thirty percent of all software for Motorola's latest phones is written in India. It also mentioned Intel's 1,400 strong (and fast-growing) operation at Bangalore, where "one floor is out of bounds to other employees as a group of engineers works on a microprocessor chip scheduled for introduction in 2006. The 32-bit processor, designed entirely in Bangalore, is to have one billion transistors (Intel's Pentium 4, its most advanced 32-bit chip for desktop computers, has 55 million transistors)."

The lead in the patents race out of India is clearly held by Texas Instruments, whose Bangalore operations (boosted in early 2001 by a unit dedicated to third generation or 3G wireless technologies[101] and collaboration with 12 Indian engineering colleges[102]) accounted in late 2003 for as many as 225 U.S. patents; in December 2003, TI's India center "developed the world's fastest chip for converting analog signals such as the human voice to digital signals."[103]

Others too are in the running. GE has filed almost 100 patents. The Indian operations of Hughes Software too had filed 13 patent applications by fall 2003.[104] On its part, after a flurry of visits in early 2003 by all its top executives, including Chairman Samuel Palmisano, President Steven Mills, Head of Technology and Manufacturing Nicholas Donofrio, and Paul Horn, Head of its key R&D unit, IBM said its India Research Laboratory was expected to generate "over $1 billion worth of innovations over the next three years."[105] During the year, IBM opened its Center for Advanced Studies (CAS) at Bangalore, one of just eight worldwide and Asia's first, wholly dedicated to futuristic R&D in life sciences, autonomic computing, speech recognition, Web technology standards, pervasive and wireless computing and grid computing.[106]

Germany's Siemens has also begun to openly acknowledge its increasing thrust on pure research in India. Siemens' Scientific Applications Centre (SAC) at Pune was set up to "establish new algorithms for its security solutions,"[107] among them a clutch of state-of-the-art biometric products (see Table II). Dutch electronics giant Philips, too, has made similar moves, re-christening its India facility as an 'Innovation Campus.'

Operational excellence in software development has long been India's forte and, as discussed later, its quality lead over other contenders, many in the U.S. and Europe included, is already massive. But the pace and scale of developments in patent filings for some of the world's most sophisticated technology powerhouses, at the highest rung of the intellectual property chain, do more than anything else to confirm the fast-growing strength of Indian IT. Once again, this indicates how inextricably India is woven into the international technology value chain.

For those carefully watching the process, this is hardly surprising. A Merrill Lynch study in 2002 found that 'core' R&D in India would account for exports of $4 billion, already by 2005.[108]

In terms of their impact on relocation, such efforts not only imply a growing repository of cost-effective high-end skills which will be a near-impossible challenge to substitute, but India's contribution at the top-end of R&D will also be difficult to reverse.

Meanwhile, although the main beneficiary of such Indian efforts still consist of international IT firms, several Indian companies too have an eye on the pie. As discussed later, small and highly specialized IT firms have begun developing intellectual property portfolios from the outset; one of the most ambitious such firms, Ittiam Systems (more below), is the brainchild of Srina Rajam, the former head of Texas Instruments' Indian operation. In early 2004, top Indian technical school BITS announced a $50 million investment in a lab wholly dedicated to creation of intellectual property in the fields of integrated circuits and embedded software.[109] The figure is comparable to effective R&D investments in these areas by leading European labs, such as Belgium's IMEC or France's LETI, and will inevitably impact on their long-term viability.

How Indian Companies Are Playing Their High Value Cards

Products, rather than services, underpin the long-term success of an industry as a global force. As discussed previously, efforts by Indian companies in the products and solutions domain date back to the 1980s, and have drawn additional force from the progressively higher-value positioning of the broader software effort in India over the years. Reflecting this, the first truly world-level success stories from Indian IT began appearing, and were steadily recognized as such, onwards from early 2003.

India's i-Flex was, somewhat belatedly, reported by British weekly the *Economist* in 2003 to be "the world's best-selling banking-software product"[110] (in reality, it already had this status for several years). i-Flex (which plans a U.S. listing in 2005) has begun making headway, for the first time, with mainstream European banks in the Netherlands, Ireland and Germany.[111] Another Indian banking software company, Polaris, is also notching up similar high-profile customers, though still on a smaller scale.[112]

An example of world-beating, cutting-edge technology from an Indian firm emerged in December 2003, when consulting firm Ernst & Young found Finacle, a core banking software solution from Infosys, establishing a clear world record, with 4,562 transactions per second, or four-and-a-half times more than the near-1000 transactions per second by its closest competitor.[113] Infosys has established an alliance with Oracle to integrate Finacle into the Oracle E-Business platform,[114] and before this, implemented Finacle in association with Sun Microsystems at banks in Jamaica, Nigeria, Abu Dhabi, Bangladesh, Sri Lanka as well as its home market, India.[115] Another win is expected in the Philippines, where its partners include Microsoft and Intel. Finacle's highest priority market is however China, where Infosys is localizing the product, and has already won ABN-Amro Bank as its first client[116] for the Greater China region, including Taiwan and the major financial services hub of Hong Kong.[117]

But it is by no means banking software alone. Indian IT services giant, Wipro, "has established leadership in the wireless LAN and IEEE 1394 space by licensing its IPs" (intellectual property), with 50 orders in 2002 and 2003 alone.[118] As mentioned, its customers include Europe's ST Microelectronics, which employs the Indian firm's know-how in its next-generation chips.[119]

There also are scores of other world-class players from India, and their number is growing rapidly. An Indian military software unit has licensed its CAD (computer-aided design) know-how for use by Airbus.[120] Yet another example is Bangalore-based Impulsesoft, which has "licensed its Bluetooth stereo technology to TEN Technology, the company that introduced the naviPod wireless remote control for Apple's iPod."[121] On its part, America's Tensilica states that "all of the algorithm solutions for the Xtensa HiFi Audio Engine," the first 24-bit audio solution for system-on-chip (SOC) designs to earn approval from Dolby Laboratories, were designed and developed by CuTe Solutions" of Hyderabad.[122] Even a giant like IBM has resorted to tapping the cutting-edge strengths of small Indian firms; Hyderabad's Software Associates, for example, has developed a VoiceXML protocol for IBM Germany; its key strength is the use of "the frame of the radio spectrum allocated for the transmission of short messages," by virtue of which it avoids encroaching on voice traffic bandwidth.[123]

Examples of Indian start-ups whose business model is focused entirely on IP licensing include Ittiam Systems' and Sasken. Within just two years of establishment, Ittiam "created a record portfolio of 30 IPs and 26 customer engagements."[124] Sasken, whose customers include a 'who's who' of the wireless industry,[125] had by end of 2003 filed "for over 30 patents in the DSL, wireless and multimedia space" and is "the leading independent provider in the world for protocol stacks" conforming to 3G wireless standards—the beacon for a consumer electronics revival in Europe;[126] it also remains one of only two independent sources for ADSL technology in the world,[127] and the solitary product company with a CMM Level 5 rating from the U.S. Defense Department-backed Software Engineering Institute. Yet another Indian firm, Mistral Software, specializes in product reference designs for consumer and defense electronics manufacturers, and "expects revenues from IP to grow at a rate of 300 percent over the next two years."[128]

Such a trend is now extending to wider mass-market products. Chip innovator MosChip (founded by DSP pioneer K. Ramachandra Reddy) has eight branded products for the global consumer appliance and datacom markets; ten more are in the pipeline.[129] A small Indian firm by the name of Softex Digital has developed the photo editor used in Siemens' newest mobile phone offering, which provides for "warping, layering, colour enhancement and adding text to the image."[130] Another start-up, founded by a Mumbai entrepreneur, has won worldwide rights (from Marvel Enterprises and Activision of the U.S.) to develop and sell a mobile phone game based on Spider Man.[131] Elsewhere, Jataayu has so far supplied eight out of the world's 15 GSM/GPRS terminal reference platform providers with its WAP browser, WAP stacks and clients,[132] while, as mentioned earlier, Soliton Automation from Coimbatore, India, was the only winner of Advanced Imaging's 'Solution of the Year Award' from outside the U.S. and Europe.

Examples like these are not rare. More importantly, they have, as discussed, been a key aspect of the Indian software industry's value-addition process since at least the late 1990s. Comprehending this kind of evidence about the upward value drive of Indian software is also crucial to understanding the impact of India on relocation, and on the future of Western technology jobs.

Equally important however is the massive effort paid by pure Indian IT service firms to gain an astounding global lead in terms of software quality processes. More than anything else, there is an undeniable analogy here with the impact of the quality focus of the Japanese automotive industry in the 1980s.

The Indian IT Lead:
More Than Price, Quality May Make it Irreversible

During the past 15 years, starting out as service providers for American customers, domestic Indian software firms paid great attention to the quality of their work. By 1996, there were more software firms in India certified to ISO-9000 quality norms of the International Standards Organization than there were in the U.S.

However, the best indicator of India's quality lead was the massive (and still-enduring) lead they obtained in acquiring prestigious Capability Maturity Model (CMM) certifications from the U.S. Defense Department-backed Software Engineering Institute at Carnegie-Mellon University, billed as the 'gold standard' for defect-free software.[133]

In 1999, BusinessWeek warned, "If U.S. software companies don't get with it in terms of quality—they could kiss big chunks of business good-bye. (India's) competitive advantage will be quality— the virtual extermination of software bugs that infest most U.S.-made packaged software."[134] Mentioning that Indian IT firms then accounted for 7 of the world's 12 CMM Level 5 ratings (the highest achievable standard), the weekly explained that "Indian programmers are snapping up new methodologies shunned by America's cowboy programmers."[135]

One year later, a paper from the University of Virginia observed that an Indian contract software developer called Advanced Information Services—"one of the few CMM Level 5 companies in existence—is cranking out code with only 0.05 defects per thousand lines of code. That's better than the space shuttle's software."[136] The paper also observed that CMM processes enabled American corporations like Raytheon to slash the cost of quality from 60 percent of software development costs to just 10 percent.

The wider (and sometimes, surprising) impact of outsourcing to CMM-certified software companies is now increasingly acknowledged. U.S. insurance giant Guardian Life, for example, "has outsourced 40 percent of its application-development work to India-based firms, and 70 percent of that work is done offshore." Other than cost-savings, the company's chief information officer, Rick Omartian, states that the offshore firms' use of CMM "has led to improved processes within its own IT department."[137] Here too, there is a close parallel with the huge impact made by Japanese automotive firms on the internal processes of their partners and customers.

Today, India's overwhelming lead in software quality remains. According to figures from the U.S. Software Engineering Institute (SEI), IT firms in India accounted in 2003 for 50 out of 74 CMM Level 5 certifications worldwide.[138] Remarkably, according to the SEI figures, several American software giants (including Oracle, HP, Honeywell, Motorola, IBM and Computer Sciences Corp, as well as smaller firms like Covansys) have their CMM Level 5 facilities in India, rather than in the U.S.[139] More astonishingly, this is in spite of the fact that American firms made six times higher applications for CMM certification (1,671 against 238 from India).[140]

Given that India has already eclipsed the United States on quality, the gap with other parts of the world is wider. In spite of also making more applications for CMM certification than Indian firms (285 against 238), there was only one IT company in Europe with the lower Level 4 rating (although three European software companies do have Level 5 operations in India). Elsewhere, helped by experts from its Indian subsidiary, Motorola obtained Level 5 certification for its operations in China, while Huawei, the Chinese high-technology star, also has Level 5 certification at its Indian software development operations,[141] (where it plans to invest $100 million and boost its headcount from 600 to 3,000 by 2006).[142] Russia, Brazil, the Philippines, Israel and Ireland (sometimes still imagined as competitors to India) have no Level 5 companies, either at home

or in India. Indeed, reflecting the country's status as a global repository of CMM quality know-how, India's Quality Assurance Institute
(QAI) has been signed up by organizations in China, Russia and
Taiwan to provide CMM consulting, while Singapore's government
awarded the firm a global tender "for improving quality of e-governance and transactional excellence in all its 28 departments;" in
February 2003 Deloitte Consulting too mandated QAI to "provide
complete CMM services across 22 centers worldwide."[143]

More than anything else, the fact that America's leading IT
firms have their CMM Level 5 certifications in India, rather than
the U.S., indicates the 'core' nature of their Indian effort, and their
inextricable commitment to the country. It also underscores the irreversibility of India's ascension in software.

This, then, is the crux of India's challenge. It is, according to
Britain's *Daily Telegraph*, "attacking the U.S. economy where it
hurts, slap-bang in the middle of its technological supremacy."[144]
Buttressed by its unique combination of cost-effective skills and
demographics, India has Wal-Marted the New Economy on a global
scale. Coupled to a concerted attack from these strengthening foundations on the higher-value service ends of the world economy,
India is showing that the Western advantage might not be permanent, and its lead therefore reversible.

Indeed, the analogy with Wal-Mart is not coincidental. The
responsiveness of the American giant's e-commerce effort today is
largely due to its deployment of patented ProactiveNet software,
winner of The CrossRoads A-list Technology Award and *Network
Computing* magazine's Well-Connected Product of the Year Award.
Proactivenet was developed in Bangalore.[145]

Skills and Scale: The Elephant's Vital Statistics

For *Washington Times* columnist Paul Craig Roberts, relocation
is the "redistribution of First World income and wealth to developing countries with excess labor supplies.[146] Given that India and
China are the only developing countries which are benefiting,
Roberts comment would have more meaning if it took note of such
a fact, as have the World Bank and several others (see Chapter VI).

India's demographics are huge, and yardsticks may help in

giving meaning to the numbers involved. Thus, for example, Indian Railways carries the population of the Netherlands every day, and about 80 percent of the world's population every year. The Mumbai stock exchange has as many investors as the population of the Benelux. In 2003, "the population of the 15-nation European Union grew by just 294,000—a figure that India, in comparison, needs only seven days to reach."[147] In January 2001, 30 million Indians, roughly equivalent to the entire population of Canada, set what might be a "new world record for the largest ever public gathering,"[148] when they collectively descended on one full-moon night to bathe in a river. On a more earthly level, the Bharat Electronics' electronic voting machines (EVMs) used by India's 668 million voters in general elections[149] could give one of every three Swiss households a voting machine of its own (with ample stocks to spare); indeed, India is now getting ready to export EVMs to Europe and the U.S.

Given such demographics, there are an ample number of Indians who will continue supporting India's pull at the lower-end services end, in spite of its industry's intense value-migration, and do so for at least a decade or two, without impacting significantly on the country's cost advantage. Indeed, India's long term-threat to the West's technology base lies in the fact that it will offer steadily escalating value at the higher-end, underpinned by cost-effective inputs at both the middle- and lower-ends, the entire pyramidical edifice seamlessly cemented with appropriate managerial skills.

As explained earlier, other new contenders for India's status as a software power may claim to possess one or the other advantages above; none can do so for the entire skills pyramid, on the kind of scale offered by India. This comprehensive shift is indeed a good example not just of India's continuing Wal-Marting of the New Economy, but also what Roger Bootle of consultants Deloitte called 'the Great Displacement.'

By the beginning of 1999, India already had the second highest number of Microsoft certified professionals in the world after the U.S., with 83,100, up in leaps from 470 in 1996, 4,700 in 1997 and 19,100 in 1998. The lead was also narrowing, especially at the higher-end of the programming community. Between July 1998 and July 1999, India recorded 2,562 new Microsoft Certified System Developers (MCSD), against 1,247 from the U.S. and just 221 from the U.K. In 2001, the Indian share of Microsoft certifications reached an estimated 65 to 70 percent[150], and during the year, American online recruitment giant Monster.com predicted that India was set to become its "top market this year not only in the region but the world."[151]

The only authoritative source for the size of the Indian software 'army' is IT federation Nasscom, whose figures show that India had a total of 650,000 IT professionals in 2002,[152] rising to 813,500 in February 2004.[153]

Putting these figures in a comparative international (and historical) context: in 2001, India was ranked by Brainbench, Inc. as just behind the U.S. in the number of total certified software professionals (with 145,517 against 194,211); in addition, it is likely that the latter figure includes tens of thousands of Indian-American software programmers. More interestingly, the Indian figure was over 30 times larger than the number of certified professionals in Europe's largest economy, Germany (with 4,802), and one hundred times more than China (1,325).[154]

Big Business Goes Public on India

Though in reality, the roots of accessing the Indian advantage go back to the early 1990s, there has since 2003 been a qualitative change in acknowledging its allure.

Firstly, statements about moves into India by Western software companies are beginning to be hedged less frequently with parallel plans for other countries like Ireland and the Philippines, or even China. This directly reflects the Indian differentiation and competitive lead.

Secondly, there now is the beginnings of a sea-change in acknowledgment of the value of the effort in India (rather than the widespread impression of just low-end efforts targeted at cost-savings).

Thirdly, reinforcing the latter, there has been a spate of public statements about the core R&D effort already accomplished in India. This fact was seldom acknowledged by Western corporations, even though in numerous cases, their Indian R&D operations were the largest outside their home countries. There were notable early exceptions, for example, Texas Instruments has since 1998 given Hindi brandnames to several of its chips,[155] but these were rare.

A fourth example of the shift in how Indian operations are regarded is that some American firms are operating their European (and other international) software operations through their Indian subsidiaries. The best example of this is Citigroup, whose global software operation, as discussed below, has long been handled by its Indian unit (now spun off as i-Flex). Another is Hughes, whose Indian software subsidiary has established its own operation in Germany to support Lucent Technologies,[156] following a previous such effort in Denmark;[157] earlier, it had won an order to set up a dedicated broadband software development center for Austria-based telecoms firm Ericsson Ahead.[158] Highlighting India's steadily-growing pull on technology jobs from across the West, the Austrian facility was previously a broadband competence center for Ericsson.

Finally, official statements about India are increasingly made by the top management of Western corporations, or released by their global headquarters, rather than their Indian subsidiaries (as was usually the case in the past).

- For example, HP's plans to center its Microsoft DotNet strategy and move even consulting operations to India were announced by Jurgen Rottler, Vice President of marketing, strategy and alliances.[159] In early 2004, HP moved software development work for two key products, OpenView and OpenCall, from the U.S. and Europe to India.[160]
- Plans to ramp up the Indian presence of Sun Microsystems and woo India's "army of software developers in the battle with rival Microsoft Corp" were announced during a visit to the country in March 2003 by its Chief Executive Scott McNealy.[161] Microsoft too announced from its Redmond headquarters that it would begin shifting programming and consulting jobs to India as part of a proposed $400 million investment. Meanwhile, Microsoft Chairman Bill Gates personally spoke in public about high-end collaboration with the Indian Institutes of Technology, including one in "very advanced compiler work."[162]
- Likewise with Intel, whose intention to triple its IT staff in India to 3,000 was announced during a visit in June 2003 by the company's President, Paul Otellini.[163]

- Similarly, Oracle's plans to double staff in India to 6,000 were announced during a conference in July 2003 with its Chairman Larry Ellison. Significantly (in the China vs. India scenario for the white-collar jobs shift), Ellison also underlined that "most companies are going for outsourcing of manufacturing activities to China and outsourcing of services to India."[164]

- This trend is now also apparent with several traditionally-secretive European software companies. SAP's plan to double its Indian headcount to 2,000 was announced in June 2003, during the first visit to Bangalore (for some time its largest development center outside Germany) by the software giant's chief executive officer Henning Kagermann.[165] Philips too announced that it would double its 1,000-strong Indian R&D staff via Gerard Kleisterlee, its Chief Executive.[166]

Not Just Aftershocks: The Wave Continues

As indicated by a glance at the technology media on any day, international IT services firms have begun massive expansion of staff and facilities in India, providing another major impetus to the relocation process. Given the ingrained advantages of their Indian rivals in operating out of India, one key issue will be how far such Western firms may also be compelled to shift higher levels of management to India, in order to bridge the gap; as discussed later, their difficulty in doing this is identified by India's Infosys as one of their key strategic handicaps.

HP was one of the first to announce, in July 2003, that it targeted Indian employment strength of 10,000-12,000 by 2007, up from 2,500.[167] Even relatively newer-entrants into India have begun implementing massive capacity expansions; for instance, Computer Sciences Corp. plans to boost its headcount from 1,350 by another 800 before end-2004, and is building a fifth Indian facility at Hyderabad,[168] while Accenture seeks to double its Indian staff to 10,000 in the same timeframe.[169] At the end of 2003, Internet search giant Google followed Yahoo in setting up an Indian R&D center,[170] and in early 2004, BearingPoint (formerly KPMG LLC) joined the bandwagon, planning two offices and 2,000 staff in India (initially with Covansys); Adam B. Frisch, an analyst for Switzerland's UBS, says that BearingPoint's Indian office 'addresses a very exposed flank,' thus "suggesting the company has probably lost business because of its absence in India."[171] The most expansive plans are however by Cincinnati, Ohio-based Convergys, which plans to increase its Indian headcount "from 7,200 to 20,000" by the end of 2004.[172]

Hundreds of specialist firms too have joined the wave, sometimes by acquiring Indian companies, such as software test and measurement star Lionbridge's buy of India's Mentorix in September 2003,[173] or by ramping up Indian operations alongside strategic moves in the U.S. One of the first moves after the merger of American quality and compliance management company MetricStream with workflow automation firm Zaplet was to more than double MetricStream's headcount in India to 100, and also transfer "development work relating to several components of Zaplet's product line" to Bangalore.[174]

For those in the West still seeking solace from an illusion about India's focus on IT services, disturbing news came in February 2004 from American IT firm Sierra Atlantic, a major product development partner for the likes of Oracle, Siebel and PeopleSoft. According to Marc Herbert, Sierra's executive vice president, "packaged software is the next offshore sweet spot."[175] The report also noted that "the majority of large Indian offshore services firms" increasingly have "a broad base of application development skills to draw from." Days later, Sierra announced the expansion of its Oracle Integration Centre of Excellence in India "for creating a hub specialising in integrating Oracle E-Business services with other software packages."[176] PeopleSoft followed suit, with an announcement by Ram Gupta, its Indian-born executive vice president of products and technology, that it intended to add 1,000 staff to its 400-strong Bangalore operation opened in May 2003, and now integrated with the Indian operations of J.D Edwards, which it also acquired during the year.[177]

The rush to India has hardly peaked. In just one week in early February 2004 (the same month of announcements by Sierra Atlantic and PeopleSoft), major expansions in Indian operations were reported by a clutch of other American software firms, among them Accelrys (drug discovery)[178], Brooks Automation (semi-conductor manufacturing),[179] eInfochips (chip design),[180] Interwoven (content-management),[181]   Lawson   (office   automation),[182] PrairieComm (3G solutions)[183] and back-office solutions provider Slash Support.[184] Announcements on Indian expansion were also made during that week by Japan's electronics giant Canon,[185] while French electrical equipment major Schneider said it was setting up a "global research and development" unit in Bangalore "for electronic design and software development;" the unit, launched with 100 staff, will grow "within two or three years" to 300.[186]

Like Schneider, several other European firms have begun stepping up the gas, among them Siemens and STMicro, as noted previously. Dutch chemicals giant Akzo started up its own Indian operations in February 2003,[187] as did German smart card firm Giesecke & Devrient[188] and French security software firm SiliComp, whose India development center is due to become its largest outside France.[189] Dutch banking group ABN-Amro said it would double staff numbers to 2,400 by the end of 2004 at its centers in Chennai, Mumbai and Delhi, which already provide support to its operations "in 18 countries."[190] Armed with orders, among others from airlines in Europe, LogicaCMG plans a quadrupling of employment to 1,500 by early 2005,[191] while Cap Gemini has started up a 1,000 strong center in Bangalore, which is due to triple in size by the end of 2004.[192] The Canadians have also joined: Canada's largest independent IT services company CGI, also plans to expand staff at its Centers of Excellence in India.[193]

It requires little imagination to extrapolate the impact of the above weekly and monthly snapshots to the years ahead.

VC Ventures Hot on India

Institutional factors supporting India's growth as a global software powerhouse include the pull and push from U.S. and Indian stock exchanges as well as the wider, international investment community, with which it has become increasingly interlocked.

The Indian IT industry has of course reciprocated, by continuing to shine. While the rest of the global IT industry floundered through the dark depths of 2003, India-based "Cognizant upped its revenue guidance for the year five times—each time by hefty amounts.... Nor is Cognizant an isolated case. After two years of cost-cutting and living with trimmed margins, other leading Indian software vendors appear to be on the same roll," noted *Asia Times* in November 2003.[194]

Currently, two of the largest Indian software firms (Infosys and Wipro) are ranked roughly on par with American giant EDS in U.S. stockmarket capitalization (in spite of at least 5-fold lower head-counts). This will also be the case after the expected listing in the near future by TCS, India's largest software exporter. Following very closely is Satyam, which boasted a U.S. stock market capitalization of $5.7 billion at the end of the year.

The American stock market performance of these Indian firms, central players in the relocation process, again highlights the growing difficulty of addressing relocation through territorial considerations; U.S. funds are among their biggest investors, and benefit directly from their gains through more relocation. Satyam Computer, for instance, counts Templeton Global, Merrill Lynch, Fidelity, Morgan Stanley Dean Witter and Warburg Pincus, among its investors; together such foreign investors held no less than 66 percent of its stock at the end of 2003.[195] General Atlantic has invested $100 million in India's sixth largest software firm Patni (the second major American investor after GE, which has a 10 percent stake in the company), while Citigroup is an investor in Polaris and Kshema, and ING of the Netherlands in MphasiS. And this process is by no means over. In April 2003, Alfred Berkeley, Vice Chairman of Nasdaq, observed that Indian companies could become a dominant foreign presence on U.S. stock exchanges. "Something really significant is going on in India. We don't want to miss what's going on."[196]

American technology firms have also invested directly in Indian IT. Intel, as mentioned before, has placed over $100 million in 30 Indian software companies, including Itanium specialist R Systems and chip designer Sasken.

But it is by no means only giants like Satyam and Patni, or midsized players like Polaris and R Systems, drawing such commitments. Much smaller Geodesic Information has extended the ceiling of foreign investment sharply up from 24 per cent; like Geodesic, there are hundreds of other such Indian IT firms, whose equity has been enthusiastically lapped up foreign investors.[197]

The longest-term indicator of the strength of Indian IT, and by some measures, its surest-footed driver, consists of private equity and venture capital. One of the earliest entrants into India was Walden International of San Francisco, which funded the high-end IT consulting firm MindTree. Others included Draper International and eVentures, formed by Rupert Murdoch's News Corp. and Japan's Softbank, joined soon after by India's own homegrown venture capitalists, including behemoths such as State-owned mutual fund giant, Unit Trust of India.

Once again, indicating the longer-term roots of this process, venture capital is also hardly new to Indian IT. In 1998, venture capital activity in India reached $687 million. A key motive: other than its skilled labor, India was already seen as "a probable place for innovative software applications and business ideas;" in addition, according to the head of one fund, "if the same Indians can succeed so well in Silicon Valley, they certainly can do it here (in India)."[198]

The pace of such investment has steadily strengthened over the years. Already in 2000, American private equity fund, Carlyle Group, said that six out of its nine Asian investments would be in India, the balance in China and Singapore.[199] 2001 saw Hong Kong-based GE Asia Pacific Capital Tech Fund earmarking 30 percent of its outlays for India, a share close to that of Taiwan, and, in a sign of the times, balanced between Indian software and Taiwanese hardware.[200] In 2002, India received $550 million in venture funding for 78 firms, second only to South Korea's $906 million in Asia.

By September 2003, venture capital investments into India had already crossed the $500 million mark,[201] but the pace was expected to accelerate further in 2004 and beyond. At the end of 2003, a delegation from 20 top-drawer U.S. venture capital firms including Sierra Ventures and Sequoia Capital, as well as Bessemer Venture Partners, Battery Ventures and Matrix Partners, spent eight days visiting IT firms in India. According to Saurabh Srivastava, chairman of the Indian Venture Capital Association, these "are all large investors who have not made any substantial investments in India so far."[202] Silicon Valley Bank, too, is now planning to set up "an office in India to support its clients."[203]

A similar pattern is also apparent in the U.S., where Indian-Americans have taken up both the first and second spots in the *Forbes* Midas List of the world's top venture capitalists. In 2003, even as global venture capital seemed to be in danger of drying up,[204] IT companies founded in the U.S. by Indians (most of which have long-running development centers in India) raised $1 billion.[205]

U.S. venture capitalists say "anywhere from one-third to three-quarters of the software, chip, and e-commerce startups they now back have Indian R&D teams from the get-go. 'We can barely imagine investing in a company without at least asking what their plans are for India,'" according to Sequoia Capital partner Michael Moritz, who nurtured Google, Flextronics, and Agile Software. India, he told *BusinessWeek*, "has seeped into the marrow" of Silicon Valley.[206] The reason for this is clear. The *BusinessWeek* article reports the case of U.S. multimedia chip and embedded software firm PortalPlayer Inc., whose Indian operations have enabled it to shave up to six months off the development cycle—and cut R&D costs by 40 percent. As a result, venture capitalists have pumped $82 million into the firm.

Other evidence of this trend comes from the fact that Indian start-ups are now attracting top-flight American managerial talent. In December, Patty Azzarello, vice-president and general manager of HP OpenView (support for which is being moved to India), left the company to join Euclid, a start-up, founded by three Indians and funded by Bay Partners and Pacesetter Capital.[207]

India's lead vis-a-vis other contenders in drawing venture capital and private equity is also widening. According to PricewaterhouseCoopers' Global Private Equity 2002, "Companies having a pan Asian presence have diverted considerable amounts ... to India."

Accompanying the Indian software industry's own growing maturity, such investment into the country is also becoming niche-specific, and (in spite of the current downturn) clearly aimed at leveraging India's growing and unbeatable advantage in cutting-edge new technologies, rather than simply software services. Examples include $130 million secured by Indian-American founded Infinera Corporation, whose Bangalore R&D lab aims to radically change perspectives on optical networking.[208] Another such firm is Insilica, founded by 'Father of the Pentium' Vinod Dham (see next chapter); it is filing three patents for its 'customized' networking chips, and has already acquired five customers.[209]

End-to-End, Top-to-Bottom

As illustrated by Insilica, one priority for venture capitalists is the core high-technology sector of chip design, where India is rapidly moving to global dominance. This is borne by the growing presence of Indian high-end R&D by scores of world chip leaders such as Texas Instruments, Motorola, Hughes and Broadcom, earlier players such as Cadence Design, and more recently, Intel, STMicro, and Adaptec—which in January 2004 announced a $25 million investment to double its Indian staff.[210]

Once again, the roots of India's rise as a chip-design powerhouse are not new. In December 2002, the International Financial Corporation (IFC), the World Bank's private-sector development arm, said it would invest in a fund to specifically incubate "chip design firms based in India."[211] Shortly afterwards, *Bloomberg News* published a report stating that India was emerging as the "world's top chip design center."[212]

The IFC, one of whose first Indian IT investments was a $250,000 (2.6 percent) stake in August 2000 in Learning Universe (the parent of software training firm egurucool.com),[213] now "plans to scale up its investments in India to $1 billion over the next two years"[214] from their present level of $700 million. Other similar high-growth niches, where India has been steadily accruing a massive lead, include the fast-growing wireless and animation sectors[215] as well as computer-based mapping, where the country "has grabbed a major slice" and "is poised to win more."[216]

Even at the top of the IT value pyramid, India's presence is not only growing, but is almost certainly here to stay.

Size Matters: Billion-Dollar Indians Force Global IT Industry Rethink

Three Indian IT firms (TCS, Infosys and Wipro) will report billion dollar revenues for 2003. Two others, Satyam Computer and

HCL, are expected to reach this status during the next year or two. Their revenues, like India's IT industry itself, are galloping. Infosys, for example, took about ten years to cross $5 million, another 8 to reach $100 million, and just five more to $1 billion.

Such Indian firms already share customers with their international rivals (such as Accenture, IBM and EDS), and their presence is rising. J.P. Morgan estimates that "probably 50% of Accenture's customer base" was using Indian vendors in early 2003, "up from about half that figure one year back."[217]

As they continue to globalize, Indian IT firms have sought to develop vertical market expertise on the home markets of customers in Western countries. One strategic accelerator for such firms is the industry-specific exposure they are systematically acquiring from back-office operations dedicated to blue-chip international customers, in sectors such as financial services, distribution and telecoms. As they grow, they are also attracting top-flight local talent, such as Jeffrey Sage, an auto-industry veteran from IBM who was hired as Chief Operating Officer for positioning India's Tata Technologies "well within the global automotive community."[218]

Meanwhile, positive perceptions about such Indian firms continue to grow in the wider business and technology community. America's Technology Business Research, for example, ranked Infosys number one in its Professional Services Business Quarterly (PSBQ) Benchmark for the 3rd quarter of 2003. PSBQ is a comprehensive analysis of the professional services industry, including management consulting, strategy consulting, system integration, outsourcing and other IT service areas.[219]

The moves by Indian firms are impacting not only deep but wide. As in China, TCS' GE-certified development operations in Hungary have brought Eastern Europe its first exposure to CMM practices. This poses an immediate challenge for access to the region's relatively small pool of qualified IT resources by firms from Western Europe seeking to build up 'ethnically-compatible' near-shore operations.

Reflecting their rising presence as a global force, Indian IT firms have also begun seeing major changes in their overseas order profile. While India's TCS and Mastek jointly won a high-profile contract worth more than $200 million from Britain's National

Health Service,[220] other orders too have been steadily rising in value, indicating growing confidence, and sometimes compulsion, on part of their customers. In July 2003, ITC Infotech won a $54 million software development order from Parametric Technology Corp of the U.S.[221] In September, Infosys bagged a $75 million order from Australian telecoms giant, Telstra, and in the following month, the former Indian government-owned CMC Ltd. (now part of the Tata conglomerate) signed a 5-year contract with TRW Automotive Inc. for over $25 million.[222] In the month of December alone, Infosys won two orders, each in the range of $25 to $30 million from ING and Kodak.[223] Satyam Computers, which had previously announced a contract with American International Group (AIG) to be an exclusive technology supplier for AIG's Web-based property-casualty insurance processing system,[224] won another bellwether order from Merrill Lynch (in a consortium which includes Microsoft and Dell) to develop a state-of-the-art research and analysis platform for the financial services giant[225]; Satyam is also setting up a 130-person offshore center for Telstra[226] (alongside the Australian firm's contract with Infosys).

While the National Health Service award in Britain for TCS and Mastek concern IT services, two big BPO wins are expected to have materialized in early 2004. The first is an over-$150 million order for HCL Technologies from an unnamed U.S. department store; HCL, which counts Federated Department Stores among its clients, already has a $160 million contract with BT.[227] Warburg Pincus-backed WNS (whose customers include British Airways and SAS), also reported a $170 million deal, again with an unnamed "U.S. financial company."[228]

Such a process is by no means confined to the largest IT firms. iGate Global Solutions, for example, secured a $20 million order from California's GreenPoint Mortgage, to manage selected "back-office processes and enhance their efficiency and operational excellence."[229]

Nor is it confined to the U.S. In Europe, mid-sized Indian IT services firm Hexaware has leveraged a strategic gamble it had previously made to focus on PeopleSoft solutions, securing a 22 million Euro order from Deutsche Leasing in Germany.[230] Following success with the National Health Service and the high-profile London Congestion Charging scheme (one of the world's largest projects on Microsoft's emerging DotNet platform, involving a daily total of 75,000 payment transactions, 250,000 vehicles and 1.5 million images),[231] Mastek went on to win a 10-year contract worth £27 million from BT's system integration arm Syntegra.[232] Kampsax India (the Indian division of Denmark's Cowi), managed to secure a lion's share of a 35 million Euro contract from the Ordnance Survey of Britain; this is considered "the world's largest mapping deal to date."[233]

On their part, Indian IT firms have become increasingly explicit about their confidence to take on international competitors. Infosys Managing Director Nandan Nilekani, for example, said "the Indian operations of global rivals" such as IBM and EDS are "piecemeal" in comparison to that of his company. "Companies coming here have a different model, which is doing local work in pockets, not in a global way. And to re-engineer that and become our model is not trivial stuff," he said.[234] Infosys Chief Financial Officer Mohandas Pai is even more skeptical. "It's not as easy as getting a bunch of guys in a room and starting work." More pertinently for relocation, he also points out that the top management of Indian IT firms is based in India, and that international firms would have to turn their business model on "its head" to cope.[235] The Gartner Group appears to endorse such confidence. Its Vice President Partha Iyengar says, "Indian companies have qualitative, time-to-market and skill advantages, augmented by low cost" and that "the single-point agenda of cost" cannot change the competitive equation significantly in the near term.[236]

The nibbling by Indian IT firms at the customer base of global giants will strengthen into a more frontal attack in the coming years. American investment bank J.P. Morgan says it would not be surprised if 2-3 years down the line offshore players begin to compete for 20-30 percent of Accenture's business.[237] In May 2003, the *New York Times* identified EDS' key global rivals to be IBM and India's Wipro,[238] and the American outsourcing company has been reported to be seeking an equity stake in India's Infosys.[239] Indeed, hostile or friendly acquisitions of some of the Indians cannot be ruled out in the years ahead.

Still, the real paradigm shift goes beyond competition on overseas markets between Indian newcomers and their long-established global competitors. The meaning of the Indian attack is seen in otherwise-smug international IT firms compelled to adapt their own delivery models to build a huge Indian presence, and doing this in the face of massive political opposition at home.

Whether through the growth of Indian IT service firms overseas or by the expansion of international firms in India, the net result will be the same: a continuous accession of India in the world's technology jobs league and an acceleration in the relocation of technology jobs.

Just Dropping In?
Indian Firms Begin Overseas Acquisitions

The outlines of India's fast-emerging software dominance should by now be coming into view. Indian IT is not new; what we see today is the cumulative impact of developments stretching back into the 1980s and before.

India's IT firms have quickly become multinational in scope, offering services around the world, and it is clear that India's low-end coding industry, while still active, is overshadowed by India's work in the most complex and creative sectors of R&D as well as in higher value packages and solutions. This lead is clearly becoming overwhelming, with the certainty of leaving behind potential competitors—not only from Russia to China—but eventually threatening European and U.S firms too.

Cementing the inexorability of this process is another new trend. Bolstered by their star status with the global financial community and bulging cash reserves, Indian IT firms have begun a careful[240] process of overseas acquisitions. The process will surely accelerate in 2004 and 2005, following the Indian government's move to ease overseas acquisition norms, discussed in more detail in a subsequent chapter. Some Indians firms are already seeking acquisitions in the near-$500 million league, directly against the likes of IBM, HP and others, for example, in a bid by TCS for Germany's Triaton (more below).

The aim behind overseas acquisitions is twofold: to acquire captive customers, and obtain more vertical-industry competencies, on par with the likes of IBM Global, EDS and Accenture. A good example of this is India's Techspan, which has merged with a 20-year old U.S. consulting firm Headstrong (2003 revenues of about $100 million). Headstrong has since appointed Arjun Malhotra (one of the founders of the large Indian IT services firm HCL) as Chief Executive of the group.[241]

In some cases, acquisitions also involve access to difficult new territories, above all Fortress Europe, still braced, sometimes numbly, against the inevitable Indian storm. For Phiroz Vandrevala, Executive Vice-President of TCS: "there are these 300-to-1,000-employee IT shops (which) have the guarantee of a three-year business waiting to be sold. In places like Europe, this will be an excellent strategy to gain entry. So, there will be action;"[242] as it happens, such 300-1,000 employee shops, form the bulk of Europe's protected IT landscape. Meanwhile, Wipro's Dutch vice president of enterprise sales in Europe, Kees Ten Nijenhuis, also confirmed at the end of 2003 that the Indian giant was "acquiring companies at the moment in continental Europe."[243] Satyam too has planned buyouts as a way to enter the European market,[244] as has Cognizant Technology, which has already acquired a Dutch IT firm and plans "smaller acquisitions in Europe in (the) revenue range of $50 to $100 million."[245]

HCL, NIIT and Wipro were among the first to venture in such a direction; all of them were careful in choosing their targets. At the end of 2001, HCL acquired BT's support center at Belfast in Northern Ireland. In 2002, NIIT made four acquisitions; these include the custom development business of Click2Learn, SAP solutions provider Osprey and DEI, an insurance industry specialist. One of NIIT's highest profile acquisitions was AD Solutions AG, itself the result of a management buy-out from IBM in Germany, with subsidiaries in Switzerland and Austria.[246] Meanwhile, Wipro acquired the energy-sector operations of American Management Systems, Nervewire (specialized in banking and financial services) as well as Ericsson's Indian IT R&D operations (which it had operated for several years).[247]

The pace of acquisitions by Indian IT firms picked up in the second half of 2003. In May, bolstered by its $100 million investment from General Atlantic, Patni acquired U.S. technology consulting firm The Reference Inc., giving it access to a clutch of top Wall Street firms, including Goldman Sachs;[248] further acquisitions are expected by Patni after the success of its early 2004 IPO, which was over-subscribed 22 times.[249] Barely days after Patni's move on Reference, two other Indian firms, Cognizant and TCS, announced acquisitions in the U.S. and Europe. While Cognizant took over ACES, a CRM company in California (thus paving its way for a coveted 'promising' rating in the field by Gartner),[250] TCS acquired Airline Financial Support Services (a joint venture between its Indian parent and SwissAir), to strengthen its offerings for the global airlines industry[251]; this was followed by TCS making two high-profile (but eventually abortive) bids in Europe, for Scandinavian IT-Group, the IT subsidiary of Scandinavian Airlines System,[252] and for Triaton, IT services unit of the German industrial giant ThyssenKrupp—in which it competed directly against some of the world's best-known IT firms, among them Cap Gemini Ernst & Young, IBM, and HP.[253]

In December 2003, Infosys announced its first overseas acquisition, of Expert Information Services in Australia, a move largely meant to politically secure its bellwether $75 million contract from Telstra.[254] Also in December, banking software firm i-Flex announced an all-cash acquisition of SuperSolutions Corporation, an American consumer lending software provider (whose clients include the likes of Harley Davidson Financial Services, Inc., Mitsubishi Motors Credit, Hyundai Motor Finance, the U.S. Small Business Administration, Onyx Acceptance Corporation, and Crescent Bank & Trust).[255] At the turn of 2003, Cognizant followed its American buy of ACES by picking up Infopulse, a Netherlands-based IT services firm specializing in the banking and financial services industry,[256] while HCL Technologies moved to take full control of DSL Software Ltd, its joint venture with Germany's Deutsche Bank in which it had acquired a 51 percent stake in 2001; DSL has exclusivity on both IT services and back-office outsourcing by the giant German financial services firm in India until 2008.[257]

Even smaller Indian players are following the acquisition route, sometimes in cutting-edge product and technology niches such as Moiria Media's buy of Silicon Valley MPEG-4 trailblazer iVast,[258] or the $13 million acquisition by India's Cranes of the Sigma product suite from SPSS of America.[259] Most however, have looked at service providers. In June 2003, Aftek Infosys acquired 49 percent of

Munich-based Arexera Information Technologies[260]; a new joint venture with a British mobile and wireless software firm is now in the pipeline.[261] In October, KPIT Infosystems acquired Houston-based PANEX Consulting, Ltd. "to aggressively tap" middle-tier U.S. companies seeking ERP implementation,[262] while Datamatics acquired U.S.-based CorPay Solutions Inc. and said it planned further acquisitions in Canada.[263] Also in October, IBS Software Services, a provider of travel and logistics solutions, took over Avient Technologies, part of Honeywell Aerospace U.K. International.[264] In November, Yash Tech acquired Global Core of the U.S., an SAP Business Partner.[265]

The process of acquisition-led immersion into overseas markets has continued, with targets in early 2004 alone including Symphoni Interactive, an American financial services consulting firm,[266] geographical information solutions provider Vargis LLC,[267] and Bristlecone, within which Indian automotive group Mahindra (parent of MBT, and a clutch of other IT services companies) plans to consolidate its consulting subsidiaries.[268]

Significantly, as illustrated by TCS' buyout of its SwissAir partner and HCL of Deutsche Bank's stake in DSL, Western non-technology partners of Indian firms now appear to acknowledge that the latter are best equipped to handle IT. A previous example of this is the U.S. stock exchange Nasdaq, whose trading platform was developed by India's SSI; in early October, SSI bought out Nasdaq's 55 percent stake in their joint venture.[269]

Overseas acquisitions are also mounting in the back-office space. Here, the motive is straightforward, to acquire customers as well as (in some cases) defend against new competitors from overseas. Bolstered by a $22 million venture capital investment from Sequoia Capital in July 2003, BPO service provide 24/7 Customer plans to make U.S. acquisitions within the six month period starting October 2003.[270] 24/7's effort will no doubt be aided by George Shaheen, former Chief Executive of Andersen Consulting (now Accenture), who joined its Board in early 2004.[271]

Further evidence of the growing strength of the Indian BPO challenge is the entry by large Indian industrial groups and conglomerates. At the end of October 2003, Hinduja TMT Ltd—part of the giant Hinduja conglomerate (transport, media, banking, chemicals and trading), said it was acquiring a controlling interest and management control in c3, an offshore call-center in Manila.[272] In November, consumer goods giant Godrej Group announced an all-cash acquisition of Upstream LLC, a U.S.-based call center company with three facilities and 600 employees.[273] Indian conglomerate Essar (steel, oil, power, construction, shipping and telecoms) made an even more ambitious move; backed by Germany's Deutsche Bank, it muscled out Britain's AllServe for an 80 percent stake in Aegis Communication Group Inc.,[274] "one of the largest call centre companies" in the U.S. with a capacity of 5,100 seats at 11 centers across the country.[275]

Thinking Global?
Local Talent Joins Indian Payrolls

Given recent developments, among them higher-value business solution offerings, acquisitions in Europe and the U.S., and a steady rise in their average order size, large Indian firms are clearly aiming to also acquire similar international identities as the likes of Accenture or EDS. At some stage, picking on the 'Indianness' of an otherwise equally international firm, as say EDS, will become untenable.

Although, after the beginnings of the offshore backlash in 2003, one of the Indian IT industry's first responses to becoming "fully engaged local citizens in local markets" was to (unhelpfully) commit to keeping Americans and Europeans "for activities like public relations, advertising and corporate communications,"[276] several individual firms have for some time recognized the need for hiring local talent, and doing so beyond simply the Board level where there already are plenty of Westerners on Indian company payrolls.

TCS made concerted beginnings for such an effort at the start of 2001, when it launched "its first training program for U.S. university graduates."[277] Ironically, the "state-of-the-art" Training Center was located in Columbus, Indiana—the very state which rescinded TCS' contract to upgrade the State's unemployment claims system in late 2003, as part of its drive to 'help' local firms.

Following its first significant overseas acquisition in Australia in late 2003, Infosys Chairman Narayana Murthy said "we want

them (Australian employees) to grow from 330 to, maybe, 3,300."[278]
Though there was an element of excessive bonhomie in these words,
the intent is serious. Satyendra Kumar, an Infosys Vice-President,
said that as part of its "effort to become a true multinational corporation"..."around 25 percent" of the company's staff would be non-
Indian by 2012.[279]

The local presence is obviously paramount at call centers, both
in India (where 20,000 foreign citizens have been recently recruited,
as Chapter VII notes) and in Indian operations overseas. These will
become the first to seriously erode attempts by Western governments to restrict contracts based on a company's origin. At its
Belfast (Northern Ireland) facility, HCL has no fewer than 861
employees, including "French, Spanish, Portuguese, German,
Dutch, Italian and English-speaking staff;" staff numbers, furthermore, rose by 30 percent in 2003.[280]

Beyond Chile, Nigeria, Pakistan: Indian Infotech 2008

By the year 2008, India's information technology services sector is on track to be chalking revenues forecast by consultants
McKinsey & Co. at $87 billion.[281] It will by then be visibly massive-
bigger, for example, than the entire economies of three otherwise-
large developing countries, namely Chile, Nigeria, or for that matter, what the world media habitually refers to as India's 'arch rival,'
Pakistan*; Pakistan's annual software exports, at $50 million,[282] cor-
responded in 2003 to 0.5 percent of India's, or just one (working)
day's worth.

The implications of such critical differences will inevitably
become clear for those who believe India is just another large developing country, and where software is just another sector.

To sum up, it is obvious that India's rise in the IT stakes is neither recent, nor etched out by global forces solely for their conven-
ience. Indeed, behind its emergence as a threat to Western white-

---

*   Based on 2001 GDPs (www.worldbank.org) and assuming a (relatively high) annual
     growth rate of 5 percent, the GDP of these countries in 2007 would be Chile ($85.97
     billion), Nigeria ($58.35 billion) and Pakistan ($81.10 billion).

collar jobs, is a process of accumulated software strengths going back to at least the early 1990s.

While Western firms, driven by strategic concerns of their highest executives, trawl aggressively across India, thereby becoming even more dependent on it, Indian IT firms too are stepping out, globalizing. Whoever leads this race, whether Indian IT firms or their Western rivals, India itself will continue to gain from both. Such an eventuality of course drives the international investment community—who provide much of the push for Indian IT's acquisition of critical mass in a progressively-higher spectrum of technologies.

In turn, invigorated by this growing spread of strengths, the pull of Indian IT on Western white-collar jobs technology is likely to rise further with time, and in some cases, become irreversible.

Before this, it may be opportune to consider whether there are any clear boundaries between Indian software and its counterparts elsewhere.

CHAPTER IV

The 'Definte Smell' Of Curry

How India Spiced Up America's Hot Industry and Beyond

How 'Indian' is World Software?

Given India's indisputable strengths in the field, this is no longer just an idle question. Indeed, as the arguments above underline, an answer may provide useful insights about where Americans, Europeans and others are on the path of the rising Elephant, and how they might be forced to relate to it. Other than moral issues about relocation (whose IT is it anyway?) this issue is also especially relevant given the close connections and synergies between the fast-growing IT industry in India and the role of Indians in the IT industry in America. Indeed, the lack of a similar Indian presence in the IT industry in Europe may be one explanation for the sequential meltdown of European New Economy companies, and their seeming inability to stage a recovery.

To go further in grasping such 'Indianness' of software, it might be especially worthwhile to look in some detail at the role of Indians in creating the American information technology industry—from chip pioneers to enablers of both the personal computer revolution in the 1980s and early 1990s, and thereafter, of the Internet Revolution and the New Economy. They have, in a sense, played a role for some years 'returning' with their know-how (both given and taken) to India. In turn, this has brought Bangalore, sometimes quietly, up to speed with, and now beyond, Silicon Valley.

The impact of this (a key part of the relocation process) has already been immense, and is unlikely to slow down in the years ahead. In the year 2000, Indian IT firms associated with the Silicon

Valley-based TiE (The Indus Entrepreneurs) forum created business with market value estimated at $235 billion,[1] in other words more than Switzerland's gross domestic product.

Fathering the Pentium: Drawing on a Blue-Chip Lineage

The IFC fund to invest in chip-design in India, referred to in the previous chapter, was the brainchild of an Indian-born engineer called Vinod Dham. Dham, who is also known as the 'Father of the Pentium' (a sobriquet acknowledged by former U.S. President Bill Clinton[2]), was Vice President and General Manager of the Microprocessor Products group at Intel. After Intel, he set up Nexgen, the company responsible for developing what eventually became the K6 processor from Advanced Micro Devices, which remains the Pentium's principal competitor.[3]

Underwriting their contribution at a fundamental level of the modern computer industry, Indian engineers also played key roles in developing the pathbreaking SPARC microprocessor for Sun Microsystems (Anant Agarwal[4]) as well as the core architecture for Silicon Graphics and its subsidiary Cray Research.[5] K. Ramachandra Reddy is "credited with having designed the world's first digital signal processor (DSP) way back in 1977."[6] In the early 1990s, Steve Sanghi rose to the helm of Microchip Technology, previously the semiconductor business unit of General Instrument Corporation, while Texas Instruments appointed another Indian to head its worldwide semiconductor R&D.[7] Shortly afterwards, Prakash Agarwal launched NeoMagic, the world's first producer of single-chip multimedia accelerators. During this period, Indians also led scores of other innovative chip firms in the U.S., among them Alliance Semiconductor (N. D. Reddy), GaSonics (Asuri Raghavan), GDA Technologies (A.G. Karunakaran), Interra (Ajoy Bose), NeST (Javad Hassan), Numerical Technologies (Y.C. Pati), Simplex Solutions (Narain Arora) and TranSwitch Corporation (Santanu Das). Ambit Design Systems, founded by Prakash Bhalerao (part of the team at CQube Microsystems which developed the now industry-standard DVD format), was sold to Cadence Design Systems for $260 million.

This blue-chip lineage continues. In 2003, Indian-born Ravi
Arumilli filed his 200th patent for IBM, along with his brother Baba
accounting for no less than 10% of the American giant's entire
patent filings out of its Austin, Texas semiconductor R&D lab.[8]
Acknowledged by IBM to be its leading expert on symmetric multipurpose systems, cache/memory hierarchies and system bus protocols, Ravi Arumilli was chief architect of IBM's Power4 chip and
lead designer of the innovative Regatta server which paved the way
for IBM's assault on Unix servers. Arumilli was also lead developer
of electronics for Pacific Blue, the advanced version of the Deep
Blue computer,[9] which bested chess grandmaster Garry Kasparov
within just one hour in May 1997.

The Early Indian Hands:
Sun, Oracle, Novell and Others

Beyond processors and integrated circuits was the early Indian
hand in founding what are today some of the largest and most successful American IT firms. As is common knowledge, Sun
Microsystems was co-founded by an Indian, Vinod Khosla, who was
also its first Chief Executive.[10] Indians also made key contributions
to the early growth of two other IT flagships, database giant Oracle,
and Novell, the world's networking leader. Umang Gupta was Vice
President and General Manager of the microcomputer products division of Oracle and wrote its first business plan in 1981,[11] while
another Indian, Kanwal Rekhi, became Novell's Vice President and
Chief Technology Officer, spearheading its rise as the leader of IT
networking. Meanwhile, at Apple Computers, Satjiv Chahil was
appointed General Manager of its Entertainment, New Media and
Internet Division (before taking over as Chief Marketing Officer at
Palm in 2000).

But this was not all. If not quite household names, several other
American IT corporate superstars were also created by Indians in the
1980s, and laid the foundations for the computer revolution. These
include the world's largest supply-chain management firm i2
Technologies (founded by Sanjiv Sidhu), chip innovator Cirrus
Logic (Suhas Patil), B2B pioneer Aspect Development (Romesh
Wadhwani), electronic design automation firm Duet Technologies

(Prabhu Goel), and ACT Networks (Suresh Nihalani)—which went on to become the world's largest independent provider of integrated frame relay access solutions.

Nearly Half of Silicon Valley...And Beyond

Through the 1990s, the Indian presence in the U.S. software industry continued to strengthen. By 1996 "nearly half of the 55,000 temporary visas issued by the U.S. government to high-tech workers went to Indians"[12]; in other words, Indian engineers in the U.S. accounted for nearly as much as the rest of the world put together. By the end of the decade, they accounted for no fewer than 20 percent of Microsoft's U.S. employees,[13] according to its Chairman Bill Gates, and 25 percent of Cisco's, according to Chief Executive John Chambers.[14]

Many Indians steadily rose to key positions in the advanced technology efforts of a sweeping range of American high-tech businesses, as varied as Apple Computers, supercomputer giant Cray Research, Deneb Robotics, Hughes Electronics, Lucent, Microsoft, Nortel, Oracle and Viacom. Rajneesh Chopra, SDRC's Director of R&D, led the team that built its flagship I-DEAS Master Series architecture, while Manu Agarwal's groundbreaking work on flash memory won Wafer Scale Integration a key U.S. patent. Elsewhere, Rajan Kulkarni was credited with spurring Fidelity.com into one of the Internet's most heavily trafficked sites. The Indian high-tech role also extended beyond IT to new-generation pharmaceutical firms such as Aviron, Theratech and Xechem, chemical companies like Raychem, as well as the auto industry: Mohammad Zaidi, for example, developed the first aluminum spaceframe for automobiles—used in the Audi A8 and the Ferrari Modena, while Haren Gandhi of Ford Motor led the company's catalyst research effort which has won over 40 patents. These were just the iceberg's tip. Beneath them were tens thousands of others; they are still there.

Table III: The Techie Tide—Vaulting Corporate Ladders

Company	Name	Title
Adobe	Shantanu Narayen	Vice President, Corporate Engineering
AlcatelTelecom	KrishPrabhu	Chief Operating Officer
Air Touch	Arun Sarin	Chief Operating Officer
Alcoa	Mohammad A. Zaidi	Chief Technical Officer
AT&TWireless	Mohan Gyani	Chief Executive Officer
Aviron	Raysam S. Prasad	Vice President, Technical Affairs
Bradley Pharmaceuticals	Dileep Bhaghwat	Chief Scientific Officer
Cable & Wireless	Gian Dilawari	Vice President
Cabletron	Piyush Patel	Chief Executive Officer
Cisco	Jayashree Ullal	Vice President
ComputerAssociates	Sanjay Kumar	President
Cray Research	Ven B. Rao	Director, New Technology Research Lab
Delphi Information	Robin Raina	President
Deneb Robotics	Rakesh Mahajan	Chief Executive
e.digital	Atul Anandpura	Vice President R&D
Ficon Technologies	Vivek Bansal	Chief Executive
GovCon.com	Raj Khera	President
Hanover Direct	Rakesh Kaul	President
HP	Pradeep Jotwani	President and General Manager, Consumer Business Organization
Hughes Electronics	S. Radhakrishnan	Chief Information Officer
Microcircuits International	Arvinder Chadha	Vice President Manufacturing
Lawson Software	Pramod Mathur	Vice President Collaborative Commerce
Lucent Technologies		
	Basant Chawla	Director (Enterprise Physical Architecture)
Matthews Studio Equipment	Anil Sharma	President
Microsoft	Sanjay Parthasarathy	Vice President (Strategy and Business Development)
	Amar NehruVice	President (Corporate Development Group)
	S. Somasegar	Vice President (Windows Engineering Group)
Neoforma.com	Bhagwan Goel	Vice President

Newbridge Networks	Satjiv Chahil	Vice President, Global Marketing
Nhancement Software Technologies	Ram V. Mani	President and Chief Technology Officer
Nortel	Krishna G. Kushwaha	Director, R&D (Access Networks)
	Shri Dodani	Director, Transmission Systems
Oracle	Jnan Dash	Vice President, Advanced Technology
	Rahul Bardhan	Senior Practice Director, Advanced Technology
PictureTel	Vinay Kumar	General Manager
Planar Systems	Balaji Krishnamurti	Chief Executive
Qualcomm	Anil Kripalani	Senior Vice President
Ramp Networks	Raghu Bathina	Vice President Broadband Unit
Raychem (Advanced Technology)	Sanjay Kasturia	Director
Santa Cruz Operation	Alok Gupta	President
SDRC	Rajneesh Chopra	Director
SoftPlus	Mohan Uttarwar	President
SSE Telecom	S. Ram Chandran	Director Engineering
STMicroelectronics	Ravi Sundaresan	Senior Manager Advanced Technology Development
Symettricom	Murli Thirumale	Vice President
TheraTech	Dinesh Patel	President
University Games	Naresh Kapahi	Co-President
US Interactive	Ajit Prabhu	Chief Technology Officer
Viacom	Jayaram Balachander	Vice President Software Engineering
Xechem	Ramesh Pandey	President
Wafer Scale Integration	Manu Agarwal	Head R&D

Even more remarkable than the sheer pervasiveness of such professionals was the massive growth in the presence of Indian-origin entrepreneurs in Silicon Valley start-ups. In early 1999, Berkeley sociologist AnnaLee Saxenian discovered that "nearly half of all Silicon Valley companies were founded by Indian entrepreneurs. The definite smell inside a Silicon Valley start-up," she observed, "was of curry."[15]

Good examples of Indian success stories in the Valley include Qube microserver developer Cobalt Networks (founded by Vivek

Mehra); online computer maintenance pioneer Cybermedia, now part of Network Associates (Unni Warrier); Internet identity management firm e-Code (Rohit Chandra); healthcare portal Healtheon-Web MD (Pavan Nigam); Hotmail, now part of Microsoft (Sabeer Bhatia); Infospace (Naveen Jain); anti-virus and security firm McAfee (Srivats Sampath); e-business pioneer NetObjects (Samir Arora); NexPrise (developer of the ipTeam Suite, used by U.S. defense contractors Lockheed Martin, Boeing and Raytheon, founded by Ram Shriram); ASP pioneer Responsys (Anand Jagannathan); enterprise application integration leader Tibco (Vivek Ranadive); networking specialist Torrent (Hemant Kanakia); payments giant Verifone, now part of HP (Hatim Tyabji); Internet/Intranet infrastructure management pioneer WebManage (Vijay Basani); and Web identity firm Yodlee.com (Anil Arora, previously technology architect of Gateway).

Through selling their own technology start-ups to larger players, Indians also acceded to the positions of Chief Technology Officers at two other high-profile firms, Amazon.com (Anand Rajaraman) and Open Markets (B.C Krishna), while Yahoo was launched with a young Indian woman, Srinija Srinivasan, as its founder Vice President and Chief Editor.

Tech firms aside, entrepreneurs from Indian also set up numerous American software service firms, including large Year 2000 specialists like Intelligroup, Syntel, IMR, Complete Business Solutions and Mastech. Nasdaq star Aristasoft had Indians concurrently holding the titles of Chief Technology Officer, Chief Information Officer, Executive Vice President Operations and Director Business Development.[16]

By the late 1990s, many such companies had huge operations in India, laying the roots for the eventual resurgence of the home-front.

The Internet's Nuts, Bolts and Wheels

Other than professional executives and dotcom start-ups, Indians also played crucial roles in providing the Internet with a good chunk of its critical technical backbone in the mid-1990s (and as it happens, even before; Indian-born Abhay Bhushan of MIT, chaired the group that wrote the key FTP file transfer protocol for the U.S. ARPANET in 1972).[17]

Four Internet technology giants started up by Indians in America, Juniper Networks, Sycamore, Exodus and Brocade, collectively attained a market capitalization of over $125 billion in March 2000, at the height of the dotcom boom.[18]

Juniper was founded by Pradeep Sindhu; its M-40 was the first router to allow Internet service providers to handle traffic at 10 gigabits per second.[19] Jagdeep Singh's Lightera Networks implemented the concept of Dense Wave Division Multiplexing to increase the capacity of optical fibers, and Sycamore Networks (founded by Gururaj Deshpande) remains a leader in optical networking technologies. Tachion (founded by Satish Sharma) developed the 'collapsed central office,' an integrated communications system allowing carriers to switch and transport both phone calls and different data formats in a fraction of the space required by traditional systems. Nexabit Networks (founded by Mukesh Chatter and sold to Lucent Technologies), delivered a router machine with speeds 160 times faster than its second-ranked competitor. At Avici Systems, Surya Panditi designed a 'next generation' router scalable to accommodate six terabits of data (amounting to 72 million simultaneous telephone calls).

Other well-known Indian-founded Silicon Valley firms playing a crucial role in making the Internet a reality include Accelerated Networks (enabling multiple voice and data services over a single access line, the brainchild of ACT Networks co-founder Suresh Nihalani); Brocade Communications (pioneer of Fibre Channel Fabric solutions which provided the intelligent backbone for SAN storage area networks, founded by Kumar Malavalli); Cerent (developer of the 454 network element, enabling service providers to customize bandwidth management, founded by Rajvir Singh and sold to Cisco for $6.9 billion; Singh also founded three other leading firms—Fibrelane, Sierra Networks and StratumOne Communications); Digital Link (founded by Vinita Gupta); Ishoni and Alopa Networks (both launched by Ambit Design founder Prakash Bhalerao, and dedicated to single-chip-based secure broadband); Intellinet (the customized 'intelligent' network pioneer, founded by Arjan Ghosal); Exterprise (the first e-collaborative,

intelligent e-business software platform, co-founded by Satyendra
Rana); Exodus (founded by K.B Chandrashekhar and B.V
Jagadeesh, which became the fastest billion dollar company in history and was declared a 'National Infrastructure Asset' by the U.S.
government in 2000); and Nextlinx (Rajiv Uppal, whose Internet
logistics suite was adopted by Cisco Systems, 3Com, Fairchild
Semiconductor, Honeywell, Rockwell Automation, Quantum,
Sotheby's and UPS; Uppal earlier led development on twelve trade
automation products for the U.S. Department of Commerce).

Harvard, Princeton and MIT—Rolled into One?

Many founders of such New Economy flagships graduated from
India's elite network of IITs (Indian Institutes of Technology),[20] in
comparison to which one of America's most competitive universities, Harvard, was described in Michael Lewis' bestseller *The New,
New Thing* as "a kind, forgiving place."[21]

This reputation continues. In January 2003, CBS News' flagship program, 60 Minutes, claimed that an IIT was "Harvard,
Princeton and MIT all rolled into one" and that "if you are a WASP
walking in for a job, you wouldn't have as much pre-assigned credibility as you do if you're an engineer from I.I.T."[22]

Beyond Tech: Riding into Finance, Mainstream American Business

Several such Indian-founded technology trailblazers were also
backed by Indians within the heart of the U.S. financial community.
Together, they pushed for early advantage in their efforts from India-
based offshore centers. The most influential Indian venture capitalists in America include ex-Sun Chief Executive Vinod Khosla, who
has been a General Partner of American venture capital powerhouse
Kleiner Perkins Caufield & Byers since 1986,[23] Promod Haque
(General Partner, Norwest Venture Partners), Yogen Dalal (partner
at another leading firm, Mayfield), Ram Shriram of NexPrise (one of
the founders of Google) and Anil Thadani (Chairman, Schroder
Capital Partners). Khosla was named by *Fortune* magazine as "the
greatest VC of all time," while the *Wall Street Journal* called him "the

hottest hand in Silicon Valley." In 2004, *Forbes'* Midas List ranked Khosla and Haque at the top of the world's venture capitalist league tables.[24]

During the 1990s, Indian technology professionals also rose to become Presidents and CEOs across large swathes of mainstream American business, among them United Airlines (Ronno Dutta), U.S. Airways (Rakesh Gangwal), Provident Financial (Shailesh Mehta), Rohm & Haas (Raj Gupta) and Citigroup (Victor Menezes—described by the *Wall Street Journal* as the rarest of corporate creatures: a Citicorp survivor[25]). Recent additions to this list include Jeet Bindra, President, Chevron Global Refining, and Pradman Kaul, Chairman and Chief Executive of space and telecoms giant Hughes Network Systems.

Going beyond their traditionally large presence in business schools, American academia and ownership of "37 percent of all hotel properties in the U.S.,"[26] Indians also headed elsewhere. The world's most influential consulting firm, McKinsey & Co., appointed Rajat Gupta as its global Managing Partner, the first non-American to hold this position in its long history. Jamshed 'Jim' Wadia became the first Indian-born worldwide Managing Partner of accountants Arthur Andersen. Another Indian, Arshad Zakaria, is in the race to become the youngest-ever President of Merrill Lynch, while Ashok Boghani and others remain stars of Arthur D. Little. Elsewhere, Sonny Mehta is (since 1987) editor-in-chief of Alfred A. Knopf, America's leading publishing house, while Fareed Zakaria has become Editor of *Newsweek International*.[27]

Though the size of the Indian tech contingent at NASA (over-30 percent[28]) is part of folklore, more remarkable has been the rise of Indians to the pinnacle of the pure scientific community in the U.S. Thus, Arun Netravali was Director of Bell Labs, the foremost U.S. R&D laboratory, and is now its President Emeritus and Chief Scientist. Robotics legend Raj Reddy headed the information technology Group of the Pentagon's secretive Defense Advanced Research Projects Agency (DARPA), and subsequently co-chaired President Clinton's Information Technology Advisory Committee. Praveen Chaudhari (developer of the erasable CD read/write and 21 other patents for IBM) is now Director of the U.S. nuclear R&D facility, Brookhaven National Laboratory. Sanjay Sarma co-founded the Auto-ID Center at MIT and has become one of the world's acknowledged gurus in the new technology frontier of Radio Frequency Identification (RFID); another Indian at MIT, Amar Bose, mixes business and pleasure as founding Chief Executive of hi-fi company Bose Corp.

Although influential Indian-Americans like these may not formally espouse an Indian dimension in American IT, informal networking within this close-linked ethnic community has played, and will continue to play, a crucial role, in cementing ever-closer links to their roots in India.[29] Thus, Arun Netravali of Bell Laboratories, is reported to be "setting up a $250-million venture capital fund" to invest in U.S.-based start-up companies "which would be outsourcing to India."[30]

The Golden Diaspora: The Political Taste of Curry

These kinds of people are clearly more than German-style IT guest laborers. Many are already American citizens. Others hold green cards, and are on their way to becoming so. More important, in terms of the domestic political impact of the relocation debate, they are all not only highly qualified, but also extremely wealthy.

The examples quoted above, however, remain shards from the iceberg's tip. Already by the 1990 Census in the U.S., the average household income of Indian-Americans "was about $60,000—more than Japanese- or Chinese-Americans and considerably above the national average of about $39,000."[31] By 1996, Indian-Americans had America's "highest median household income and highest proportion of college graduates, according to a Harvard study."[32] By all accounts, this lead strengthened further in the 1990s in the New Economy. In 1999, gushed *Salon* magazine, "IIT has produced more millionaires (per capita) than any other undergraduate institution." According to a recent Merrill Lynch survey, there are no fewer than 200,000 Indian millionaires in the U.S.

In 2000, *Time* magazine featured the extraordinary success of Indian-Americans vis-a-vis Asian and other immigrants—as "a triumph of quality over quantity"—in a feature titled 'The Golden Diaspora.'[33] This is a striking change. For decades (and in spite of the 1990 census), the American media resisted anointing yet another immigrant group as "the smartest" of an era. Whatever the merits of doing so, it is an important sign that 'Asians' who occupied this perception space for decades have now been displaced.

The Golden Diaspora has played a role in the emergence of the Indian-American community as one of the U.S.' most powerful lobby groups.[34] This is not just in Silicon Valley. In Virginia, the Indian Chief Executive High Tech Council was described by Don Upson, the State's Secretary of Technology: "They've got the A-list. I mean, it's just that simple." Mark Warner, (now) Governor of Virginia, describes the Council as "maybe the singularly most successful association that's taken place in the last decade." Both these quotes appeared in the *Washington Post*,[35] which also mentioned how the Indian Council had immediate access not only to leading American politicians, powerbrokers and financiers, but also to others ranging from the British Ambassador in America to the President of Egypt.

Indian-Americans have become assertive in the relocation debate. For example, Vinod Khosla, the Sun Microsystems co-founder and top-ranked venture capitalist in the *Forbes* list, has publicly urged India to "use World Trade Organization (WTO) rules" to fend off "protectionist attacks in an election year."[36]

By now, it ought to be clear that there is no clear demarcation, certainly in information technology, between 'us' and 'them,' between Indian IT and American IT. Thus, the argument about American technology jobs 'going to India' clearly remains a semantic puzzle, even were it possible to magically put a stop to the process.

Going further (territorially speaking), an American connection is also instrumental in the arrival of Indians at the top rungs of corporate Europe.[37] Europe's largest technology firm Vodafone, for example, inherited its Indian Chief Executive, Arun Sarin, from AirTouch of the U.S.[38] Earlier, it was his tenure at Citibank which propelled Michael deSa to become what the *Wall Street Journal* said was one of Deutsche Bank's "most successful executives"; "in less than four years," deSa "put Deutsche Bank's foreign-exchange operation on the map," ranked "just behind Citibank globally."[39] For European business, the strength of the Indian-American connection[40] was even more strongly demonstrated when the U.S.' most powerful business daily, the *Wall Street Journal*, appointed Indian-born Raju Narisetti as Managing Editor of its European edition at the end of 2002.

While such issues will continue to erode simple homilies and contexts about territorial delimitation, what is equally clear is the fact that, in the cold calculus of American electoral politics, both the votes and (even more, the) money of Indian-Americans will prove a continuing, complicating counterweight to the voices of laid-off American tech workers.

The political implications of the Indian ascendancy in the U.S. were evident in 2003, when Bobby Jindal, a 32-year old son of Indian immigrants, won the Republican candidacy for Louisiana governor. Jindal ran the Louisiana medical system at 24, became President of the University of Louisiana at 27, and White House health policy czar at 30. His campaign was heavily backed by Indian-Americans, and did not seem to face any hurdles, in spite of the fact, as the *Guardian* observed, that Louisiana was "a state where 12 years ago a former grand dragon of the Ku Klux Klan, David Duke, won a majority of the white vote.[41] Though Jindal was narrowly defeated by the Democrats, his campaign illustrated both the real political clout of Indian-Americans and their competency in maneuvering through the evidently-complex minefield of ethnic minority, racial and partisan issues—indeed, as Chapter VII illustrates, rather like they would have done in elections back home.

Such complexities have emerged in the U.S. presidential elections, too. Democratic contender Gen. Wesley Clark, for example, was forced to withdraw comments from his Website inviting Indian IIT graduates to take up American citizenship and start-up software firms. "Let's all be wealthy and prosperous and happy together," he suggested. In November, Gen. Clark stepped into the gaping chasm outlined in Chapter I—regarding the fact that few people, least of all experts, seem to know what will replace high-end, white-collar New Economy jobs relocating to India. His comment during an Iowa debate, "Let them do the software in India; we'll do other things in this country,"[42] provoked howls of protest across the U.S. Though Gen. Clark had earlier stated that "energy and environmental engineering are two very fertile areas for the growth of American jobs," in a subsequent email exchange with Gen. Clark's New Hampshire

Policy Director Cristina Posa, a questioner asked: "Please explain why he doesn't think this work can be done in India. I'm an engineer, and let me tell you—it CAN be done in India."[43]

Beyond Borg?

Those who have seen the movie First Contact might already be drawing analogies. The Indian ascension is relentless and pervasive. Starting small, it has grown incrementally to now pose an incredible, deep-rooted and wide-ranging impact.

However, such fears would, above all, be grounded in unawareness. As mentioned on several occasions, there has been a universal and often-perverse disinclination, above all by the Western media, to acknowledge and fill-in what for this author, would best be described as the Great Indian Absence. For multi-cultural America, it has evidently also been difficult to be alerted to the Indian (as opposed to Asian) emergence in their country. Indians have, of course, not helped such understanding, by having—or adopting—names and surnames such as Arun, Bobby, Jim, Reddy, Ronno, Sunny and Victor (mentioned above), or, for that matter, Tosh (like this author).

As Indians move beyond the American techscape and into mainstream business and political life, such a lack of awareness will no doubt reverse. On the other hand, it is equally important to understand a corresponding process of change in their home country.

In the light of estimates of up to 800 American jobs relocating to India every working day, it may be useful to look at the consequences of such a process. These go beyond IT into realms of economics and geopolitics, where India has begun leveraging its technology advantage to make its impact felt on the world outside, and begin reshaping it according to its own longer-term interests. Such issues remain generally unknown to the outside world, but are already beginning to heavily determine the framework within which Western governments will be forced to respond to the growing Indian challenge and seek to 'manage' relocation.

CHAPTER V

The Elephant's
Mounting Weight

India's software success has become integral to its quietly-intensify-
ing combination of push-and-pull processes on the world economy,
and the global system. In October 2003, Britain's Deputy Prime
Minister John Prescott made a strong pitch for British trade unions
to give India "a chance to develop" its software skills, but he also
hammered home the inherent trade-offs in today's globalising world
by thanking the Indian government for a huge order of Hawk train-
er jets—three times larger than one by Britain's own air force"—as
it "saved many jobs in his constituency."[1]

As high-level policy makers in the West like Mr. Prescott
appreciate, India's size and strengths, above all the accelerating
growth of its giant high tech-turbocharged market, provide another
point of complexity for resisting relocation. Indeed, in 2003,
Britain's exports to India "rose by a whopping 30 per cent, and to
China by 29 per cent," while exports to France "fell by 0.2 per cent,"
and to Germany "by a hefty 6.2 percent."[2]

Having considered some underlying causes and effects on relocation related to the Rising Elephant, it is opportune to go further
in understanding what the Indian challenge really entails, both in
terms of its depth and its sweeping breadth. This ranges from issues
of economics and policy, investment and trade, and will eventually
extend to international military concerns and geopolitics. Above
all, the Indian challenge is accompanied by a carefully calibrated set
of actions and responses, juicy carrots and sometimes-weighty sticks.
Largely due to the vapid time-warp of its media, much of the
Western public has unfortunately been asleep while the Elephant
has awakened, stirred and begun to step out.

Behind some of the more perturbing details is a fact largely
undisclosed until now. Measured in U.S. dollar terms (a currency
not used in the country), India's entire economy, not just its technology sector, is $529 billion, or more unexpectedly, the size "of the

five-county area of Los Angeles, Orange, San Bernardino, Riverside and Ventura."[3] What, then, is all the fuss about?

The real worry would be underlined by a more meaningful measuring stick, Purchasing Power Parity (PPP), which is used, among others, by the IMF, the World Bank, the American Central Intelligence Agency and, increasingly, by the mass media.[4] In PPP terms, the Indian economy is now the world's fourth largest—after the U.S., China and Japan. Given its faster 7-8 percent growth rate, India is expected to displace Japan in the near future..

The numbers speak for themselves: According to the World Bank,[5] India's PPP-adjusted gross domestic product (GDP) in 2002 was $2.7 trillion ($2,695 billion). The figure was $2.17 trillion for Germany, $1.55 trillion for France, $1.51 trillion for the U.K., $1.31 trillion for Brazil and $1.14 trillion for Russia. In other words, the Indian economy is nearly two and a half times the size of Russia, and almost as large as France or Britain and Brazil combined.

The relevance of PPP should be obvious from just one example. Given local prices averaging one-sixth those in the West, India's 210 million tonne annual output of food grains alone would add almost half to its U.S. dollar-denominated GDP.[6] But in India, food, like milk, fruit and vegetables, bicycles and motorcycles, cement and steel, detergents, electricity and medicines (in each of which it is among the world's largest producers), is priced in rupees, and is 'cheap' in dollar terms. So too are bus, rail and cinema tickets, toys, eggs, books and school fees, newspapers and much else. Up to a point, these 'cheap' items are bought by 'cheap' workers who also live in 'cheap' houses, use 'cheap' forms of transportation, eat 'cheap' food, and of course, also supply 'cheap' white-collar services—all very cheap indeed, as long as everything is calculated in American dollars, which are not used in India.

PPP is especially crucial to understand giants like India and China, who produce a full-range of goods and services and, unlike smaller economies, do not require to both earn and pay dollars for the bulk of their imports. Worse, as discussed later, both India and China threaten to deflate the exchange-rate yardsticks of the global economy, not only because they can (and will) produce nearly everything; they would also export to other developing countries, and to Western markets—as they have indeed begun to.[7]

For the purpose of this book, the key point is this: Suppose an Indian IT worker earns 20 percent of what an American doing a similar job earns, but a house comparable to the one an American IT worker can afford is, in India, also priced at one-fifth of its cost in the U.S. Through the lens of comparing currencies, an American only sees that his Indian rival earns 20 percent of his salary—and cries unfair! Exploitation! But if both can purchase houses of comparable value (and not just houses, but other goods and services too, many of which are equivalently cheaper in India), then the living standards of the American and the Indian move much closer—even though the Indian, by the measuring stick of straight currency comparison, still earns 20 percent of the American's wage.

In a rare instance of understanding PPP by the mainstream media, the *Los Angeles Times* expressed it thus: "If you look at purchasing power, $20,000 in India can buy you goods and services worth three or four times what it can in the U.S. Put differently, a job offering that much in India is like having one worth close to $80,000 here."[8]

The Future of Exchange Rates

As seen above, the difference between India's dollar GDP and its measurement in PPP terms is approximately $2.5 trillion. This is not an inconsequential sum. The missing amount is larger than the real purchasing power of Europe's largest economy, Germany, and almost twice that of Brazil.

Even the best efforts of economic alchemists cannot bury or wish away such a momentous fact. In the longer term, through a concerted attack, (crucially) at its higher-value services end, the Elephant will impact on the underlying exchange rate structure of the world economy, with or without an overt or leave-it-to-the-market depreciation of the U.S. dollar. Several factors justify such a prognosis.

The Deloitte Research study referred to in Chapter II[9] estimates a net addition to Indian output of $118 billion over five years in one single sector: financial services by Top 100 firms (the difference between "$356 billion" which relocates and the "cost saving of $138 billion"). In addition, if we factor in the huge expansion in the wider back-office industry (the 11-fold increase forecast by The Gartner Group), the continuing 20-30 percent annual rise in India's traditional software exports and the comfortable cushion of its $100 billion in foreign exchange reserves at the end of 2003, few would argue that the country's dollar-denominated GDP cannot make sense much longer—unless the global order can sustain one of its largest economies growing at 15-20 percent a year.[10]

Such massive figures do not still touch the limit. In 2001, Michel Dertouzos, Director of MIT's Laboratory of Computer Science, estimated that relocation of white-collar jobs (or what he called 'office work proffered across space and time') could add a total of $1 trillion to India's GDP.[11]

Similar challenges can be found elsewhere, for example, the eventual impact of India's aggressive emergence in markets such as automobiles—its drive ultimately anchored in the country's low-cost, rupee base. The giant Tata group, owner of one of India's leading and fast-globalizing automotive companies, is now planning to launch a car which would be priced at below $2,200. According to group Chairman Ratan Tata, "despite its seemingly impossible pricing" (less impossible, of course, in PPP terms) the car "will offer safety and all-weather protection features that the traditional passenger car offers."[12]

Some observers have already hinted at this exchange-rate realignment—due to the 'deflationary impact' of giant, fast-growing countries like India and China. One example is Eisuke Sakakibara, previously vice minister for international affairs in Japan's Finance Ministry and currently director of Keio University's Global Security Research Center in Tokyo. Sakakibara notes that, other than technological innovation, "globalization has been dramatically altering the patterns of production, distribution and transactions. The re-emergence of former economic powers, particularly China and India, is helping to drive this increase in productivity and output. China and India together had the dominant share—nearly 45 percent—of world gross domestic product in 1820. As (they) re-establish their position in today's globalized economy, it should not come as a surprise that prices are falling," he concludes.[13]

The long-term inevitability of this scenario is sometimes also apparent to the general public. A letter to the Los Angeles Times, for example, notes: "American companies can, of course, be discouraged from laying off American workers and moving jobs overseas. Temporarily. Until far cheaper goods and services from India and China put the American companies out of business."[14]

A *UPI* column was forthright. In a detailed discussion on the current state of flux in the global exchange rate regime and the stagnant world economy, it concluded:

> Finally, the one winner, India. The rupee will strengthen against the dollar, yet India will still be competitive in cost terms both in the United States and in the EU. The competitiveness of its outsourcing and software services in the EU will increase, yet EU protectionism will find these imports more difficult to block than conventional imports of goods. As a largely self-sufficient economy, India will be damaged less than most by the hiccups in world trade that the next decade will inevitably bring. And its stock market, undervalued by Western standards yet now largely open to foreign investment, should perform quite well against competitors hampered by capital outflows (the United States) or deep recession (the EU.)[15]

Five California Counties...
or the World's Fourth Largest Economy

PPP is real. Otherwise, five California counties would hardly merit strategic attention at the top levels of companies as diverse as GE and Cincinnati Milacron, British Gas, Hughes and Ford, Nortel, Qualcomm, Ericsson and Western Union,[16] for all of who India is by many measures among their top markets. French cosmetics giant L'Oreal saw 2003 sales in India gallop by 33 percent.[17] For Coca-Cola, Indian revenues in 2003 rose by 22 percent, over five times its global average, and compared to 4-5 percent in Latin America, Europe and the Middle East and just 2 percent in North America; (Indian Coke sales also outstripped China's 16 percent).[18] In February 2004, Motorola announced $307 million in Indian orders "to provide telecom gear for future expansion in one of the world's fastest growing markets."[19]

Meanwhile, the Indian market's across-the-board growth potential is apparent elsewhere: the global per capita consumption of steel is 150 kilograms a year, as against the Indian average of only

27, even now.[20]

Evidence of India's rise will not only grow steadily, but begin to impact on areas sacrosanct to the West's self-image as a rich, leisure society. Formula One racing supremo Bernie Ecclestone, for example, expects motor sports in India and, later, South Korea, to "largely supplant Europe" in the second half of this decade.[21]

The Indian market's pull has impacted on several mainstream American IT firms. For Sun Microsystems, India is its fastest-growing global market, with revenues "almost doubling" every year[22]; one of the largest customers for Sun's new Java Desktop, for example, is India's United Insurance Company.[23] For Oracle, India is the company's "fastest growing market in the entire Asia-Pacific,"[24] and is set to become its "second largest market in the region behind China."[25]

The unremitting rise of India is best reflected in strategic plans by American firms to position themselves for the country's massive e-government projects, alongside the emergence of tens and (potentially hundreds) of millions of Indian language IT users. Part of Oracle's huge expansion plans in India, for example, reflect the fact that its software will be used in e-government projects, nine of which already run on Oracle databases.[26] After launching Indian-language versions of Windows 2000, Exchange 2000 and SQL Server, Microsoft's Project Bhasha is localizing its XP and Office product suites into 14 Indian languages—billed as a strategic move "to attain a stronger foothold in the Government segment."[27] IBM has been there earlier, working on Indian-language applications since 2000, when it launched Hindi versions of Lotus Notes and Domino.[28] For Adobe, too, a decision to localize its products into Hindi and other Indian languages "was driven by the demand of e-governance projects in India," according to Bruce Chizen, its President and Chief Executive.[29] Meanwhile, with India seen by proponents of the Linux system as a "back door into the lucrative global business software market,"[30] Red Hat has also joined the club, planning a rollout of a Hindi version of its Linux operating system.[31]

It is not only giant corporations who are succumbing to the Elephant's pull. American CAD firm Bentley Systems, for instance, is reported to be "pinning its growth hopes" on India's $16 billion roadworks mega-plan as well as "new airport projects, the map updating projects of (the) Survey of India, military plans to become a digital enabled army, rail quadrilateral projects, metro rail projects, flyovers and bridges."[32] Elsewhere, India's revving up automotive powerhouses are all huge users of Parametric Technology's software, while Borland expects its Indian sales to overtake even Japan's in the near future.[33]

Within India, information technology remains just one, if still the most prominent facet, of broader economic, technological, political and even social developments. Nevertheless, the Indian system has, in a sense, become heavily dependent on continuing to notch further successes in the field of information technology. An across-the-board consensus now exists within the country that its success in software is fuelling not only its emergence as a global player but also offers the only long-term solution to poverty. As discussed later, even communist-led state governments and trade unions view IT as India's Golden Goose, its new Sacred Cow.

It is an opportune occasion to look at the wider context, and underlying geopolitical implications, of India's IT-fed economic boom, which will continue to drive the Elephant's emergence.

Entering the Golden Era: Preparing for Lift Off

"India has grown by a Brazil in the last ten years, and will grow by another Brazil in this decade," says Richard Celeste, a former governor of Ohio and U.S. Ambassador to India.[34]

In early August 2003, a study by the Economist Intelligence Unit found that "China and India are forecast to drive Asia's economy between now and 2007 to keep it the world's fastest growing region, but the rest of Asia is expected to post only modest expansion."[35] Three months later, the *Guardian* added, "Along with India, China is one of the few sources of world demand outside the U.S."[36]

Since then, amidst the global slowdown, India's economic growth has accelerated further. In the July-September 2003 quarter, it grew at a scorching 8.4 percent, its fastest pace in five years. In early 2004, the respected National Council of Applied Economic Research (NCAER) revised its forecast of India's annual GDP growth upwards to 8 percent,[37] which would of course bring it very close to China.

At the end of 2003, French daily *Le Monde* said India's 'lift-off' was the 'News of the Year.'[38] Specific points highlighted by the newspaper included growing foreign investment in India which reached $6 billion in 2003, the stabilization of the rupee after decades of depreciation, the Indian stock markets' 60 percent appreciation during the year, the country's $100 billion in foreign exchange reserves and its economic growth rate accelerating to 7.5 percent, after 'merely' 5-6 percent in the 1990s.

Indeed, the pace of change in India since it opened up its economy in the 1990s not only continues to be staggering; unlike Southeast Asia, this has been achieved without any major upheavals.[39] Even today, in spite of a consumer spending boom, "retail credit is barely 4 percent of the GDP compared to 60-plus in Korea, 40-plus in Malaysia and 20-plus in Thailand,"[40] while India's mortgage-to-GDP ratio is 2.5 per cent, over twenty times lower than the U.S. and Britain, and about one-third that of China.[41] Nevertheless, the conservative nature of the Indian system is borne out by the fact that its central bank has already called for a review and tightening of consumer credit risk appraisal and management systems. Such evidence also comes from India's government: "Contrary to some market expectations of an overtly populist pre-election budget in February 2004," it announced no tax concessions.[42]

In May 2003, in a move that sent a clear signal of the country's growing strength around the world, India stopped taking development aid from over 20 countries.[43] It also announced plans to pre-pay $3.5 billion in loans from the Asian Development Bank and World Bank, following a $3 billion advance clearance for both institutions last year.[44] Finally, India joined the International Monetary Fund's pool of lenders, marking yet another step to herald its emergence as a global economic power.

Meanwhile, the country's economic reforms have continued to strengthen. The process remains systematic, but, inspired by the government's growing confidence, it is less hesitant than before. Though not quite a Big Bang (as explained, the Elephant is unlikely to ever seek such one-shot displays of showmanship), India's reform process has clearly metamorphosed into a series of targeted booms, which have systematically grown in force, and will also do so in their eventual impact. Bar some hiccups over issues like the pace of privatization of state-owned companies—central to democratic

India's deeply-ingrained processes of early warning and self-correction—reforms will continue to strengthen, regardless of the political party or coalitions running the government.

In early 2004, India reduced duties across a range of goods (a move expected in particular to boost the fast-emerging sectors of auto-components, plastics as well as consumer electronics and white goods).[45] In addition, the government kickstarted a privatization program for sale of stakes in two large energy monopolies (Oil and Natural Gas Company, and Gas Authority of India); the "lightning speed at which the process moved has astounded"[46] five leading investment banks invited to underwrite the sale, including Merrill Lynch and Morgan Stanley.

To conserve and build what has now become a war-chest of foreign currency holdings, India had previously imposed a longstanding $100 million ceiling on investments overseas by domestic companies; the government in January 2004 raised this ceiling to 100 percent of a company's net worth. Also relaxed were restrictions on the ability of individual Indians to invest directly on overseas stock markets, a far cry from the pre-reform days when Indians traveling abroad had to get special permits to acquire the princely sum of $100 in foreign currency.[47]

Such liberalization will cause considerable impact on world markets. As one Indian newspaper noted, "India Inc. can now swoop for the M&A kill."[48]

This is hardly hyperbole. In just over a decade since economic reforms, India's net international investment position is already heading towards parity (balancing of inward and outward investments); last year, India's outward foreign investments were close to two-thirds of foreign direct investment into the country. In 2004, Indian companies have plans for $2.5 billion in overseas acquisitions; this figure may be just the beginning.

There are, of course, obvious advantages in buying assets amidst a serious global economic downturn. In October 2003, India's Reliance conglomerate paid $207 million for acquiring the international undersea cable operator Flag Telecom; Flag was worth $7 billion just two years ago.[49]

Expected to first go "on the prowl" for global companies and "bid big against competition for the target takeovers" are India's IT and pharmaceutical companies, who are "slated to benefit the most from this relaxation"[50] and, as a result, will quickly become international players. Companies in other sectors, too, are moving in for the kill, as discussed later.

Overseas acquisitions, however, do not give the full story of the revving up by corporate India. Back home, "almost 600 (Indian) companies are getting ready to go public this year,"[51] and no less than "$13 billion worth of public offerings are expected," in the near future, according to Prime Database, a capital market research firm based in New Delhi.[52]

In a strong endorsement of India's economic fundamentals in January 2004, American credit rating agency Moody's upgraded India's sovereign foreign-currency debt to investment grade, opening the door "for a new class of international investors, including pension and certain types of mutual funds, to invest in Indian debt and equities."[53] Within weeks, Moody's rival, Standard & Poor's, noted Indian stock market returns of 65 percent, and recommended investment in India's own mutual funds. S&P also noted that India, "long ignored by Western investors," may have finally begun closing the gap with China.[54]

India's engagement with the world will acquire further momentum after full convertibility of the rupee (which is still not freely traded on international currency markets). In early 2004, the International Monetary Fund's deputy managing director Anne Krueger made an explicit call for floating the Indian currency.[55]

International investors have welcomed such developments. According to James Goulding, Chief Executive, Asia-Pacific Region of Deutsche Asset Management Group, "India is entering a golden era. It has set out on a path of fabulous economic growth and is way ahead in the game in comparison to other Asian countries."[56]

The Force of a 300 Million Strong Middle Class Modernizing...

The data and statistics above mean a number of major things for the relocation debate. There is, however, another issue worth pursuing at this juncture: India's growing power and increasingly-interlocking engagement with the rest of the world establish impor-

tant pre-conditions before one can think of solutions. One set of circumstances that both complicates and creates an opportunity is the
force created by one billion people modernizing their lives.

The impact of India's IT-fed growth is already resonating powerfully through the lives of its people, and beyond. DSP Merrill
Lynch estimates that household consumer spending in India could
double to $510 billion by 2008.

In a feature 'Sizzling Economy Revitalizes India,' the *New York
Times* noted[57]:

> Just over a decade after the Indian economy began shak-
> ing off its statist shackles and opening to the outside world, it is
> booming. The surge is based on strong industry and agriculture,
> rising Indian and foreign investment and American-style con-
> sumer spending by a growing middle class, including the people
> under age 25 who now make up half the country's population....
> The growth of the past decade has put more money in the pock-
> ets of an expanding middle class, 250 million to 300 million
> strong, and more choices in front of them. Their appetites are
> helping to fuel demand-led growth for the first time in decades.
>
> India is now the world's fastest growing telecom market,
> with more than one million new mobile phone subscriptions
> sold each month. Indians are buying about 10,000 motorcycles
> a day. Banks are now making $15 billion a year in home loans,
> with the lowest interest rates in decades helping to spur the
> spending, building and borrowing. Credit and debit cards are
> slowly gaining.
>
> The potential for even more market growth is enormous,
> a fact recognized by multinationals and Indian companies alike.

In November 2003, a news report noted that "thanks to rock-
bottom call rates," India is set to meet its target of increasing the
number of phones to 70 million (or seven for every 100 people)
much ahead of its scheduled date; this target, set for 2005, was in
fact achieved by end-2003, while a level of 15 per 100 (150 million
phones) is expected "in 2005 or 2006," instead of 2010. For the sake
of comparison, teledensity was just 2 per 100 (20 million) in 1999.[58]

But the lift-off is also broad based, making it clear that India is
riding a wave as both a future global industrial powerhouse, and a
hotspot market for international business. Indian automotive group
Mahindra's tractor sales in January 2004, for example, were up 56
per cent from the previous year, other vehicles by 32 percent.[59] As

the Indian software powerhouse now also seeks to become "a large-scale hardware manufacturer on the back of explosive sales growth,"[60] it plans to install no less than 50 million pay TV set-top boxes in just the 2004-2007 period.

Fuelled by India's IT-led boom, the real-estate market too is accelerating. Giant builders such as the Hiranandanis, DLF and the Ansals alone have orders for over 50 million square feet of office space, shopping complexes, dedicated jewelry, furniture and automobile marts, and residential buildings. Around India's IT centers, 100- to 500-acre townships are sprouting, with homes and apartments boasting closed-circuit television, swimming pools, Internet connections and piped gas—all unheard of in the country as recently as 2000. Even once-obscure mid-sized builders, such as Omaxe, Ambience and IDEB, are seeing 100 percent growth in annual revenues. Omaxe's 1.4 million square feet facility at New Delhi's Connaught Place is billed as the largest shopping complex in India. IDEB is close to completing almost 2 million square feet of malls, residential apartments and a software park, and plans to start work on a similar scale in early 2004. Meanwhile, much room remains for still-further growth, notwithstanding warnings of a real-estate bubble in the Indian media. In spite of a scorching 76 percent rise in home mortgages in 2003, India's mortgage-to-GDP ratio is 2.5 per cent, against 54 and 57 per cent for the U.S. and the U.K., and still way behind China's 7 per cent or Thailand's 14 per cent.[61]

Foreign firms are beginning to get locked into Indian real estate. The Vatika City township, for example, scheduled to be ready by 2005, has been designed by the British architects behind London's prestigious Canary Wharf. Los Angeles-based Oakwood, with a $2 billion real estate portfolio, is set to shortly introduce luxury apartments initially in Bangalore, Hyderabad and Mumbai, followed by Chennai, Delhi and Jaipur, and expects "India to become one of its largest markets exceeding 10% of its global business by 2010."[62]

Running Ahead of Schedule:
India's Infrastructure Train

Even in articles heightening its rapid transformation, media coverage of the underlying breadth and pace of India's emergence continues to lag. For example, in a February 19, 2004, article cover-ing American investment in India, the *Wall Street Journal* warned that "...poor infrastructure—from roads and highways to ports and power supply—must be improved to cut transportation costs and boost gross domestic product." Absent from its sermon was the fact that India has begun to massively and rapidly modernize its infra-structure, as evident, most prominently, in a 14,000 km computer-supported national highway network (so, far "the largest highway construction programme in the world")[63]; nine months before the *Journal's* report, the network was already 80 percent complete, and, what was more, running "ahead of schedule."[64] Neither did the *Journal* take note of New Delhi's spanking new underground metro, the new multi-modal transport systems flagged off in 2003 in two other Indian cities, Chennai and Hyderabad,[65] or much other evi-dence.

Giant infrastructural projects have indeed begun lift-off in other areas. On the cards now is a $100 billion mega-project, which aims to connect nearly 30 rivers across the country to combat floods and drought, and boost farm productivity,[66] as well as a $25 billion port modernization program.

India also plans to electrify 600,000 villages by 2007 and add another 100,000 MW power generating capacity by 2012, in a bid to make electricity available to all the country's households. In October 2003, India switched on Nathpa Jhakri, its biggest hydroelectricity project to date, on one of the world's fastest-flowing rivers. The 1,500 MW project established a clutch of world engineering records, including the largest-ever underground de-silting complex, a 28 kilo-meter long power tunnel, and Asia's biggest power house. The exca-vated material could be spread "into an eight-meter wide and 12-metre thick carpet on the Great Wall of China," noted the plant's ebullient Chairman; the steel used "is enough to lay a rail line con-necting India's four metropolitan cities," while 14 million bags of cement would "provide a 75-metre pavement around the earth."[67]

Like India's highway building program, two other giant power projects by the National Thermal Power Corporation's and National Hydroelectric Power Corporation's Chamera Hydro project have been completed "ahead of time" while a power transmission project by Power Grid Corporation in the North East remains on schedule.[68]

Elsewhere, the Reliance conglomerate has begun work on a $2.2 billion project to build what the *Financial Times* has called "the world's largest gas-fired power station, with 3,500 megawatts of generating capacity." It would "almost double electricity supply in the backward northern state of Uttar Pradesh." Most importantly, the move is "the strongest sign so far that New Delhi's reform of the power sector is bearing fruit, six months after it enacted new legislation."[69]

Such efforts, aimed directly at what were hitherto bottlenecks on development (that is, in fields other than software), will serve to further accelerate economic growth over the next decades. In spite of the usual debates and controversies accompanying such large-scale changes in India's contentious democracy, they are being achieved through internal resources (rather than foreign direct investment) and have already begun impacting on other industrial and economic sectors. As *Bloomberg News* noted, India's highway-building program (as well as cheap consumer credit) have led to a near-tripling in profits for Tata Motors, India's largest truck manufacturer;[70] in the nine months to January 2004, Indian commercial vehicle sales rose 36 percent, medium-and heavy trucks by 44 percent.[71] Such figures, in turn, explain why India's MPRL refinery has stopped exports of petroleum products.[72]

All this will of course intensify opportunities for Western business. But it will also increase interdependency.

No Solitary Tangos: The Elephant Plays Hardball

Whether it is consumer goods, aircraft or building materials, access to the massive and fast-growing Indian market by Western manufacturers will be a trade-off for access by Indians to supply technology services to the West. The Indian view is simple: the West cannot be expected to participate in tomorrow's growth opportunities, without conceding something in return. For rapidly developing India, such participation is clearly no longer about philanthropy, NGOs, warm feelings and foreign aid. As the founder of Indian call center 24/7 explained at his offices to *New York Times* columnist Thomas Friedman: "All the computers (here) are from Compaq. The basic software is from Microsoft. The phones are from Lucent. The air-conditioning is by Carrier, and even the bottled water is by

Coke." Friedman's conclusion was simple: "What goes around comes around, and also benefits Americans."[73]

As mentioned before, it will call for more than dexterity by Western governments to oppose the workings of free markets, especially after this has begun to benefit (at least some) developing countries.

So far, such dexterity has often been little more than doublespeak. Thus, while George Newstrom, Washington's Secretary of Technology, said at a U.S. conference in early September 2003 that "IT workers were justified in feeling paranoid about offshore outsourcing",[74] Washington's Secretary of State Sam Reed explained around the same time in Bangalore that "there was not much of a backlash issue" in Washington and that it was "relegated to pretty isolated pockets in other states."[75] Reed was heading a broad-based business delegation to India (rather than one focused on IT) and, as expected, also made a pitch for "more commerce" between India and his state.

With information technology fast on its way to become one of the Indian economy's largest sectors, such a trade-off is explicit for its government. In June 2003, India's Commerce Minister Arun Jaitley warned that attempts in the U.S. to ban information technology outsourcing from other countries amounted to a denial of market access "in an area in which India has core competence"—legalspeak for a possible complaint to the World Trade Organization (WTO).[76] In November, Indian foreign secretary Kanwal Sibal drew a direct connection between offshore outsourcing and the fast-growing Indo-American military-strategic relationship. At a meeting of the India-U.S. High Technology Group, he noted that restrictions on offshore outsourcing in the U.S. would "hinder ongoing progress" in defense and other high-technology areas between India and the U.S.[77]

The calibrated Indian riposte gathered momentum after the passage of the U.S. Senate's anti-offshore outsourcing bill in January 2004. Although that move is seen as anodyne (see Chapter I), India plans to vigorously contest it. It still "sends a far from insignificant signal," Jaitley protested to the *Financial Times*. "Here you have a country (the US) whose main mantra is 'market access' and whose argument is that opening markets to competition is the solution to poverty in countries like India."[78] Jaitley will no doubt remind his

American counterparts that India too is not just a large market, but also a democracy; as he warned the *Financial Times*, the U.S. Senate move will "make it more difficult for New Delhi to sell trade liberalization measures to the Indian electorate." In February, Jaitley upped the ante further, when he said that prospects for the Doha world trade round "were at risk" because of the U.S. Senate move;[79] this is a particularly meaningful threat given Jaitley's personal role in causing the collapse of the previous Cancun summit of the World Trade Organization in September 2003, a topic discussed later. Indeed, a draft report from the UN Conference on Trade and Development advised India to take just this step—by challenging U.S. Senate restrictions within the framework of multilateral trade negotiations.[80]

The complex international implications of the U.S. Senate anti-offshore outsourcing move were also central to a warning by Bruce Josten, executive vice president of the U.S. Chamber of Commerce. For Josten, the move is "counter to the general procurement agreement under the World Trade Organization," which provides for open trade in government purchases of goods and services, and has already been signed by the U.S. government, 37 American states and 46 other nations. "This (ban)," he stated, could also "open the door to retaliatory action against (the) U.S., and hinder job growth and economic growth."[81]

American technology corporations are aware of the fact that India holds several aces, not least because of the already-huge and irreversible commitment they have made there, but also because of the lure of its market. 'Choose to Compete,' a position paper from the CSPP lobby group comprised of eight American IT industry Chief Executives (see Chapter I), points out that 60 percent of revenues of American IT companies come from outside the U.S. Microsoft Chairman Bill Gates, too, has warned the West against dismantling free trade "in a knee-jerk reaction to increasing competition from the burgeoning Chinese and Indian economies."[82]

India's IT industry federation Nasscom is keenly aware of such leverage. Soon after passage of the U.S. Senate anti-offshore outsourcing bill, Nasscom President Kiran Karnik noted that India's government had itself awarded huge IT contracts for its income tax department to American companies, thus hinting at retaliatory actions.[83] Another Indian IT industry heavyweight, Saurabh Srivastava, Chairman of Xansa India, and of the Indian Venture Capital Association, says: "The U.S. stand on outsourcing is similar to what we might take here on—why not ban Coke or Ford Ikon or any other consumer items from there?"[84]

Given the complex politics of the issue in the American election season, the Indians have by and large been low-key in their response. Referring to a report in the *Wall Street Journal*, an Indian newspaper noted that "in recent months, without much fanfare, a coalition of Indian Government officials, business groups and wealthy Indian-Americans have quietly launched an extensive lobbying campaign" (using Washington DC-based law firms and lobbyists) to counteract the backlash against India.[85] Indian companies, on their part, have also been advised by Paul Laudicina, Managing Director, A.T. Kearney, to employ 'third party surrogates' to do this work, principally in the form of their customers, who would "communicate to U.S. political leaders and administrators the benefits arising from offshore outsourcing deals."[86]

Powerful support for India is expected to come from non-IT American businesses, for who the fast-growing Indian market is a major lifeline. In October, 45 members of the U.S. Congress urged the Indian Prime Minister to authorize purchase by Air India of 22 Boeing aircraft (with an option on another 13), noting that it would not only serve as a 'great demonstration' of 'strengthened' Indo-U.S. commercial ties, but also "provide the struggling economy (of the U.S.) with a shot in the arm when it needs it most."[87] Such efforts by Congress on behalf of U.S. businesses are exceptional. Even more indicative of the Elephant's growing clout is the reference to a 'struggling' American economy which needs help. At the time of writing, India may still of course threaten to shift the deal to Boeing's European rival Airbus. Whether or not it does, the linkage between access into the huge Indian market by American firms and India's continuing play in the relocation game is likely to strengthen further.

The calibrated (and sometimes choreographed) ballet of mutual global trade give-and-take picked up in February 2004. Following passage of the Senate bill, U.S. Charge d'Affaires in India, Robert Blake, said, "The most important step India can take to counter efforts to restrict outsourcing is to continue to open its markets" to ensure U.S. investors have as many opportunities in India, as Indians in the U.S. He commended the Indian government for already taking "some important steps" in this direction, including tariff and investment liberalization measures announced in early January.[88] Crucially, Blake acknowledged India's post-Cancun trump card, with a call for the U.S. and India to work together in the Doha round of the WTO.

Shortly after, David A. Gross, Deputy Assistant Secretary of State, noted in public that the Senate anti-offshore outsourcing bill was 'narrow in scope,' and moreover, would be in effect only till November.[89]

However, the best indicator of the shape of things to come is a statement by Jeffrey Schott, senior fellow at the Washington think tank, the International Institute for Economics. "Given the complexities and the political sensitivities I don't see an agreement (on the WTO) being reached this year.... But if they don't make progress this year (2004) one could see retrenchment or diversion of political capital to other priorities."[92] In other words, the end of the jockeying and posturing coincides directly with the conclusion of American elections in November 2004, before which, as Deputy Assistant Secretary Gross noted, the bill is due to expire.

India has also begun advance positioning its trade cards in Europe. In July 2003, Indian information technology firms closed ranks to formally press the government to move the outsourcing issue (as well as questions on taxes and Europe's burdensome social security payments) at the WTO. In October, the government formally indicated that India was "mostly interested" under the WTO regime in "cross-border trade in services (Mode 1)," and the "movement of natural persons (Mode 4)."[93]

Fortress Europe has resisted much of the relocation wave, at least until the middle of 2003, with a melange of regulatory overkill. Some examples include separate high-tech visa regimes for different EU countries and never-to-be-claimed pension and healthcare contributions from IT professionals on limited, short-term assignments.[94]

India has since formally asked the EU to make it easier for Indian professionals to visit and move freely within Europe. As

Bloomberg News noted, what is at stake behind the request "is India's goal of doubling two-way trade with the European Union to $50 billion, or $60 billion, over the next five years."[95] In parallel, India has also begun tightening the screws, with anti-dumping measures across a range of EU exports, including "chemicals and pharmaceuticals, textiles and steel."[96]

Responding to such pressures (and in spite of protests by white-collar trade unions[97]), the European Union has announced new guidelines to provide Indians easier access to EU countries, and extending eligibility beyond software professionals to other categories (once again showing the convergence between Indian information technology and the wider white-collar sector). In a clear indication of the underlying reciprocity issues discussed above, officials said in July 2003 that the proposal was aimed at "cementing (the) trade partnership between India and the EU."[98] Barely two weeks later, the European Union signed a Trade and Investment Development Programme (TIDP) with India, its first such alliance with a country outside the EU.[99]

Shortly after the EU proposals, Germany's Labour Minister Wolfgang Clement announced that he was extending a 'high-tech visa' scheme (bringing mainly Indian professionals to his country) by another 18 months.[100] Also, in seeming acknowledgment of the inevitability of such trends, Mike O'Brien, Britain's Minister for the Foreign and Commonwealth Office, said just before the EU proposals that India had become the "preferred global hub" for software development and business process outsourcing.[101] O'Brien also accepted that the U.K. had "benefited substantially" from this process.

In September 2003, Gavyn Arthur, Lord Mayor of the City of London, went further in dismissing protests by British unions against relocation. During a 10-day visit to India, he said, "There may be a protest here, there may be a protest there but nonetheless outsourcing is a fact of life. This is not something in which the government tries to interfere."[102]

Following passage of the U.S. Senate's anti-offshore outsourcing bill, another British Minister, Stephen Timms, took note of a massive $200 million government contract for two Indian software companies, and insisted that Britain would not put up barriers, since such firms helped his country's global competitiveness.[103] Within days, yet another senior British Minister, Foreign Secretary Jack Straw, told reporters the same thing during a visit to India.[104] In February 2004, European Union Commissioner for External Relations Chris Patten underlined that there would be "no backlash against outsourcing. What you can expect is that some politicians will raise questions and make a fuss."[105]

A convincing indicator of India's growing clout is that, in spite of massive protests from white-collar trade unions, the British government appointed a powerful Indian lobby group on an official panel set up to review visa procedures for visiting foreign professionals. According to a British newspaper, "The India Business Group, which is supported by the Indian High Commission (Embassy), will represent Indian software suppliers on the Government's IT sector skills panel. This plays an influential role in deciding what types of IT jobs qualify for work permits."[106]

Yet another sign of tokenism in the U.K. with regard to union concerns on relocation was a government statement: "Companies which fail to consult their employees over major changes including layoffs could face fines up to 75,000 pounds"[107]—hardly a princely sum given the scale of the problem.

India/China: The Asian Centennial Choice

For 40 years, through its policy of 'nonalignment,' India skillfully played the U.S. against the Soviet Union. This was a geopolitical game. India no doubt has accumulated the know-how to play Europe against the U.S., and the two against other parts of the world, in terms of the politics of world trade.

In parallel, of course, for the rest of the world, there is also the question of playing the two giants from Asia, India and China, developments both of which will clearly shape the 21st century.

Whether IT and back-office services, or pharmaceuticals and biotechnology, India is central to the white-collar job relocation debate. China remains focused on relocating blue-collar manufacturing skills, and whether it will first of all seriously choose, and then manage, to close the huge gap with India in the white-collar field, remains uncertain. For India, on the other hand, a move down the value chain into blue-collar skills may be easier. As discussed later, there are strong signs that such a process may have already begun.

Though both India and China share similar demographic advantages, blurring the differences between the two Asian giants derails some of the finer points in the relocation debate. One of the most important issues here is that India's challenge to Western economic supremacy is focused on the white-collar services sector, which in the U.S., for example, accounts for 60 percent of the economy; this compares to manufacturing's 14 percent (high-tech fields such as chip-making and consumer electronics included), where China has laid its stake. Reflecting this, services have become the fastest-growing sector of India's economy, up from growth of 6.8 percent in 2002 and 7.1 percent in 2003 to a forecast 8.4 percent in 2004.[108]

Correspondingly, India has also built uniquely robust foundations for its white-collar assault. As stated previously, it produces six times more engineering graduates than China, and according to American management guru Peter Drucker's interview with *Fortune* magazine at the end of 2003, India's huge lead in higher education explains why its progress is "far more impressive" than that of China.

Still, India's increasing engagement with the world is not limited solely to exporting white-collar skills, but is anchored within a broader-based (and in the long-term, more durable) political and economic and business context. Unlike China, India has the advantages of a long-standing entrepreneurial culture; its stock exchanges are, for example, Asia's oldest.[109] They are also mature. Not only have peak trading volumes in Mumbai (which lists over 5,000 companies) often rivaled New York; unlike some of its Western counterparts, India's National Stock Exchange is completely electronic, and 'paperless.'

Indian IT services giant Wipro is a good example of such contexts. Its name is an abbreviation for Western India Products, reflecting its roots as a vegetable oil trading firm launched in 1945. Over decades, Wipro has steadily, systematically and profitably grown into other fields: from soaps to hydraulic cylinders, and then computer hardware, medical equipment, and finally software; in tandem, India too has grown and developed, as has the wider Indian economic system, which has accommodated Wipro's changes and growth.

Such systemic and contextual differences between India and China have begun drawing attention, as illustrated by the observations of Peter Drucker above. A poll by Britain's *Euromoney* magazine in December 2002 found that Indian companies were Asia's best managed in a swathe of sectors, among them IT of course, but also in banking, chemicals and pharmaceuticals. One reason for this is India's critical lead over China in terms of middle and upper levels of professional management; among other things, even pre-reform India had managers running private companies (multinationals included), while a 55-year old manager in China in 2003 was unlikely to have had much of a career in his 20s, just after the Cultural Revolution.

In an article 'Can India Overtake China?' published in the July-August 2003 issue of influential American publication *Foreign Policy*, two scholars observe that although India is not outperforming China overall, it is doing better in certain key areas; in turn, such success may enable India to catch up with and perhaps even overtake China. The authors, professors Yasheng Huang of the Massachusetts Institute of Technology and Tarun Khanna of Harvard Business School, observe that foreign investment in China was an "accident" of history, and that "by relying primarily on organic growth," India has managed "to spawn a number of companies that now compete internationally with Europe and the U.S."[110] The difference here, of course, is of more than academic interest. One conclusion of the above study was that "Can India surpass China is no longer a silly question," and "if it turns out that India has indeed made a wiser bet, the implications for China's future growth and for how policy experts think about economic development generally could be enormous."[111]

While China's seeming decisiveness, and its clearly more sophisticated perception management machine, has engendered a pro-Chinese constituency, especially in Europe, others, especially those drawing parallels with Southeast Asia in 1997, are less sure. As *BusinessWeek* notes: Some China boosters still "argue that the Middle Kingdom beats India on political stability. That might seem a bit odd, given that China is the last surviving communist power, while India is the world's largest democracy."[112] Such an angle is also taken by Ross Terrill's 'The New Chinese Empire and What it Means for the United States,' which makes a convincing case that

China is the only empire left on earth today, a multicultural, multi-ethnic system held together essentially by force; in other words, not necessarily either predictable or stable.[113]

In his interview with *Fortune* magazine, Peter Drucker also warns that China faces a huge undeveloped hinterland with excess rural population, but the likelihood of the absorption of rural workers into the cities without upheaval seemed doubtful; as a result, "the chances of very serious social unrest in China in the next 10 years are greater than 50 percent." India does not have this problem "because they have already done an amazing job of absorbing excess rural population into the cities. India's rural population has gone from 90 percent to 54 percent without any upheaval." No upheavals indeed. Elections and changes in government, both national and state-level, have assured a safe process for the management of change.

As much as its consensual democracy, India's open market system stands out in stark contrast to China's, once again in terms of providing immunities against sudden, violent surprises. A *UPI* article in May 2003 states that China will have to reverse "false output statistics, bailing out state companies with loans and pretending that all is well." Otherwise, this will trigger a protectionist backlash in the West and "the option of using its export success to solve its economic problems will no longer remain."[114]

In terms of the long-term political impact of technology job relocation, confusing India and China may be a dangerous distraction. *BusinessWeek* recognized this at the end of 2003. As a "deep source of low-cost, high-IQ, English-speaking brainpower, (India) may soon have a more far-reaching impact on the U.S. than China.... Indian knowledge workers are making their way up the New Economy food chain, mastering tasks requiring analysis, marketing acumen, and creativity. This means India is penetrating America's economic core."[115]

The India-versus-China question will remain intriguing for decades. Its outcome, however, will clearly have a major impact on the shape of the world economy. Already, in terms of the critical issue of managing globalization, India's open and responsible free-market system has seen it playing by the rules of the game, even when this is to its disadvantage. For example, while China has refused to allow its currency to appreciate (in order to permit a classical realignment of terms of trade and take some of the pressure off U.S. exporters),[116] the Indian rupee has strengthened significantly since early 2003 against the dollar,[117] and is expected by leading international banks to appreciate still further.[118] Among other things, this has led to huge pressures on the margins of India's star software industry.[119] In marked contrast, even U.S. supporters of free-trade "complain that the Chinese enjoy a 40 percent competitive advantage because they won't let their currency 'float' to a realistic level."[120] After increasing pressure from U.S. President Bush, Treasury Secretary John Snow and Secretary of Commerce Donald Evans, the Chinese finally relented, but did so in the form of a complex, opaque and hard-to-monitor solution to cut tax rebates on exports.[121]

On its part, influential Indian economists are lobbying the government to use its now-huge foreign reserves to collateralize domestic investment by Indian companies.[122] This would be a novel and obviously autonomous means to address one of India's seeming weaknesses vis-a-vis China, namely its relative lack of foreign direct investment, without, of course, the threat of becoming an 'accident of history.'

Behind the Elephant's White Collar: Manufacturing Businesses Globalize

Although white-collar competencies will remain its mainstay strength, India's emergence as an international actor in a variety of other industries, ranging from motor vehicles to metals and minerals and even food, will further bolster its growing global presence. The impact of the rising Elephant in such contexts will also be significant for the world economy—for example, in terms of very real plans by the Indian Tata conglomerate to build a $2,200 passenger car, as mentioned previously. Indeed, less than a decade after economic reforms made it possible, India became only the world's ninth country to design and produce a wholly-local vehicle on its own; as we shall see, these are already being exported to Europe, one of the world's most competitive and protected markets.

Suditpto Mundle, chief economist at the Asian Development Bank, echoes the findings of the MIT and Harvard professors referred to above. "Large parts of corporate India," he notes, "are slowly but surely becoming globally competitive."[123] Among other factors, such global-level competitiveness derives from the fact that, over the 1990s, many of India's large corporate groups too invested significantly in cost-effective Indian information technology.

This was a process with immense synergies. In many cases, domestic corporate groups not only supported the evolution of their own in-house IT divisions into software firms, but also used the growing international expertise of the latter to boost their own productivity. For example, Ramco's Marshall enterprise resource planning (ERP) program (see Chapter III), was test-bedded in the premises of its parent, a large Indian building materials company. Already by 1998, the now fast-internationalizing Mahindra automotive group had become "the world's largest Windows NT and SAP site",[124] achieving 30 percent cost reduction in its operations; other large groups, including Indian Oil, and India's Tata industrial conglomerate, were also early adopters of ERP.

Such synergies continue to emerge. KPMG Consulting, for example, has advised India to use lessons from its IT success to mount an attack on the world's jewelery and diamond industries.[125] With India long being the world's biggest buyer of gold[126] and cutting "nine out of every ten diamonds in the world,"[127] once again, both volume and value would underpin its position in such a business. In May 2003, the *Wall Street Journal* noted Indians had displaced the Jewish community in Antwerp, accounting, in just two decades, for 65 percent of the $25 billion global diamond trade. Indians, the newspaper said, have "reinvigorated the jewellery districts in New York and Hong Kong," and were "challenging Jewish dealers, even in Tel Aviv."[128]

Like much else in the growingly-seamless world economy, there is no permanent breakwater point between manufacturing and services, blue- and white-collar, especially as both globalize. With information technology an increasingly-integral part of manufacturing processes, India has also begun to pull the more-purely blue-collar parts of the global economic edifice towards itself, riding and drawing strength from its increased predominance in the higher value white-collar segment. Here again, India has an inherent lead over China, which will no doubt strive to do the same, but from the opposite, lower-value direction.

Henner Klein, Chief Executive of global consultants A.T. Kearney, says "India is very much on the radar for manufacturing outsourcing"—a mid-way between blue- and white-collar, which he describes as "the next big wave" after IT software services and BPO services.[129] As Chapter I explains, an A.T. Kearney survey of American auto executives ranked India "as the top outsourcing destination with 24 percent of the respondents giving it the thumbs up," compared to just 15 percent for China.

More significantly, drawing upon the lead in competitiveness of its homegrown multinationals (and its broad-based strengths in science and engineering), Indian manufacturing businesses are also vigorously globalizing. As the *Wall Street Journal* observed in February 2004, India's "vast manufacturing sector, long sluggish and inefficient, is becoming a new global force...taking the nation's economy beyond its well-known strengths in technology and back-office outsourcing."... India's key advantage, it noted, was "a deep reservoir of home-grown engineering muscle that goes well beyond software."[130] Such developments will no doubt further confuse and complicate the core debate about India's pull on white-collar jobs. On the other hand, they also underline India's ambitions to not remain content with its status as a global back-office, but use such additional strengths to fuel its drive into becoming a world power— incapable of being locked into any box of definitions.

The best evidence of this is the remarkable success by Indian manufacturers on the highly-protected Western European market. For example, Indian Tata sports utility vehicles are being imported into Italy and Spain.[131] An Indian-designed Tata-built car is now a lifeline for MG, one of Britain's erstwhile flagship motor car brands, which "plans to import about 50,000 of the cars a year and sell them in Europe through their existing dealerships."[132] Indian companies are also nibbling at markets in Eastern Europe—as another foothold for entry into the Fortress. In Romania, where Indians have already made major acquisitions in steel and telecoms, the Prime Minister of that country has called for aggressive Indian investments in a sweeping range of other areas, including oil exploration, pharmaceuticals, agriculture, education, health and infrastructure.[133] Access to the Fortress is also being offered from elsewhere, such as Switzerland,

which is not part of the EU but belongs to the European Economic
Area free trade zone. Francis Sermet, General Manager of the Swiss
government's investment promotion body DEWS, has sought to
tempt Indian firms, among other things, holding forth the carrot of
a corporation tax rate of just 10 percent.[134]

Large emerging markets, some of which might otherwise be
considered as competitors to India but cannot claim any similar success in that country, are also in the sights of Indian business; these,
to some, surprisingly, include China.

The Mahindra group plans to assemble its jeeps in China,
Indonesia and Russia,[135] and in Turkey too,[136] while Hindustan
Motors is believed to be a candidate for a stake in Malaysia's struggling 'national' car company Proton.[137] The most ambitious move so
far was made by the Tata group in late 2003, when it announced the
acquisition of Daewoo Commercial Vehicle Company, the second-
largest maker of heavy commercial vehicles in South Korea—essentially seen as a 'springboard' into the Chinese market,[138] where Tata
is also targeting investments in steel, telecoms and hotels.[139]
Meanwhile, motor scooter giant Bajaj is seeking to boost its presence
in Southeast Asia through a local manufacturing operation in
Indonesia, and plans to set up in Brazil too.[140] At the start of 2004,
another Indian motorcycle company, TVS Motors, said it was planning to "set up a manufacturing base in Indonesia or Thailand to
penetrate into the South-East Asian markets."[141]

Given India's cost advantages, Africa is of course an obvious
target. Mahindra, for example, has sold jeeps and tractors in
Nigeria.[142] In Senegal, the Tata group won a global tender for locally building 500 buses, and on a visit to India, Senegalese President
Abdoulaye Wade said he believed India's automobile industry would
be an optimal partner to design and build a "car for African people."[143] Tata is also developing a new 'World Truck,' targeted for
launch in 2005, and almost certainly meant to leverage the Indian
advantage in other developing country markets.[144]

Meanwhile, to access the tightly-knit world of European and
U.S. car manufacturers, Indian auto component manufacturers have
begun a flurry of acquisitions overseas. While the Tata group already
supplies plastic parts to Ford and wiring harness to Yazaki,[145] smaller, specialized players have also joined the bandwagon. In October

2003, India's Amtek Auto acquired the £120-million GWK group, Britain's largest independently-owned auto components company. The next month saw Bharat Forge (already one of the largest suppliers of lorry axles to North America) announce acquisition of a major German forging company, Carl Dan Peddinghaus, whose customers include Western automotive giants such as Volkswagen, BMW, DaimlerChrysler and Audi; the acquisition immediately made the Indian firm the world's second largest forging company, after Thyssen Krupp of Germany. One day after Bharat Forge's announcement, India's Sundram Fasteners (a leading supplier to GM) disclosed its own impending acquisition of another blue-chip brand, Dana Spicer Europe's precision forge unit in the U.K., which supplies to the likes of Sweden's Volvo and Scania. Another Indian auto parts firm, G.G Automotive Gears, has also disclosed that it is in talks to acquire a $114-million, 80-year-old U.S. company, which manufactures high precision custom gears and planetary gears.[146]

Going further down the traditional economic value chain (and now well below what are understood as white-collar services), Ispat (run by India's Mittal group) is now the world's second largest steel group after Europe's Arcelor, according to the International Iron and Steel Institute,[147] following acquisitions in Mexico, Trinidad, Ireland, Canada, the U.K., Algeria, France, Germany, Indonesia, Kazakhstan, the U.S., the Czech Republic, South Africa, Romania and recently, Poland.[148] Another Indian steel giant, Tata Steel, is in talks for a stake in South Korea's Hanbo Iron and Steel Company (to acquire a foothold for the Chinese market), while the AV Birla group "acquired a carbon black facility in China to supply exclusively to Michelin."[149] Vedanta, part of the acquisitive Sterlite mining and metals group, has made huge inroads in Africa and became the London Stock Exchange's largest listing in 2003.[150]

With 70 percent of India's oil needs met by imports,[151] India's energy companies, too, have begun globalizing. The NTPC utility has been "roped in by a foreign investor to bid for an operations and maintenance (O&M) contract" for a 430 MW power station owned by Carron Energy in the U.K.[152] Indian Oil is "managing terminals and refineries" in Nigeria, Madagascar, Zambia, Mauritius and Sri Lanka. Gas Authority of India has offered Iran a $1 billion liquefaction plant.[153] Other Indian petroleum companies have acquired assets in Iraq, Sudan, Russia, Myanmar, Vietnam and Libya, and recently bid (jointly with IPR International of the U.S.) for an exploration and production contract in Syria; the aim of such efforts is to reduce India's dependence on its fast-growing oil imports by increasing overseas production.[154] For Vladimir Ivanov of the Economic Research Institute for Northeast Asia, "Russian mainstream thinking is to put Japan, Russia and China into one consortium to develop the (oil) reserves in Eastern Siberia, plus maybe the U.S. and India."[155]

Where required, India has begun to use its growing political weight to muscle into contracts, especially in its Asian neighborhood. In December 2003, for example, Malaysia re-invited India (and China) to bid for a $3.8 billion rail project, previously awarded to a Japanese consortium headed by a close business ally of Mahathir Mohamad, the former prime minister.[156]

As the examples above illustrate, the Elephant's ascension, though recent, is rapid and comprehensive, and its impact on the world economy will clearly be sweeping. While white-collar skills build high-value leverage on world markets, blue-collar businesses are also riding the wave. For Indian-American management guru C.K. Prahlad (founder of the 'core competency' theory in business), manufacturing is a crucial requirement for India to not only become a world power, but also the only way to address the enormous challenge of jobs for its growing population in the years ahead.[157]

The result of a push overseas by Indian manufacturing firms will become increasingly dual-edged and impact on white-collar jobs too. It is for instance, highly unlikely that the Tata conglomerate, whose TCS subsidiary is already ensconced as a high-profile software company in Hungary (counting GE among its clients) will not use this presence to seek opportunities for its car or other businesses, or that other Indian firms will not use the Mittal group's status as eastern Europe's largest steel producer, to add in their own wares, for example white-goods, or software. As mentioned in Chapters II and III, the Tatas aside, several Indian manufacturing conglomerates have entered the global IT and back-office game.

A Taste of the Threat to Britain: Tea, Anyone?

In early 2000, the Tata group took control of Britain's largest tea brand Tetley's ("inventor of the teabag").[158] The Indian emergence however goes well beyond "the traditional English cuppa," to politically sensitive world food markets, marked by a high-profile drive to export its growing surpluses to 'traditional' Western markets in the Middle East, Southeast and Africa.[159] Indian foodgrain exports, reached 5 million tonnes in 2003, and target these very same 'traditional' Western markets.[160]

Blue Tide Colors White-Collar Relocation Debate

Such examples are clearly unique, certainly for an otherwise-poor, developing country, and given India's size, another source for trade spats,[161] which will further muddle those already expected in the area of white-collar service exports.

One sign of the real complexities which lie in wait was India's joining forces with China and Brazil to cause a collapse of the Cancun summit of the World Trade Organization in September 2003, largely on the issue of the huge agricultural subsidies paid to farmers in Europe and the U.S. (including the wheat exporters who had sought to 'help' India after its nuclear tests) and the impact of this overload of cut-price surpluses by rich countries on world grain markets. British daily the *Guardian*, in its post-mortem of Cancun, endorsed the success of this new alliance, contrasting them with small nations which, "are too weak to resist policies foisted on them from outside."[162]

In sharp contrast, an editorial in the *Washington Post* took this group of countries to task for "joining much poorer countries in a bloc, claiming to share their interests and inveighing against a deal."[163] However, the *Post* warned that international trade was not a zero-sum game but rather a way of facilitating growth across the board, and concluded that one consequence of the failure would be a higher premium on bilateral deals.

The latter is precisely the trade-off India seeks and encourages. Given the relative novelty of its emergence in a still-unregulated field like white-collar offshore services, quid pro quo arrangements can be effectively established only on a bilateral (that is country-to-country) basis. In October, 2003, the *Financial Times* confirmed this view by observing that "India appears totally unfazed by the collapse of the WTO meeting in Cancun last month—having already signed three bilateral trade agreements with other Asian partners in its aftermath. Many believe India pursues the deals as a substitute for progress at the multilateral forum."[164]

India's resolve to make what *BBC News* called "more of a mark on the world stage"[165] was reflected in two preferential trade deals signed in 2003, with the Association of South East Asian Nations (ASEAN) and with the Mercosur grouping in South America. As explained above, both these regions will inevitably become huge markets for India's exports of not only higher-end services but also Indian industry's fast-growing flood of manufactured products (cars and trucks, scooters and motorcycles, white-goods, construction materials and medicines, and even food).

For ASEAN countries, their agreement with India also has a political dimension—as a means "to counter-balance China's growing economic dominance of the region."[166] India's trade arrangement with Mercosur too is seen "as a counter weight to dependence on trade with rich nations,"[167] and concerns the U.S.' traditional 'backyard'; its context is all the more significant since a similar trade deal with the EU is floundering.[168] The Mercosur agreement was signed during a visit to India at the end of January 2004 by Brazilian President Luiz Inacio Lula da Silva, who was Chief Guest at India's Republic Day, the country's annual display of military-technological might; just one month previously, Brazilian Defense Minister Jose Veiges Filho signed an agreement in India to "explore the possibilities of cooperating in air-surveillance systems, as well as in exploring co-production and co-development of aircraft, warship building and sub-systems such as software avionics and ordnance."[169]

Such potentially-dramatic extensions in India's spheres of engagement are also evident in the Middle East, where the six-nation Gulf Cooperation Council (comprising Saudi Arabia, Kuwait, Bahrain, Qatar, Oman and the United Arab Emirates) has invited India "to join its exclusive club as 'dialogue partner'"—a status so far accorded only to the U.S. and Japan,[170] and in a region with which the European Union's relationship is strained.[171] Responding to such overtures, India has recently offered "to help Oman maintain and upgrade its military aircraft and give technical training to its air force in electronics and communications."[172] In early 2003, Oman became the first Arab country to provide Indians with automatic entry visas on arrival.

On the wider international trade front, the implications of such developments are self-evident, above all in increasing mutual inter-dependency between India and the West (both of the cooperative and competitive kind), while reducing room for one-way pressures from the West on single issues, such as the relocation of white-collar jobs. These considerations become especially relevant given the Elephant's increasing autonomy in military technologies as well as its determination to be viewed as a major world power.[173]

The Elephant Muscles Into Technology's Final Frontier

As the process of skills-fuelled enablement sweeps across several high-technology fields and massively bolsters the broader foundations of its economy, one result is India's rapid empowerment with globally significant military-technological competencies. Such a trend has, in turn, created a powerful military-technology constituency in India. Its proponents are already integrated deeply as opinion formers within the Indian system and continue propelling the country's rise as the world's leading offshore supplier of technology services.

The intimate connection between Indian military technology and its success in software was noted as far back as 1997 by *Asia Times*, which suggested that the credit for Bangalore's success as a global software center must be given to India's military and aerospace program; this provided 'rich pickings' for U.S. corporations. Yale University professor Paul Kennedy too was prophetic in the early 1990s with his observation about India's "powerful and technologically sophisticated military-industrial complex," whose "seventeen hundred research establishments" stimulated the broader landscape of Indian science and engineering.[174]

Since then, leveraging its strengths in software, India has begun making impressive headway in cutting-edge, militarily relevant information technologies ranging from supercomputing to aerospace. The new Indian Param Padma supercomputer, for example, is teraflops-rated (the first outside the U.S. and Japan); integral to India's nuclear program, previous supercomputers in this series have already been exported to institutes and universities in Singapore, Canada and Germany,[175] and by the year 2000, Russia already had three of the machines.[176] Though delayed, India's supersonic, "fifth-generation" Light Combat Aircraft (LCA) program[177] had, by end of 2003, seen the completion of a record 125 test flights without a single crash[178]; the high-level software skills employed in this program are evident from the fact that Autolay, a computer-aided design and simulation package developed in India specifically for the LCA, is now being used for the Airbus A-380 'superjumbo.'[179] Software from the LCA program will also be deployed for the new IL-214 military transport aircraft under co-development by Russia and India in a 50-50 joint venture.[180]

In the space industry, India's third-generation INSAT-3 communications satellite (the fourteenth so far) is now in orbit, and is the only satellite responsible for search and rescue from Europe to Australia.[181] Indian remote-sensing satellites are widely acknowledged to be as good as those of the U.S. and Europe.[182] As *SpaceNews* noted in 1999, "With resolution of up to 19.0 feet (5.8 meters), the four Indian Remote Sensing Satellites (IRS) are the best money can buy." Since then, the IRS constellation has doubled to eight. IRS-P6 has increased resolution to 2.5 meters, while the latest TES satellite has brought resolutions down to 1 meter (providing for explicit military surveillance applications).[183]

Though a little known fact, both the U.S. and Europe are already significant users of Indian satellite data. In Europe, IRS data has been used to monitor pollution[184] and forest fires,[185] while the U.S. military resorted to Indian satellites for information on Iraq (as noted by John Pike of the Federation of American Scientists[186]) and more recently, in Afghanistan, too.[187] In early 2004, U.S.-based Space Imaging extended by six years a global agreement to sell data from India's IRS-P6 (Resourcesat) satellite as well as the IRS 1-C, IRS 1-D, and the IRS P-5 (Cartosat) satellites.[188]

Recent Indian launches include a dedicated locally-built weather satellite[189]; other satellites are shortly planned exclusively for telemedicine, rural education and disaster management[190]; each of these, as this author noted in a *Financial Times* commentary comparing the Indian and Chinese space effort, would be world-firsts.[191] India is now building a complex 500-cluster radar imaging satellite;

its cost is estimated to be 15-fold lower than the U.S.,[192] posing another profound Indian challenge at yet another edge of the satellite technology value-chain.

With a second launch pad commissioned,[193] India is fast increasing its autonomy for satellite launches; so far, India has lofted 17 satellites built domestically. As the *New York Times* observed, "Unlike space programs in other developing countries, including Brazil, low costs have not meant catastrophic launching failures. Only 6 of India's 37 satellite launchings have failed"[194] —as it happens, at a rate comparable to Europe's and much better than Japan.

The 1-tonne payload of the Indian PSLV rocket already gives India a quick intercontinental ballistic missile (ICBM) capability according to the CIA.[195] The PSLV has also successfully launched the country's own IRS satellites as well as those from Belgium, Germany, South Korea and others.[196] In May 2003, India completed the second development test of the larger Ariane IV-class GSLV launcher[197]; later in the year, India announced successful test of a homegrown cryogenic rocket engine, joining a handful of countries, "including the United States, Russia and France" with such a capability which "would allow it to launch high-altitude satellites, send a man to the moon"—or again, "build intercontinental ballistic missiles."[198]

The GSLV's payload is over 2 tonnes and would suffice for India's INSAT communication satellites, now launched by Russia and Europe. Steady progress is also being made on the GSLV-Mark III project, which would put a four-tonne satellite into orbit by 2006 or 2007.[199] For the sake of comparison, Israel's Shavit has so far managed to loft only a 300 kg satellite (the Ofeq-5)[200] into orbit, while Brazil failed again in August 2003 (for the third time since 1997) to launch a similar sub-500 kg satellite[201]; such a capability was acquired by India in the early 1980s. In December 2003, Israel dropped Russia in favor of India, for the launch of Tauvex, "a set of three telescopes able to image ultraviolet sky," soon to be placed on board a forthcoming Indian satellite.[202]

Rather than resist such trends, the U.S. has been urged to endorse India's efforts. One suggestion in an American report was to help India's space effort through "a role in future NASA lunar research missions and in some Mars missions as well as promoting multilateral satellites for Indian launchers"[203] (though this would hardly be welcomed by Europe's Arianespace).

On the other hand, India's determination to act in its own interests is amply demonstrated by its decision to invest £210 million in the 30-satellite European Galileo navigation system (compared to £140 million by China). Galileo, for which India is expected to build "six to eight satellites",[204] is being designed as an alternative to the U.S. GPS Global Positioning System and the move has been described by a British daily as an endorsement by two rising Asian powers of "Europe's bid to challenge American supremacy in space."[205]

In nuclear power too, India's fiercely autonomous nuclear energy program is not only two times larger but more advanced than China's,[206] and includes both a functioning fast-breeder as well as the world's first thorium-fuelled reactor;[207] both these, in turn, have major implications for the Indian nuclear weapons program.

Do-It-Yourself: The Great Sanctions Strike-Back

The roots of India's potentially-sweeping high-technology military capabilities are, ironically, anchored in a drive for self-sufficiency central not only to the philosophy of the country's freedom movement and its pre-reform 'license Raj,' but to a resolve to go-it-alone following U.S. sanctions after India's first nuclear tests in 1974.

The Param supercomputer, for example, was developed in response to U.S. sanctions, which blocked India from importing Cray supercomputers. Like Param, India's space program, too, is the outcome of an effort to become self-sufficient in the face of sanctions. These are just two examples. Though acquisitions of high-technology know-how by India may have shortened its learning curves, their long-term viability would be obviously less, and the country's dependency on external suppliers greater. Instead, India has now clearly come to a stage where such past efforts could quickly pay dividends, should it choose to become a military-technology exporter.

Ready to Compete for a Piece of the Arms Bazaar

India's techno-superstructure, intimately interconnected with information technology, is also part of its wider high-technology military capabilities. The country's eventual emergence as a military technology exporter will have major implications, both strategic and commercial, in Southeast Asia, Africa and the Middle East.

Though India's arms exports are still negligible, its capacity is surely not, especially in terms of military-related high-tech know-how, rather than just weapons platforms in the pure sense. Nevertheless, in the latter too, the potential is truly immense. Already in 2001, American think-tank Stratfor alerted its readers that India was getting "ready to compete for a piece of the Southeast Asian weapons market in several arms sectors." India, it noted, "produces surface-to-surface missiles, tanks, artillery pieces, howitzers, unmanned air vehicles (UAVs), ground sensors for battlefield intelligence and a variety of small arms" as well as "destroyers, guided-missile and other frigates, fast attack vessels, landing ships and even aircraft carriers and destroyers with 'stealth' technology to evade radar."[208]

In August 2003, India made its first formal offer to sell warships and train naval personnel from Vietnam.[209] Earlier, Stanley Weiss, founding chairman of the American pressure group Business Executives for National Security, wrote in the *International Herald Tribune* about India's offer of "advanced Indian military technology" to Iran, in return for Indian "access to Iranian military bases in the event of war with Pakistan."[210]

As if such a major step into the Middle Eastern imbroglio was not remarkable enough, India's fast-developing military-political alliance with Israel may see the latter marketing the civilian version of the Indian helicopter Dhruv,[211] which is designed to meet U.S. standards,[212] and versions of which are already in use by India's army, navy and air force; the first result of this combined Indo-Israeli effort is likely to be an order from the U.S. Customs, for 10 helicopters.[213] More tellingly, Bell Helicopters of the U.S. has sent a team of engineers to study India's efforts to control vibrations in its own helicopters, by the use of smart materials such as piezoelectric ceramics and magnetostrictives; the key effort, however, is a software 'control algorithm' being developed at the Indian Institute of Science, which would be integrated into an onboard electronic engine management system aboard the Dhruv—once again highlighting the close connection between Indian IT and its growing military technology capabilities.[214]

Shifting the Balance of Power

Few 'experts' understand that though smaller in numbers, the Indian military is technologically more advanced than China's.[215] One of the rare exceptions was Jim Rohwer, a correspondent for British weekly the *Economist*. Rohwer's 1995 book *Asia Rising* explicitly referred in an analysis of Big Powers in Asia to "India's crack army and formidable navy, much more modern than China's."[216,217]

Many analysts did not actually see India's arrival. For example, in *The Coming Conflict With China*,[218] Richard Bernstein and Ross H. Munro, former Asia correspondents with *Time* magazine, pay great attention to Chinese acquisition of top-line Russian military hardware such as Su-27 fighters, Kilo-class submarines and (C-141 Starlifter class) IL-76 long-range heavy-lift transport aircraft, and its impact in the Asian context. As it happens, India's acquisitions from Russia of Kilo-class submarines and IL-76 transporters were far more numerous than China's,[219] and in the case of the Su-27 vis-a-vis India's thrust-vectored Su-30 MKI, technologically more advanced.[220] A more serious flaw is the authors' inordinate emphasis on Chinese naval power projection capabilities, which mulls over a startling gap in this field, namely China's lack of an aircraft carrier, as well as the 10-15 years which would be required to learn how to effectively operate a carrier battle group.

India, in contrast, has not only operated carriers since the early 1960s, but has purchased the 45,000-tonne Gorshkov from Russia,[221] while also building its own 32,000-tonne carrier.[222] Sometime early in the next decade (2010-), this would give India three aircraft carriers, in other words more than France or Britain, and second only to the U.S. Well before this, India's own secretive ATV (Advanced Technology Vessel) program for building nuclear submarines is also expected to have yielded results.[223]

The most dramatic example of the limitations in Bernstein's and Munro's analysis was their fear about the South China Sea "being turned into a Chinese lake."[224] Two years after publication of their book and close on the heels of a high-profile recapture by the Indian Navy of a hijacked Japanese cargo ship (described later), India sent a naval task force into the very same South China Sea, ostensibly to conduct anti-piracy exercises with the South Korean and Japanese navies. Stratfor, the American think-tank, commented on its implications in 2000: The Indian navy's move "to expand operations from the north of the Arabian Sea through the South China Sea and to establish an expeditionary-capable force not only threatens China's areas of operation but also alters the balance of naval power in the region.... In creating a viable blue-water reach, including refueling and support craft, India will significantly surpass China's naval capabilities as well."[225]

Such blue-water naval ambitions are quantified in a statement by India's Chief of Naval Staff in December 2003: a strength of at least 200 ships, 40 frigates and destroyers and the requisite number of support and auxiliary craft.[226]

China itself has few illusions. In a sweeping review of the country's strategic thinking, U.S. expert Michael Pillsbury of the National Defense University, noted that "One area where Chinese authors assess India as having significant power is in military affairs."[227] Indeed, Chinese military analysts refer admiringly to India's comprehensive military-technological base. Given China's lack of an aircraft carrier, some (Chinese analysts) are almost wistful about this advantage held by "India's powerful Navy."[228]

No Swashbuckling: Quietly Harnessing IT for Command and Control

More pointedly, Chinese experts, according to Pillsbury, also "explain that India's stress on the development of science and technology has been a key factor in developing its military power. 'India currently has 3 million scientists and technicians, following only the United States and Russia, to be third in the world. These science and technology troops are India's precious intelligence resource, and play a decisive role in national defense studies and war production.'"[229]

India is determined to retain such a high-tech edge, mainly by continuing to harness its lead in information technology, and by implication, further encourage its pull on Western white-collar jobs. In short, it will resist restrictions in such fields—a difficult enough task, given the growing complexities of its engagement with the world.

India's ability to harness its substantial military and technology capacities were amply demonstrated in the aftermath of a massive earthquake in Gujarat in January 2001. Within hours, Indian Air Force IL-76 transporters had begun delivering supplies round-the-clock (in one case using oil lamps in lieu of runway landing lights). On its part, the Indian Navy dispatched two hospital ships, equipped with helicopters for airlift of urgent cases. In just the first three days, a total of 1,184 air evacuations were conducted, while military doctors performed 11,090 surgeries. Meanwhile, Indian IRS remote-sensing satellites began beaming images to aid planning for the relief effort, while VSAT uplinks to Indian INSAT satellites mediated a total of over 750 telemedicine sessions by military doctors, or more than one every six minutes.[230]

The direct connection between India's growing capabilities in IT, their military dimension and India's strength as a future military technology exporter came in early 2004 in the form of Samyuktha, a state-of-the-art electronic warfare communication system to identify and jam radar and communication frequency bands. Samyuktha, which will be offered for export, has been billed as India's "largest ever" defense IT project.[231]

The role of information technology in India's military muscle is however best illustrated by a high-seas drama in late 1999. Described by the *International Herald Tribune* as "the first such incident in recent memory," it involved an Indian Navy missile corvette, aided by other warships and patrol aircraft, conducting an armed interception and boarding on the high seas of a Japanese-owned freighter, MV Alondra Rainbow, which had been hijacked by Indonesian pirates.[232] Rather than emphasize the dramatic swashbuckling military elements of this incident, Indian General Ashok Mehta, a respected commentator on strategic affairs, stressed what was perhaps the more subtle and all the more impressive element of total control through IT:

> My main concern is to harness infotech, technicalising manpower to build a robust command and control. We showed

our future potential for this through international networking in
the run up to the seizure of the MV Alondra Rainbow. The communication network established brought the International
Maritime Bureau, Tokyo, the Piracy Reporting Centre, Kuala
Lumpur, the Coast Guard, the Western Naval command, Naval
Headquarters and fleet units at sea on one grid. This was no
mean achievement.[233]

Making Sense of Military Spending with PPP

As explained previously, purchasing power parity (PPP) is a
useful yardstick to measure economies. PPP may also be crucial to
obtain a more meaningful idea about military spending and key to
understanding India's new assertiveness in international affairs.

For example, there is a huge disparity between India's defense
budget (measured in U.S. dollars as approximately $15 billion in
2004) and its status as one of the world's largest arms importers (and
producers). One of the few to note this point is Peter Robinson from
the London-based Institute for Public Policy Research. Writing in
the *Financial Times*, Robinson contested Yale University professor
Paul Kennedy's widely-quoted statement after the Iraq war in 2003
that the U.S. is in a class of its own by spending more on its military
"than the next nine countries combined." Instead, Robinson argues
that adding China's and India's PPP-weighted military budgets
means that "the U.S. does not even reach a two-power standard"; in
other words, rather than being more than the next nine, American
military spending was less than that of India and China taken
together.[234]

An India That Can Say No:
Is the West More Dependent on Indian High-Tech
Than It Cares to Admit?

Given the complex but dense interconnections of U.S. information technology with Indian software, it would be naive to escape
the implications of the growing American dependency on India. In
October 1999, the *Washington Times* hinted at such concerns, when
it identified India as one of the "most sophisticated" countries with
"the capacity to engage in state-sponsored, surreptitious electronic

raids" against the U.S.[235]

Another scenario, even if still-subtle, may be more pertinent.

After the first Gulf War, a controversial book *The Japan that Can Say No*[236] underscored the U.S.' military-strategic dependency on Japan in terms of the high-tech chips used to guide intercontinental ballistic missiles. A key point in the book was that even if the U.S. had the know-how to design its own chips, it lacked the manpower and other support resources to do this quickly and effectively.

It may be worthwhile revisiting this issue today. The U.S.' dependency on Indian software is more significant, given the fact that the know-how is much more diffused and 'virtual,' and therefore more difficult to identify, control and reverse (than would have been the case with Japan). This goes far beyond the clutch of American military technology firms with Indian connections, such as San Diego-based Science and Applied Technologies Inc., developing an advanced missile guidance system under a $60 million contract with the U.S. Navy,[237] Alabama-based Systems, Studies & Simulation, now scouting for acquisitions in India,[238] or firms like Digite Enterprises, which supplies program management software to the likes of National Air Intelligence Center (NAIC) and the Federal Judiciary Center, and has a Mumbai product development center.[239] It also goes beyond Indian-Americans and visiting Indians at DARPA or NASA, although top American defense electronics firms like Rockwell have sounded red alerts on their inevitable loss of competitiveness "to countries such as China and India" following cutbacks on H-1B visas in October 2003.[240]

Instead, the issue here concerns the longstanding presence of American firms in India, especially those with military technology businesses. The CIO of United Technologies, for instance, calls his Indian effort an "outsourcing success story."[241] Today, nearly every major U.S. military technology company (Honeywell, GE, Texas Instruments, Motorola) not only has long-established software development facilities in India; as explained in a previous section, in several cases the Indian facilities have higher U.S. military-standard CMM certifications than their U.S. operations. Though their overt military-related work can be nominally compartmentalized, it is again imperative, as in Chapter I, to point out the difficulties with territorially segregating the intrinsic cross-border creep of complex software processes.

In some cases, however, the connections are more explicit. In June 2003, GE announce it would buy out its Indian partner TCS in their CMM Level 5 Engineering Analysis Center of Excellence (EACoE) joint venture. A little-noticed news report listed some of the Indian inputs involved in this equation: "EACoE provides high-end engineering analysis, design and software development services to GE Aircraft Engines (GEAE) and GE Power Systems (GEPS) as part of the joint venture since its inception in July of 1999. These services include solid parametric and finite element modeling for the purposes of conducting stress, heat transfer and computational fluid dynamics (CFD) analyses of aircraft engines and power turbine components. EACoE also develops and maintains in-house analysis software needed to conduct and enhance such engineering analysis."[242] Finely differentiating the overlaps in such efforts on a GE engine in a warplane, as opposed to a civilian aircraft, is hardly straightforward. Nor would it be the case with a Texas Instruments chip or a Honeywell avionics package.

Such linkages are already strong and pervasive, and therefore very likely to continue. In January 2004, Dr. James Carafano, a specialist on defense and homeland security at The Heritage Foundation, told Indian software firms about their opportunity for partnering with American IT companies in the Department of Homeland Security's plan to integrate disparate IT systems at various administrations, with a focus on 'disaster preparedness' and security framework modules. The integration objective is central to a $44 billion investment plan by the Department.[243] Though Dr. Carafano acknowledged that there would be a 'political' factor to be overcome, he was no doubt aware of the especially strong global competency and capacity of Indian firms in exactly such areas.

Can the U.S. keep a secret? Even if American policy makers remain unaware of the implications of such trends, Indians are conscious of their own techno-strategic dependency on the U.S., and have actively sought to neutralize it where possible. For example, in 1999, the Indian Defense Research and Development Organization issued a 'red alert' warning against all American-made network-security software, stating that the (64- or 128-bit) limits placed by the U.S. on encryption exports implied that only 'insecure' products were exported.[244] Indeed, more than a year previously, India's Signitron had launched a 448-bit encryption package, which, according to one news report, provided 'a virtually unbreakable method of encrypting data.'"[245]

Indian IT is also thinking ahead, and positioning itself in advance to not only meet challenges on security concerns, but prime itself for new opportunities. This is especially relevant given the inevitability of privacy, confidentiality and data protection issues lending ammunition to the American anti-offshore outsourcing effort in the years ahead. Already, for example, a letter to the *Los Angeles Times* asks: "With the concern over cyber-security and terrorism at its all-time high, what is the Indian government doing to secure my family's data, which has now been sent overseas like spam?"[246]

Security was one of the hot flavors for IT federation Nasscom's summit in early 2004, at which its President Kiran Karnik pledged to work jointly with the U.S. "to evolve global standards to boost confidence in online transactions and address fears as far as privacy of sensitive information, such as healthcare and financial data, were concerned."[247] Such policy efforts will moreover allow India to derive further strengths, given that they would surely juxtapose into the secretive high-level anti-terrorism working groups set up by India, the U.S. and Israel, as discussed later in this chapter.

The Indian government's infotech R&D heavyweight C-DAC (developer of the Param supercomputer) has developed a suite of evidence tracking and compilation tools at its Technical Resource Centre for Cyber Forensics,[248] which "benchmark themselves against the very best available worldwide."[249] Indian IT firms are also preparing for mastering the highest American digital security standards. Bangalore-based SISA Information Security, for example, has established "a strategic tie-up with the Software Engineering Institute and Carnegie Mellon University"[250] on the latter's Pentagon-endorsed Octave Information Security Risk Assessment. SISA will train Indian IT firms on Octave, and expects them to acquire a similar star status as they have with CMM certifications, also issued by the very same American institutions.

India is setting the stage for a day when it may be futile for anti-offshore outsourcing groups in the U.S. to raise concerns about security and privacy, as far as Indian IT is concerned.

Ankoors Away?
The Difficulty of Caging the Elephant

Three different examples of India's high-tech autonomy severely limiting room for maneuver by the West were underlined in U.S. and European media comments by this author, just after the Indian nuclear tests in 1998.

In an interview with the Belgian monthly *ID-Side*, he noted the role of an Indian software breakthrough in Hydrogen Bomb-enabling tritium technology which had previously been described by the authoritative defense publication *Jane's Intelligence Review* as "the first of its kind anywhere in the world," and one which "may have tipped the strategic scale (against China and Pakistan) in New Delhi's favour." This author also observed that "U.S. military contractors like Honeywell, GE, Allied Signal and Hughes employ an estimated 15,000 Indian software engineers" and Indian hawks "look at facts like this to shrug away any threat from sanctions to the country's software industry. Indeed, barely ten days after the first Indian nuclear tests, Motorola announced it would set up a very large scale integration (VLSI) design center in Gurgaon, near Delhi, for an investment of $50 million."[251]

In a July 1998 commentary in the *Washington Post*, this author argued that even if there was some truth to the claim (made previously in the *Post*) that most of the military plutonium stocks used for the Indian nuclear tests came from two (1960s vintage) U.S.-supplied reactors, American pressure would at best be "feeble because India depends little on external technology in this field. It could simply increase extraction of plutonium from its 10 domestically designed, pressurized water reactors."[252]

In the *Washington Post* of January 4, 1999, this author noted the futility of American sanctions on Indian supercomputing efforts, especially given the key role of Indian scientists in designing chips such as Intel's Pentium and Sun Microsystems' SPARC as well as the country's position as "a world leader in the field of massively parallel software." The commentary emphasized that "India's capability in such fields" is what brought U.S. companies like IBM and Digital to the country to begin with, and that it would also be "counterproductive for the U.S. to restrict chip sales to a country like India for another reason. U.S. corporations such as Texas Instruments,

Hughes, Motorola and Cypress have huge (chip) design facilities in the country. In fact, TI's latest DSP chip bears the Hindi name, Ankoor."[253]

The Elephant Goes Calling: India's Year of Assertions

Given below are some typical examples of India's relentless drive to attain a stronger geopolitical profile, along with a brief analysis of their implications, over twelve months of 2003.

- In January, the U.S. and India were reported to be planning joint air exercises to pit America's top of the line F-15 Eagle fighter against the Russian-built SU-30MKI (the world's only operational warplane to use advanced thrust-vectoring technologies). As noted by the *Washington Post*, this would be "the first time that the highest-performing fighters built by the United States and Russia would be pitted against each other."[254] The thrust-vectored SU-30 is currently operated to any significance by only the Indian Air Force, and over 140 are due to be license-built in India; the Russian Air Force can hardly afford to operate them. Indeed, like the SU-30MKI, Russia's latest warships (e.g. Krivak class stealth frigates) and battle tanks (the T-90) are almost wholly destined for India (and China), who in a sense, subsidize its continuing relevance as a military-industrial player. India is now "helping Russia to co-produce a fifth-generation stealth fighter," a transport plane for the air forces of the two countries,[255] as well as a beyond visual range (BVR) air-to-air missile.
- In February, the director of UN affairs on former U.S. President Clinton's National Security Council underscored "rapidly emerging technological capacity," when he suggested that India alone should obtain American support for permanent membership in the UN Security Council (rather than with Japan and Germany).[256] Continuing this trend, in both February and March, a series of editorials and commentaries (among others, by influential columnists in the *Washington Post*[257] and *New York Times*) urged giving India permanent membership of the UN Security Council, in some cases even suggesting that India replace France.[258] Since

then, major European nations have also endorsed India's candidacy, most recently Sweden, whose Prime Minister Goran Persson noted, after a three-day conference on 'Preventing Genocide' that what was at stake was "the future credibility of the United Nations."[259]

• In March, India sought to forcefully demonstrate its interests in Afghanistan by delivering its hundred and ninety-second bus and its third Airbus aircraft to that country, in addition to continuing work on building highways and hospitals there.[260] India also said it was investing an additional $100 million to modernize the Afghan phone system, including delivery of exchanges and satellite communications equipment,[261] while preparing for completion of a program to train no fewer than 700 Afghan diplomats and other officials at New Delhi.[262]

• In April, India began work on INS Shivalik, the first of 12 planned 'stealth' warships for its navy. Alongside three Russian-built Krivak-class stealth frigates in service, all these vessels are being equipped with the PJ-10 Brahmos, the world's first, and so far, only supersonic (Mach 2.8+) air- and sea-launched cruise missile. The hardware in Brahmos is Russian; reflecting Indian IT skills, its guidance system is Indian.[263]

• In May, the Indian government decided to stop taking development aid from over 20 countries, and instead doubled its own existing aid commitments to Africa and Asia (already on par with what will be terminated). The ostensible reason was that smaller aid programs were too expensive to administer, but the real cause was the moralizing 'sermons' from Europe, Canada and Australia which accompanied the aid.[264] Shortly after, India joined the International Monetary Fund's pool of lenders (the so-called Financial Transaction Plan), thus shedding its decades-old image as a borrower.[265]

• In June, the *Los Angeles Times* suggested that the U.S. should "support India's participation" not only as a permanent member of the UN Security Council, but also "in an expanded G8 economic summit."[266] During the same month, aware of the Indian military's combat readiness as well as its long-range heavy airlift and naval capabilities, the *Washington Post* remarked that "no country (but India) could provide more immediate help for the beleaguered U.S. presence (in

Iraq)."267 A few weeks later, the *New York Times* noted that
although Poland was ready to supply troops for Iraq, "it is
willing, but the question is, how able," while India, which
"was expected to provide a division, a unit with an established system of command and control" was clearly "able but
not willing".268 On yet another note, the *Financial Times*
observed that, drawing on its experience in Kashmir, India
was probably one of the few countries which could help the
U.S. manage the type of low-intensity conflict it would
inevitably face in Iraq.269

* In July, while U.S. President George Bush was visiting
  Africa, Indian warships were providing security for the Africa
  Union Summit in Mozambique270 (a role traditionally associated with France), planning show-the-flag visits to South
  Africa and Nigeria271 and readying for a permanent deployment to protect the exclusive economic zone for the Indian
  Ocean island nation of Mauritius.272 Meanwhile, back in the
  U.S., for the first time, Indians and Jews, two of the most
  "highly educated, affluent" ethnic communities in the country, celebrated a "burgeoning political alliance" between
  themselves.273

* In August, a front-page article in the *Financial Times*
  announced India's $80 million plans for a moon mission by
  2007.274 Just over two months later, a science correspondent
  for *UPI* reviewed India's space successes and projects, including the "all-Indian design" in both the PSLV and GSLV rockets, and acknowledged that a moon mission was well within
  India's "resources and capabilities."275 Indeed, in 2004 or
  early 2005, India is due to launch a recoverable 450 kg satellite as part of its Space Recovery Experiment (SRE), a critical step towards the moon mission.

* In September, the Indian Defense Minister said that the
  Indian LCA warplane might be exported "to friendly countries within the next four to five years."276 During the same
  month, Israeli Prime Minister Ariel Sharon's landmark visit
  to New Delhi (timed for the anniversary of the September 11
  terror attacks on the World Trade Center in the U.S.) set the
  stage for a strategic partnership between the two countries,
  with enormous geopolitical implications.277 The *Jerusalem
  Post* observed in an editorial, "It's important that Israel show

it can make friends other than America and Micronesia in this unfriendly world, and especially secure the cooperation of an emerging great power."[278] Sharon's delegation included Chief Executives of numerous Israeli high-technology firms, from both the military and civilian IT sectors.[279] One of the key items on the agenda was Israel's largest-ever military order, for a $1.1 billion purchase by India of three Phalcon AWACS (airborne warning and control systems),[280] jointly developed with the U.S.; the sale of Phalcons to China was previously vetoed by the U.S. Even as India continues work on its own AWACS system,[281] the Phalcons will give the Indian Air Force a massive edge over all its Asian rivals, China included.

- In October, as mentioned previously, Indian conglomerate Reliance acquired Flag Telecom, owner and operator of a 50,000km network of undersea optic-fiber cable connecting key business markets in Asia, Europe, the Middle East and the U.S.; Flag's customers include all the top 10 international telecoms carriers. Alongside the Tata-Indicom 3,175-km India-Singapore cable due for completion by end 2004[282] (part of a $3.5 billion investment by the Tata conglomerate in the telecom sector), the Reliance acquisition adds teeth to India's global communications reach. Soon after the Flag buyout, a leading Pakistani daily voiced the apprehension that Indian ownership of one of the world's largest global undersea cable networks, rendered Pakistan's electronic data insecure, since it would enable India to "eavesdrop on the country's communications."[283]

- In November, after beating of a Canadian challenge for the 2010 Commonwealth Games, India emerged as a front-runner for hosting the 2016 Olympics.[284]

- In December, Stephen Blank, an American commentator on defense issues, wrote about India's acquisition of an operational air base in Tajikistan, which "could be used to counter Central Asian insurgents or Pakistan, or to support a friendly government. This probably will not be India's last base, and it probably will not remain a small one. Certainly it appears to spearhead New Delhi's deepening involvement in Central Asian defense," he said.[285] In spite of its overtures to Iran, the Tajikistan facility will be "India's first-ever military base in a foreign country,"[286] and will allow stationing of Special Forces, combat troops as well as "fighter and heavy lift transport aircraft." The aim will be to secure India's fast growing need for oil and gas supplies from energy-rich Central Asia; Indian oil company ONGC Videsh Limited has since tied up with the Kazakhstan government "for oil exploration in Alibekmola and Kurmangazi fields."[287]

So this too is India—an Elephant finally on the move: sitting atop a hundred billion dollars in foreign reserves, debts begun to be prepaid, a lender to other developing countries, businesses reaching out worldwide, granaries 'overflowing' with food surpluses,[288] its Navy guarding African seas, producing stealth warships, warplanes and supersonic cruise missiles, allied with both Iran and Israel, and now possessing its first overseas base.

Will India ever become aggressive, 'imperial'? New Empires have seldom been built by victims of previous ones, and given India's history, this is all the more unlikely. India's Ashoka was, after all, the world's first (and so far, only) Emperor to renounce violence in the 3rd century BC, disband his army—after winning a major war—and become key to Buddhism's eventual spread. In spite of the massive naval power of the turn-of-the-millennium Cholas, India's history in Asia too was clearly benevolent[289]; Cambodia's celebrated Angkor Vat is ancient Indian architecture, Indonesia's Javanese traditions and language are clearly the result of strong Indian influence (the name of its national airline, Garuda, is taken from the Indian epic *Ramayana*), while myths and legends in Malaysia and Singapore draw heavily from two thousand year old Indian compilations such as the *Hitopadesha* or the *Tantri Kamandaha*, and what in the West is the better-known *Panchatantra*.[290] None of the history books of these countries complain about an aggressive India.

More pertinent to the above question may be the way modern India deals with some of its smaller neighbors, and has done before. Thus, unlike the U.S. or France, Indian troops for example, have not remained in liberated Bangladesh, while its 'Hindu nationalist' government has been one of the most resolute backers of democracy in the world's only Hindu Kingdom, Nepal. Even Bhutan seems to be doing well so far as India's neighbor: India has not only built up that country's roads and electricity infrastructure since 1961[291]; in spite of

Bhutan's vocal criticism of its 1998 nuclear tests, the new, wholly Indian-funded Tala hydropower project will result in Bhutan's per capita income almost doubling,[292] indeed to become more than India's own.[293]

Still, as India emerges from behind its externally cast veil of Gandhian nonviolence and general good-neighborliness (with the obvious exception of Pakistan), it is also important to take close note of the fact that the Elephant has never hesitated to act in its own interests. At present, a strategic alliance with America is a clear priority, and in spite of the inevitable ups and downs expected from mature democracies, irreversible. The speed of progress of this alliance is breathtaking and its implications profound, once again in terms of complicating and limiting space for a single issue like white-collar job relocation.

The Indian-American Strategic Partnership: Hope or Inevitability

In early 2003, former American Senator Larry Pressler wrote: "It is time for (President) Bush to embrace India—as a key ally, democratic torchbearer and trading partner—for the sake of security in a post war world,"[294] and urged the U.S. to set up a free trading arrangement with India.

Indeed, few serious observers doubt any longer that India is a fast-rising world power, and its growing presence will have to be accepted. This process has already begun.

In November 2003, U.S. Under Secretary of Commerce Kenneth Juster noted that "in the aftermath of lifting of (post-1998 nuclear test) sanctions, the rate of license approvals for Indian imports of sensitive technology had reached "over 90 percent" and that the 700 licenses to Indian firms was "more than what has been given to British firms with 500 licenses' and next only to Japan's 900."[294]

For the U.S. in particular, India's emergence (and the two countries' growing mutual interdependency in IT and high-technology) poses both geostrategic opportunities and challenges. Unlike, say, Pakistan, a giant like India is hardly likely to present itself as what a Pakistani journalist memorably called a 'condom,'[296] to be used and thrown away. In very sharp contrast to both Pakistan and China, or for that matter Brazil and Russia, India is an established democracy and an open society. Its motives are transparent and its workings there for all to see. As the late U.S. Senator Moynihan emphasized to American critics of India's 1998 nuclear tests, there were really few reasons for surprise; they should have, he suggested, been reading Indian newspapers—which would include some of the world's largest English-language dailies.

The implications of such factors cannot be exaggerated, and go back several years. In February 1999 (or just months after India's controversial nuclear tests), America's National Endowment of Democracy chose India for its first, high profile global Conference.

The mutual dependency has since moved closer. As the *Associated Press* observed, "Indians today are linked to the United States in ways unimaginable only a few years ago. The two cultures are learning to interact more closely, particularly in the war on terrorism."[297]

Since September 2001, Indian-American military ties in particular have grown by leaps and bounds, in some cases to reach levels of cooperation conducted by either, if at all, with only a handful of other countries. In May 2002, Indian and U.S. special forces undertook no less than three weeks of joint day-and-night operations, including paratroop and bundle drops with "swapped chutes and airplanes" at India's largest airbase, Agra, in temperatures of up to 115 degrees F.[298] In October 2002, India sent a heavy-airlift transporter to Alaska with 80 soldiers (including representatives of a crack para-commando regiment) to conduct joint exercises with the U.S. Army and U.S. Air Force; the aim of this effort was to "increase interoperability in Airborne Operations and integrate USAF and IAF (Indian Air Force) forces into Joint and Combined Operations."[299] In August 2003, the Indo-American joint Defense Policy Group met to take stock of cooperation; among the points for discussion was a "combined Special Forces counterinsurgency exercise in northeast India."[300] Over the next month, U.S. and Indian soldiers simulated three weeks of high-altitude mountain warfare (at heights of 15,000 feet) as part of military exercises in Kashmir—the very region whose control by India is bitterly disputed by Pakistan. Once again, the goal was "to increase the interoperability of

American and Indian troops and to optimize their commonalities" according to Indian Army Lieutenant General Arvind Sharma.[301]

Even as both countries prepare the Cope India '04 joint air exercises to pit their top-of-the-line warplanes against each other in "simulated beyond visual range combat, high value asset protection and...low and high altitude combat missions,"[302] it is in the naval area that U.S.-Indian military cooperation is possibly closest knit. Onwards from March 2002, the Indian Navy has escorted American ships in the Malacca Straits off Indonesia, the Andaman Sea and the South China Sea.[303] In October 2003, nearly 1,500 Indian and American sailors, accompanied by warships (and for the first time, submarines), played out scenarios involving "contraband control, anti-submarine maritime interdiction operations, air defense, counter-terrorism maneuvers and sea control operations. Cross defense flying or landing helicopters on each other's deck for familiarization; surface shoot, that is, firing at a target by the ship's surface guns; and UNREP (replenishment when the ships are under way) were also conducted jointly," with the aim, yet again, of "allowing the two navies to familiarize themselves with each other's operating philosophy and improve inter-operability."[304] The U.S. brought to this exercise some of its top naval assets: a Ticonderoga class cruiser, an Arleigh-Burke class destroyer, a Los Angeles class nuclear-powered submarine, and a 62,000-tonne tanker; two P3C-Orion long-range maritime patrol aircraft also took part. On their side, the Indians fielded a guided-missile frigate, a guided-missile destroyer, a diesel-electric powered submarine and a replenishment tanker, along with helicopters for anti-submarine exercises.

In early 2004, a closed-door meeting in Goa saw no fewer than 40 of America's and India's leading scientists explore ways to use science and technology to fight terrorism, including "cyber-terrorism, bio-terrorism, threats to nuclear facilities and other topics."[305] The political equivalent of that gathering took place in Herzliya, Israel, at the end of February, when Indian and American intelligence experts were joined in a so-called Trialogue by three Israeli cabinet ministers, the chairman of the Knesset Foreign Affairs and Defense Committee, the Commander of the Israeli Navy, and a former head of the Mossad intelligence agency.[306]

During the week of the Goa conclave, U.S. President George

Bush pledged to sharply intensify a "strategic partnership"[307] with India as part of what was described as a "groundbreaking pact on missile defense, nuclear safety and space technology."[308] Bush's announcement was made at the Summit of the Americas in Mexico, in tacit acknowledgment of India's emergence as a global player. Military sources have told this author that Indian Jaguar warplanes and aerial refuellers are due to be invited to participate at America's joint exercises with five NATO nations in Alaska in July 2004.

Notwithstanding such momentum, as a contentious democracy, India is by no means going to be a pliable ally. In spite of the seeming American desperation to secure Indian military participation in Iraq, India did not budge from its initial stance that it would do so only under UN authorization. Also, as noted earlier, India has made overtures to Iran to supply it with 'advanced military technology' in exchange for military bases in that country. Such self-interest is also evident in the sphere of international trade. After scuttling the Cancun talks of the World Trade Organization, India continues to lead a combined developing country bloc seeking to slash agricultural subsidies in the U.S. and the European Union.

India's engagement with the U.S. in the military sphere has also been guarded. For instance, the submarine it brought to their October 2003 joint naval exercises was one of its German-designed (but Indian-built) Type 209s. Absent, despite persistent U.S. requests, were any of the Indian Navy's fleet of Russian-built Type 877 EKM Kilo-class submarines, also called Black Holes "because of their noiseless operation."[309] The Indians, meanwhile, are also aware of greater American benefits from joint exercises in high-altitude warfare, jungle warfare and low-intensity conflict. According to an Indian instructor, "India has more to give away in this art of warfare than the Americans can." Others asked: "If we have not perfected our mountain warfare techniques in more than half a century of fighting in the worst terrains, then those Generals, who are advising the defense minister on offering of reciprocal facilities, must be naive if not irresponsible."[310]

Such calculating self-interest is present in India's agreement to join the U.S. 'missile defense' shield[311]—part of the broader Indo-U.S. pact on missile defense, nuclear safety and space technology announced by President Bush at the Summit of the Americas. As borne out by India's participation in Europe's Galileo project (and its success in developing the guidance system for the Indo-Russian Brahmos supersonic cruise missile), only the naive would believe that the country does not expect even more in return—namely, direct involvement in contributing to development of the software for the missile shield.

But the self-interest process is by no means confined to the military-political realms. Even in software, India's chosen field of world stardom, the country ejected the prestigious Massachusetts Institute of Technology from a flagship billion-dollar project, Media Lab Asia (a venture which, in the words of one observer, most countries would have 'killed for'). The Indians were upset about MIT's $5 million fee to use the Media Lab name, and claimed it had also run adrift from its pre-agreed development and social empowerment objectives, rather than simply churning out intellectual property.[312]

Such measured pragmatism does not mean India has abandoned all its once-lofty principles. While the West bends over on its knees to accommodate China,[313] an editorial in the *International Herald Tribune* calls for "a quiet, dignified note (to show) that we have not forgotten Tiananmen, or the Dalai Lama, or followers of Falun Gong, or any of the other victims of a system that is still undemocratic and oppressive."[314] The newspaper (like almost all coverage on Tibet in the world media) may have done well to also note that the Dalai Lama heads a government-in-exile in Dharamsala, India, and that India shelters and finances no fewer than "1.3 million Tibetan exiles,"[315] some of who too, like India itself, are now tired of "the stereotypical view of Tibetans as peace-loving monks."

Given the West's growing military-technological dependence on the country, on the one hand, and attempts by some to play India against China on the other, one pertinent topic is a recent book by General K. Padmanabhan, who retired as Indian army chief in 2003. Called *The Writing On The Wall: India Checkmates America 2017*, the book predicts a U.S.-India armed conflict late in the next decade, where, interestingly, China is on the Indian side.[316]

Shaking Up Stereotypes:
Reversing the Great Absence

The implications of India's emergence as a world military power remain feebly understood. As with Indian information technology, this is wholly the result of twisted, time-warped perceptions about India—from Gandhi, hippies and the Beatles, to castes, famines and poverty. In spite of some recent change in views, especially at the upper echelons of Western policy makers, there still is truth in what the Cato Institute observed in 2000—that many still see India as a "Third World, poverty-stricken giant" rather than "an emerging world power with an influence felt far from Asian shores."[317]

There are several examples, some striking, of this phenomenon, described previously as the Great Indian Absence. One is the commonplace reference that India "helped" Bangladesh in its 1971 war of Independence,[318] a misleading term, when one considers such 'help' involved sheltering 10 million refugees, one of post-World War II's largest airdrop of troopers, supported by artillery and bombers, and the surrender of 90,000 Pakistani combat troops. India's massive military engagement at the time is held up by the linguist, pacifist and noted critic of international affairs, Noam Chomsky, as one of just two cases for justified military force after the Second World War.[319]

In 1988, both India's quick reaction and force-projection capacities were illustrated after it reacted within hours to a coup d'etat in the Indian Ocean island of the Maldives by airlifting 400 commandos, backed by warplanes; the leaders of the coup were captured by Indian Navy warships, and jailed.

In 1999, during India's near-war with Pakistan on the Kargil peaks, the world media almost universally assumed (and reported) that it was U.S. President Bill Clinton's intervention which resulted in Kashmiri militants backing off.[320] The truth was somewhat different, and was exactly what India had stated all along. Rather than militants, the Kargil conflict involved Pakistani Army regulars; more pertinently, they were soon at the edge of defeat. Thus, in April 2000, a noted expert on Pakistan, British-based Tariq Ali, reported in the American journal the *Nation* that "after two months of fighting, the Clinton Administration persuaded Prime Minister Sharif to withdraw support for the militants."[321] Exactly one year later, Ali effortlessly turned 180 degrees. In the *London Review of*

Books, he wrote: "In the war-zone itself, India suffered initial reverses, then brought in more troops, helicopter gunships and fighter jets and began to bomb Pakistani installations across the border.... By May 1999, as the yellow roses were about to bloom, the Indian Army had retaken most of the ridges it had lost. A month later its forces were poised to cross the Line of Control. Pakistan's political leaders panicked and, falling back on an old habit, made a desperate appeal to the White House;"[322] an altogether opposite case from what he, like much of the world media, earlier suggested.

Whether under the United Nations flag or directly in its neighborhood, India has rarely been less than assertive, when the occasion has demanded it. Examples of this go back decades. As far back as 1961, an Indian-led UN mission saw the country's air force and army resolutely bring order into the fast-deteriorating political minefield of the Congo, where a panicking Belgian colonial government was fighting Congolese troops and irregulars, as well as heavily-armed mercenaries from Britain, France, Belgium and South Africa. The mission has been described as the "most difficult" and complicated peace-keeping mission "ever undertaken" by the UN,[323] but was achieved with complete professionalism; in an interview with the Institute of International Studies at Berkeley, veteran British diplomat Sir Brian Urquhart recalled the matter-of-fact manner in which Indian troops freed him after his kidnapping by Congolese secessionists.[324]

The habit of overlooking India is sometimes amusing. In 2000, for instance, Indian forces with the UN mounted a "classic example of joint Army-Air" assault on rebel forces in Sierra Leone in what Britain's *Air Forces Monthly* described as "the most resolute United Nations (UN) military action of recent decades."[325] The assault, in "extremely adverse weather conditions—incessant rain and low-cloud" involved 98 armed sorties by Indian gunships as well as helicopter transporters for troops and 105mm howitzers; on occasion, there was "only one meter clearance from the tips of the helicopter rotor blades." Backed by gunships and ground artillery, detachments from India's 8th Gurkha Rifles and 18th Grenadiers "successfully extricated 222 Indian troops"..."encircled and held hostage" by rebels. Also freed was "one British officer," Major Andrew Harrison. On July 16, 2000, as *Air Forces Monthly* noted, his photograph beamed from one of Britain's largest newspapers the *Sunday Times*, under the headline 'Daring Raid by British Troops Frees Hostages.'

Such instances might be funny. But the complex implications of miscalculating, underestimating, or being simply unaware, of, changing geopolitical realities, were best illustrated by the near-collapse of the government of Belgium in 2003—about the moral consequences of exporting a few thousand-odd machine guns to India's neighbour Nepal, fighting a Communist insurgency. Over several months, much of the Belgian print and TV media were near-surreally convulsed amidst their small country's exaggerated sense of self-importance. While the possibility of external military aid was confined to Europe's classic Big Brother the U.S. (or Britain), there were barely a handful of references to India and China; those that did, usually mentioned Nepal's geography, sandwiched as the country is between the two giants. Rather than the make-or-break implications of a consignment of small arms, no experts seemed aware about the real political issue (China and India), or the extent of heavy, high-technology weapons flooding in from India. As *Reuters* noted in late November: "Nepal's prime minister will ask his kingdom's biggest arms supplier (India) for more aid to help break a military stalemate with Maoist rebels.... Nepal's army desperately needs more helicopters for the mountainous region, as well as better communications and surveillance gear and night vision equipment.... India, anxious for a stable buffer state between it and China and keen to avoid trouble spreading among its own rebel groups in bordering areas, is Nepal's biggest arms supplier and has given counter-insurgency training to the army and donated helicopters."[326]

One however must not focus only on politicians and the media. In 1997, a highly-reputed military analyst, Eric Arnett, of the Stockholm International Peace Research Institute, was categorical in asserting that two domestic Indian warship programs—for the 'Delhi' class guided missile destroyer and the 'Brahmaputra' frigate—were definitely "suspended,"[327] insinuating that India lacked the capacity to go through with its ambitions. As it happens, both warships rolled out within just one year. While a Brahmaputra-class frigate was used by India in its October 2003 naval exercises with the U.S., plans by India to export 6,700 tonne Delhi-class destroyers (the other "suspended" program) could seriously shake up the balance of power in southeast Asia, as explained previously.

In May 1998, when India 'stunned' and 'shocked' the world

with its series of nuclear tests, few Western newspapers noted the key issue: India's first nuclear test was in 1974, and rather than international agreements which it had consistently refused to sign, India was simply breaking a 24-year old self-imposed moratorium on tests, as its newly-elected government had promised in its campaign. The jacket of American scholar George Perkovich's seminal work 'India's Nuclear Bomb' observes simply: India departed from "decades of nuclear restraint, a control that no other nations with similar capacities had displayed."[328]

More pertinent than this kind of media oversight were other reactions, even helpful ones. Thus, pressed by its farm export lobby, the U.S. Congress partially lifted post-test sanctions for 'humanitarian reasons,' in order to allow "India and Pakistan" to buy wheat. But, generally unknown to Congress, India was, as explained previously, uninterested in American wheat. It was already the world's second largest producer of wheat, on its way to record a bumper 76.4 million tonne harvest of wheat[329] (compared to the U.S.'s 65 million tonnes) and was instead seeking to export millions of tonnes of its own surpluses to Africa, the Middle East and central Asia; as mentioned previously, Indian foodgrain exports in 2003 reached 5 million tonnes.

Such examples of the Great Indian Absence have been cited at length for two reasons. First, whether in Africa or its Southeast Asian neighborhood, the impact of emerging India is going to be a lot louder than it was previously, and even soporific Western journalists will find this difficult to ignore. More relevant, however, to the white-collar relocation debate is another factor: it is precisely such a Great Indian Absence, which underlines reactions to India's seemingly-sudden emergence as a threat to technology jobs. Thus, a recent collection of essays on the American downturn dated between December 1997 and March 2003 by New York Times columnist and one of the Bush administration's foremost critics, Paul Krugman, makes no reference to India in either a heading or the index.[330]

As the year 2003 turned, and the flurry of peace initiatives in south Asia underlined that Pakistan may have finally accepted the pointlessness of seeking equivalence with an 'arch-rival' eight times its size[331] (one can think of Belgium and Germany, or Canada and the US), we can still read a compilation of yesterday's wisdom from U.S.-based Control Risks Group, in its forecast for 2004: "Tensions between new U.S. allies Pakistan and India can be expected to rise again in the spring with the thawing of the Kashmir snows."[332] This is poignant, when one considers a letter to the *New York Times* questioning the jobs drift to India and other 'unstable' countries: "Not very long ago, it was feared that India and Pakistan, among the potential providers of labor, would fire nuclear weapons at each other."[333]

Indeed, given the increasingly shaky nature of Pakistan, the likelihood of another volley of distractions by that perennially near-failing State (already by 1999 bailed out 17 times by the IMF[334]) will accompany the 'thawing of the snows' for some years. India's steady ascension will however bring home one fact to even the most recalcitrant experts. The Pakistani experiment, like that of East Germany built around a 'separated' but exclusivistic national identity, is condemned to self-limitation. Home now to more Muslims than its Islamic neighbour,[335] India's conflicts with Pakistan do not only involve differences of religion, but also those of culture and outlook—between sectarianism and secularism, between medievalism and modernity, ideology and pragmatism. It is therefore hardly surprising that in a forward-looking field like IT, Pakistan's software industry is no more than a flea on its rival Elephant's hide—as explained earlier, annually exporting the equivalent of one (working) day's worth out of India, a share of 0.5 percent; this is the case too with several other civilian sectors, from automobiles to pharmaceuticals.

In spite of their common history, Pakistan has not managed to harness the free-thinking and sometimes irreverent, tradition-threatening characteristics of the Internet and the New Economy, as has India—described, for example, in a feature on changing Indian 'values' in the *International Herald Tribune* at the end of February 2003.[336] More indicative may be another little-noticed statistic. Although their parents have similar social backgrounds, *the Guardian* reported on May 11, 2000 that children in the U.K. "from Indian families are outperforming white children in exams. But black, Pakistani and Bangladeshi pupils do less well."

As illustrated in the next chapter by the presence of elected, IT-championing Communist governments in India, such issues—on modernity and pragmatism, history and the future, change and resistance—have significant implications for relocation.

CHAPTER VI

Back to the Future

The Indian Context

Arguments against globalization often focus on the idea that the U.S. and the wider West are continuously exploiting the Third World, a kind of homogenous entity, in a somewhat static relationship immortalized in the 1970s by German Chancellor Willy Brandt's concept of North and South. While certain elements of such a view (and by no means just a few) may be true, the process is neither simple nor is it merely a zero-sum game.

In the broadest terms, countries like India and China are clear net beneficiaries of globalization, even if there are (and will continue to be) regions and population sections within the two countries that benefit less than others. University of Texas economist James Galbraith explains it: "The income gap between rich and poor societies is widening, not narrowing. 'The real world is one of rising inequality and—outside China and India—zero per capita growth.'"[1]

Indeed, as demonstrated by the growing exodus of white-collar jobs to India (and manufacturing jobs to China), the two countries have begun to benefit more from globalization than do segments (and sometimes entire regions) of Western industrialized economies. Given the size of India's and China's populations, their 150-year struggle against poverty, and their still very low incomes relative to the West, such a trade-off seems hardly undesirable, above all, to more than 2 billion Indians and Chinese, who are pulling the process.

But the process will go further. In the longer term, the inescapable result of relocation—and one of its key drivers—will be a leveling down of vast global differences in incomes and living standards. This not only benefits India and China (as it seems to be); given some of the wider structural challenges from the two giants to the Western-dominated global trading system, it may also benefit countries like Haiti and Gabon, Indonesia and others.

In turn, the leveling down would also lead to the elimination of the more extreme differences in wages and costs of living, and reduce the incentive in the future for violent processes of relocation- from the U.S. and Europe, or from whatever country/countries replace them as the value-centers of the world economy over the next decades. India and China, of course, look most like becoming such replacements.

The root of much of the debate about relocation involves a question of national identity—displacing a job from one country to another. Given the scope of India's otherwise-unexpected pull on Western white-collar jobs, it may be helpful to consider where India is coming from, and some of its more-unusual contexts, implications and consequences.

Is 200 Years of History Reversing for 5,000-Year Civilizations?

For both India and China, globalization's benefits involve as much a relative rise, as a return, to their previous historical status— and one really not so long ago, given their 5,000-year long histories. The two countries see themselves as victims of a previous cycle of 'globalization,' namely European colonialism, and its child, the modern Western system. This cycle was accompanied by a precipitous decline from their status in the 19th century, when India and China accounted for almost half of the world's economic output.

Robert Radtke explains this in the *International Herald Tribune.*" "Both (China and India) see themselves as great powers fallen on bad times centuries ago, but well on their way back to reclaiming their rightful places as preeminent nations."[2] The writer also warns: "China and India think in terms of generations, not quarterly results."

Roger Bootle, an economic adviser to consultants Deloitte, endorses Radtke. "By the early 19th century," he writes, "although India had already begun its long relative decline and the U.K. its long relative ascent, India's economy was still some three times the size of Britain's. Once I had grasped it, this fact immediately solved something that had puzzled me for years, namely how could the conquest of India have meant so much for Britain?"[3]

Bootle would have benefited earlier from such insights had he accompanied Robert Clive, who became the first representative in India of King George III. Clive, whose "plunder" of a "staggering" treasure from India was auctioned in Britain in early 2004,[4] remarked that the Indian city of Murshidabad was "as extensive, populous, and rich as the city of London, with the difference that there are individuals in the first possessing infinitely greater property than the last."

Others have perceived why India was the 'Jewel' in Britain's crown well before Bootle. In 1908, the American journal *Atlantic Monthly* published a statement by Lord Curzon, then Viceroy of India: "Powerful Empires existed and flourished here (in India) while Englishmen were still wandering painted in the woods, and while the British Colonies were a wilderness and a jungle." India, said Curzon "has left a deeper mark upon the history, the philosophy, and the religion of mankind, than any other terrestrial unit in the universe."

More significant than the Indian Jewel's luster were the links between what Bootle called the ascent of Britain and the 'long relative decline' of India. According to historian Mike Davis,[5] in the last half of 19th century, India's income fell by 50 percent, and in the 190 years prior to independence in 1947, its economy literally experienced zero growth. Between 1872 and 1921, he writes, life expectancy fell by 20 percent. A 1938 report by the International Labor Organization (ILO) on 'Industrial Labor in India' reveals that longevity in India was barely 25 years in 1921 (compared to 55 for England), and fell further to 23 in 1931.

The 1908 issue of the *Atlantic Monthly* also debunked a still-lingering myth, that Britain 'gave' India its education system. It noted the lead of several Indian princely states (which were independent of Britain) "in the important matter of popular education. Mysore is spending on education more than three times as much per capita as is British India, while Baroda has made her education free and compulsory."[6]

Historians will no doubt remain divided on how much Britain 'gave' and how much it 'took' from India, and the link between British supremacy in India and its impact on Europe and the world beyond. They will also continue to argue about setting standards for such 'relative' equivalences.

In the face of this, a new constituency—both within today's India and abroad—has begun to simplify the terms of the debate. Instead of 'exploitation' in the pure sense of the term, it may be argued, Britain's presence simply served to keep India out of the Industrial Revolution. One good example of such rethinking, reported in the *Los Angeles Times*, is that, rather than "an insulated civilization overripe for colonial picking and conquest," India was a commercially, culturally and militarily-advanced one, "in many respects more advanced and refined" than Britain's, and which had therefore to be won over "from the inside."[7]

Tuning in to Patents, Cultural and Historical Theft: Lessons from the Hijacking of the Fashion Runway

Such a degree of 'advancement,' even if eclipsed, does not vanish. There is now a growing belief that the tide is reversing, among others, in areas evidently connected to India's historical and cultural prominence. Defining such a process, of course, is India's rise in software, but it is by no means limited to this.

One good example is the fashion industry, a particularly relevant one given the serious damage done by the British Empire to India's world-pioneering textiles industry. For the *New York Times*: "Considering that it is the country historically credited with giving the world paisley, seersucker, calico, chintz, cashmere, crewel and the entire technique of printing on cloth, it is anybody's guess why India barely registers on the global map of fashion."[8] It really may not be just a guess, as the newspaper itself acknowledges, quoting the wife of a former American ambassador to India: "Western designers have been coming to India and 'borrowing' for 50 years." However, the Ambassador's wife also described how India was getting set to reverse this, and again make its mark on global fashion. Confirming this, in December 2003, India's IT capital Bangalore became one of 12 cities named by American magazine *Newsweek* as "the world's top hot spots for design."[9]

Other instances of this reversal of the historical tide have been mentioned previously: the acquisition by an Indian firm of Britain's tea market leader Tetley, a classic flagship of the colonial era, where, like textiles, the British relocated value-addition homewards; or Britain's MG automotive brand now depending for survival on an Indian-designed car. More such reversals will inevitably emerge in the years ahead.

On its part, a newly assertive India has also successfully resisted efforts to continue pirating its ancient know-how, in areas such as traditional medicine and agriculture. It has fought legal battles against efforts by W.R Grace to patent the neem pesticide,[10] against RiceTec of Texas—over basmati rice[11] and against a patent on turmeric for wound care.[12] While encouraging promising efforts— such as those by Rochester's Wilmot Cancer Center or the Anderson Cancer Center in Texas—to investigate traditional Indian remedies for diseases such as colon cancer, radiation burns, multiple myeloma and Alzheimer's,[13] India—named by the *New York Times* as "probably the largest victim" of such piracy with "2,000 or 3,000 cases of misappropriation"—is also making sure it will not have to pay for fighting fraudulent patent claims by publishing the resources of its millennia-old Ayurveda health system on the Internet.[14]

Such assertiveness and (technology-leveraged) pre-emption will surely underpin some elements of a sophisticated Indian riposte to secure its place in the white-collar relocation stakes.

It would also contrast dramatically with what may be one of the world's most brazen instances of intellectual piracy—namely the use and lack of attribution by Italy's Nobel Prize winning scientist, Guglielmo Marconi, of an Indian scientist's know-how in a path-breaking invention at the turn of the 20th century, the radio. After decades of controversy, the respected international journal *Science* noted in 1998, "It now appears the coherer used in (Marconi's) famous transmission was invented and published from Calcutta in the British Proceedings of the Royal Society 1899 by (Indian) biol-ogist and physicist Jagadish Chandra Bose, who was never men-tioned later by the Europeans, never acknowledged by Marconi, and who probably ought to have shared the Nobel Prize in Physics with Marconi and Braun in 1909." Bose, who was also "a pioneer of mil-limetric wave research, and developed the first solid-state diode in 1899," did not protest and is portrayed as "uninterested in the commercialization of scientific inventions."[15]

The best example of such rethinking about history, however, goes to the heart of post-World War II identities, and touches upon a delicate subject—one, where the ugliness of the Great Indian Absence extends to the school books of every American or European child. As Kevin Meyers observed in Britain's *Daily Telegraph*, just before Remembrance Day celebrations in November 2003:

> In all the acts of remembrance today, who will remember the greatest volunteer army for freedom the world has ever seen?...
>
> The Burma campaign was fought and won in large part by Indian troops.... But what is more surprising, and even more unforgivable, is the vital role of the Indians in defeating the Nazis has almost vanished entirely from the public imagination.
>
> Tens of thousands of Indian troops served in the war against Hitler's Germany and Mussolini's Italy. The 4th Indians—one of the very finest divisions of any allied army—restored independence to Abyssinia, and from first to last participated in the battles against and the victory over Rommel's Afrika Korps and Italy's 10th and 15th Armies. After victory in Africa, the next stage was the mainland of Europe: and three full Indian divisions served in the brutal, bloody liberation of Italy.
>
> For some, this was a return to Europe; Indian troops had served in France in 1940, and now they took part in some of the most savage, bloody fighting of the entire war....
>
> Why did they serve? For economic reasons, mostly—but having taken a soldier's oath, they clung to it, unto death if necessary: and not just the fabled Gurkhas and Sikhs, but also the Rajputs, Pathans, Punjabis, Garwhalis, Jats, Ranghars and Dogras. Had British military historians not so disgracefully neglected the achievements of these men, usually in order to focus on the more accessible accounts of British units, their story might be better known. For who now remembers that the mighty battle of Kohima, which gave rise to the most unforgettable memorial dedication of the war ('When you go home, tell them of us...'), was essentially won by the 33rd Indian Corps?[16]

Of Arabic Numbers, Nalanda University, Backus-Normal and Panini

As Indians and others tune into recapturing India's immense historical presence, some argue that the country's emergence as a global force in software is simply fed by what French philosopher Henri Bergson called an 'Èlan vital' or vital spirit—as the birthplace of mathematics and several other sciences, including medicine.[17] Few still are indeed aware of the sheer magnitude of the highly structured breakthroughs made in that country a thousand years before Europe.

American software guru Capers Jones is one exception. He describes India's ancient Nalanda University (founded in the 5th century BC) as "the largest in the world for more than 1,200 years," with "a scientific curriculum that would not be far behind contemporary universities."[18]

It is now generally accepted that 'Arabic numerals' are really 'Indian' and, as explained in depth by Denis Guedj of the University of Paris, India invented the "wonderful system" of the zero and positional notation, as well as the decimal system.[19] Still to be widely understood are the massive advances made by ancient India in areas such as advanced number theory, negative numbers, computational mathematics, algebra and trigonometry. These not only laid the foundations for modern science and technology, but were in many cases simply 'rediscovered' in Europe. It does not, of course, require effort to recognize that the Industrial Revolution, let alone the New Economy, may not have got very far with Roman numerals.

British researchers at the University of St. Andrews in Scotland have studied this subject at considerable length. "It is without doubt," they state, "that mathematics today owes a huge debt to the outstanding contributions made by Indian mathematicians over many hundreds of years. What is quite surprising is that there has been a reluctance to recognize this.... Quite a few results of Indian mathematicians have been rediscovered by Europeans. For instance, the development of number theory, the theory of indeterminates, infinite series expressions for sine, cosine and tangent, computational mathematics, etc...." They provide other 'rediscovered' examples: "a formula for the ecliptic; the Newton-Gauss interpolation formula; the formula for the sum of an infinite series; Lhuilier's formula for the circumradius of a cyclic quadrilateral."[20]

Two of the St. Andrews' research papers concern the 5th century Indian mathematician and astronomer Aryabhata, and Brahmagupta, who lived two centuries later. Aryabhata calculated

'pi' to the 8th decimal place (3.14159265) and valued "the length of
the year at 365 days 6 hours 12 minutes 30 seconds," remarkably
close to the current figure of 365 days 5 hours, 48 minutes and 46.5
seconds. More strikingly, over 500 years before Copernicus and
Galileo, Aryabhata also "believed that the apparent rotation of the
heavens was due to the axial rotation of the Earth," that "the Moon
and planets shine by reflected sunlight,"..."that the orbits of the
planets are ellipses" and "correctly" explained "the causes of eclipses
of the Sun and the Moon."[21]

Brahmagupta, who headed an astronomical Observatory at
Ujjain in the 7th century, contributed the following: "mean longitudes of the planets; true longitudes of the planets; the three problems of diurnal rotation; lunar eclipses; solar eclipses; risings and settings; the moon's crescent; the moon's shadow; conjunctions of the
planets with each other; and conjunctions of the planets with the
fixed stars." He extended arithmetic to "negative numbers and the
zero", developed an "algorithm for computing square roots"—which
is shown to be "equivalent to the Newton-Raphson iterative formula"—and solved "quadratic indeterminate equations." Also developed by Brahmagupta fourteen centuries ago was "an interpolation
formula to compute values of sines" and "formulas for the area of a
cyclic quadrilateral and for the lengths of the diagonals in terms of
the sides."[22]

In the specific field of computer programming, such arguments
become truly striking. According to another paper from St.
Andrews, Panini (an Indian grammarian who lived in the 5th century BC and compiled 4,000 rules and metarules of Sanskrit) "should
be thought of as the forerunner of the modern formal language theory used to specify computer languages." Though the Backus-
Normal Form was discovered independently by John Backus in
1959, Panini's notation, say the British researchers, "is equivalent in
its power to that of Backus and has many similar properties. It is
remarkable to think that concepts which are fundamental to today's
theoretical computer science should have their origin with an
Indian genius around 2,500 years ago,"[23] the paper concludes.

These remarkable achievements are of little utilitarian value
today, having long been eclipsed by subsequent work. But they provide a strong source of teleological confidence to a rebounding

India. For foreigners in particular, an important issue to take note of is India's continuity as a culture, grasped by some viewers of Vedic rites at Banaras, such as American writer Mark Twain, who described the city as being "older than history, older than tradition, older even than legend, and looks twice as old as all of them put together"; unlike ancient Greece and Egypt, Babylon or the Incas and Mayas, India's customs, cultural practices and expectations, have changed little over the past five or six thousand years.[24]

While past glories are one thing, India—clearly emerging from its historical eclipse—is also increasingly aware that one of the reasons for this was its caste-fragmented innards. Economically and militarily, but above all socially and politically, re-emerging India is clearly seeking to address such weaknesses.

In turn, the country's unique development pathways can reveal much about not only its eventually formidable nature as a global competitor but also how to learn from it, and effectively respond.

From Hellhole to Future Global Model: Touching Lives With High-Tech

One topic previously discussed is the impact of the 250-300 million strong Indian middle class, who pull the country's modernization. But recent developments have begun to go further, and deeper. Here too, there is a specific Indian context to the process of change under way, in terms of harnessing technology as a powerful engine for social and political empowerment. Through this, not just the middle class, but the rest of the country, another 700-750 million strong, are participating and becoming stakeholders in the future. Such ambitious experiments have never been attempted before, and their results—within a relatively short period of just one decade—though still largely unseen, may already be remarkable.

U.S. President Bill Clinton's visit in the year 2000 marked a high point for demonstrating India's success in imaginatively leveraging technology for development goals, involving a living, working model with hugely-positive synergies between private- and public-sector firms, NGOs, as well as the federal and provincial governments. The Indian effort in using high-technology for potentially sweeping results in mass empowerment, often on what are shoestring budgets, will demolish a clutch of pontificating 'either-or' clichés and carries lessons both for other developing countries as well as the West.

Commenting on an e-literacy program in India's Kerala state, Kenneth Keniston, Andrew Mellon Professor of Human Development at MIT, observed that out of the 210 member States at the UN, he knew of "no country or government" that had made such a commitment.[25] The efforts are also dramatic, even if unnoticed, in sometimes-unexpected realms. For example, an Indian NGO-led computer-training program for women inmates at Asia's largest jail, Tihar, is the kind of initiative credited for its transformation, according to *Time* magazine in December 2001, from a "hellhole to a global model for prison reform."

During his India tour in early 2000, Clinton was visibly impressed by his ability to obtain a driving license online, as well as an all-women's computerized cooperative deep in rural Rajasthan which had made its members "one of the richest milk producers in the state."[26] Such trends were, however, only the tip of the iceberg. The empowerment process had already gone beyond simply enamoring Clinton, and was continuing to gather force. In certain cases, it already involved some of the world's most sophisticated technologies.

Back in 1999, *Space News* commented: "For over 10 years, India's Earth-pointing space cameras have helped farmers sow their fields, fishermen cast their nets, city planners design new towns, and navigators move around the sea." Using its satellites, the country "can now prevent the destruction that millions of locusts cause throughout India's western states.... And in the coastal areas, tens of thousands of fishermen have been trained to read color satellite images of the ocean to pick the best locations and times to unfurl their nets.... In Rajasthan, where deserts sprawl, villagers have had to walk up to 25 kilometers to find potable water. India's remote sensing satellites have eliminated that distance in 60 villages by finding untapped well sites within town limits."[27]

Since then, even as it continued to lay the foundations for its emergence as a global software power, democratic India was also using its fast-growing expertise (and revenues from the white-collar job relocation process) to harness the IT revolution to further touch the lives of its billion-strong population.

On August 28, 2001, Britain's *Financial Times* commented on the e-government experience of one pioneering Indian state, Andhra Pradesh, which by then had already built a high-speed broadband network, providing real-time connection of the State administrative headquarters with all major cities and as many as 1,100 rural administrative blocks:

> A network of computerised one-stop shops...will enable 'customers' to clear 18 separate bureaucratic hurdles in one visit. Services on offer...will include payment of utility bills, applications for driving licences and passports and the registration of property. Up to now most bureaucratic procedures were a nightmare because they had to be conducted in person. Previously, transferring a title deed, for example, could take months or even years. Now, according to the state government, the process will take an average of one hour.

The project met its targets and was steadily extended over the next two years to no less than 30 services,[28] including tax payments, phone bills, electricity and water connections, property statements, birth and death certificates, several forms of banking, and in early 2004, to online medical consultation. Among other mediums, e-government services have begun to be delivered through Internet-enabled touch-screen kiosks in rural heartlands, of which 6,000 are being established in the state of Andhra Pradesh alone.[29]

Numerous other Indian States have also begun to set up similar schemes, as well as a host of other IT empowerment initiatives, from education to crime prevention and farming support, as a sample in Table IV shows. Such a process is driven further by (informal but powerful) inter-State competition within India's multi-party federal system for attainment of targets and milestones, and its dynamics have become irreversible.

As a result, India may be showing a way out from one of the most recalcitrant challenges for development in the Third World, namely the rural-urban divide. True, it will be several years before the benefits become tangible, but the Internet's novelties are being used to provide the strongest-possible foundations for long-term rural empowerment—above all, by whittling down the role of (city-based) middlemen, as well as village money lenders and political touts. In Andhra Pradesh, an online tendering system for government contracts has, for example, yielded savings of 6 billion rupees within just one year of its launch; much of this would have mutated into kickbacks, involving contractors from all sides of the political spectrum. In this respect, more than his familiarity with Bill Gates, Andhra Pradesh's trailblazing 'Laptop' Chief Minister Chandrababu Naidu deserves to be congratulated.

In spite of the electoral risks from his growing unpopularity in rural areas of the state, Naidu has stuck to his vision: investing in the imaginative use of new technologies, and harnessing India's world-class but cost-effective technical skills, may—for the first time any-where—offer wholly new ways to address the seemingly intractable challenges of both under-development and poverty. This, as we shall learn from examples in the rest of this chapter, may possibly be the only way to provide real foundations for achieving such goals durably—more durably than the time-tested pap of populist Third World politicians promising 'free' electricity, other freebies and a perennially-magical reversal of under-development. The INR 6 billion rupee savings referred to above is 'real' money for state investment in education, healthcare, or even 'free' electricity.

Table IV: Examples of Internet Empowerment Initiatives in Indian States

Andhra Pradesh

- Following the growing success of its E-Seva e-government scheme, the State has computerized its entire transport network of 212 bus depots and implemented a GPS-equipped 'Real Time Information System.' Other states such as Maharashtra are also following by equipping their transport fleets with GPS.

Bihar

- The E-Swashthya (e-health) project is providing smart cards to agricultural workers carrying "their entire health history, which can be accessed at local community health centers."

Karnataka

- Karnataka has digitized 17 million land records, and handwritten deeds "are no longer valid." It also became the first state in which all police stations are connected through computers and crime-related information is accessible online round the clock; two other states, Gujarat and Maharashtra, are close on the heels of Karnataka, in this effort.

Kerala

- Akshaya digital literacy project. The aim is to equip at least one member of the State's 6.4 million families with ICT literacy. 9,000 centers will provide 6 Mb/s connectivity across the State—with access points within 2 kilometers from even the remotest household.

Madhya Pradesh

- Gyandoot E-literacy program seeks to replicate Kerala's Akshaya (see above).

Maharashtra

- Warana 'wired village project' provides farmers access to individualized information such as optimal time for planting and harvesting, current market rates for their produce and payments made by factories. Warana links up to the federal MANAGE program for online weather forecasts, market prices for seeds, fertilisers, implements, government credit and subsidy schemes, practice packages, organic farming, plant protection, farm machinery etc. The aim is to enable farmers to make informed decisions on choice of crop, hold on to stock when prices are low, and buy inputs at best rates. The main benefit will be the elimination of middlemen.

Pondicherry
- Establishment of 'knowledge centers' in each village has enabled online access to commodity prices, government entitlement schemes and even real-time prediction of wave heights for fishermen in coastal areas.

Tamil Nadu
- E-literacy program has already covered "80 percent of the Government Higher Secondary Schools."

The federal government, too, has been active in efforts to leverage IT and is spending $2.7 billion towards bridging the digital divide. The government has, above all, been instrumental in providing e-empowerment projects with their key communications and satellite backbones.

Federal projects have also established frameworks for State efforts. For example, Karnataka's Internet-enabling of its crime information system (see Table IV) will interface into a nationwide biometrics-based facial recognition system under development for the federal government.[30] Likewise with efforts such as the Warana wired village agro-Internet project in Maharashtra, which would back into a round-the-clock, free-of-charge network of call-centers for farmers to query multi-lingual agricultural science graduates "trained to troubleshoot farming problems."[31]

Federal IT initiatives also aim to enhance the efficiency of the country's revving-up economic machine. After computerizing the reservation system of its railways (the world's largest, carrying 5 billion passengers a year), the Indian government stepped-up a program for purchasing rail tickets, both on the Internet and via mobile phones.[32] The speed of such initiatives is impressive. On the same day the Internet/mobile telephone railway-ticketing initiative was announced in late January 2004, the government also launched an online system for the country's entire foreign trade paperwork, via a new encrypted digital signature and electronic funds facility.[33]

As India prepares to launch the world's first dedicated satellites for telemedicine, disaster management and education, its space program is already yielding benefits in new areas.[34] Data from an ongoing satellite-fed geographical information system (GIS) project helped Indian health workers to vaccinate 98 million children against polio in just one day. The *Associated Press* noted this was the "largest immunization drive ever against the disease."[35]

Beyond Zero-Sum Debates and White Elephants

One enabler for the success of Indian e-government initiatives, as discussed previously, consists of Internet-enabled touch-screen kiosks in rural areas. Such kiosks are widely considered a 'silver bullet' to bridge the digital divide[36] and the Indian government is paying for converting the country's 900,000-strong stock of public call-offices into kiosks. The target for achieving this is the end of 2005.

Most such call-offices are privately owned. For the *Washington Post*, the zero-sum debate of investing in information technology, or education and health services, has been "rendered irrelevant by turning over the job of connecting rural India to the Internet to profit-minded entrepreneurs."[37] Others too have hailed such synergies. U.S.-based Digital Partners, for example, finds the strength of the public-private partnership in kiosks a key reason for India's huge e-governance lead over other developing countries. As it states: "in Latin America commercial ICT centers developed by the private sector are a healthy business" but "they don't often succeed in reaching the poor."[38]

Telemedicine provides another excellent example of mature, early-stage coordination between India's private and public sectors, for both maximizing reach and providing long-term economic sustainability. In the 1990s, the Indian military's permanent mission in Antarctica demonstrated the country's already-impressive capabilities in telemedicine; since then, India's National Telemedicine Network[39] has been quickly accessed by private hospitals, and, following the forthcoming launch of a dedicated telemedicine satellite, "nearly 600,000 villages will be able to consult specialist doctors in the cities through live video."[40] Several of these projects have already gone live, such as one run out of the Bangalore-based Narayana Hrudayalaya hospital which, according to a *BBC News* report, consists of "13 satellite video links with distant hospitals within India" and to places such as Malaysia and Mauritius, Tanzania, Bangladesh "and even Pakistan."[41] The telemedicine program is not only provided free to parts of far-flung rural India, but also to the Bangalore prison, described by *BBC News* as "a highly unusual jail: it already has a video link-up with the law courts so the inmates' cases and appeals can be heard without them being transferred."[42] Other private hospitals too are plugging into the opportunity, in some cases directly interfacing with State empowerment schemes. In February 2004, for example, Apollo Hospitals decided to offer live consultations at 37 kiosks connected to the Andhra Pradesh e-government system.[43]

More Bucks for the Broadband Bang

As evidenced by its space program, unlike much of the developing world, India's high-tech autonomy permits affording otherwise prohibitively expensive, long-term 'social' goals. Few developing countries, for instance, could obtain the kind of low-cost 6 Mb/second broadband connectivity integral to the success of the Akshaya digital literacy program in the Indian state of Kerala, the subject of MIT Professor Kenneth Keniston's adulation. Using another measure, 85 percent of India's 650,000 villages and 700 million people already have potential access to broadband through a homegrown telecoms technology called CorDECT, which is discussed later.[44] Such lessons, learned within the Indian context, have obvious relevance for other developing countries.

But India's billowing electronic infrastructure goes beyond rural empowerment to making other areas of public life more efficient, and less vulnerable to corruption. Several States are already deploying the Internet for school examinations. In Maharashtra, for example, a pilot project has extended this capability to 18,000 students; interestingly, just 4,000 of these were in the metropolitan city of Mumbai.[45] The number is expected to rise dramatically in the near future, and has quickly spread beyond the State.

India's Wi-Fi infrastructure too has begun to bloom. Given its status as the country's IT capital, Bangalore took an early lead, followed soon after by arch-rival Hyderabad. However, several other cities have followed suit, as have universities; in February 2004, the

University of Pune became India's first to have its entire 414-acre campus ("roads, departments, hostel rooms, canteen and library") Wi-Fi enabled.[46] In Kashmir, the tourist hotspot of Dal Lake staked a claim in late 2003 to be the world's first Wi-Fi lake.

Healthy synergies in separate efforts by private and public sectors are apparent in India's fast-growing broadband infrastructure, which by mid-2002 already covered 85 percent of the country.[47] State-run Indian Railways (which has already begun offering Internet connectivity on some of its trains) is upgrading its huge 62,900 km network with STM1 and STM4 grade broadband (offering data and voice on the same channel); this is connecting 200 towns across the country.[48]

Meanwhile, Indian conglomerate Reliance Industries completed its own 60,000-km countrywide optic fiber backbone project,[49] and announced the "largest infrastructure and services rollout in the information and communications sector by any new entrant anywhere in the world." Reliance has a powerful supporter, in the form of the Indian government, which needs its help (as well as that of other private operators) to invest an estimated $12 billion in telecoms infrastructure required to support 100 million Indian cell phone users by December 2005.[50] By the end of 2004, Reliance expects its newly launched CDMA mobile phone subscribers alone to leap to 25 million, trebling its market share within just one year.[51]

The Reliance network also supports a countrywide network of consumer 'Webstores' (800-strong by the end of 2003), offering a swathe of broadband services such as "video conferencing, video chat, digital movies and download of digital music",[52] as well as low-cost data, PABX and VPN services directed at households and small businesses.[53] In October 2003, Reliance extended its infrastructural reach to a global scale, after acquiring the undersea optic-fiber cable operator Flag Telecom; as mentioned previously, the 50,000km Flag network connects key business markets in Asia, Europe, the Middle East and the U.S.

Profits from high-value international customers will allow Reliance to continue cross-subsidizing its target markets, up until today's poor will begin to afford higher tariffs, provide a volume boost to the company's bottom-line, and join the next wave of India's middle class. In effect, Reliance will live up to the dream of its founder that mobile phones "should be cheaper than a postcard so that even the poorest of the poor can reap the rich dividends of the technology revolution."[54]

Such developments, especially in terms of giving India multiplying advantages in the global high-technology stakes, have not gone unnoticed. Gene B. Sperling, chairman of former U.S. President Clinton's National Economic Council, has called for the American government to subsidize "the kind of infrastructure expansions that are heavily underwritten by the governments of India and China. 'One may not be able to control whether wages are lower in Bangalore than Buffalo, but you could make sure broadband access isn't better there,' he said."[55]

Made in India:
IT Solutions For the World's Digital Divide

As much as political will, know-how at the top of the high-tech chain (fed by both its drive for autonomy and by the relocation process) are also instrumental in India's accumulating strengths. For example, the data warehouse in the Andhra Pradesh e-government system is hosted on an Indian Param supercomputer. But aside from Param, three other innovative, cost-effective, high-technology solutions from India may offer solutions to address some of the chronic problems of the Third World.

At the end of 2001, the *New York Times* credited the year's "most significant innovation in computer technology" to be the Simputer, an Indian Linux-based, Internet-enabled, portable and technologically state-of-the-art but still inexpensive computer, "intended to bring the computer revolution to the third world." The Simputer translates "English-language Web sites into local Indian languages, reading the content aloud to illiterate users."[56] The outcome of a joint government-private sector effort, the Simputer is now being plugged into India's Internet-enabled public communications infrastructure. Among the Simputer's commercial applications are its use as a handheld solution for electricity billing in the state of Karnataka[57] and in Kerala's Akshaya digital literacy program.[58]

Another such success story—with huge potential for developing countries—is India's homegrown corDECT wireless-in-local-loop technology from Midas Communication, which leverages know-how acquired from the country's e-governance projects. corDECT telephone exchanges, developed by a team at one of the Indian Institutes of Technology, have already found markets in 10 countries—"South Africa, Nigeria, Kenya, Russia, Brazil, Argentina, Madagascar, Fiji, the Philippines, and Indonesia"[59]—but could clearly go much further. Though less fast than GSM or CDMA, corDECT's key advantage is sustainability of speed, a key issue for transmission conditions common to developing countries. Midas has since come up with yet another solution called optima, which is a fiber-in-local-loop system for ISDN and broadband services, again without being hampered by infrastructural bottlenecks common to developing countries.

The third technology solution with direct relevance for developing countries is a wholly computer-based adult literacy program developed after a four-year effort by researchers at Indian IT giant TCS. The "novel scheme," to quote *BBC News*,[60] teaches "whole words rather than individual letters," imparting recognition of "pictures and images, so each word is taught as a picture." To bring adults to functional literacy with such a system, requires just "10 weeks before they could read a paper," and costs merely $2.20 per person.

The TCS computer literacy initiative includes five Indian languages, and another 13 are planned, again indicating that India's own New Economy is not simply the preserve of the country's English-speaking elite. Instead, it parallels efforts by the likes of Microsoft, Oracle, Adobe and others (who have all developed Indian-language versions of their software) as well as initiatives like Thamizha (an Open Source Internet browser and Open Office suite in Tamil)[61] and the Indian government's C-DAC (developer of the Param supercomputer), whose Graphics and Intelligence Script Technology (GIST) has led to Indian-language and -script interfaces for a full range of applications.[62]

While such grassroots efforts will impact in democratic India, they also need to be urgently taken account of for use elsewhere by NGOs, developing country governments and international development organizations such as the World Bank. More than just being a possible model for beneficial globalization, India's experience with technology-led empowerment provides both suitable and tested tools for propagation in other developing countries. Indeed, such uniquely new social/high-technology paradigms may very well mean that the Elephant is sitting on a New Third World Thing.

Such a possibility is in fact acknowledged by some sections of the world media. In October 2003, the *Washington Post* reported: "In many ways, India is the perfect laboratory for adapting the Internet to development needs, bringing together abundant technological expertise with an estimated 700 million people in 600,000 rural villages."[63]

And Beyond the Third World...

As Chapter II explains, Indian hospitals already perform cost-effective surgeries on Americans and Europeans and target $2 billion in revenues from such forms of 'healthcare tourism.' The Indian telemedicine projects described above will inevitably have an impact on relocation. The Apollo hospital group, for example, which is participating in Andhra Pradesh state's e-government system, is also a major player in India's healthcare tourism industry.

During his visit in 2000, American President Bill Clinton "described watching as an Indian woman carrying her baby in her arms walked into a village health center that was equipped with a Web-ready computer and downloaded a child care manual that rivaled the quality of advice provided by expensive health care experts in the United States."[64] It requires little imagination to see the opportunity for Indian firms here, in terms of not only health advice, but also consultations with foreign patients, provided cost-effectively through the country's telemedicine network, which will be boosted further by the world's first dedicated telemedicine satellite.

Apollo is surely looking at such business, as would be a score of other Indian hospital groups.

Globalization's New Advocates:
A Billion Indian Stakeholders

Crucial though it may be, empowerment tools are only part of the solution to development. Like rock star Bob Geldof's efforts in Africa, such efforts rely on philanthropy, good feelings and benefaction—even within a democratic society; when the benefactors stop feeling concerned, the benefacted might be left in the lurch. The only meaningful alternative is to leverage empowerment with economic capacity.

In India, this seems to be the case. From shampoos and soaps, to tractors, motorcycles and mobile phones, rural markets drive long-term business in India. Although the success of consumer goods companies like Procter & Gamble and Unilever in India's villages is now business-school folklore, a more recent development involves focused marketing of even industrial products like steel and building materials in non-urban markets[65]—confirming the steadily growing participation by its huge rural population in the Indian market.

The foundations for this have, once again, also been laid in India's New Economy. Good examples of India's efforts in using information technology to actively empower its population include e-Shakti, an initiative by consumer goods giant Unilever's Indian subsidiary to bring electronic commerce (alongside direct support for self-help schemes and micro-credit) for 100 million rural people, by the end of 2006.[66] Another scheme, by tobacco giant ITC Ltd., called e-choupal, was described by the *New York Times* as "offering a model for all developing countries."[67] The satellite- and solar-power supported e-choupal network allows farmers to compare world futures prices with local prices, before going to market; it also gives them access to local weather conditions, soil-testing techniques and other expert knowledge that will increase their "productivity and income." According to the *New York Times*, e-choupals have "the means to reach into some of India's 600,000 villages, where 72 percent of the people live and where the greatest potential markets lie." Eventually, ITC "expects to sell everything from microcredit to tractors via e-choupals-and hopes to use them," it concludes, "to become the Wal-Mart of India."

e-choupals were born in the year 2000 from ITC's determination to improve the quality of its soybean crop purchases, which it turns into oil to sell in India and into animal feed for export. Alongside the Indian government's own initiatives, such enlightened efforts by the private sector once again drive home the stable long-term foundations of India's free-market system.

The Growing Suction of Trickle Down

Examples like e-Shakti and e-choupals establish that, within India, there are strong institutional mechanisms for ensuring that the trickle-in benefits from relocation are trickling down; indeed, they have good reason to continue doing so. The Indian government, any Indian government, will continue to need votes. As illustrated by e-Shakti and e-choupals, the Indian private sector too simply cannot afford to ignore the huge volumes of business and profits in rural areas, home to the majority of its population, as it slowly and steadily—but in India, always stably and surely—comes into its own.

While the *Associated Press* observes the Indian middle class emerging "amid a surge in conspicuous consumption,"[68] a *UPI* reporter finds that "Indian consumers, irrespective of their socio-economic origin, are suddenly on a self-appeasement mission, where greed is good and hence, so is consumption."[69]

In reality, as with government empowerment schemes—which will provide large-scale access to the New Economy—the effects of India's technology-fed economic boom are permeating deep into the country. Fuelled directly by relocation, "small businesses ranging from carpentry shops to corner groceries have hired some 25 million new workers" over the past 10 years,[70] notes *BusinessWeek*. For every new call center, "there are numerous support systems springing up in retailing, catering and entertainment."[71] Over the years, the drive by India's billion for more (and faster) benefits from globalization is going to strengthen the relocation process.

More Equal than Most:
Doing the Sums on Indian Inequality

Other than the above arguments, to understand the durability of India's technology-fed development (and the deep roots of its pull on relocation), it is imperative to firstly look in detail at one wrong but much touted cliché—about India's income distribution.

For example, with nary an attempt at attribution about a nation accounting for one-sixth of the human race, the correspondent of Belgium's leading *Le Soir* daily, Philippe Regnier, opened his coverage of the anti-globalization World Social Forum in Mumbai in January 2004 with a tirade against India—one of "the world's most unequal countries."[72]

The truth is hugely different.

India has long had one of the world's most-equal distributions of income. According to the World Bank's 'World Development Indicators' for 2000, the poorest 20 percent in India earned as much as 8.1 percent of national income, over three times the 2.3 percent level in the Philippines or Brazil's 2.5 percent, well over double South Africa's 2.9 percent and Mexico's 3.6 percent, and still comfortably ahead of Russia's 4.4, the U.S.'s 5.2 percent, China's 5.9 percent and Britain's 6.6 percent. More surprisingly, India's poor have as much of a share in national income as those in Europe's rich and often smug Welfare states: compared to India's 8.1 percent, national income shares for the bottom fifth of the population were 6.7 percent in Ireland, 7.5 percent in Spain, 8.4 percent in France, and only slightly better in Belgium (9.5 percent) and Scandinavia (9.6 percent).

Meanwhile, the wealthiest 20 percent in India earned 46.1 percent of national income, in huge contrast to a 64.8 percent share in South Africa, 63.8 percent in Brazil, 58.2 percent in Mexico, and 53.7 percent in Russia. The Indian share, in fact, again corresponds to that of Western countries: 46.4 percent in America and close to France's 41.7 percent or Britain's 43 percent.

Gurgling even deeper behind Regnier's pap is the widespread Western lack of awareness about India's implementation of the world's oldest and most ambitious program of positive discrimination,[73] even though hints of it do come across in occasionally catchy headlines such as 'Crownless maharajahs brave dust and grind of electoral battle' (*Agence France-Presse*, November 26, 2003) or 'Indian kings proud amid poverty' (*BBC News*, December 18, 2003). The *Washington Post* was one exception, highlighting the "vast experiment in social engineering that already bestows preferential treatment on roughly half of India's billion-plus people"; more strikingly for Americans and Europeans concerned with social justice, it acknowledged that "the concept of affirmative action as it is understood in the West began in India."[74]

Other than such policies, India's social mobility is demonstrated by some striking, real-life cases. The $22 billion Reliance group, for example, was founded by a former gas-station employee.[75] Outside business, it would no doubt also be hard to find the Prime

Minister of any other developing country, whose humble roots are best illustrated by the report that his murdered nephew was an "employee in the Jindal Pipe Factory in the Kosikalan industrial area,"[76] or for that matter, to come across a scientist-President like India's Abdul Kalam, the "son of a boatman who once sold newspapers at a railway station"[77]

Meanwhile, globalizing India has also refrained from unbridling a free-for-all, survival-of-the-fittest free market. In 2003, it launched a one rupee-per-day "insurance-linked pension scheme for senior citizens."[78] Also, coinciding directly with India's economic reforms is what *BusinessWeek* calls "a surge in school spending in the villages. Young Indians today get five more years of schooling, on average, than their parents, and there is nearly universal primary education."[79]

Thus, in spite of India's economic lift-off, the government's social justice objectives seem to remain in place. They will have to. India's media, its voters, will see to it. The country's robust democracy, which has, uniquely, handled the challenge of decades of grinding poverty, is clearly equipped to cope with the new and far more comfortable test of its emergence from poverty. As a result, arguing about the 'evil' of globalization, without seeking to understand the differences between the Indian experience with it, and that of say Haiti and Bolivia, might prove to be a painfully short-lived process.

A World Unto Itself

Other than the inherent balance in economic growth given by its equitable income distribution, India's political stability is also a crucial factor in making its rise a long-term certainty.

In spite of Mr. Regnier of *Le Soir*, whose tirade also covered the host country's "sectarian Hindu" government, India is actually a rare example of a developing country, which is very secular and stable. Such inherent strengths are underwritten further by both an independent judiciary and an aggressively free media. Unlike most developing countries (British colonies included[80]), India's powerful military has never interfered in civil society.

From pollution control to child labour and education, India's

Supreme Court continues to set new global milestones in socially-aware judicial activism[81]—for example playing a direct role in New Delhi's success "in converting the entire public transport to CNG-propelled vehicles...on a scale unparalleled anywhere else"[82]; its independence was hailed by Britain's Lord Chief Justice[83] as a lesson for the United Kingdom.[84] In February 2004, the Court ruled for a massive 80 percent cut in fees at the elite Indian Institutes of Management[85], which are increasingly compared to Harvard and Europe's INSEAD; similar moves are expected with India's world-class technology universities, the IITs.

The freedom of the Indian media is demonstrated by indefatigable campaigns to unearth corruption at the highest levels of government, among them the decades-old Bofors howitzers scandal (involving Sweden's largest-ever defense order)[86], the so-called JMM bribery and Pathak allegations plaguing former Prime Minister Narasimha Rao[87], the notorious Tehelka arms-for-bribes stings in 2001,[88] or those which in 2003 led to resignations by top leaders of both the BJP party and the Congress.[89]

In the context of this book, the perpetually corrective influence of the Indian media is demonstrated by its detached, professional assessment of India's IT success; on February 5, 2004, Indian papers widely reported Infosys' Chairman Narayana Murthy's warning that the country was "not yet" an IT superpower, and carefully explained why.[90] Such an approach contrasts starkly, for example, with the hype in Malaysia about the now-defunct Multimedia Super Corridor,[91] in Belgium about its onetime software superstar, Lernout & Hauspie (see Chapter I) or the assortment of Silicon Valley wannabes on which huge sums of taxpayers' money were wasted.[92] It also stands out against the orgy of self-congratulation in the U.S. media during the dotty years of the dotcom boom.

India, and its institutions, have maintained such a status in spite of some of the world's most-extreme challenges of poverty, and the unparalleled heterogeneity of the country. Equally crucial: unlike the West, India's development process is not accompanied by officially-sanctioned slavery, colonies or Empire, or the value-adding, surplus population sink of a 'New World'; again, very unlike the West, modern India's nation-building is accompanied by universal suffrage.

India is indeed a functioning world unto itself. It has 18 official languages (most with their own scripts), five States led in 2003 by women Chief Ministers,[93] trade unions and mass movements (including a million non-governmental organizations) having what France's *Le Monde* described as a weight without parallel anywhere in the world,[94] as well as religious minorities present across all walks of life.[95]

Two Indian States boast the world's longest-running—and elected—Communist governments. Both are intense champions of information technology as a means for mass empowerment. One U.S. newspaper noted the irony: "Even the Communist government of the state of West Bengal, of which Calcutta is the capital, is getting in on the act: It is promoting the city as India's newest information-technology hub. In the last few years, say officials from the Communist Party of India (Marxist), which has run the state for 26 years, 172 such companies have set up shop in the area, including IBM and a firm that develops software for United Airlines."[96]

In brief, India will surely continue to surprise. But unlike yesterday's Indonesia (or even tomorrow's China?) there will be no unexpected shocks, unpleasant surprises. This, quite simply, is the real meaning of its democracy, above all its secular democracy.

Indian Secularism: A World in Denial

In 1995, this author commented to a conference in Europe:

> India has now long since reached a stage where members of such 'minority groups' have become cabinet ministers, chiefs of the armed forces, judges of the court, ambassadors and chief ministers, and of course leaders of business. Indeed, both India's longest serving cabinet minister, Jagjivan Ram, and Mayavati, a former Chief Minister of India's largest State, Uttar Pradesh, came from the so-called 'untouchable' (or Dalit) community.[97]

Since then, another Dalit, veteran Indian diplomat K.R. Narayanan, was appointed as the country's President (in 1997),[98] and during his five years in office, became one of India's most socially-activist heads of State. But Ram, Mayavati and Narayanan are hardly exceptions. A report in a random issue of newsweekly *India Today* (November 29, 1999) yields the remarkably routine profile of

Pratibha Bharathi, a "five-time MLA (legislator), whose father and grandfather were also legislators. A Dalit, she is the first woman Speaker of the Andhra Pradesh Assembly."

Given that globalization, among other things, involves a growth in contact and interdependency between different cultures, ethnic and religious groups, the Indian model deserves, indeed requires, close study. Other than its huge edifice of affirmative action, this also concerns the relatively unique presence of 'minorities' across the country's mainstream, and at its top.

At the end of 2003, instances of religious minorities at the pinnacle of 'Hindu-dominated India' included Abdul Kalam, the country's missile-scientist President (and its third Muslim Head of State since independence); George Fernandes, a former Jesuit and Defense Minister in the country's 'Hindu fundamentalist' government; James Michael Lyngdoh, also a Christian, heading India's all-powerful Election Commission; Sonia Gandhi, an Italian-born Roman Catholic Leader of Congress, the largest opposition party; Ratan Tata, a Zoroastrian Parsi, (originally from Persia), whose family controls the Tata conglomerate, India's largest business group; and Azim Premji,[99] whose majority holding in software giant Wipro makes him one of the world's richest Muslims.

Such a presence stretches wide and deep, and, like reports about influential Dalits, rarely provokes excitement or comment. Thus, with no extra attention, the Indian media refers to the 'miraculous escape' from a helicopter crash of Waris Hayat Khan, the (Muslim) Director General of Police of Bihar State,[100] or to Mufti Mohammed Syed, the Chief Minister and other Muslim political leaders in the 'disputed State' of Jammu and Kashmir. Elsewhere, Hindu Indians revere Muslim musicians such as sitarist Vilayat Khan or sarod maestro Bismillah Khan, sports personalities like former cricket captain Mohammad Azharuddin as well as the huge contingent of Muslim superstars in India's cinema capital Bollywood, such as Salman Khan, Shah Rukh Khan and Aamir Khan.[101] The Indian legal system too continues to draw inspiration from one of the pioneers of its extraordinary record of judicial activism, former Supreme Court Chief Justice A.M. Ahmadi, also a Muslim. In parallel, Aligarh Muslim University retains its title as one of India's leading universities, while Vellore's Christian Medical College remains one of its top medical schools.

These kind of examples are hardly to be found in China (with its Tibetans, for example), most other developing countries, or for that matter, in continental Europe. Unlike India, which has (and according to the *Financial Times*,[102] plans to cut down on) separate holidays for Christians, Sikhs, Buddhists, Jains, Muslims and Hindus, most national holidays in 'secular France' remain Catholic; as the *International Herald Tribune* reported, French President Chirac in February 2004 "rejected a proposal that France move toward treating its faiths equally" by creating at least "one school holiday apiece for Jews and Muslims."[103]

However, this overwhelming secular reality is neither recent, nor a politically-correct afterthought to India's emergence. Thus, in 1971, the surrender of a Pakistani general and 90,000 troops to the Indian Army "was demanded by a Parsi, chief of army staff Gen. Sam Manekshaw. The terms were prepared by a Jew, chief of staff of eastern command Maj.-Gen. J.F.R. Jacob. The actual surrender was before a Sikh, general officer commanding-in-chief of the eastern command, Lt.-Gen. Jasjit Singh Aurora."[104]

Equally striking is the rare, reciprocal resonance of India's Islamic community. *BBC News* described Daud Sharifa from Tamil Nadu, leading a 3,000-strong group movement in Tamil Nadu seeking to build a mosque for women.[105] The *Washington Post* reports about an all-women Muslim panel (a 'muftia')—possibly "the first of its kind" in the entire Sunni Muslim world. The panel rules on issues of modernity and religious tradition, replying to queries sent in by writing as well as email, and makes India a proving ground for "female Islamic jurisprudence." "You have to study Indian Muslims quite apart from the rest of the world," Anwar Moazzam, the retired head of the department of Islamic studies at India's Osmania University, told the newspaper.[106]

To assess where India is in terms of secularism, it may be opportune to compare the above kind of examples to the 'developed' continent of bucolic Europe, currently luxuriating in debates about whether or not Muslim girls should be allowed to wear head-scarves to school[107]; "what constitutes a religious beard, as opposed to some other type;"[108] if a bandana "presented by young girls" is religious[109]; and whether Athens should permit a mosque, its first ever, to be built in the city.[110] To top it off we have this enlightened question from Croatia: can a Muslim girl be a beauty queen in a Catholic country?[111] To nations like these, the meaning of 'Hindu' India's secularism, where Prayag, one of Hinduism's most sacred cities, retains the 'Allahabad' name given by its erstwhile Muslim conquerors, is simply beyond the realm of comprehension.

The Message of the Miracle...

As much as other factors, secularism illustrates and underpins the durability of the Indian system, as it has through the country's long history. Alongside India's other attributes, it may hold relevance to some of the key challenges accompanying globalization— above all the ease with which 'others' are seemingly connected, sometimes unexpectedly, into one another's lives.

Unlike Mr. Regnier of *Le Soir*, *New York Times* columnist Thomas Friedman was positively gushing: "The more time you spend in India the more you realize that this teeming, multiethnic, multireligious, multilingual country is one of the world's great wonders—a miracle with message."[112] Such a verdict was also given by a *Fortune* cover story at the end of 2003 on India's rise to global leadership in software. "India at its best is a lot like the U.S. at its best—a nation of staggering ethnic and religious diversity that somehow holds together by dint of tolerance and a sense of shared destiny."[113] It is, in fact, 'somehow' difficult to imagine a Pakistani parallel to the proposal that American rock legend Tina Turner play a cinema role as a Hindu goddess,[114] any less than it is to conceive of an Indian or Chinese actress proposed for the role of the Virgin Mary in European cinema.

In spite of its poverty and complexity, India's mature secular democracy underscores why the runaway success of its IT industry has not run out-of-control, as happened in Nigeria's oil-fed boom of the 1980s, Southeast Asia's foreign investment-led successes of the 1990s, or more recently in Latin America.[115] Indeed, the irony today is that, following its accession to the International Monetary Fund's Financial Transaction Plan, yesterday's laggard India, deaf to the sermons of Western open-up-everything-at-once pundits, will be financing balance of payments deficits in other, once-miracle developing countries.

To summarize, India's IT-fed economic boom is neither mainly benefiting the rich, nor any religious or ethnic group. Important enough as the latter factor is anywhere in today's fast-globalizing world, the cement of the Indian system's neutrality is even more remarkable within the huge heterogeneity of the country. As a result, India's pull on white-collar jobs is not going to disappear because it collapses under its own weight, or, like some erstwhile 'miracle' economies, vanishes suddenly without trace.

...Its Challenge and Promise

Still, even the Indian 'miracle' does have flip sides. Agglomerating India's open democratic society with its rare level of secularism would be straightforward, were this not also accompanied by its concomitant status as one of the largest and poorest countries in the world.

India is hardly a simple case, and seldom offers an easy ride, especially for those seeking a quick buck. One of the world's most powerful corporations, Coca-Cola, only succeeded, after a decade-long effort, to bury the popular Indian 'Thums Up' cola, in spite of having acquired the brand in the 1990s. Coke continues to face problems with Indian NGOs over allegations of pesticide residues in its soft drinks[116] as well as a ban in early 2004 on its bottling operation in the Communist-controlled, water-starved Indian state of Kerala.[117] And yet, as Coca-Cola's world record sales in India show, India justifies the effort.

Such opportunities and challenges go beyond soft-drink sales. Thus, in spite of lingering caste disputes inside its rural heartland, pockets of new poverty in places like Orissa, armed Maoist struggles in Andhra Pradesh and Bihar (disconnected, of course from the still, semi-officially Maoist government of China), terrorism in Kashmir and the Chinese-influenced northeast, a notorious widow-burning incident some years ago, and numerous other blemishes, the over-whelming majority of India's billion people—like those in the West-go about their daily lives in peace.

As discussed previously (in examples on India's demographics), such everyday lives often involve extraordinary challenges, and function in the face of power failures, heat waves and monsoons, and above everything, the country's still-high levels of poverty. It remains important to again note that even after reforms, the average Indian's purchasing power income of $2,529 per year (based on the World Bank's income distribution calculations) remains less than half that of a Bosnian's $5,249 or a Colombian's $6,003, the latter living in nations which hardly qualify as working models of stability.

In other words, even by Third World standards, India is a very poor country, but all the more remarkable for that. Although incomes will rise rapidly, the facts are clear: on such foundations, India's challenge to the Western world at its highest-value economic frontiers is clearly extraordinary.

In addition, the Indian 'miracle' is a working one, and durable too. As a result, India will continue to offer a rare model for absorbing the benefits of globalization, especially as its growing economy continues to heal the inescapable internal fault-lines of India's 200 year legacy of poverty, the key reason for some of its still-shocking aberrations.

Poverty Rollback:
The Indian Lesson and the World

Like its hugely equitable income distribution, another little-emphasized fact is that India's 65 percent rate of poverty when it won independence from Britain in 1947, had fallen to 26 percent by 2002.[118] India achieved this in spite of its population more than tripling over the period, from about 350 million to over a billion. In other words, the Indian system has provided livelihoods for more than six hundred million people (or almost equal to the populations of Western Europe and the U.S.), and their number continues to grow.

Given India's size, its success in fighting poverty has, in turn, directly impacted on the poverty rate of the whole world's population. As noted in 2002 by the World Bank: "Rapid economic development in India and China over the past two decades has underpinned the first reduction in the number of poor people in the world."[119] In 2004, the UN added that India and China's growth not only continued to reduce global poverty, but that this should "serve as an incentive to other developing countries."[120]

Nevertheless, for critics, increases in average income for the huge populations of India and China conceal the fact that this was untrue for much of the developing world, as France's *Le Monde* pointed out.[121] In fact, such warnings provide an excellent opportunity to do some homework, on an unavoidable question: what makes India and China different, and how to use their lessons in other countries of the Third World, which are adversely impacted by globalization. Few would, for instance, refute the fact that it is better that a billion people, within China and India, get lifted out of poverty than an entire country with a far smaller population such as Singapore, or for that matter, Haiti—where globalization has clearly failed.

To go further, it may be necessary to devise other yardsticks for success, but there is unlikely to be a more compelling argument than winning the fight against poverty. Whether it is a blight like infant mortality or illiteracy, poverty clearly correlates to such indicators, and in India's case, a fall in poverty has been accompanied by declines in each of the above. Infant mortality in India, for instance, was 59.6 per 1,000 live births in 2003, down from 64.9 in 2000, according to the CIA's *World Factbook*. Though this still lagged China's 25.3, it was comfortably better than Pakistan's 76.5; what is more, poverty in India is clearly declining (by 10 percent in the three year period 2000-2003). So too is illiteracy, down from more than 85 percent at the time of Britain's exit to 35 percent in 2001,[122] and like poverty, achieved in spite of a tripling in the Indian population; meanwhile, accompanying the 'surge' in school spending referred to above by *BusinessWeek*, the Indian government's Sarva Shiksha Abhiyan program aims at ensuring that all 6-14 year olds complete eight years of schooling by 2010.

India is achieving such steady progress without Empire or colonies, or the ruthlessly efficient upliftment of a totalitarian success story like China. This, in turn, poses a question which is uncomfortable for some: what differentiates India's success from that of China? Is it, for example, 'better' that a totalitarian State like China succeeds in eliminating poverty more quickly than a free country like India? Is the former kind of success necessarily more durable, especially given the example of the massive resurgence of poverty after the failure of the manufactured miracle in southeast Asia—which may have parallels to China, as some experts argue?

Given previous discussions and examples, these are questions of relevance not just for proponents and critics of globalization, but given India's and China's rise, for the epic challenges of the forthcoming decades.

The Moral Imperative of Growing the Pie

Though long-standing Indian attributes such as secularism, democracy and fair distribution of incomes could, for some, be commendable ends in themselves, they did little to address the issue of the country's poverty until reforms in 1991 freed up the country's economy. This permitted India to more-rapidly grow its economic pie, rather than equitably distribute slices of a small one—as it had been doing since Independence in 1947.

Largely due to reforms, India's economy has seen increased economic growth rates, up from its derided 2-3 percent 'Hindu' rate, to the current 7-8 percent and enabled it to become an active participant and net beneficiary of today's globalization trend.

India's economic boom is driven by relocation. Software exports already account for over 3 percent of the Indian economy and are growing four times faster than gross domestic product. The impact of such a connection is explained in the *Washington Post*: "Twelve years after the (Indian) government began liberalizing the economy (in 1991), service industries such as banking, insurance, health care-and, most visibly, anything related to information technology—are booming in the world's second-most populous nation, driving an unprecedented and long-awaited expansion in the ranks of the middle and upper classes."[123]

And yet, like the West's growing jobs crisis, India too faces major challenges in the years ahead. As mentioned before, it has one of the world's youngest demographic profiles, with 68 percent of its one billion population under the age of 35; no fewer than 100 million people are expected to join the labour force in the next 10 years, and 335 million over the next 30.

In addition, support for reform and globalization in India is hardly universal. Such concepts, in a country where Gandhian 'swaraj' or economic self-sufficiency was one of the most powerful tools in its fight for independence, are still associated in many quarters with the worst of the colonial era.

Above all, India's embrace of economic reform has massively reduced the capacity of the State to create new jobs, as was the norm under the pre-reform patronage system.[124] In recent years, public sector employment has fallen from 2.5 million to 1.6 million, and in the short-term, this has begun to impact on the lowest rungs of Indian society, the so-called 'untouchables' or Dalits, who counted heavily on affirmative action job schemes created by the State; their poverty rate in 2000 was 43 percent, much higher than that of the country as a whole.[125]

In the face of this, influential Indian weekly *Outlook* asks: "Even with all the new call centers and the boom in services, employment in the organized private sector grew by only 1 percent last year. So when and how will the 40 million jobs the Prime Minister keeps promising be created?"[126] Another report in *Outlook* notes that India's jobless has "grown to 27 million people, or 7.32 percent of the work force" and will "rise to 40 million" by 2007.[127] More than the media, such concerns leaped to the fore in February 2004, when 50 million Indians, backed by a dozen of the country's powerful trade unions, went on strike, to protest against "the fraud being perpetrated by way of the feel good factor by the Government" as part of the BJP's 'shining India' election campaign. "If India is really shining," said general secretary Gurudas Dasgupta of the All-India Trade Unions Congress, "the response would not have been so massive."[128]

Protests like this (even given its scale) are part-and-parcel of life in democratic India, but indicate something else: Unlike several other countries, India cannot manufacture or conjure an economic 'miracle.' The rewards of globalization still have a very long way to go before reaching everyone in the country, and being accepted as a universal good. Those yet to tangibly and significantly obtain such rewards, do have a vote, and can force governments to change policy, or throw them out.

The relevance of such factors must not be under-estimated in a country with free elections, one of the world's most socially activist judiciaries, potent trade unions and a perpetually alert media. The challenge of India's miracle is expressed by Rob Jenkins of London's Birkbeck College: "How can we explain the ability of economic reform to become rooted in India, despite the daunting array of political obstacles placed in its path? India is not only a democracy; it has been one continuously for the past fifty years: unlike newly democratizing countries in the developing world, or in the former Eastern bloc, there are no discredited authoritarian regimes on which past failures can be blamed."[129]

In effect, globalization's, beneficiaries, both current and future, will continue to encourage India's pull on the world's white-collar services, which provides the oxygen for its continued growth and development. As a Boston Consulting Group (BSG) vice-president observed, India has the "potential to generate 30 million jobs" by 2020, simply as spin-offs from the outsourcing business.[130]

Globalization 2.0

As discussed previously, the derailment of the Cancun summit of the WTO showed that only India and China (and to an extent, Brazil and South Africa) have the strength to challenge the West, and forge what the *New York Times* described as "a powerful bloc"[131] to reshape the world order—of which, the rest of the Third World's failures constitute an integral part.

One of the strongest (and widely accepted) reasons for such Third World failures is the enormous overhang of agricultural subsidies in the rich West. A study sometime ago, for example, found that the average European cow is paid £1.20 in daily subsidy; although not quite a Sacred Cow, its earnings are more than double that of many African farmers, such as Senegal's Douda Dia "who makes just £180 a year."[132] Even if this is just one, extreme case, such examples underline why it is cheaper to buy Western foodstuffs than it is to produce locally in huge swathes of Africa and Latin America, and the reason why "10,000 farmers have lost their jobs in the dairy industry in the Dominican Republic over the last twenty years."

In dramatic contrast, when the Indian Prime Minister launched his one-rupee-a-day insurance scheme, he noted that "we are able to provide food to the poor at the cheapest rate anywhere in the world." This is, of course, largely because India has been able to not only steadily grow its foodgrains output and, as discussed, boast granaries 'overflowing' with food surpluses; it has also successfully resisted European and American pressure to reduce its agricultural subsidies[133]—a particularly crude demand given average Indian living standards. Instead, at Cancun (and since), India refused to budge from its demand that the rich West begins the subsidy roll-back, before it provides more access—amidst the global slowdown—to its giant and fast-growing market.

Such market-access issues, as explained, are also linked up further to that of white-collar job relocation, and within this complex cascade of carrot-and-stick, what is clear is that India (and China) will continue draining Western jobs.

Evading such interlocked complexities will prove fruitless, although it still remains a habit. In February 2004, a report for the UN called *A Fair Globalization*, whose authors include Nobel Laureate Joseph Stiglitz, again noted that, in spite of the proliferation of black spots across the world, there were "two bright spots: China and India, the two Asian nations with a third of the world's population."[134] But: one day later, gloomy coverage of the same report by the left-leaning anti-globalization British daily, the *Guardian* failed completely to mention these two huge and portentous exceptions.[135]

Like the *Guardian*, this kind of perverse melancholia (remaining fixated on problems from a rich Western perch rather than seeking to come to grips with increasingly-evident solutions) was demonstrated at the January 2004 anti-globalization World Social Forum at Mumbai, India, which preceded the World Economic Forum at Davos, Switzerland. At Mumbai, there was little effort by Western activists to learn either answers, or find new questions, from their Indian hosts. Worse: as French news agency *Agence France-Presse* reported, while Indian activists stayed in makeshift accommodation, most of their "Western allies at the World Social Forum were driven off to comfortable hotels..." Even as "the longest food lines were exclusively Indian," some "foreigners preferred dishes such as the Thai red curry and Tibetan momos, costing up to $4 a serving, or stopped by the 'Croissants, Etc.' stall."[136]

Potentially-pathbreaking lessons from India for a New, New

Third World Thing, such as the use of Indian satellites for telemedicine, for controlling deforestation and fighting locusts or finding
water, did not figure on the agenda. Neither did the possibility of
replicating unique Indian-inspired digital-divide bridges such as the
Simputer, corDECT telecom networks and TCS' revolutionary computer literacy program (unveiled only days before the Summit).
Indeed, with nary a glance at the workings (or defects) of India's
massive affirmative action program, one of the movement's pontiffs,
France's anti-McDonalds campaigner Jose Bove, unleashed a patronizing outburst against India's 'failure' with respect to its 'untouchables'; as a Paris-based American film-maker remarked to this
author, Bove's pulpit would have been better deployed explaining
Europe's record on secularism or its phenomenal lack of response to
its "largest transnational minority"—its "persecuted, suppressed,
abused" gypsies.[137]

Nevertheless, in the years ahead, even the most leisurely anti-
globalization crusaders will have to face up to the fact that the tide
is turning. The first cracks in this Western edifice appeared on
February 21, 2004, when an *Associated Press* feature reported 'U.S.
urges EU to eliminate subsidies on farm exports.' It quoted Robert
Zoellick, the U.S. Trade Representative, speaking from Geneva, the
headquarters of the World Trade Organization: "Let's quit fooling
around. Let's eliminate them all."[138] Three days later, India reciprocated, as borne out by a *Financial Times* headline: 'India ready to shift
stance on farm subsidies."[139] The dance is by no means over, and the
calibration of give-and-take will last for several years.

The key to India's 'shift in stance' on farm subsidies, however,
is that it does not involve "endangering" the livelihoods of Indian
farmers. The issue of defining livelihoods in relative terms between
India and the West (both for farmers, as well as white-collar and
blue-collar workers), and finding long-term mechanisms to level
down such differences is also intrinsic to the longer-term agenda of
the relocation debate, as discussed in the next chapter.

CHAPTER VII

Linking Here and There— Boom to Bust

Previous chapters have underlined India's key role at the heart of the global information technology revolution. They also provided facts and figures on the impact of relocation on the Indian economy, and sought to explain some causes for India's profound and evidently strengthening pull on Western white-collar jobs.

This still leaves a burning question: Can relocation be managed, especially to mitigate its worst effects—above all, for its victims? Before addressing this, however, it is important to go beyond facts and figures, investigate sometimes-strong assumptions, which are central to the relocation debate. Above all, these include issues of identity and territoriality, a timeframing of the Western economic downturn and its new 'crisis' mindset, and benchmarking cross-border standards and equivalences within the flow of globalization.

One of the first steps for managing relocation involves acknowledging the difficulty, indeed the impossibility, of finding a single issue to explain the trend, or a single pressure point, to reverse it. Indeed, until the wider totality of factors—including some misleading assumptions—are taken into account, there is a risk that the debate moves in circles of misconceptions, rather than help find solutions for a real and growing problem.

Identity: U.S. and Them...

Today's globalization is unique in that it involves brains and know-how, not just mobile capital and blue-collar armies which can be quickly trained or retrained, and dispatched elsewhere. This fact, in turn, throws into relief a key issue: How different would be the shape of the 'American' or 'global' IT industry, without the 'Indian' contribution?

In 1996, a survey of U.S. computer companies "found that one of every 10 jobs could not be filled because of a shortage of trained technology workers. The industry was expanding so fast that colleges and training schools couldn't keep up."[1] At the height of the dotcom boom in the year 2000, *eCompany Now* observed: "India has been a key recruiting territory of U.S. tech firms for years. But now the demand for skilled programmers has become so intense that even small businesses...are tapping India's work force."[2] Referring to an Indian IT professional by the name of Sudah Durairaj, it wrote that he "can't get enough of the United States. The U.S. tech sector can't get enough Sudah Durairajs."

Considering that a total of roughly 400,000 Indian-origin H-1B visa holders in by the U.S.[3] accounted for a very significant share of America's skilled IT population through the 1990s, built up some of its most-successful IT firms, and provided often-dramatic intellectual contributions to its technology flagships (ranging from Intel and IBM to Bell Labs), the question arises: without such a contribution, would the American information technology industry have been as much a provider of territorially-demarcated American livelihoods—or high pay, "bountiful benefits and sterling opportunities"[4] and, after the downturn, be as worth 'saving?' Or would it have grown much slower, but retained its 'American' identity?[5]

These are complex questions, and underscore the difficulty of territorial dissimulation, either from America or Europe. Even after the downturn, the proportion of Indians in U.S. H-1B visa allocations has remained at the same near-50 percent level,[6] endorsing the complex but seamless and persisting bonds between Indian and American IT.

One obvious answer is that India's contribution to America, and the huge skills shortage there, fuelled and made feasible the New Economy. There was nothing calculated here. India, like any other country, was simply seeking an opportunity to live up to its capacities. Like "the greatest volunteer army for freedom" in World War II, Indians were finding out what they were good, indeed excellent, at doing, in order to make a living, even if their huge presence and contributions went unacknowledged.

Such contributions were not directed at just high-tech firms and Big Business but fed into huge swathes of the American system. The mechanical engineering department of the University of Maryland, for example, had one-fourth of its students from India, while nearby, George Mason University had "hatched a plan to go out to India and woo up to 60 students each year with scholarships, a housing allowance, and a paid internship at a sponsor's company."[7]

Catherine Mann of the Institute for International Economics in Washington acknowledges the context of this contribution.[8] Firstly, she says, "the end of the technology boom, the general economic slump, and the downturn in manufacturing—not foreign programming competition—account for most job losses" in the U.S. Most estimates, she states, "compare the peak of the business cycle and technology boom with today's sluggish economy. That's not a valid comparison."

In addition, she points out that the value advantage from offshore programmers made "information technology affordable to business sectors" which had not yet joined the IT productivity boom, among them "small and medium-size businesses, health care and construction;" in turn, this added significantly to U.S. economic growth, and therefore, that of the wider Western and global economy.

The relevance of this cannot be under-estimated. Firstly, a refusal to accept India's distinct and massive contribution to making the New Economy possible is counterproductive—given that the world IT industry is headed to that country anyway. Secondly, conjuring up the Indian contribution as a disposable item (as some are wont to do) would, more than a free ride, equate to intellectual theft on a similar scale as Europe's unacknowledged use of key Indian contributions in mathematics, or Marconi's appropriation of Bose's coherer—the kind of theft today's India is making amply clear will not happen again. Indeed, if nothing else, the pace at with which Indian labs of American IT firms have begun filing patents since 2001 (Chapter III) is clear evidence of both the scale and quality of their past contributions.

...And Those in Between

White-collar job relocation does not involve shifts from California to Oregon. It therefore brings up questions of national origin and identity.

In addition, since the relocated jobs are not moving from the

U.S. to Britain or Europe, it also involves issues of both Western versus non-Western cultures as well as white-versus non-white ethnicity.

In such contexts, one vexatious issue is to segregate Indian-born American citizens from Indian permanent residents in the U.S.—and then one step further, from those Indians (or other foreigners) who are equally talented H-1B visa holders, but still merely visitors, possibly awaiting permanent residency and/or citizenship.

As it happens, one of the most outspoken advocates for capping the H-1B (and now the L-1) visa is Ron Hira, reported to be an American of "Indian ethnicity,"[9] who is a professor at Rochester Institute of Technology and head of an immigration policy committee for the Institute of Electrical and Electronics Engineers.

The right of Indian-origin Hira staking territorial claim to America, and keeping out others originating from India (or still to be born there), is not only a problem of who-caught-the-earlier-bus. It also flies in the face of America's own complex identity as a land of opportunity and a nation of immigrants, both from ethnically-white Europe and elsewhere.

Such factors will remain troubling. They lie at the root of the outcry which followed Democratic presidential candidate Gen. Wesley Clark's suggestion that the U.S. invite Indian IIT graduates to become American citizens and set up IT companies. They also illustrate the immense, and inevitably, continuing, complexities, of relocation.

When is a Company Really American?

One of the strongest assumptions in the relocation debate is that Indians (today, after the downturn) are somehow 'stealing' Western jobs, and that American companies have a moral obligation to protect jobs in America. As demonstrated by Gen. Clark's troubles, the idea that an Indian-founded IT company in America could be as American as one founded by someone else (not necessarily born in America) also seems anathema, evidently not just to a few—given that he had to withdraw his invitation to India's IIT graduates from his campaign's Web site.

Proceeding from such an assumption, it becomes necessary to

ask what exactly is an American company, and how long does it retain this American-ness? This is a key factor behind any meaningful effort to territorially localize business, and seek to prevent offshore outsourcing.

- Is a company American because it was incorporated in the U.S., and pays taxes there? Indians, for example, believe that if an Indian IT company "starts an outfit in the U.S., it is as much entitled as any 'American' company to bid for contracts or take any subcontracts."[10] In contrast, one also thinks of several such 'American' companies, which have rechartered (legally known as 'inversion') in jurisdictions with lower taxes such as the Cayman Islands, or Bermuda, where IT consulting giant Accenture, for example, is incorporated. Meanwhile, with some exceptions, the decades-old system of double-taxation treaties seem to have done its job well enough—both through boom and dotcom bust.
- Is a company American because its founding capital originated in the U.S.? This is a difficult question in the age of complex cross-border financial systems, especially when one considers that the massive $3 trillion U.S. national debt is underwritten by the rest of the world's savings, "most of that" from Asia[11]; meanwhile, an American today is born with debts of $124,000,[12] a large part owed by his or her government and 'American' corporations, and this will no doubt continue to be financed, mainly from Asia.
- Is a company American because it was founded by Americans, or American-born Americans? As Chapter III illustrates, this would pose considerable difficulties for the huge mass of Silicon Valley companies, including some of the strongest technology brands in the world, set up by Indians or Indian-born Americans.
- Is a company American because its workforce is (mainly) American? Here, one could think of GE, whose Indian employment overtook the U.S. in 2001,[13] well before the dotcom bust—that is, before anyone paid attention to such questions, and few saw India as anything more than a warehouse of just-in-time skills to continue fuelling the New Economy. More strikingly, such an argument would lead in another unpleasant direction: many American technology

companies now employ more IT staff in India than they do in any single country of Europe. Would this entail management of relocation by winding down their European operations (or at least new job creation in Europe), and preserving activities in the United States and India?

- Another challenge of territorial delimiting of corporate identity involves countries in which companies do their business; as mentioned in Chapter I, 60 percent of revenues of American IT companies already come from outside the U.S. For a country like Sweden, most of its large enterprises (some of which, such as Volvo and Saab, are now in American hands) have long accepted that limiting their activity to country of origin would have left them minnows, and may not therefore have permitted to built up their size, both in terms of revenues (crowns, dollars or other currencies), as well as local-born staff. For decades, Swedish companies have accepted that their homeland was by no means their largest market, by any measure. Indeed, like many others from Europe, they have viewed the U.S. in this role, both in terms of sales and local employment. Like the Swedes, Americans will have to learn that their largest markets will some time in the future lie elsewhere, almost surely in China and India. This is no doubt exactly what India will be explaining in the years ahead, as it continues to open its own markets, in return for more white-collar jobs.

Out of Britain's Dark Satanic Mills

The alleged 'theft' of jobs, and its role as the First Cause of much that seems to be going wrong with Western economies, needs to also be looked at from another direction.

For example, the *Los Angeles Times* explains what it calls California's new Gilded Age: "the income gap between rich and poor wider than at almost any time in history and magnified by the sudden wealth and lavish living of a growing elite. California's super rich haven't been this flush or freewheeling—and the poor and middle classes haven't languished this far behind—since the last days of the Roaring '20s."[14]

This news item appeared at the beginning of 2000, well before the dotcom bust and the relocation wave three years later.

Such evidence also exists outside America. In early 2001, over two years before the Indian threat emerged, British Trades Union Congress general secretary John Monks described Britain's call-centers as "dark, satanic mills" and the *Financial Times* devoted a special review on "problems facing U.K. call centers as they sought to improve their image" of, yes, being "sweatshops."[15]

Issue Goes Beyond Dotcoms and IT

Complicating matters further is the fact that white-collar job relocation is by no means limited to IT services,[16] but goes beyond (for at least four decades) to broader fields of science and technology, to research labs, hospitals and universities, and more.

Like IBM's 'King of Patents' Ravi Arumilli, GE's oil-gulping bacteria wizard Ananda Chakraborty and Narendra Karmarkar of Bell Labs (whose eponymous patented algorithm pioneered the 'interior point revolution' in complex business computing), hundreds of thousands of other skilled Indian scientists, physicians, engineers and academics moved to the West onward from the 1960s. There are, for example, an estimated 20,000 alumni in the U.S. from the elite Indian Institutes of Technology (*Salon* magazine's millionaire-record club), which would correspond to 20 percent of the 100,000 graduates they have produced since 1951.

During the 1990s, graduates from India's top business schools, the Indian Institutes of Management (IIM), were also voraciously lapped up by American firms, and like the IITs, saw a multitude of American job offers as they completed their programs. For example, in early 2000, an Indian newspaper reported that "FatWire Corporation USA (a leading Internet content management company) made 10 job offers within a few hours of Zero Day"[17] for freshly-minted IIM graduates.

This high-end brainpower remains in great demand elsewhere too; once again, supplied mainly by India. Britain, for example, launched a Highly Skilled Migrant Programme in early 2002, aimed at "uniquely talented people" whose visas make them automatically eligible for indefinite stay. British Foreign Office Minister Beverley Hughes said, "There is a real demand in sectors such as research and development and financial services for maths, science and engineering specialists." Here too, Indians comfortably lead, with 832 awardees, against China's 126 and Russia's 123.[18]

Such non-IT skills too continue to be needed, sometimes desperately. In Ohio, according to the *Akron Beacon Journal*, Summa Health plans to shut down its 36-year-old transplant program at Akron City Hospital, unless Dr. Tanmay Girish Lal, an Indian-born doctor, gets "special permission from the federal government to continue working in the United States."[19] Across the U.S. border, residents of Windsor, Canada, are in a similar position, and have recently offered two Indian neurosurgeons free food "for the rest of their lives" as well as free massages, haircuts and automobile leases, in order to dissuade them from moving south to the U.S.[20]

The question goes further than scientists and surgeons. One such scenario has already begun to play out. Although not as dramatic as the dotcom demand for Indian software professionals, there are intriguing parallels, especially in terms of territory-specific jobs held by the locally-born. According to the American Bureau of Labor Statistics, one of the fastest-growing professions in the U.S. in the 2000-2010 period is expected to be nursing.[21] And yet, we also read elsewhere that "demand for nurses in the U.S. has set off another migration from India.... U.S. Consulate officials confirm that nurses and teachers can get immigrant visas for themselves and their families."[22] Yes, teachers too. In early March 2004, the *Washington Post* portrayed India's Vivek Agarwal who teaches science at Houston's M.B. Smiley High School, and complained that H-1B visa cutbacks threatened to curtail a crucial supply of teachers for America.[23]

Economists could no doubt construct hundreds of different scenarios to answer these questions, but as much as profitability and competitive concerns, or territoriality, such questions also lie at the roots of the relocation debate.

It is unfortunate that neither the Western media, international firms nor Indians themselves, sought to crack this conspiracy of silence during the go-go years of the Silicon Valley boom, symbolized by now-ironic cover stories in the *Economist*—"When companies connect—How the Internet will change business" (June 26, 1999), or *BusinessWeek* in its issue of January 31, 2000: "The New Economy. It Works in America. Will It Go Global?" Neither of them mentioned India.

Had there been adequate attention to India's huge role in the New Economy, there would have been two outcomes:

First, victims of relocation would have been better prepared to comprehend what is happening and why, rather than being walloped out of the blue; what is more, they may have even been proactive in finding alternatives, at least on a personal level. Thus, to take two examples, awareness about India's longstanding contributions to Siemens and Sprint may have prevented Western programmers from being subject to the "most humiliating experience" of their lives, after Siemens relocated from Florida,[24] or been wrongly surprised when Sprint 'begins' outsourcing to India[25]—a country where its joint venture with RPG Group rolled out SprintNet as far back as 1994.

Second, as a result of this awareness, the political context for managing relocation too may have been more meaningful than it appears now.

Ripped By Van Winkle

It is obvious that the Western public can hardly afford another surprise, by under-estimating or misreading India. The responsibility for this will again lie with the media, the interpreters of global change. It is however, by no means certain, that Western journalists will manage quickly enough to reverse their compulsive love for time-warped Indianisms, and avoid encouraging readers to remain patronizingly shut-eyed, primed juicily for another volley of bewilderment.

Thus, the widespread coverage in 2003 about Indian elephants wearing reflector lights on their backsides to avoid being hit by traffic:[26] most news items failed to report the equally intriguing fact that such elephants in India also have court-ordered pension rights at age 65,[27] and go to regular holiday camps[28] where they are given free anti-stress massages.

Reinforcing such clichés is the Western media's continuing focus on aberrations, especially those connected to India's huge population levels, such as the 'hundreds' and 'thousands' of casualties from bus and train accidents or heat waves; these, in fact, correspond remarkably to similar calamities in the West, on a per capita basis (or fall behind, as in the case of Europe's summer 2003 heat wave). Worse, after high-profile coverage of such incidents, few report outcomes.

For both the media and others, one key challenge over the coming years will be to understand that, unlike the West, India is not a 'form' but a 'content' culture. Some may do well to learn from Karen Elliott House, President of The Dow Jones Company. Unlike China, she noted as far back as 1997, India was 'chaotic' on the surface but 'stable' underneath.

Like much else in the country, this is why, in spite of the seeming chaos at its railway stations, India's 14,000 trains fare better on timings than do Britain's, as British newspaper the *Sunday Times* discovered in September 1998. An even more striking content-versus-form example from India would touch the soul of business process quality experts: *Forbes* magazine reported that the 175,000 daily deliveries of lunchboxes on foot, bicycles and trains by Mumbai's redoubtable 'tiffinwallahs,' amidst the city's dust, grime and seeming chaos, yields just "one error in every 8 million" deliveries.[29] For enterprise software portal ERPWeb.com, this is one of a handful of achievements worldwide to the futuristic Six Sigma quality standard.

Such a focus on content rather than form explains why, even as the Western media focused on low-end 'tandoori' software, India had, since the 1990s, silently been building strong foundations for its seemingly-meteoric rise today. It may also be a reason why few in Silicon Valley noticed the otherwise-quiet presence of 400,000 Indian engineers, and the growing strength of their contributions to the New Economy. Indeed, any future excesses in India's growing assault on white-collar jobs can only be avoided if the Western media (and its readers) do their homework, rather than simply blurt out worn-out clichés.

Give and Take: Cashing the post-dated Cheque

While Indians emigrating abroad have gained from relocation, so too have their host countries. Britain's Highly Skilled Migrant Programme, as mentioned above, is explicit about such mutual benefits.

What has clearly not benefited (until recently) is the emigrants' country of origin, India. The United Nations Development Program has assessed India's losses from emigration by software professionals at $2 billion per year.[30]

The cost to India is, of course, far higher, if one takes account of not just what is spent on educating future emigres, but also the opportunity cost of what the Indian economy loses by not using their skills at home. *BusinessWeek* noted this in October 2000: "As Indian graduates emigrate en masse, (Indian) high-tech companies are crying for help."[31]

These losses go beyond the New Economy. In the 1970s and 1980s, several academics sought to quantify the impact of the Indian 'brain drain' to the West, and reached impressive figures, sometimes in the hundreds of billions of dollars. One study estimates that the purely fiscal impact of Indian emigration to the U.S. is up to 0.58 percent of India's GDP per year[32]—year after year.

With the IITs growing reputation as some of the world's best engineering schools, they have obviously been a target for critics in India's aggressive media. Asks India's *Economic Times*: "Questions have always been raised about the ethical correctness of the government subsidizing IIT education. A large chunk of those who graduate from the elite institutes go abroad and do not offer much to their home country."[33]

Such a scenario has begun changing, and this too is part and parcel of the relocation process, its other new side. *BBC News* recently reported: "India's brain drain is coming full circle"[34] from the U.S. Consultants from McKinsey estimate that "some 40,000 H-1B visa holders returned to India in the past two years."[35] Not surprisingly, some in the U.S. fear that this exodus could eventually hurt America itself, which is losing "some of the world's smartest and most entrepreneurial people."[36]

Returning Indians comprise more than just casualties of the dotcom meltdown. Well before the bust, in July 2000, *Far Eastern Economic Review* noted: "For the first time, the brains of India are returning and powering New Economy companies back home. They are also transforming other parts of the economy, taking traditional, low value-added companies such as copycat pharmaceutical firms and pushing them up the value-added curve."[37] Less than a year later, the *Economist* described an Indian "expert in optical network-ing," who left IBM's Thomas Watson R&D center and then "poached engineers not only from the Indian labs of Cisco and Lucent but from as far away as Bell Labs in New Jersey" to launch his start-up Tejas. Another high-profile returnee was Bell Labs' algo-rithm guru Narendra Karmarkar, who joined an Indian research lab. Upon such foundations, the pull on technology jobs from India has accelerated, and will continue to strengthen.

In the broadest sense of the term, Indian-Americans are now clearly returning to India, and, in a sense, 'going back' with their know-how, returning their advantage. To some, India has finally begun to reap some fruits from its decades-old export of skills to the West. For example, the state-of-the-art $50 million chip lab at Indian technical school BITS mentioned in Chapter II is funded wholly by its alumni. It will inevitably impact on the viability of similar efforts in the West, whose principal advantage so far has been an ability to cover the last intellectual property mile through their deeper pockets.

More importantly, many more Indian engineers do not want to even leave India. *BusinessWeek* sensed this in a cover story in February 2003, when it referred to the "dazzling new technology parks rising on the dusty outskirts" of India's cities and to 26-year old Dharin Shah, a designer of third-generation mobile phones for Texas Instruments. "Five years ago, an engineer like Shah would have made a beeline for Silicon Valley. Now, he says, 'the sky is the limit here.'"38

Indeed, as borne out by the previous chapter, India has been "transformed into a place" where, according to the *Los Angeles Times*, for the first time, high-tech employment allows engineers "to own a home and a car and to settle into a middle-class lifestyle as comfortable as—maybe more comfortable than—the one they lived in the United States."39

In July 2003, Oracle's Chief Executive Larry Ellison demon-strated his usual savvy in grabbing moral mileage by seizing the Elephant by its trunk. "Globalization is controversial," he said. "Yet isn't it remarkable that right now Oracle employs 3,200 Indian citi-zens, paying increasing salaries, and providing a very high standard of living, helping to create a new middle class."40

'The Sky is the Limit?' Not Yet, But...

Though Dharin Shah and Oracle's 3,200 Indians might enjoy a lifestyle "maybe more comfortable" than in the U.S., they still represent the tip of an iceberg. Hundreds of millions of Indians have yet to see such dramatic gains.

But the waters are receding, and will do so further in the decades ahead. As previous chapters explain, India is seeking to ensure the continuing access to globalization's new opportunities for steadily larger chunks of its population. Given the mature and highly competitive nature of the country's democracy, above all in terms of populist opposition parties and the media, any sluggishness in such a process will be political suicide, for governments from any and all political parties.

On the other hand, following the political trade-offs inherent to India's decade-old economic reforms, it will also remain important for India to continue growing its economic pie. Not doing so would be equally suicidal.

Given its high value elements, and India's already strong position in the process, white-collar job relocation will clearly remain a vehicle of choice for the country. If anything could be a given in today's uncertain world, this is it.

Wages and Costs: Riddle or Creative Accounting?

Relocation involves striking a complex balance. Though wages are only one component of the costs of business, very few, especially in the media (and therefore, in its readership, among them trade unions, politicians and the general public) seem to take account of this fact.

Britain's *Daily Telegraph* claims simply that "Tesco, the country's largest retailer, has joined a host of other British companies in relocating parts of its operation to India to save on labour costs."[41] For David Clarke, chief executive of the British Computer Society, the argument is different: "Customers don't want low-wage suppliers, they want low-cost, high-quality suppliers."[42]

Cost and quality aside, other intangibles too are often at issue in relocation. Sir Keith Whitson, the outgoing chief executive of HSBC, provoked outrage in 2003, when he suggested the bank's

Indian workers were more motivated and harder working than their British counterparts.[43]

It is however on the issue of wage costs that much of the relocation debate tends to veer off track. As it happens, most operational and living costs in India, from food, fuel and electricity, to transport and telecommunications are also 'cheaper.' Carl Guardino, Chief Executive of the Silicon Valley Manufacturing Group, underlines this: India and China not only offer "incredibly high-skilled workers" but also "much lower costs of living and doing business."[44]

However, the benefits from such savings do not appear immediately and explains why India's pull on Western jobs is a complex issue. As revealed in Chapter II, Bain & Co. estimates that outsourcing in the life assurance sector brings the cost per policy down from "above £20" in the U.K. to just "under £15" in India. According to Deloitte Consulting, "while direct wage costs may be 80 percent lower in India, total labor cost savings are much more modest—10 percent to 15 percent for most companies."[45]

One explanation for the above is that there are important added costs to doing business in India that eat up much of the saving,[46] such as travel costs. For Dean Davison, a META Group analyst: "If you send four people to India once a year, you've just spent $50,000 to $60,000.... That's half of a person in terms of salaries and things."[47] Of course, a large number of Indian IT operations have now mastered the offshore process to such an extent that travel is no longer a major requirement for efficiency.

Whose Goalposts: Cheap India or Overpriced West?

Closely related to the question of relative costs is another underlying issue, a moral one, of exploitation of Indian workers—for example, in the frequent references to 'poverty-level wages'[48] and 'sweatshops,'[49] by virtue of which relocation is strongly viewed, from the moral high ground of the rich West, as a Bad Thing. Once again, such judgements, whose roots are strong and pervasive (for example, in anti-globalization debates about Nike shoes[50]), confuse an essential distinction between blue- and white-collar relocation.

There are, in fact, three crucial differences. First, Nike can move around relatively easily with its factory; it is unlikely that Motorola or Texas Instruments can replicate the accumulated chip-design know-how of their Indian staff as easily as, say in Cambodia. Second, Nike's transfer to a Vietnamese manufacturing location was unaccompanied by the emergence of globally competitive Vietnamese shoe brands; for Indian IT (as well as several other sectors), this is not the case. Third, it is arguable that, at the very least, higher-end skills should be difficult to replicate—among other reasons, by virtue of being predefined as high-value. Indeed, one may propose that reloca-tion of higher-end skills, or in the words of an American newspaper, "high-paying, highly sought-after jobs that often require advanced degrees and years of study to attain,"[51] simply means a move out from (artificially) expensive suppliers in similarly expensive settings towards more realistic alternatives. In software in particular, the huge lead in Indian quality[52] clearly demonstrates the irony of a situation where a 'cheaper' workforce seems to also be at least as good, in one of the highest skilled activities of the modern age.

The 'at least as good' qualifier is important, in the face of asser-tions, such as an unattributed one from American columnist Thomas Sowell, that, "by and large," "the average productivity of Indian (IT) workers is about 15 percent of that of American work-ers."[53] This claim projects a similar story as a 'bunch' of Indians doing an American IT job (see Chapter I), but, unless Sowell has confused wages with productivity, it is hardly true. The respected Capers Jones Software Productivity Research, for example, finds the performance of an average Indian programmer, expressed according to the industry standard of function points per month, is almost 650, compared to just 500-550 for the U.K., the U.S. and France, 550-600 for Brazil, and much higher than Russia's 400-450.

Exploitation: Shafting them Down the E-coal Mine?

Purchasing power parity (PPP), which as explained previously gives an indication of revenues related to local costs in local curren-cies, may again provide the best way to extricate the truth from alle-gations about exploitation. Though becoming popular as a measure of GDP, very few, if any, arguments about job relocation pay any attention to the impact of PPP as an indicator of real versus nominal wages.*

In simple terms, India's PPP multiplier is accepted to be roughly 5—or the ratio between its GDP in purchasing power parity to that in U.S. dollars.[54] This would mean that workers in India are not being 'exploited,' as long as they earn more than one-fifth of their counterparts in the West.

Indeed, a multiple of five is accepted to be the prevailing ratio between Indian and American software wages,[55] although differences vary considerably, especially when skill levels and non-wage costs are taken into account. For Cap Gemini Ernst & Young, the "average" computer programmer in India costs $20 per hour in wages and benefits, "compared to $65 per hour for an American with a comparable degree and experience."[56] At the other end of the scale is a report that "big U.S. investment banks, it seems, are outsourcing analytical work to India, on salaries one eighth the going rate in Manhattan,"[57] or even further, the comparison by McKinsey Global Institute of "a $60-an-hour software job" shipped to "a $6-an-hour code writer in India."[58]

In real life, as the examples above show, the PPP-adjusted gap varies considerably, based on the level of skills in question. As a rule of thumb, the gap narrows as one goes up the skills (and wages) spectrum.[59]

A key complexity with wage and cost assessments is that employers frequently relocate various permutations and combinations of white-collar skills. They have been doing so for some time. In 1998, this author explained such issues in British magazine *Business Eye*:

> Though much emphasis has been given to cost advantages, international companies increasingly see a differentiated mix of advantages in determining the benefits of an Indian presence.... For maintenance, customization and migration, companies choose India for inexpensive talent, and one that (like much else in the country) is available in large numbers. At the other end, many employ world-class (and not necessarily less expensive) Indian talents to design and improve products.... For most middle-sized international companies, however, India's promise lies in leveraging a mix of skills from across the spectrum, and paying adequate attention to devising the most appropriate cost-benefit combination, that is vis-a-vis home country operations.[60]

---

*Possibly the most violent depiction of this is the World Bank's widely-quoted definition that $1 a day in income represents a "minimum standard of living," and that 28.3 percent of the world's population live below it. It defeats imagination how anyone could survive on less than a third of the $3.49 cost of a box of Ritz crackers or Chips Ahoy cookies at Kroger's.

In turn, the use of PPP would also underline to top talent in India, such as designers and inventors, that they are not being exploited. For example, referring to a new release of one of the world's most popular software programs, Adobe's PageMaker, India's *Hindustan Times* asked its readers in January 2002 whether they were aware it was "created by an Indian team out of its New Delhi office. While the new package may do wonders for the company's bottom line, all that the Indian software pros got to take home was $7,000 for each patent granted."[61] Referring to the Merrill Lynch study which found 'core' R&D exports from India reaching $4 billion, the newspaper concluded that "e-coal mines" created intellectual property "that makes billions for shareholders back home while their Indian lab coats are handed a pittance." The $7,000 paid per patent would, of course, have a very different meaning if it was PPP-weighted with a multiple of 5, to $35,000, corresponding much more closely to payments by IT companies to American inventors.

The final argument for using PPP is straightforward. Suppose, as an alternative, Indian workers were paid the same as American workers were, and in U.S. dollars. This would create a new over-class of obscenely rich people in India, in glaring opposition to the country's successes in not only creating one of the world's most equal societies but also in distributing benefits of its software-led globalization to a steadily-increasing share of its population.

Though such arguments may deflect complaints about cheap Indian techno-coolies slaving in sweatshops, PPP (accompanied by exchange rate realignment) will eventually impact on the issue of whether it is India which is cheap, or the West which is over-priced.

The best example of PPP at work is the still-novel sight in India, of white Americans and Europeans beginning to work for Indian employers. According to news agency UPI: "Headhunters say that over 20,000 expats were recently recruited by Indian companies.... Drop in at India's new dollar spinning back-office outfits, and you will find French, German, Swedish, Finnish, Norwegian, Swiss, Japanese, besides English rubbing shoulders with Indian executives and working at 25 percent of the salary levels of their home countries."

These expatriates, in fact, understand and live by the rules of PPP. "'The cost of living is lower in India; I responded to an ad and here I am,' says 29-year old Ethel Graff of back office service provider Technovate Solutions."[62]

The Global Context of Relocation

As much as countries, globalization (and relocation) involves people, inhabitants of countries. The difference between these two is often overlooked. Some figures,[63] placed in a comparative context, may help address this distinction—about the difference between the composite threat from India, and the position of Indians, who underwrite such a challenge and seek to reap its benefits.

In spite of its impressive development since economic reforms in the early 1990s and India's impending status in the very near future as the world's third biggest economy, the average American's $34,479 purchasing power income in 2002 (based on a breakdown of World Bank statistics) was still 13.6 times higher than the $2,529 for an Indian. In other words, a typical American earns and consumes more in one month than an average Indian does in an entire year[64]; the figure for Europeans, the clear beneficiaries of globalization's 19th century round, is only slightly less impressive. Still worse, the average income of the poorest 20 percent of Americans at $8,964, was still significantly above the $5,868 for the richest 20 percent of Indians.

Morally, therefore, resisting relocation across-the-board will be a tough call, given such huge income gaps, and the fact that the process is one way to close it, as it has begun to do. Indeed, it requires little effort to appreciate the interconnection between the following facts:

- In the U.S., "you are forced out of a $25-an-hour job and, after six months of job hunting, find work at $20 an hour. Two years later, having struggled back to $23 an hour, you are laid off again, and you slip back into the next job at $21 an hour."[65] Other evidence too justifies this decline. In its March 1, 2004, issue, *BusinessWeek* cited data from Foote Partners showing average pay in America for application developers fell by 17.5 percent in 2002-2003. For database administrators, the drop was 14.7 percent and for system administrators 5.4 percent.

- But America's loss was India's gain. Led by India's IT and BPO boom, global human resources firm Hewitt Associates found that "Indian workers gained an average salary increase of 14 percent in 2003. This was twice as much as second placed Philippines, where pay was up about 7 percent."[66]

...and its implications

Whatever one's verdict on the process, global income leveling is clearly another side of the relocation coin. From Bob Geldof's Band Aid to the 1970s UN Fund for Commodities, other solutions to Third World poverty have failed, and only India and China—relocation's white-collar and blue-collar entrepots—are managing to show an alternative way.

To mark the outer boundaries of the relocation debate requires a straightforward exercise with numbers. If the world's entire economic output of $47.4 trillion in 2002 (again, World Bank figures) is redistributed equally (as some anti-globalization proponents may unwittingly wish for), everyone—Americans and Europeans, Indians, Chinese, Croats, Colombians, Fijians and Ghanaians—would have a per capita purchasing power of $7,526, that is, just after Russia's current $7,971, but still some way behind Mexico's $8,493. This would make Americans four times poorer, but it would still be over three times the average Indian's income in 2002. Equal redistribution of world income would of course be hardly desirable (for Americans at least), or feasible: the Soviet Union attempted such a miracle in the early 20th century; the Great Depression partially achieved it less than two decades later. Clearly, the world economy will have to continue growing to make leveling more than a zero-sum game, and part of this growth will involve new centers of productivity and excellence.

Indeed, this should be obvious. Relocation is driven as much by 'wages' as by costs and disparities in global, inter-country standards of living. For the first time in history, a 'poor' country like India is acquiring some of the best-paying jobs from the 'rich' world. The leveling down of often-obscene differences in living standards between rich and poor countries is both part of the process and a sine qua non for finding a way out of poverty in poor countries. There are simply no alternatives.

Meanwhile, in the long term, relocation-led income leveling, between countries, within an expanding world economy, is also the only way to reduce the huge difference in costs of living. In turn, such leveling would prevent upheavals from another future round of relocation: American jobs are after all not going to Britain, Germany or other rich Western countries, and as the example of telemarketing wages in Virginia show (Chapter II), at the lower-end of white-collar jobs at least, this leveling may have already begun to dam the tide.

Alongside such a process, giant economies like India and China, may as discussed, eventually force the global exchange rate system towards closer parity between the longer-term purchasing power of their currencies and the U.S. dollar. Such a long-term trend has already begun (the American government has, after all, been pressing China to revalue, and India's rupee has steadily strengthened). Although some blips cannot be ruled out in the medium-term, it will inevitably have consequences for America's predominant position in the global economy. This would parallel Great Britain's eclipse by America itself after it abandoned the gold standard in September 1931.

Indeed, like Britain in 1931, America's fundamental challenge is simple. The country has been living beyond its means, and has become heavily dependent on the outside world, to both build and pay for its success. In engineering, for example, "43% of the master's degrees and 54% of the doctoral degrees awarded by U.S. universities go to foreign-born students."[67] On its part, the National Science Foundation estimates "foreign-born workers with bachelor's degrees represented 17 percent of all science and engineering positions..., 29 (percent) of master's degree positions and 38 percent of PhDs" in the U.S. But as previous examples show, America's shortage goes beyond this, to nurses, high-school science teachers and more.

Whether or not the American quandary is 'imperial overstretch' or, like Gibbons' Rome, a result of 'immoderate greatness' is beyond the scope of this book. It is nevertheless a fact of life that America has become immensely dependent on India, on China, and on Asia. Such dependence goes beyond its massive reliance on Indians to build the New Economy, or the continuing role of skilled Indians and others to prop up its science and technology superstructure. There is another, more alarming statistic: America's $3 trillion debt (more than the purchasing power GDP of India) is going to become untenable. The bulk of this debt is held by Asians, who will inevitably see alternative opportunities emerging, in India and China, as indeed already has the American investment community.

Meanwhile, with or without a depreciation of the dollar, India's own rapid economic growth will eventually see a growing number of Indians earning as much as the average American or European; based on the World Bank's income distribution figures, the number in 2003 would be no more than 25-30 million. At some point in the next decade, when this figure reaches, say, 100 million, India will clearly possess the critical mass of wealth to invest more in its own success (for example, pay for scores more IITs) and accelerate its advantage further. This is only a matter of time.

Living and Leveling—Who Pays the Price?

Someone in the West losing a white-collar job is a victim of the relocation tide, no matter what the explanation. However, getting a grip on the underlying forces at play is imperative to forge an effective response, and do so without feeling victimized and helpless. Resisting such a powerful tide, through anger or comforting cliches, is simply a way to paralysis.

To summarize the key issues:

Relocation does not move white-collar jobs to a sweatshop; most workers receiving these jobs will have at least an approximately comparable standard of living. There also are cost and numerous other advantages for Western employers in moving out such jobs, at least some of which are too compelling to resist.

The Indian challenge has not emerged as a bolt from the blue. India's growing role as a repositary for relocated jobs derives principally from its contribution to building the New Economy, including provision of both its bounties and sometimes, its previous 'salary madness.' India will therefore encourage relocation; it is India's job to do so.

Meanwhile, legislative restrictions on relocation will be meaningless, given the complex, massive and enduring interconnections between Indian and global IT, as well as the lure of the huge, fast-growing Indian market on which Western exporters will become increasingly dependent. Blanket laws against relocation, especially in the current global economic climate, would only trigger equal and opposite responses, marking a return to the navel-gazing, beggar-thy-neighbor process which sparked the Great Depression's race to the bottom. Few, especially in politics and Big Business, but also outside such circles, would wish for this.

As the first chapter shows, anti-offshore outsourcing laws are already little more than token, and, while wading their way through congressional committees, most will serve to simply buy time. Powerful, countervailing pressures are already in play, at the World Trade Organization, within India's strengthening military-strategic partnership with the U.S., and elsewhere. Some of these will come forcefully into view after the American election.

In the years ahead, it is clear that to become effective, the key debate about relocation will have to shift away from India-versus-America to what American (and other Western) IT professionals need to do about retaining both their relevance and excellence. Meanwhile, Americans will also have to seek ways to address systemic challenges within their own country as a result of this round of globalization—rather like India has done so far.

Though relocation has clearly started to bridge obscene, static and sometimes worsening, differences, in incomes between the West and the rest of the world, only the naive would imagine that relocating corporations are deeply concerned about its moral consequences. Paying overseas workers less, even if they do acquire the same purchasing power as Americans, means corporations acquire very tangible benefits from the global leveling process, while American workers lose because their jobs are outsourced.

One landmark test for the future is therefore internal to the American system, in terms of finding ways to better manage and redistribute its own wealth. This would clearly offer a more meaningful way to coping with relocation instead of fighting the profoundly structural roots of this historical, economic, political and moral tide. Another unavoidable priority will be to prop up American education, so that it brings its own skills into more balance with the requirements of its economy. Even if this does not solve problems associated with the current relocation round, it will prevent the eventual deskilling of America. This is hardly fantasy, as shown by examples in this book.

These two responses would form the only real foundations for a reasoned response to relocation. The final chapter offers more.

CHAPTER VIII

Preparing America for the New Age of Globalization

Relocation is a major challenge within the Western world for three different actors. Individuals seek jobs and financial security, companies are driven by profits (and, in many cases, quarterly results), while governments are concerned with elections, economic growth and retention of strategic, long-term national advantage in a changing world.

Reconciling these different and sometimes-opposed concerns has always been a challenge. It is now even more so, given the unexpected new directions taken by globalization, in the form of the exodus of economically high-value, white-collar jobs. For all three actors, the government, companies and employees, it is important that relocation neither be left to run its course freely, rampaging through America's economic innards, nor demonized and resisted with words and emotions, like a futile Last Stand.

Though it is obvious that no policy can reverse the long-term dynamics of the global leveling process, anchored as it is in demographics and the Himalayan gaps in worldwide living costs/standards, the very nature of the Internet does offer some intriguing new possibilities to think-out-of-the-Box, creating new definitions and paradigms for IT jobs. Some of these may dampen the worst effects of the relocation process.

Given below are some suggestions to manage relocation, for both individuals and the American government. The list is by no means a Silver Bullet, but, against the backdrop of discussions in this book, is meant to be a useful set of first steps.

Several of its suggestions also apply to Europe, tied closely as it is to the American political and economic umbrella, and facing similar quandaries about its future—not least a near-zero rate of growth, its shaky public finances, its faster-aging population, and as mentioned in Chapter I, the very real risk of moving on to 'history's exit ramp.'

IT workers

To Avoid

- Waiting for economic recovery. As discussed previously, the timing of such a recovery remains unclear. So do its parameters. The shape of the Western territorial technology jobs market in 2005 or 2006 is likely to bear little resemblance to that of the 1990s. In addition, there is no guarantee (quite the contrary, in fact) that yet another round of relocation will not follow economic recovery.

To Do at home

- Identify and train for emerging skill niches. A recent feature on offshore-proofing IT careers suggests American IT staff focus on five areas: requirements analysis, business process design, contract management, business relationship management and architecture planning.[1] Although the writer acknowledges that "11 percent of companies had outsourced system and architecture planning offshore despite the fact that this is one of two categories that analysts and chief information officers have predicted would never leave the home shores," this still leaves opportunities in almost nine out of 10 employers.

- Identify and train for 'sensitive' sectors. John Challenger, chief executive of international outplacement consultants Challenger, Gray & Christmas recommends tech workers look at more 'sensitive' sectors, such as "government and military technology, health care and pharmaceuticals." Although India is clearly gearing up for addressing IT security and privacy concerns, such fields are unlikely to quickly fall under its suction. They also provide more viable fields for legislation to dampen the speed of relocation, than do blanket restrictions on offshore outsourcing.

To Do abroad

- Reverse relocation. Headhunters in India, notes the *International Herald Tribune*, corroborate that "inquiries have begun coming in from top-level and middle-level executives from the West, seeking jobs with top Indian technology firms."[2] If outsourcing to India continues unabated, "India can soon become a global job hub," says one recruiter.[3] On its part, the Indian government is evidently serious about encouraging reverse relocation. Its new Science and Technology Policy framework has called for "attracting expatriate talent" as a way to develop high-end management and R&D, and has also urged "special fiscal incentives" to meet such goals.[4]

- Think beyond Top IT firms. The boom in Indian IT and the industry's intensive value-migration has created a gap for technology and project management skills, especially in small- and middle-sized Indian firms. In early 2004, for example, the CEO of a systems integration firm in southern India "could manage to find only three out of ten support engineers that he was supposed to provide on his client-site, as part of the deliverables."[5] While getting a newly qualified graduate was not a problem for mid-sized Indian firm Ontrack, "finding a Microsoft or Cisco-certified engineer with three or four years experience, who can do justice to complex technical requirements at the client-site, is increasingly becoming difficult." This is of course precisely the job profile which continues to face the axe in the West.

- Make an opportunity out of threat. Help smaller Indian IT firms acquire global competencies. Over the years, programming has changed from bottom-up methods of first mastering business processes and then building IT systems, to a top-down approach, where software packages permit definition of future requirements and the design of more-complex and agile IT systems. For many businesses, which require leveraging of cutting-edge technologies, being 'local' provides an edge, which cannot be fully compensated by the cost- and scale advantages of a pureplay offshore facility.

Given that cost is one of the factors driving IT companies to offshore, and it is usually larger firms who are doing this, there may be room for entirely new offshore paradigms; these would be devoid of one of the biggest handicaps of the large firms, namely their huge overheads.

In such a model, requirements design and analysis would be handled by loosely-structured but well-informed and proactive networks of Western technology professionals, who have the advantage of business/cultural affinity with customers, as well as proximity. They could, in turn, link up to smaller Indian firms (who, unlike their larger counterparts, cannot do-it-themselves and are desperate for such assistance).

The American Government

To Avoid

- Pretending there is no relocation problem; there very clearly is, and it threatens some cherished assumptions. Doing nothing will make the problem a crisis, or worse. As Bob Herbert writes in the *New York Times*, "One of the things that sank with the Titanic was the theory that it was unsinkable."[6]
- Playing election campaign footsie with territorial anti-offshore outsourcing laws, which miss the point, and whose limitations will become increasingly evident in the months and years ahead.
- Focusing on short-term, self-canceling solutions. As this book has repeatedly shown, India's challenge sweeps across the entire range of skills. The $8.1 million lost by preventing Indian IT firm TCS from a contract in Indiana (see Chapter I) would have provided one full year of training support under the Bush administration's proposed "personal re-employment account bill" for 2,700 Americans. This may even have been offered out of TCS' own "state-of-the-art" Training Center in Columbus, Indiana. The end result would clearly have been more meaningful.

To Do:
Assist Relocated Workers
Such assistance will not only be far cheaper than denying the huge benefits of international trade to 300 million consumers by protectionism; it is also more sustainable, given changes in geopolitical realities.

- Implement job insurance. The 1960s-era Trade Adjustment Assistance Program, which provides employee-funded insurance for laid-off workers, does not cover programmers and other information workers, and in the absence of an alternative program, is unjustifiable. In early 2004, a lawsuit in the U.S. Court of International Trade in New York accused the Labor Department of illegally denying them such benefits; the suit seeks class-action status, and may involve up to 10,000 claimants.[7]

To Do:
Fund Such Assistance

- Implement an offshore outsourcing tax, along the lines of suggestions by Congressman Dan Manzullo[8] and former Clinton Administration Labor Secretary Robert Reich,[9] and thereby pay for transition by Americans. As Deloitte Consulting's figures show in the previous chapter, cost savings from offshore outsourcing are no more than 10-15 percent for most companies. This, of course, may be inaccurate, apply only to certain kinds of offshore effort, or do so in a short-term timeframe alone; for Nariman Behravesh, chief economist at Global Insight, "unthinkably large tax incentives" would be required to offset lower wages in countries like India and China.[10] However, such a move (or in Britain, scrapping of a 'crackpot' exemption on value-added tax by offshore firms[11]) would at least prevent a lemming-like rush to cash in on the offshore bonanza and dampen potential excesses of relocation, at least for the much larger mass of low-end jobs.

- Make offshore outsourcing businesses contribute to job insurance. Based on a study conducted by scholars at the University of California and the Brookings Institution, McKinsey Global Institute estimates that "for as little as 4 to 5 percent of the savings companies realized from offshore outsourcing, they could insure all full-time workers who lost jobs as a result."[12] Such a step would not penalize companies for real business decisions but, in the wake of the dotcom bust, seek to prevent a self-fuelling cycle of short-termism. It could also form part of a rationalization of federal regulatory costs, estimated by the Office of Advocacy of the U.S. Small Business Administration, at $7,000 per employee for small businesses (20, or fewer employees) and $4,300-4,400 per employee for larger ones.

To Do:
Train for the Future

Given the virtual world of the Internet, the absence of local employment does not mean that skilled/re-skilled IT professionals cannot find new opportunities elsewhere—as explained previously, even in India. But it is equally important to know which way skills requirements are evolving.

- Require technology firms to publish rolling five-year Jobs Plans. Such baseline information is already collected routinely by large companies, although for internal audits. A first step in this direction was taken in Britain in February 2004, after financial services giant HSBC agreed to provide unions with two years' notice of its 'global resourcing' plans.[13] A meaningful Jobs Plan would provide both historical and current data on the age groups, income-levels and technical skill-sets lost as part of relocation,[14] and those expected to replace them.[15] Aggregated into national-level data, it could be leveraged to identify the shape of nascent, next-generation skillsets towards which training and education could be directed. One aim would be to add a quality element to whatever be the shape of new job creation in 2004 and beyond.

  To be more meaningful, the Jobs Plan should also be accompanied by territorial breakdown,[16] in order to assess any volume-based pull from India on new skills. Such a Plan may, therefore, avoid another roller-coaster relocation round, by compelling American corporations to think concretely about how they plan to avoid a new (domestic) high-tech skills shortage after economic recovery.

- Establish IT training schemes. In spite of critics of federal training programs (such as Gordon Lafer of the University of Oregon),[17] most efforts so far have concerned blue-collar jobs. Meanwhile, the sheer unexpectedness of white-collar job relocation, as well as its speed and violence, have clearly conspired to numb some of its victims. A catalyst for reversing such numbing, such as a structured federal IT training program, may prove to be useful—especially since it has not been tried before.

  IT training might even be provided, efficiently, in India, or through cost-effective Indian online IT training firms, such as NIIT's netvarsity.com or Aptech. Alex Taylor, head of technology services at British telecoms giant BT, has already suggested that managers "be sent to India to attend training courses because these are significantly cheaper than courses at home."[18] An Indian training input would yield more than simple savings; it would be an efficient multiplier in terms of the crucial goal of acquiring and staying in touch with new skills, especially at it would be closely connected to India's own inevitable rise in the world IT stakes.

To Do:
Pay for Training

- Implement a human investment tax credit. This has been proposed by Catherine Mann of the Institute for International Economics in Washington,[20] and would be similar to what electronics makers got after free-trade agreements in the 1990s. Such credits would provide incentives for American business (and others) to retrain engineers, focused on emerging skill requirements (as explained above).

To Do:
Think Globally, Act Futuristically.

- Establish a bipartisan, cross-sectoral, employer-union framework. In November 2003, Alan Tonelson, a researcher with the U.S. Business and Industrial Council, noted that though the relocation trend was clearly nationwide, "there is virtually no national political response."[20] Such a response is clearly an immediate requirement. However, it should not only provide immediate remedies to victims of relocation, but also seek realistic long-term responses to the structural challenges faced by America.
- Provide tax credits and other forms of support to encourage Indian IT firms to hire Americans. Indian firms clearly hold the long-term advantage and will eventually emerge as winners, against both the higher-cost (and higher-overhead) constraints of their American and European competitors. Participating actively in such an inevitability would be a way to ride the relocation tide, and help its victims.
- Consider similar support to encourage Americans to find jobs in India, or otherwise establish connections to Indian IT.

Like Indian firms, India also possesses clear long-term structural advantages in the global IT stakes. Encouraging Americans to directly participate in its success would provide obvious mutual benefits.

- Bolster basic science education. *New York Times* columnist Nicholas Kristof notes that children in Bangalore study algebra in elementary school and hopes "that the loss of jobs in medicine and computers to India and elsewhere will again jolt us into bolstering our own teaching of math and science."[21] Such a step should form part of a wider revamp of education discussed below.

- Learn from the Indian example in fostering globally competitive skills, in spite of the country's massive handicaps. Instances of openly seeking to learn from India are growing. Thus, according to the *Washington Post*, the University of Denver's Chancellor has modified admissions procedures after he "visited a business school in India."[22] Following the U.S. blackouts in August 2003, a delegation of American energy regulators "turned to India for help. The country is a world leader in managing blackouts,"[23] observed the *Financial Times*. One key lesson may be the undisputed excellence of the Indian Institutes of Technology (IITs). Such institutes have produced some of the world's best engineers, because the Indian government heavily subsidizes them, and provides relatively equal opportunity for qualified entrants, regardless of their ability to pay. As India's economy grows, such access will broaden and deepen further, even as subsidies remain or increase further; in January 2004, the Indian Supreme Court appeared to be setting the stage for mandating cuts in IIT fees, to a targeted level of one-third India's per capita GDP.[24] On such a yardstick, a top U.S. engineering school like MIT would have fees of about $11,000 a year, three-and-a-half times below its level of $39,200.[25]

Most of the above suggestions are simply meant to manage relocation. Given its demographics, and its decades of dependence on India and other countries, America has, as mentioned, clearly begun to live beyond its means. By contrast, India's challenge to the West on white-collar jobs is simply an attempt by the country to live up to its capacities. This too is a moral issue accompanying relocation.

In the years ahead, in spite of the clearly world-class stature of American universities, the looming shortage of high-school science teachers and the huge share of foreign-born engineers, graduates and Ph.Ds in America, shows that the entire U.S. education system is lopsided. More than Nobel Prizes, both the education provision and access deficit demand high-level political attention. Although not an answer to the immediate crisis, such a deficit explains several structural shortcomings associated with relocation. It also offers the only long-term solution.

Should the reach of the American educational system not be quickly extended, within a few years the quality threat from the burgeoning mass of a younger population in a richer India (with a still-heavily-subsidized technical education system) will clearly become an irreversible onslaught.

The start of this chapter noted that retention of strategic, long-term national advantage was a priority for any government. In the face of the massive and complex challenges of white-collar job relocation, America can simply not afford to be an exception.

Notes

Author's Note

1 Communists From India Seek the Help of Capitalists, *New York Times*, May 16, 2004.
2 India Election Shock Won't Hurt Business -US Execs, *Reuters*, May 13, 2004.

Chapter One

1 More 'Can I Help You?' Jobs Migrate From U.S. to India, *New York Times*: May 11, 2003.
2 Around The Markets: Outsourcing Hits Wall Street, *Boston Globe*: May 7, 2003.
3 One in 10 U.S. Tech Jobs May Move Overseas by End-2004—Gartner Report, *Reuters*: July 30, 2003.
4 Job Cuts to Continue Till '05? *Cyber India Online*: December 4, 2003.
5 Phone Inquiries Ring in New Jobs, *BBC News*: February 19, 2003.
6 Perot Aims for 40% Growth in India, *Cyber India Online*: February 5, 2004.
7 Over 40 percent of New Development Activity Is Now Outsourced, Says META Group, *Business Wire*: November 12, 2003.
8 IT Outsourcing: Not All Gloom and Doom, *CIOToday.com*: November 21, 2003.
9 Outlandish Outsourcing: What Are Its Long-Term Effects, *TechWeb*: November 3, 2003.
10 Intel Chairman Says U.S. Is Losing Edge, *Washington Post*: October 10, 2003.
11 Where Your Job Is Going? *Fortune*: November 24, 2003.
12 The Rise of India, *BusinessWeek*: December 8, 2003.
13 Business In Brief, *Washington Post*: February 13, 2004.
14 Making Software to Help Manage Business Processes, *Washington Post*: February 16, 2004.
15 Now Playing: New Epic War Over U.S. Jobs, *Free Press Detroit*: July 25, 2003.
16 Real Estate Center Economist Says U.S. Job Market in Jeopardy, *Business Wire*: November 12, 2003.
17 IT Jobs Rapidly Moving Off Shore, *Washington Times*: October 16, 2003.
18 U.S. Loses 540,000 Tech Jobs, *Reuters*: November 20, 2003.
19 Exec Outlines Perils of Offshore Outsourcing, *Tech Web*: October 1, 2003.
20 The Programmer's Future, *Information Week*, November 17, 2003.
21 Prés des Trois Quarts des Salariés Français Travaillent Aujourd'hui Dans Les Services, *Le Monde*: February 20, 2004.
22 High-Tech Degrees Don't Guarantee Jobs, *Associated Press*: January 26, 2004.
23 Survey: Outsourcing May Hit Information Technology Careers, *CNET News.com*: July 9, 2003
24 Anxious About Outsourcing, *Washington Post*: January 31, 2004.
25 The Coming Job Boom, *Business 3.0*, September 2003.
26 Jobs Lost Abroad: Host of New Causes for an Old Problem, *New York Times*: February 15, 2004.
27 Welcome The Rise of China and India, *The Telegraph Online*: October 12, 2003.
28 Paul Craig Roberts, Seeking Jobs in the USA, *Washington Times*: August 6, 2003.
29 Brussels to Set Out Why EU Is Trailing U.S., *Financial Times*: January 20, 2004.
30 La Commission Prend Conscience Du Retard European, *Le Monde*: February 20, 2004.

31 UN Chief Kofi Annan Accepts Invitation to Address Canadian Parliament, *Canadian Press*: January 23, 2004.
32 The British-U.S. Axis No Longer Makes Any Sense, *Guardian*: February 21, 2004.
33 Putting Job Flight in Perspective, *New York Times*: December 22, 2003.
34 One in 10 U.S. Tech Jobs May Move Offshore-Report, *Reuters*: July 30, 2003.
35 White-Collar Jobs Moving Abroad, *Christian Science Monitor*: July 29, 2003. This figure stands in stark contrast to a claim by U.S. consulting firm Evalueserve (in a study funded by the Indian IT industry lobby group Nasscom), that "only about 0.2 percent of American workers lose their jobs and remain unemployed for more than three months because of outsourcing." See 'India to U.S.: Outsourcing Good for U.S., Good for You,' *Reuters*: October 9, 2003.
36 The Bright Side of Sending Jobs Overseas, *New York Times*: February 15, 2004.
37 Experts Urge Strong Education Rather Than Big Tariffs, *New York Times*: July 28, 2003.
38 Jobs Migrating Overseas, But It's A Two-Way Street, *Los Angeles Times*: July 20, 2003.
39 High-Tech Jobs Are Going Abroad! But That's Okay, *Washington Post*: November 26, 2003.
40 Losing Jobs Is Always Painful, *Cyber India Online*: November 12, 2003.
41 Experts Urge Strong Education Rather Than Big Tariffs, *New York Times*: July 28, 2003
42 A New Crop of Tech Titans, *New York Post*: September 17, 2003.
43 The Indian Machine, *Wired*: February 2004.
44 Are You Ready for a Nanotechnology Career, *Reuters*: February 3, 2004.
45 HP: Protectionism Won't Save Europe's Jobs, *CNET News.com*: January 23, 2004.
46 HP to Set up Captive Call Center, *Cyber India Online*: October 8, 2003.
47 HP's OpenCall to Enhance Telco Services, *Cyber India Online*: February 13, 2004.
48 The New HP Way: World's Cheapest Consultants, *Forbes*: December 12, 2003.
49 The Globalization of White-Collar Jobs: Can America Lose These Jobs and Still Prosper? *House Committee on Small Business*: June 18, 2003.
50 Millions of U.K. Jobs Seem Ripe for Export, *FT.com*: October 17, 2003.
51 Education Is No Protection, *New York Times*: January 26, 2004.
52 Reuters Takes Outsourcing to a New Level With Journalists, *New York Times*: February 9, 2004.
53 Outsourcing America, *Washington Post*: February 21, 2004.
54 We Import Cars and Stereos, So Why Not CEOs, *Los Angeles Times*, February 6, 2004.
55 At Forum, White-Collar Job Migration Is A Hot Topic, *International Herald Tribune*: January 24, 2004.
56 Nation Losing More Than Unskilled Work, *Los Angeles Times*: October 20, 2003.
57 Jobless Say Economic Recovery Is A Mirage, *Associated Press*: August 3, 2003
58 Job Exports May Imperil U.S. Programmers, *Associated Press*: July 13, 2003.
59 To Ease Fears About Jobs, Put Imagination to Work, *Los Angeles Times*: January 4, 2004.
60 North American Firms Set Pace for World's Vehicle Supplier Industry, Says New A.T. Kearney Study, *Canada Newswire*: August 6, 2003.
61 India's Auto Industry Drives Offshore, *Washington Times*: October 1, 2003.
62 Blessed Are the Underdeveloped, *Forbes.com*: December 1, 1997.
63 Why Is Indian IT A Success, *ID Side*: May 1998
64 White-Collar Jobs Moving Abroad, *Christian Science Monitor*: July 29, 2003
65 The New IT Worker: Angry and Proactive, *Computerworld*: April 28, 2003.
66 U.K. Offshore IT Staffing Debate Heats Up, *CBR Magazine*: September 24, 2003.
67 U.S. Economy to Benefit From Offshoring: Mckinsey Report, *Hindu*: November 27, 2003.
68 Jobs Cut Since 2001 Gone for Good: U.S. Study, *Business Times*: September 29, 2003
69 U.S. IT Cos Join Fight Against BPO Backlash, *Financial Express*: January 20, 2004.

70 Call Centres Take The Passage to India, *Daily Telegraph*: May 25, 2003.
71 The Rise of India, *Business Week*: December 8, 2003.
72 See, for example, "Coming and Going" in "Survey of Corporate Leadership," *The Economist*: October 25, 2003.
73 Where The Good Jobs Are Going, *Time*: July 28, 2003.
74 Two Steps to Protecting Your Job From Offshore Outsourcing, *CNET Networks*: October 16, 2003.
75 The Coming Job Boom, *Business 2.0*, September 30, 2003.
76 India May Gain From U.S. Labour Shortage: Study, *Hindu*: October 10, 2003.
77 A Global Demographic Time Bomb, *BusinessWeek Online*: January 24, 2004.
78 Greenspan Pushes Social Security Cuts, *Associated Press*: February 26, 2004.
79 The article begins: "Kofi Annan, the UN secretary-general, has launched a scathing attack on 'fortress Europe,' warning that its 'dehumanising' policies towards immigrants are leading many to their deaths." See 'Annan attacks fortress Europe over migrants,' *The Guardian*: January 30, 2004.
80 U.N.: Rich Nations Mixed on Immigration: *Associated Press*, January 29, 2004.
81 A Global Demographic Time Bomb, *BusinessWeek* Online: January 24, 2003.
82 Young, Indian and A Gandhi—But Can Priyanka Boost Congress Party at Polls? *Financial Times*: January 24, 2004.
83 New Reality Is Leaving Growth in The Mire, *New York Times*: July 20, 2003.
84 A Missing Statistic: U.S. Jobs That Went Overseas, *New York Times*: October 6, 2003.
85 If You Get the Ax, Don't Blame India, *Los Angeles Times*: February 6, 2004.
86 Casualties of the Recovery, *Washington Post*: September 5, 2003.
87 The Reality of The Jobless Recovery, *International Herald Tribune*: October 28, 2003.
88 Jobless Count Skips millions, *Los Angeles Times*: December 29, 2003.
89 As High-Income Jobs Vanish, Professionals Struggle to Get by, *International Herald Tribune*: December 1, 2003.
90 Setting the Bar Too Low for U.S. Jobs, *International Herald Tribune*: October 25, 2003.
91 Economic Scene: Reasons to Fret Despite A Spurt of Jobs in The U.S, *International Herald Tribune*: November 10, 2003.
92 America's Recovery is strictly for the Elite, *New York Times*: December 31, 2003.
93 Les Entreprises Embauchent, Sans Augmenter L'emploi, *Le Monde*: January 18, 2004.
94 Buildup of Cash Isn't Swaying Hiring, *Los Angeles Times*: February 8, 2004.
95 Microsoft Keeps $51.6B Cash Hoard For Legal Contingencies: No Dividend Boost, *Associated Press*: November 11, 2003.
96 New York Is Seen as Looming Large in Edwards Run, *New York Times*: February 20, 2004.
97 Aviva Beats Year Forecasts by £200m, *Daily Telegraph Online*: February 7, 2004.
98 Free Trade Emerges as Hot Issue in U.S. Presidential Race, *New York Times*: January 31, 2004.
99 Democrats Talk Back on Jobs and Iraq War, *International Herald Tribune*: January 22, 2004.
100 Mr. Mankiw is Right, *Washington Post*: February 13, 2004.
101 Wanted: A Campaign of Ideas, *Washington Post*: January 11, 2004.
102 Kissinger for U.S. Offering Sops to Curb Outsourcing, *Financial Express*: July 15, 2003.
103 Concern over Outsourcing, But No Solutions, *IANS*: October 24, 2003.
104 Outlandish Outsourcing: What Are Its Long-Term Effects, *Tech Republic*: November 3, 2003.
105 Shourie Suggests Low-Key Approach to Outsourcing Concerns, *Hindu*: November 26, 2003.
106 U.S. Bill 'May Hurt Indian IT Sector in The Long Run,' *Hindu*: January 25, 2004.

107 "For all the alarms being sounded here, however, officials acknowledged that the effect of the proposed legislation in the United States was likely to be minimal." See 'Indians Fearing Repercussions of U.S. Technology Outsourcing,' *New York Times*: February 9, 2004.

108 Indians Fearing Repercussions of U.S. Technology Outsourcing, *New York Times*, February 9, 2004.

109 Federal Bill Targets Offshore Labor, *CNet News.com*, February 20, 2004.

110 Outsourcing Issue In U.S. Driven By Politics, *Hindu*: February 22, 2004.

111 After the downturn, petitions for H-1B visas dropped by 75 percent in 2002, to 26,659, according to the American Electronics Association. The total number of H-1B visas issued stands at about 900,000.

112 U.S. to Sharply Cut Number of High-Tech Visas, *Reuters*: September 22, 2003.

113 U.S. Examines L-1 Visa Misuse, *IANS*: May 31, 2003.

114 What Do The Proposed Restrictions on the L-1 Visas Mean, *Tech Republic*: September 24, 2003.

115 U.S. Study Supports Inflow of Foreign Skilled Professionals, *PTI*: September 14, 2003.

116 India Pushes EU on Barriers to Labor, *Bloomberg News*: December 1, 2003.

117 U.S. May Ease Entry for Overseas Hi-Tech Workers, *PTI*: October 27, 2003.

118 U.S. Business Groups Protest Outsourcing Restrictions, *New Indian Express*: January 26, 2004.

119 India Fires Back at U.S. in the Outsourcing War, *washingtonpost.com*, February 10, 2004.

120 ITI Questions MTNL Contract to Huawei, *Hindu*: February 11, 2004.

121 Airtel Services Outsourced to Ericsson—Bharti Signs 3-Year Agreement for Over 400 *Hindu*: February 10, 2004.

122 'Offshoring' Trend Casting a Wider Net, *Los Angeles Times*, January 4, 2004.

123 Controversial Offshore Deal Scrapped by Indiana, *CBR Magazine*: November 26, 2003.

124 Backlash Brews As White-Collar Jobs Move, *Associated Press*: January 18, 2004.

125 U.S. Tech Cos Wary of Offshore Legislation, *Reuters*: December 3, 2003.

126 Keane Finalizes $137 million Outsourcing Contract With The National Life Group, *PR Newswire*: January 14, 2003.

127 Accenture to Double Staff in India to 10,000, *Reuters*: December 4, 2003.

128 U.S. Tech Services Giants Shifting Offshore, *Reuters*: November 26, 2003.

129 GAO Criticizes Awarding of Contract to EDS, *CBR Magazine*: January 7, 2004.

130 Telstra Under Fire Over Outsourcing Jobs, *FT.com*: January 23, 2004.

131 Australian Union Upset Over Telstra HR Job Shifts, *Hindu*: February 5, 2004.

132 U.S. Lawmakers Seek To Punish Companies That Outsource, *IANS*: January 30, 2004.

133 Covansys Reports Fourth Quarter and Full-Year Results, Press Release: February 11, 2004.

134 This, along with the spectacle of the World Social Forum in Mumbai, where Western 'activists' ensconced themselves in luxury hotels and stayed aloof from their highly-organized but still 'Indian' counterparts, is discussed in more detail in Chapter VI.

135 Collection Bureau of America Pledges to Keep Investing in American Labor, *PR Newswire*: January 20, 2004.

136 Too Many Visas for Techies, *BusinessWeek*: August 25, 2003.

137 Visa Program Robs U.S. Technology Workers of Jobs, Dignity, *Associated Press*: August 11, 2003.

138 'Doughnut Days' May Give Clue to Election Result, *Daily Telegraph Online*: November 12, 2003.

139 Offshore Outsourcing: Keeping Your Plans Hush-Hush Can Hurt You, *TechWeb*: July 22, 2003.

140 Union Warns of India Jobs 'Decimation', BBC News: June 21, 2003.
141 After U.S., Indians Face BPO Backlash in UK, IANS: September 9, 2003.
142 U.K. Unions Now Brandish A Survey, Economic Times: December 31, 2003.
143 Round Table On Jobs Outsourcing, Guardian: February 3, 2004.
144 Now, UK's National Rail Inquiry Services to Move to India, Hindustan Times: October 15, 2003.
145 Telstra Under Fire Over Outsourcing Jobs, FT.com: January 23, 2004.
146 Australians Protest Outsourcing to Indian Tech Firms, IANS: September 13, 2003.
147 Getting A Job in The Valley Is Easy, If You're Perfect, New York Times: November 19, 2003.
148 Efforts on to Free i-Flex Arm Chief Executive, Hindu: March 29, 2003.
149 Although the U.S. has not yet ventured into arresting Chief Executives in January 2000 (that is, before 9/11), 40 Indian programmers were arrested and handcuffed by the U.S. Immigration and Naturalization Service at the Randolph Air Force Base; the Indian Embassy was even four days after the incident. All of them had valid H-1B visas, but were not carrying it on their persons. See 'Arrest of Indian experts not notified,' PTI: January 24, 2000.
150 House Passes Drug Measure, but Faces Fight With Senate, New York Times: July 25, 2003.
151 Techno-Coolies No More—Does India Need Its Own Software Brands? The Economist: May 8, 2003.
152 Indian IT Services Industry Set to Grow 23% This Year, Computer Business Review: February 27, 2004.
153 Call in the Lawyers, Frankfurter Algemeine Zeitung [English edition]: August 19, 2001.
154 Dell Cuts Back India Customer Service Venture, Financial Times: November 25, 2003.
155 Dell Moves Some Customer Service Operations Back to The U.S., New York Times: December 8, 2003.
156 Lehman Moves Jobs Back From India, BBC News: December 16, 2003.
157 Offshore Backlash Grows as Lehman Pulls Out', CBR Magazine: December 17, 2003.
158 Overseas Outsourcing Trend Is Seen Persisting, Financial Times: December 28, 2003.
159 IBM Exports High Pay Jobs to India, China: Report, AFP: December 15, 2003.
160 Call Centre Decline Is Myth, Says Hewitt, Daily Telegraph Online: December 6, 2003.
161 HSBC to Cut 4,000 Jobs in Switch to Asia, Reuters: October 16, 2003.
162 Lloyds Under Fire as Jobs Go to India, Guardian: October 31, 2003.
163 More British Banking Jobs to Move to India, Guardian: October 30, 2003.
164 Abbey Will Use Outside Firms to Run Funds, Daily Telegraph Online: January 23, 2004.
165 Abbey Closes Call Centre, BBC News: January 14, 2004.
166 Boss Backs India Call-Centre Move, BBC News: November 12, 2003.
167 Aviva Says to Move 2,350 U.K. Jobs to India, Reuters: December 2, 2003.
168 Prudential Upbeat About Indian Captive Centre, Express Computer: December 22, 2003.
169 Aviva Pact With Wipro, Hindu: February 19, 2004.
170 Infosys, BT in Joint Development Pact, Hindu: February 17, 2004.
171 BT Outlines Exact Offshore Strategy, CBR Magazine: December 3, 2003.
172 Outsourcing—A Hush-Hush Affair, Cyber India Online: September 15, 2003.
173 CORRECTED: U.S. Companies Quietly Moving More Jobs Overseas: December 30, 2003.
174 The Dark Side of The Outsourcing Revolution, AlterNet: January 25, 2004.
175 Outsourcing—A Hush-Hush Affair, Cyber India Online: September 15, 2003.
176 Fallout of Outsourcing Backlash: IT Services Firms Keep New Client Wins Under Wraps, Hindu: July 28, 2003.

177 WashTech Reveals Microsoft Secret Layoff Plan, *Communication Workers of America*: July 3, 2003.

178 I.B.M. Explores Shift of White-Collar Jobs Overseas, *New York Times*: July 22, 2003.

179 Kyocera to Shift Software Jobs to India From U.S., *Hindu*: October 13, 2003.

180 Getting A Job in The Valley Is Easy, If You're Perfect, *New York Times*: November 19, 2003.

181 Bush Adviser Draws Ire for Job Comments, *Associated Press*: February 12, 2004.

182 Bush Economic Team Under Fire, *Associated Press*: February 19, 2004.

183 Bush Aide Seeks to Stem Damage Over Exporting Jobs, *Reuters*: February 12, 2004.

184 Bush's Call For Job Training: Cruel Joke On Unemployed, *Los Angeles Times*: January 25, 2004.

185 Christopher Jencks, "The Low-Wage Puzzle," The American Prospect vol. 15 no. 1, January 1, 2004 .

186 Low-Pay Sectors Dominate U.S. and State Job Growth, *Los Angeles Times*: January 22, 2004.

187 French GDP Inches Up, *Reuters*: January 7, 2004.

188 German Economy Grew Less Than Expected in Q4, *Financial Times*: February 12, 2004.

189 Germany and France Return to Growth, *Financial Times*: November 13, 2003.

190 The Fall of Baan, *BusinessWeek*: August 14, 2000.

191 "Hype has been part of the company since its birth," said *BusinessWeek* in a reference to Lernout & Hauspie (September 11, 2000).

192 Wim De Preter, 'De verborgen agenda van L&H,' *De Standaard*: December 30, 2000.

193 IBM Plans Regional Research Hub in Asia, *PTI*: March 14, 2003.

194 French Government Decides to "Forgive" 90% of Bull Loan, *Computer Business Review*, November 24, 2003.

195 France Telecom Cuts 15,000 Jobs, *Computer Business Review*, January 21, 2004.

196 This Constitution Will Propel Europe on to 'History's Exit Ramp,' *Daily Telegraph Online*, December 1, 2003.

Chapter Two

1   More 'Can I Help You?' Jobs Migrate From U.S. to India, *New York Times*: May 11, 2003.

2   The Productivity Advantage in Trade, *Washington Times*: August 27, 2003.

3   The Rise of India, *BusinessWeek*: December 8, 2003.

4   'India An Economic Powerhouse, Better Than China,' *Economic Times*: January 5, 2004.

5   Backlash Can't Harm Offshoring: Gartner, *Cyber India Online*: June 24, 2003.

6   China Syndrome, *Forbes.com*: October 9, 2003.

7   Who's Reading Your X-Ray, *New York Times*: November 16, 2003.

8   Countrywide to 'Offshore' 250 Jobs to India, *American Banker*, February 2, 2004.

9   New GGS Book Services Division Launches Its Innovative `Power of One' Concept to Book Publishers, Press Release: February 13, 2004.

10 *Reuters* Takes Outsourcing to a New Level With Journalists, *New York Times*: February 9, 2004.

11 The Rise of India, *BusinessWeek*: December 8, 2003.

12 Unilever Research & Development: Website (Research.Unilever.Com).

13 Cadbury's India Arm to Be 'Innovation Centre,' *Financial Express*: August 18, 2003.

14 Bell Labs Opens R&D Facility at Hyderabad, *Hindu*: February 9, 2001.

15 Indian Labs Working on 'Terminator' Gene Technology, *Financial Express*: January 18, 1999.
16 Scientists Develop GM 'Protato' to Feed India's Poorest Children, *Guardian*: June 12, 2003.
17 Indians Find SARS Virus Genes, *Hindu*: December 30, 2003.
18 India's Auto Industry Comes of Age, *Asia Times*: September 3, 2003.
19 GM Sets Up R&D Center at Bangalore, *Cyber India Online*: November 11, 2003.
20 Wipro Inks Master Service Pact With GM, *Hindu*: December 9, 2003.
21 The Rise of India, *BusinessWeek*: December 8, 2003.
22 Fluent to Open Global Operations Hub in India, *CFD Review*: December 8, 2003.
23 Quantech Global to Invest $2 m in India Centres: *Hindu*: February 21, 2004.
24 Advanced Imaging Magazine Announces Imaging Solutions of the Year Award Winners for 2004, *Business Wire*: January 23, 2003.
25 Reva on a PET Ride, *Cyber India Online*: February 12, 2004.
26 India's Auto Industry Comes of Age, *Asia Times*: September 3, 2003.
27 I2IT to Offer Courses in Russia, *Hindu*: January 22, 2004.
28 Guess Who Wants a Byte of India's Supercomputer? *Indian Express*, February 11, 2004.
29 India To Frame Roadmap For Using Hydrogen Energy, *IANS*: February 24, 2004.
30 The Rise of India, *BusinessWeek*: December 8, 2003.
31 ibid.
32 Second Take-Off, *Far Eastern Economic Review*: July 20, 2000.
33 TCS Initial Offer Likely by Early Next Fiscal, *Indian Express*: September 21, 2003.
34 Wipro Confident of $1 Billion Status This Year, *Hindu*: October 17, 2003.
35 Offshore Business: China Threat 'Over-Estimated,' *Hindu*: October 17, 2003.
36 HSBC Exporting 4,000 Jobs to Asian Centres, *Daily Telegraph Online*: October 17, 2003.
37 A Simple Choice: Outsource Or Die, *Financial Times*: October 17, 2003.
38 India Is Becoming a Testing Ground for Pharmaceuticals, *Los Angeles Times*: October 20, 2003.
39 How India Could Export Drug Deflation, *BusinessWeek*: February 24, 2003.
40 Singapore PM Warns of Trade Struggle, *Reuters*: November 2, 2003.
41 Outsourcing Abroad Applies to Tax Returns, Too, *New York Times*: February 15, 2004.
42 The Dark Side of the Outsourcing Revolution, *AlterNet*: January 25, 2004.
43 Outsourcing Abroad Applies to Tax Returns, Too, *New York Times*: February 15, 2004.
44 Reuters to Shift Core Unit to India, *BBC News*: August 5, 2003.
45 Legal Papers Jobs Head to India, *BBC News*: December 9, 2003.
46 Passage to India, *Boston Globe*: May 7, 2003.
47 Wall Street to Ship Research Jobs to India, *Reuters*: May 2, 2003.
48 Bank of New York Warns on 2004 Profits, *Associated Press*: January 26, 2004.
49 Bank of America to Hire 1,000 in India, *Reuters:* February 18, 2004.
50 Bank of America to Step Up Outsourcing to India, *Reuters:* October 13, 2003.
51 Demand for Fund Compliance Managers Up, *Reuters:* January 17, 2004.
52 The Productivity Advantage in Trade, *Washington Times*: August 27, 2003.
53 India May Gain From U.S. Labour Shortage: Study, *Hindu*: October 10, 2003.
54 Philippines, India, China to Enjoy Sharp Rise in Call Centers: Expert, *AFP*: September 25, 2003.
55 Indian BPO Industry Fights Attrition Trap, *Cyber India Online*: December 3, 2003.
56 Value-Added BPO Is New Outsourcing Mantra, *Express Computer*: July 14, 2003.
57 Progeon to Cap Voice Work at 30 percent of Income, *Hindu*: October 29, 2003.
58 Spectramind to Focus on Non-Voice Business, *Hindu*: January 26, 2004.
59 This Wave Is for Doctors to Surf, *Economic Times*: December 31, 2003.

60 Rick Simmonds, a director of British outsourcing advisers ALS Consulting noted that China are beginning to undercut India—but only "on some of the more menial contracts." See 'Exodus to Asia Moves up the Corporate Ladder,' *Daily Telegraph Online*: October 20, 2003.

61 Xansa Says Three-Quarters of Clients Want Offshore, CBR Magazine: November 4, 2003.

62 Xansa Unfazed; to Beef up India Team, *Hindu*, February 6, 2004.

63 Hinduja Buys Manila BPO Firm, *Cyber India Online*: October 31, 2003.

64 Daksh Expands to Philippines, *Reuters:* January 7, 2004.

65 Infotech Opens 'Near Shore' Centre in U.S., *Hindu*: September 1, 2003.

66 Daksh Expands to Philippines, *Reuters:* January 7, 2004.

67 Datamatics Plans Foray Into Canada, *Hindu*: October 17, 2003.

68 Beyond Borders, *Business World*: December 23, 2002.

69 Daksh Expands to Philippines, *Reuters:* January 7, 2004.

70 SPI Tech to Acquire Kolam Services, *Financial Express*: November 18, 2003.

71 Keane's Indian Buy Highlights BPO Crossover, CBR Magazine: October 23, 2003.

72 HLL Sets Up BPO Subsidiary, *Cyber India Online*: September 8, 2003.

73 Wobbling Out of The Past: India Accepts It Is Time for A New Life Cycle, *Independent*: October 4, 2003.

74 Transworks to Add 1000 Jobs, *Reuters:* November 25, 2003.

75 'India An Economic Powerhouse, Better Than China,' *Economic Times*: January 5, 2004.

76 Pakistani Baby Treated in India, *BBC News*: July 15, 2003.

77 Afghan Girl Gets Life-Saving Surgery, *BBC News*: September 3, 2002.

78 High-Tech Surgical Procedure Demonstrated to Paris Live From Chennai, *Frontline*: July 4, 2003.

79 Healthcare: India's Next Tourism Booster, *UPI*: August 18, 2003.

80 Patient Outsourcing: No Stopping This One, *Asia Times*: March 17, 2004.

81 India Fosters Growing 'Medical Tourism' Sector, *Financial Times*: July 2, 2003.

82 India Lures Briton for Knee Surgery, *BBC News*: September 29, 2003.

83 India's 'Five-Star' Hospitals, *BBC News*: September 29, 2003.

84 ibid.

85 India Fosters Growing 'Medical Tourism' Sector, *Financial Times*: July 2, 2003.

86 SRL-Ranbaxy to Invest Rs 1,000 Cr Over 5 Years, Eyes West Asia Markets, *Financial Express*: November 6, 2003.

87 Medical Tourism - Winning Hearts Overseas, *Hindu*: August 3, 2003

88 How India Could Export Drug Deflation, *BusinessWeek*: February 24, 2003.

89 India-U.S. Bilateral Trade Zooms in 2002, Press Release, Embassy of India, Washington DC, March 3, 2003.

90 Indian Pharma Industry Takes Giant Strides, *Rediff.Com:* December 29, 2001.

91 India Drugmakers Focus on West, *International Herald Tribune*: December 27, 2003.

92 India Set to Tap $48 Billion Pharma Outsourcing Market, *Rediff.com*, October 31, 2003.

93 RLL Embarks on Road to E-R&D, *Express Pharma Pulse*: November 20, 2003.

94 Companies to Watch in 2004, *Business Today*: December 21, 2004.

95 In 2001, the U.S. National Institutes of Health announced the existence of 64 stem cell lines in five countries worldwide. The bulk was held in Sweden (24) and the U.S. (20). Two Indian labs, one government and the other private, accounted for a total of 10 lines, placing India ahead of Australia (6) and Israel (4). See 'U.S. details stem-cell lines eligible for funding,' *Japan Today*: August 28, 2001.

96 DNA fingerprinting is now "both cheap and easily available in India." See 'DNA Tests Come of Age,' *BBC News*: June 2, 2003.

97 India Is Becoming a Testing Ground for Pharmaceuticals, *Los Angeles Times*: October 20, 2003. .

98 India's Potential for Clinical Research—Quality vs. Cost, *Express Pharma Pulse*: June 19, 2003.

99 Bill Clinton Backs Indian Drug Makers, *Associated Press*: November 21, 2003.

100 Brazil's Drug Copying Industry, CBS News.com, September 25, 2003.

101 India Eyes Brazil for Military Hardware, and More, *Asia Times*: December 11, 2003.

102 Dr. Reddy's Q3 FY04 Revenue at Rs.5138 million, *Business Wire*: January 30, 2004.

103 Ranbaxy to Expand Operations in Russia, *Hindu*, February 13, 2004.

104 U.K. Drugs Giant in India Tie-Up, *BBC News*: October 23, 2003.

105 Ranbaxy Gains Approval for Generic Augmentin, FDAnews, *Daily Bulletin*: December 9, 2003.

106 U.S. Ready to Ease Trade Rules on Some Generic Drug Sales, *New York Times*: August 27, 2003.

107 rDNA Insulin, 2 New Vaccines from Bharat Biotech, *Express Pharma Pulse*, June 26, 2003.

108 Wockhardt's Human Insulin to Hit Market Next Month, *Express Pharma Pulse*: July 17, 2003.

109 VCs, PrivateEquity Firms Pump in $304 million in Q3, *Times News Network*: January 6, 2004.

110 Health Costs Surge Amid U.S. Slump, *New York Times*: January 9, 2004.

111 Glaxo Settles Patent Suit, *International Herald Tribune*: February 7, 2004.

112 Indian Drug Firms Eye Generic Market, *Financial Times*: December 29, 2003.

113 Dr. Reddy's Receives Final Approval for AmVaz—Amlodipine Maleate, *Business Wire*: November 2, 2003.

114 Generic Drug Worries Mute Sanofi Results, Outlook, *Reuters:* September 2, 2003.

115 UCB Unmoved by Possible Keppra Generic Threat, Dow Jones: January 22, 2004.

116 Ranbaxy to Acquire Aventis' Generics Arm, *Reuters:* December 13, 2003.

117 Dr. Reddy's Organizes International Symposium on Drug Discovery: January 16, 2004.

118 Ranbaxy Gets 3rd Milestone Payment from Bayer AG, *Business Standard*: December 12, 2002.

119 Survey: Outsourcing May Hit Information Technology Careers, *CNET News.Com*: July 9, 2003.

120 BPO to India Seen Surging to $13.8 Billion by 2007, *Reuters:* July 8, 2003.

121 Opportunity on The Line, *TechWeb*: October 21, 2003.

122 ISRO Signs MOU With Indonesia, *Space Daily*: April 5, 2002.

123 This is of course also true for China. as argued by a leading French politician 'Par la masse de leur paysannerie, la Chine et l'Inde disposent d'une "armée industrielle de réserve", et, par conséquent, d'un avantage comparatif de longue durée—un bas niveau de salaire combiné avec un haut niveau de productivité—contre lequel les pays anciennement industrialisés se trouvent démunis." La Gauche Face A La Mondialisation, Par Jean-Pierre Chevénement, *Le Monde*: October 15, 2003.

124 Wipro Owner Sees no India Staffing Shortages—Paper, *Reuters:* February 20, 2004.

125 Malaysian Project to produce 1 million 'ICT' Youths, *Hindu*: December 19, 2003.

126 NIIT Says Q4 Software Orders Worth $42.3 million, *Reuters:* October 24, 2003.

127 Call Centre Decline Is Myth, Says Hewitt, *Daily Telegraph Online*: December 6, 2003.

128 Banishing the 'Sweatshop' Label, *Financial Times*: April 4, 2001.

129 City Briefs, *Daily Telegraph Online*: October 28, 2003.

130 British Firm Announces Wind Up of India Call-Centre, *IANS*: January 26, 2004.

131 U.K. Firms Challenged on India Jobs, *BBC News*: January 20, 2004.

132 Telemarketers Find a Welcome, *Washington Post*: November 9, 2003.

133 BPO Sector Has Reached Critical Mass: McKinsey, *Hindu*: January 14, 2004.

134 Indian BPO Industry Fights Attrition Trap, *Cyber India Online*: December 3, 2003.

135 Anxious About Outsourcing, *Washington Post*: January 31, 2004.

136 Outsourcing Backlash: Globalization in The Knowledge Economy, CNET Network: September 19, 2003.

137 Outsourcing Is Volgende Ronde Van Globalisering, *De Standaard*: June 17, 2003.

Chapter Three

1   The Lotus Files: Technology Entrepreneurship in China and India, *The Fletcher Forum of World Affairs*: April 2003.

2   Indian IT industry to Touch $15b Next Year, *Cyber India Online*: February 3, 2004.

3   IT Ministry Plans 8-Year Strategy, Rediff on the Net: January 31, 2000.

4   Indian IT Services to Grow Five-Fold, *CBR Magazine*: January 21, 2004.

5   India's Software Exports Grow by 30 Pc, Express India Online: March 8, 2004.

6   Where Your Job Is Going? , *Fortune*: November 24, 2003.

7   L'Inde Met Ses Cerveaux Au Service De L'industrie Occidentale, *Le Monde*: December 9, 2003.

8   L'information Economique De L'année? Le Décollage De l'Inde, *Le Monde*: December 21, 2003.

9   What an American writer called a 'boastful' headline in the January 5 edition of the *Times of India* to this effect was actually already about one month old, when it first appeared in *BusinessWeek* and France's *Le Monde*. Erroneously patronizing the Indian media further, he goes on to write: "And if we can believe the *Times of India* (and I think we can)".... See 'Forum: What's the plan for future jobs?,' The *Washington Times*: January 18, 2004. In 2002, the *Times of India*, with a circulation of 2.14 million overtook *USA Today* to become the world's "largest circulated English broadsheet daily."

10 Their Jobs Are on The Line, *Independent*: November 10, 2003.

11 For example, at Silicon Valley "programmers from China, Russia, India and elsewhere tap away at desktop computers in close proximity with Americans.... Many of the Chinese, who seem to predominate among the valley's foreign high-tech workers, can program in the languages of computers but speak little English." See 'Visa Program, High-Tech Workers Exploited, Critics Say,' *Washington Post*: July 26, 1998.

12 "According to estimates by the American Immigration Lawyers' Association, there are about 900,000 H-1B employees in the United States now, and as many as 45 percent of those are from India." See 'Curb on U.S. Visas Confronts India's Tech Industry,' *International Herald Tribune*: October 1, 2003.

13 Cisco to Boost investments, Headcount in India, *Reuters:* January 17, 2001.

14 Microsoft's Gates Says 20 percent of Engineers Indian, *Inquirer*: November 1, 2002.

15 Indians Issued Most U.K. Work Permits in IT in 2002, *IANS*: November 8, 2003.

16 Visa Program, High-Tech Workers Exploited, Critics Say, *Washington Post*: July 26, 1998.

17 The 'Cyber Coolie' Is Here, *Hindu*: December 8, 2003. The article describes how undercurrents of Raj-nostalgia in Britain (alongside an awareness that India was now turning into an economic threat) led to creation of this pejorative term.

18 H1-B Pay: Are You Being Shortchanged, *Economic Times*, January 6, 2004.

19 Silicon Subcontinent, *Financial Times*: March 15, 1999.

20 India Optimistically Prepares for Slump in the U.S, *New York Times*: March 13, 2001.

21 India Software Stocks Hit The Bargain Bin, CNN (online): September 21, 2001.

22 The Asians Are Coming, Again, *The Economist*: April 28, 2001.

23 China to Boost Software Exports, *China Daily*: November 11, 2002.

24 Software Wars: China vs. India, *wired.com*: April 25, 2002.

25 China Ambitious on Software, *China Daily*: October 15, 2003.

26 Year of The Monkey Will See China IT Swing Higher, *CBR* Magazine: January 23, 2004.

27 This is not just the author's personal opinion. According to The World Bank: "In many respects, India...stands out from other countries in terms of its tradition of data collection and its pioneering of many of the techniques of data analysis, which have now become common currency throughout the world." See 'India—Achievements and Challenges in Reducing Poverty," The World Bank: June 30, 1997.

28 The Dragon Is No Imminent Threat: Nasscom, *Hindu*: February 23, 2004.

29 Oracle's India Recruitment Drive Angers U.S. Employees, *CBR* Magazine: July 14, 2003.

30 Oracle Accelerates Investments in China, *CNET Asia*: October 30, 2003.

31 Russia to Go the Indian Outsourcing Route? *Star Software*: July 24, 2003.

32 Russia Says Cannot Repeat India's Information Technology Bonanza, *Reuters*: December 20, 2002.

33 Uitbesteden in Lagelonenlanden Niet Zo 'Hot', *Datanews*: December 10, 2003.

34 IBM Heeft 15.000 Vacatures, *Datanews*: January 19, 2004.

35 Het Onverwoestbare Optimisme Van Silicon Valley, *Datanews*: October 15, 2003.

36 HP Bedankt 1300 Werknemers, *Datanews*: August 21, 2003.

37 Prague Becoming Outsource Magnet, *Financial Times*: November 24, 2003.

38 Infosys' DHL Account may touch $54 million, *Hindu*: September 23, 2003.

39 Outsourcing: Make Way for China, *BusinessWeek* online: July 29, 2003.

40 NIIT Plans More Centres in China, *Hindu*: February 1, 2002.

41 China Means $11bn for Indian Software Industry, *Asia Times*: January 31, 2003.

42 Tata Eyes Auto, Steel, Telecom & Hospitality Sectors In China, *Financial Express*: February 13, 2004.

43 Europe, Asia Roll Out Red Carpet for Indian Firms to Slow Outsourcing, AFP: November 2, 2003.

44 China Beckons Indian IT Firms to Set Shop in Dalian, *IANS*: February 16, 2004.

45 Cognizant Expanding in a Big Way — Development Centre in China on Cards, *Cyber India Online*: February 20, 2004.

46 Infinite Plans China Foray: *Hindu*, February 20, 2004.

47 India's New Outsourcing Rival—Romania? *ZD Net*: September 12, 2003.

48 Romania Hopes to Forge Close Ties with India in Software Sector, AFP: January 30, 2004.

49 Indian Software Giant Targets Europe, *BBC News*: August 30, 2001.

50 Abbey Changes Brand and Joins Passage to India, *Guardian*: September 25, 2003.

51 U.S. Lawmakers Seek to Punish Companies That Outsource: *IANS*, January 30, 2004.

52 Study Assures Offshoring Jobs Not A Concern, *Reuters*: January 24, 2004.

53 Made in India: The Other Country for Software, *ID-Side*: May 1998.

54 Planet Computer, *Forbes*: February 24, 1986.

55 Computervision To Invest $30 m In India R&D Base, *Newsbytes*: February 24, 1997.

56 Silicon Valley Goes East-Way East, *Forbes*: November 17, 1997.

57 Personal Touch: The Notes Look Handwritten, But a Computer Did The Work, *Time*: January 7, 1991.

58 NIIT Develops Interactive TV Model, *Express Computer*: December 30, 1996.

59 Surprise in the Bidding Process, *Financial Times*: December 6, 1995.

60 Adrian Slywotzky, Value Migration: How to Think Several Moves Ahead of the Competition, Harvard Business School Press, 1996.
61 Details from 'Here Comes The Package,' *Dataquest*: January 16-31, 1995.
62 Maars Launches Plug And Play ERP Product, *Express Computer*: August 21, 2000.
63 India—An Emerging IT Superpower, *Business Eye*: September 1998.
64 Continuing its relentless march into higher levels of intellectual property, Geometric Software was recently awarded a U.S. patent for a new 'Hole Recognition' algorithm, key to its feature recognition (FR) technology. See 'Geometric Software Bags U.S. Patent,' *Cyber India Online*: September 17, 2003.
65 Should Indian IT Dive into IP Licensing, *Express Computer*: September 1, 2003.
66 Revenues of $5 bn By End of Decade, *Financial Times*: December 6, 1995.
67 The Information Technology Market in India, Find-SVP Inc., New York, 1997.
68 IT Industry Struggles Towards Globalization, *Financial Times*: September 3, 1997.
69 India—An Emerging IT Superpower, *Business Eye*: September 1998.
70 Inside Outsourcing in India, *CIO* Magazine: June 1, 2003.
71 Dateline Bangalore - Third World Technopolis, *Foreign Policy*, Spring 1996.
72 Biography of Roger J. Feulner, Vice President Honeywell Inc., Purdue University, Distinguished Engineering Alumni, 2000.
73 Sequent to Set Up Global Support Centre, *Express Computer*: December 30, 1996.
74 Analog Devices India Merged with Parent's Liaison Office, Rediff on the Net: July 30, 1998.
75 HCL America Bags Datamation Award, *Dataquest*: January 16-31, 1995.
76 Euro Prisma, Hardsoft Solutions All Set to Form Joint Venture, *Indian Express*: April 19, 1998.
77 Computer Associates to Float 3 New Joint Ventures in India, *Financial Express*: August 15, 2000.
78 Think Local—Mahindra-BT Develops Location-Based WAP Services, *Financial Express*: August 17, 2000.
79 India—An Emerging IT Superpower? *Business Eye*: September 1998.
80 Siemens Arm Unveils MSB Version, *Hindu*: January 31, 2001.
81 Chipmaker STMicro to Invest $100 Mln in India, Reuters, February 19, 2004.
82 Wipro licenses WLAN IPs to STMicroelectronics, *Cyber India Online*: August 4, 2003.
83 Most Siemens Software Jobs Moving East, *Associated Press*, February 16, 2004.
84 3Com to Set Up Test Laboratory in India, *Business Standard*: September 11, 2000.
85 Computer Associates to Float 3 New Joint Ventures In India, *Financial Express*: August 15, 2000.
86 Kanbay Int Starts Consulting Centre for E-Solutions, *Financial Express*: January 19, 2001.
87 Ford Plans India Software Unit, *The Observer of Business & Politics*: January 29, 2001.
88 America Online Rs 460-cr FDI Proposal Gets FIPB Approval, *Financial Express*: March 3, 2001.
89 Broadcom Acquires Armedia, Indian Chip Designer, *EE Times*: July 2, 1999.
90 Adobe to Invest $50 million in R&D, *Hindu*: January 24, 2001.
91 India, Pakistan and G.E., *New York Times*, August 11, 2002.
92 Nokia Sets Up R&D Lab In Hyderabad, *Hindu*: February 2, 2001.
93 Rainbow Tech Set to Buy Viman Software, *Hindu*: February 12, 2001.
94 Sun in Research with Top India Institutes, *Reuters*: September 7, 2000.
95 See Symbian website (http://www.symbian.com/partners/wipro.html).
96 Wipro to Provide Competence Center for the Series 60, *Business Wire*: February 23, 2004.
97 Interwoven expects 150 jobs at new Indian R&D unit, *Reuters*: February 9, 2004.

98 Source: MNC R&D Centres Mushroom in India, *Express Computer*: June 9, 2003, and author's research.

99 In India, a High-Tech Outpost for U.S. Patents, *New York Times*: December 15, 2003.

100 Thirty Thousand Patents and Counting, Press Release, Lucent Technologies, March 10, 2003.

101 Texas Instruments Opens 3G Wireless Center in Bangalore, *Cyber India Online*: January 11, 2001.

102 Texas Instruments to Set Up End-Equipment Labs in 12 Top Institutes, *Financial Express*: February 23, 2001.

103 Texas Instruments Unveils High-Speed Chip, *Associated Press*: December 2, 2003.

104 Hughes Banks on BPO for Growth, *Cyber India Online*: September 22, 2003.

105 $1 bn Innovations Likely out of IBM India, *Cyber India Online*, November 6, 2003.

106 IBM Launches New Center for Advanced Studies at Bangalore, *Cyber India Online*: June 18, 2003.

107 Pune Is Destination R&D, *Express Computer*: September 22, 2003.

108 Indian IT Pros Get a Raw Deal in IT, *Hindustan Times*, January 7, 2002.

109 BITS Alumni Seed $50 Mn Into IP Lab, *Indian Express*: March 15, 2004.

110 Techno-Coolies No More—Does India Need Its Own Software Brands? *The Economist*: May 8, 2003.

111 i-Flex Says HVB to Install Flexcube at German Bank, *Reuters*: May 28, 2003.

112 Retail Banking Systems: January 2003.

113 Finacle Humbles Competitors, *Cyber India Online*: December 9, 2003.

114 Infy, Oracle Join Forces for Banking, *Cyber India Online*: October 23, 2003.

115 Sun Helps National Commercial Bank Jamaica Limited Reinvent Its Business, *Reuters*: September 8, 2003.

116 Infosys Bets on Finacle for China Growth — Plans to Localise Product Suite at Proposed Subsidiary, *Hindu*: October 27, 2003.

117 IDBI Taps Infosys for Tech Platform, *Financial Express*, January 26, 2004.

118 Should Indian IT Dive Into IP Licensing? *Express Computer*: September 1, 2003.

119 Wipro Licenses WLAN IPs to STMicroelectronics, *Cyber India Online*: August 4, 2003.

120 ADA in $3 million Deal to Supply Software to U.S. Firm for Airbus, *Economic Times*: July 17, 2001.

121 TEN Technology Licenses Impulsesoft's Wireless Stereo Technology for iPod Adapter, *PR Newswire*: January 20, 2004.

122 Tensilica's Xtensa HiFi Audio Engine is First 24-bit SOC Solution to Receive Dolby Approval, Press Release: February 9, 2004.

123 Hyderabad Firm Working on VoiceXML Protocol, *Hindu*: January 25, 2001.

124 Should Indian IT Dive Into IP Licensing? *Express Computer*: September 1, 2003.

125 Sasken to Set Up New Centre in Pune, Hire 100 Staff, *Reuters*: February 4, 2004.

126 Mobile Operators to Shop in Cannes for 3G Build-Up, *Reuters*: February 20, 2004.

127 Should Indian IT Dive Into IP Licensing? *Express Computer*: September 1, 2003.

128 ibid.

129 Companies to Watch in 2004, *Business Today*: December 21, 2003.

130 Softex Digital Photo Editor for Siemens Mobiles, *Hindu*: October 6, 2003.

131 India Games Startup Gets Spider-Man Deal for Mobiles, *Reuters*: September 16, 2003.

132 Jataayu Ties Up with UbiNetics, *Hindu*: February 25, 2004.

133 Metrics for Application Development, *CIO*: January 31, 2003.

134 Will Bugs Eat Up U.S. Lead in Software?, *BusinessWeek*: December 6, 1999.

135 ibid.

136 The U.S. Software Industry and Software Quality: Another Detroit in The Making? Bryan Pfaffenberger, *University of Virginia*: May 3, 2000.

137 Fall Conference: Get The Most From Outsourcing, *Tech Web*: September 24, 2003.

138 List of High Maturity Organizations, Software Engineering Institute, Cranegie Mellon University: October 2002.

139 ibid.

140 CBA IPI and SPA Appraisal Result: 2002 Year End Update, Software Engineering Institute, Carnegie-Mellon University: April 2003.

141 Huawei Technologies India achieves SEI-CMM Level-5, *Express Computer*: August 25, 2003.

142 Huawei Plans to Outsource 1,000 Jobs to Indian Vendors, *Hindu*: February 2, 2004.

143 Booting Up Software Quality, *Business Today*: December 21, 2003.

144 Nilekani's Outsourcery, *Daily Telegraph Online*, February 15, 2004.

145 Walmart.com Expands use of ProactiveNet, Press Release: February 11, 2004.

146 The Jobs Problem..., *Washington Times*: January 18, 2004.

147 U.N.: Rich Nations Mixed on Immigration, *Associated Press*: January 29, 2004.

148 Millions Plunge into Holy Ganges, *BBC News*: January 24, 2001.

149 Gearing Up For India's Electronic Election, *BBC News*: February 27, 2004.

150 The Globalization of Software: *Sloan Foundation*, Pittsburgh, 2001.

151 India Will Be the Top Market for Monster.Com this Year, *Financial Express*: March 12, 2001.

152 1.1 Million IT Jobs to Be Created by 2008, *Cyber India Online*: February 14, 2003.

153 India's IT Sector Creates 152,500 Jobs in Year, *Reuters:* February 25, 2004.

154 Global IT IQ Report: March 2002, *Brainbench*, Inc.

155 Texas Instruments Develops Modem Chip, *Associated Press*: May 29, 2003.

156 India's Hughes in Software Deal With Lucent, *Reuters:* February 26, 2003.

157 India's Hughes Wins Order From Danish Firm, *Reuters:* June 5, 2002.

158 Hughes to Build Software for Ericsson Ahead, *The Observer of Business & Politics:* January 6, 2001.

159 The New HP Way: World's Cheapest Consultants, *Forbes*: December 12, 2003.

160 Hewlett-Packard to Move R&D to India, *Financial Express*: January 22, 2004.

161 Sun Chief to Woo India in Software War, *Reuters:* March 4, 2003.

162 Bill Gates Speech at IIT '50, *IIT Bombay*: January 17, 2003.

163 Intel Chief Open to Setting Up Manufacturing Base in India, *AFP*: June 9, 2003.

164 Oracle to Double Staff in India to 6,000, Times News Network: July 10, 2003.

165 SAP AG to Double Headcount in India Within Three Years: Kagermann, *AFP*: June 30, 2003.

166 Philips to Double Software Staff in India, Reuters, September 3, 2003.

167 Digital's Army To Touch 12,000, *Cyber India Online*, July 22, 2003.

168 US-Based Computer Sciences Corp to Increase Headcount in India, *IANS*: January 28, 2004.

169 Accenture India to be 10,000 by Dec'04, *Cyber India Online*: December 3, 2003.

170 Google Plans Indian R&D Center, *Computer Business Review*: December 16, 2003.

171 BearingPoint Opens India Office, *Washington Post*: February 12, 2004.

172 Indian Job Migration Defies Backlash, *Computer Business Review*: March 10, 2004.

173 Lionbridge Announces Fourth Quarter and FY 2003 Results, Press Release: February 2, 2004.

174 Metricstream to Take Over Zaplet; Double India Staff, *Hindu*: February 23, 2004.

175 Sierra Says Packaged Software is Next Offshore Sweet Spot, *Computer Business Review*: February 13, 2004.

176 Sierra Expanding Oracle Centre, *Hindu*: February 16, 2004.

177 PeopleSoft to Triple Staff in India, *CNet News.com*: February 17, 2004.

178 Pharmacopeia Announces Fourth Quarter And Full Year 2003 Financial Results, *PR Newswire*: February 5, 2004.

179 U.S. Firm Sets Up Centre in Chennai, *Hindu*: February 6, 2004.

180 eInfochips Expands Use of Verisity's VPA Solutions, Press Release: February 3, 2004.

181 Interwoven Expects 150 Jobs at New Indian R&D Unit, *Reuters*: February 9, 2004.

182 Xansa to set up ODC for Lawson Software, *Cyber India Online*, February 4, 2004.

183 PrairieComm Furthers Its Investment in 3G with Expansion of Bangalore Development Center, Press Release, February 3, 2004.

184 Slash Support to Add 1200 in Chennai, *Cyber India Online*: February 3, 2004.

185 Canon Sets Up Digital Imaging Solutions Lab, *Cyber India Online*: February 6, 2004.

186 Schneider to Set Up Global R&D Centre in Bangalore, *Reuters*: February 5, 2004.

187 Akzo Opens ICT Center in Bangalore, *Hindu*: February 25, 2004.

188 G&D to Invest 10 Million Euro in India, *Cyber India Online*: February 23, 2004.

189 French IT Firm Sets Up Indian ODC, *Cyber India Online*: February 20, 2004.

190 ABN Amro Expands Indian Operations, *Computer Business Review*: March 2, 2004.

191 Logica-CMG to Recruit 1000 in India, *Cyber India Online*: September 5, 2003.

192 Cap Gemini to Begin Bangalore Operations, *Hindu*, October 15, 2003.

193 Clarence Chandran Steps Down From Current Position but Remains in Advisory Role at CGI, Press Release: February 13, 2004.

194 Global Software Bounces Back, *Asia Times*: November 13, 2003.

195 ICFAIPRESS -Analyst: April, 2003.

196 Morgan Stanley Dean Witter, Govt of Singapore Buy Satyam Stock, *Hindu*, January 27, 2004.

197 Geodesic Okays Extension Of FII Investment Limit, January 7, 2004.

198 Feature -Tech Boom Fuels Venture Capital in India, *Reuters*: November 18, 1999.

199 Hongkong Technology Venture Group to Invest in 6 Indian Firms, *The Observer of Business & Politics*: August 18, 2000.

200 GE Asia Tech Fund to Focus on India, *Hindu*: February 23, 2001.

201 U.S. Venture Capitalists on the Hunt in India, *Reuters*: November 13, 2003.

202 ibid.

203 India A Big Draw for Venture Capitalists, *UPI*: November 17, 2003.

204 Venture Capital Outlook Remains Bleak, *Washington Post*: May 5, 2003.

205 Despite A Significant Drop, Asian Indian-Founded Companies Increase Their Share of Venture Capital Distribution in the United States, Raise $1 Billion, *Business Wire*: June 23, 2003.

206 The Rise of India, *BusinessWeek*: December 8, 2003.

207 Former HP Lady VP Joins Indian Start-Up, *Cyber India Online*: December 4, 2003.

208 Infinera Closes $53m Funding, *Cyber India Online*: August 7, 2003.

209 Customized Chip to Roll Out of B'lore, *Cyber India Online*: February 20, 2004.

210 Adaptec To Boost Indian Development, *Computer Business Review*: January 16, 2004.

211 International Finance Corporation to Invest in Indian-U.S. Chip Fund, *Reuters*: December 2, 2002.

212 India Emerges as World's Top Chip Design Centre, *Bloomberg News*: December 7, 2002.

213 IFC Picks Up 2.6% in Egurucool.Com, *Economic Times*: August 24, 2000.

214 IFC to Raise Investments in India to $1 Billion, *Express Computer*: December 8, 2003.

215 India to Star in Animation Scene, *Reuters*: September 18, 2001.

216 India Grabs Major Slice of Global Computer-Based Mapping Business, *AFP*: January 29, 2004.

217 Are Global IT Players a Threat to Indian Firms? *CNBC India*: February 18, 2003.

218 New Tata Tech COO, *Hindu*: February 25, 1994.

219 Infy Tops Tech Business Ranking, *Cyber India Online*: February 12, 2004.

220 U.K. Backs India Outsourcing, *BBC News:* February 4, 2004.

221 ITC Infotech Wins $54 million Deal from Parametric, *Reuters:* July 22, 2003.

222 CMC Signs Up With U.S.-Based TRW Automotive, *Hindu:* October 17, 2003.

223 Infosys Bags ING, Kodak Orders, *Hindu:* November 28, 2003.

224 AIG Company Signs Outsourcing Deal With Satyam, *Cyber India Online:* October 30, 2003.

225 Satyam in Merrill Order Win, *Reuters:* December 5, 2003.

226 Telstra Under Fire Over Outsourcing Jobs, *FT.com:* January 23, 2004.

227 HCL Tech Bags Big Order; to Triple BPO Headcount, *Hindu,* January 12, 2004.

228 WNS Wins Largest BPO Deal in the Country, *Cyber India Online:* February 4, 2004.

229 iGate strikes $20 million Contract, *Cyber India Online:* January 19, 2004.

230 Hexaware Bet on Peoplesoft Has Paid Off, *Hindu:* November 6, 2003.

231 Indian Developers Get Serious About .Net, *Indian Express:* October 20, 2003.

232 Mastek Gets 27 million Pound Order From BT Arm, *Reuters:* December 9, 2003.

233 Indian Firm Gets World's Largest GIS Deal, *Computer Business Review:* February 18, 2004.

234 Infosys Sees Large-Sized Outsourcing Deals, *Reuters:* September 19, 2003.

235 Not Easy for Global Majors to Ramp Up Centres Here, *Hindu,* February 6, 2004.

236 Are Global IT Players a Threat to Indian Firms, *CNBC:* February 18, 2003.

237 Are Global IT Players a Threat to Indian Firms, *CNBC:* February 18, 2003.

238 In A Low Key, New EDS Chief Hopes to Regain Skeptics' Trust, *New York Times:* May 13, 2003.

239 EDS in Strategic Talks with Microsoft, Hewlett-Packard, *Dow Jones Business News:* March 23, 2003.

240 The term 'careful' cannot be over-emphasized, and in fact, underlines the durability of India's emergence. Most Indian IT firms have been highly conservative, in spite of cash reserves of about $500 million each for the larger IT firms such as Infosys, Wipro and Satyam, $200 million for companies like Cognizant, and $75 million for the likes of iGate Global. In spite of its star status on Nasdaq, Infosys held back on acquisitions through 2000, and, after its refusal to take the plunge on U.S.-based Cambridge Technology Partners, was criticized by analysts for its excessive caution. Likewise with Wipro, which during the New Economy boom, was repeatedly rumoured to be close to buying U.S. IT services firm, Sapient.

241 HCL Co-Founder, Arjun Malhotra, Named Chief Executive of Headstrong, *Business Wire:* January 26, 2004.

242 Enough Meat on Offshoring Bone, *Hindu:* February 18, 2004.

243 Wipro Eyes Acquisitions to Expand Presence Across Europe, *Hindustan Times:* November 5, 2003.

244 Satyam Says Seeks Acquisitions for Growth, *Reuters:* January 14, 2003-4.

245 Cognizant Eyeing High-End BPO Buys, *Hindu:* November 3, 2003.

246 NIIT Acquires AD Solutions of Germany, *Cyber India Online:* November 14, 2002.

247 Can Acquisitions Help Wipro Join The Big League, *Express Computer:* June 30, 2003.

248 Patni Buys U.S. Firm, Taps Financial Clients, *Reuters:* May 6, 2003.

249 Patni Over-Subscribed 22 Times in IPO Boom, *Reuters:* February 6, 2004.

250 Gartner rates Cognizant high in CRM services, *Hindu:* February 3, 2004.

251 TCS Buys Airlines Outsourcing Services Provider, *Reuters:* May 6, 2003.

252 TCS Loses Bid to Acquire SAS Group Arm, *Hindu:* December 19, 2003.

253 HP Boosts German IT Services Unit with Triaton Buy, *CBR Magazine:* February 24, 2004.

254 Infosys Buys Telstra Contractor in Australia, *CBR Magazine:* December 19, 2003.

255 i-Flex Buys U.S. Firm for $11.5 million, *Cyber India Online:* December 16, 2003.

256 Cognizant Acquires IT Services Firm Infopulse in the Netherlands as Part of European Expansion, *Business Wire*: December 2, 2003.
257 HCL to Acquire Deutsche Bank's Stake in DSL Software, *CBR Magazine*: December 5, 2003.
258 Ivast Sale Highlights MPEG-4 Woes, *CNET News.Com*: February 20, 2004.
259 Acquire... and Be Sure, *Hindu*: February 18, 2004.
260 Aftek Eyes Europe for Rapid Growth, *IRIS*: June 3, 2003.
261 Aftek Infosys Picks Up 49 pc Stake in German Firm, *Hindu*, May 30, 2003.
262 KPIT to Tap Mid-Tier U.S. Companies, *Hindu*: October 15, 2003.
263 Datamatics Plans Foray Into Canada, *Hindu*: October 17, 2003.
264 IBS Acquires Honeywell Unit, *Hindu*: October 23, 2003.
265 Yash Tech acquires U.S.-based firm, *Hindu* November 25, 2003.
266 iGATE Net Loss at Rs 2.65 Cr; to Acquire Symphoni Interactive, *Hindu*: January 22, 2004.
267 Infotech Buys Vargis, *Hindu*: January 22, 2004.
268 Mahindra to Buy Majority Stake in U.S. Software Firm, *Reuters:* February 9, 2004.
269 SSI Buys Nasdaq Share in JV, *Cyber India Online*: October 3, 2003.
270 24/7 Customer Eyes U.S. Acquisitions, *Cyber India Online*: October 30, 2003.
271 Accenture Ex-CEO joins 24/7 Customer, *Cyber India Online*: February 12, 2004.
272 Hinduja Buys Manila BPO Firm, *Cyber India Online*: October 31, 2003.
273 Godrej Buys U.S. Call Centre Company, *Hindu* November 15, 2003.
274 Aegis Communications Group Terminates Merger Agreement with AllServe; Announces Investment by Deutsche Bank and Essar Group, *PR Newswire*: November 5, 2003.
275 Essar, Deutsche Bank Acquire U.S. BPO Firm for $28 million, *Hindustan Times*: November 7, 2003.
276 'Backlash' Will Fizzle Out by '04: Gartner, *Cyber India Online*: July 17, 2003.
277 TCS America Launches Aggressive Plan to Train Next Generation of U.S. Technology Professionals, *Business Wire*: January 30, 2001.
278 India's Infosys to Buy Australian Firm, *The Age*: December 19, 2003.
279 Infosys to Be MNC Staff-Wise Too, *Hindu*: November 18, 2003.
280 Now, Indian Firm Creates Jobs in Britain, *IANS*: February 11, 2004.
281 Nasscom-Mckinsey Study Predicts $80-Billion Potential for Indian Information Technology Sector in 2008, *Rediff.com*: June 10, 2002.
282 Pakistani Software Major Eyes Indian Firm, *IANS*: January 29, 2004.

Chapter Four

1 Upstarts, *Asiaweek*: November 23, 2001.
2 Inderfurth Remarks on U.S.-India Relations, United States Information Service: July 3, 2000.
3 For example, "With two smash hit chips to his credit -the Pentium and the K6 -can Vinod Dham score one more time at Silicon Spice," See 'Dham Good?' *Forbes*: October 7, 1998.
4 Sun Forms New Unit to Explore Data Center Options, EE Times: March 21, 2001.
5 (Jim) Clark (founder of Silicon Graphics and Netscape) "had a thing for Indians...as some of the sharpest technical minds he had ever encountered." *The New, New Thing* Michael Lewis, Hodder and Stoughton, 1999.
6 Companies to Watch in 2004, *Business Today*: December 21, 2004.

7   For instance, Mike Watson, then managing director of Texas Instruments in India, told a British weekly in 1991 that that his 130 staff would "more than hold their own" against U.S., Japanese or English rivals. As the newspaper observed, "That is not too surprising. The head of the company's worldwide semiconductor research is an Indian." Skills Exporter, *The Economist*: May 4, 1991.

8   IBM's Indian is Patent Raja, *Times of India*: January 19, 2004.

9   Prolific EE Decorates IBM's Patent Crown, *EE Times*: January 20, 2003.

10 CTO Forum: Sun Founder Touts 'Real-Time Enterprise', *Infoworld*: April 9, 2002.

11 Umang Gupta Joins Peninsula Community Foundation Board, Press Release Peninsula Community Foundation: March 13, 2003.

12 Michael Lewis, *The New, New Thing*, Hodder and Stoughton, 1999. Indeed, even after the downturn, the proportion has stayed at the same near-50 percent level, establishing the tight connections between India and American IT. See 'Indian IT Will Be Hard Hit by H1-B Visa Cut,' *IANS*: September 24, 2003

13 Microsoft's Gates Says 20 percent of Engineers Indian, *Inquirer*: November 1, 2002.

14 Cisco to Invest Another $50 Mn In India, *Indian Express*: January 18, 2001.

15 Michael Lewis, *The New, New Thing*, Hodder and Stoughton, 1999.

16 High-profile recent additions include Prof. Anoop Gupta, head-hunted from Stanford University to become a personal technology adviser to Microsoft Chairman Bill Gates, and Padmasree Warrior, Chief Technology Officer of Motorola.

17 Funding a Revolution, National Academy Press, 1999.

18 Juniper returned to the limelight in early February 2004, after paying $4 billion for Netscreen, the highest value acquisition since the collapse of the dotcom bubble, and designed to enable it to compete with Cisco.

19 Sindhu has been described as 'the unsung hero of the Internet' since "he permanently changed the definition of what a router does and got Internet protocol on a robust footing." See 'Sculptors of Silicon India,' *Asia Times*: June 20, 2002.

20 According to the ëInternational Herald Tribune', the IITs "train a disproportionate number of the world's leading Internet-era entrepreneurs." See 'Wizards of High Tech on the Subcontinent,' *International Herald Tribune*: April 20, 2000.

21 Michael Lewis, *The New, New Thing*, Hodder and Stoughton, 1999.

22 60 Minutes, CBS News (US): January 12, 2003.

23 CTO Forum: Sun Founder Touts 'Real-Time Enterprise', *Infoworld*: April 9, 2002.

24 Midas List 2004, *Forbes.com*: January 29, 2004.

25 Victor Menezes Is A Survivor At Citicorp, *Wall Street Journal*: November 3, 1998.

26 NRIS to Introduce New Trends in Gujarat Hotel Industry, *IANS*: January 7, 2004.

27 For an informative (but by no-means exhaustive) analysis of Indians at the top of the U.S. information technology and business establishment, see 'India's Whiz Kids,' *BusinessWeek*: December 7, 1998.

28 India on Threshold of Becoming Developed Nation: Lord Paul, *PTI*: February 16, 2004.

29 The principal Indian IT lobby group in the U.S. is Silicon Valley-based 'The Indus Entrepreneurs,' whose membership extends to several of the people named above.

30 Arun Netravali to Set Up $250-M Fund for Start-Ups, *Hindu*: November 2, 2003.

31 A Capital Idea for the High Tech Elite, *Washington Post*: May 26, 2000.

32 Indian-American A Candidate for La. Gov, *Associated Press*: October 25, 2003.

33 The Golden Diaspora, *Time*: June 19, 2000.

34 The Congressional Caucus on India is the largest country caucus in the U.S. Congress, composed of over 170 members of the U.S. House of Representatives.

35 A Capital Idea for the High Tech Elite, *Washington Post*: May 26, 2000.

36 Use WTO to Bolster Outsourcing, Says Pro-Bush Tech Guru, *Reuters:* February 23, 2004.
37 And other sectors, too. In December 2002, Raju Narisetti was appointed Managing Editor of *Wall Street Journal Europe.*
38 A New Voice at Vodafone, *The Economist:* July 31, 2003.
39 Deutsche Bank Moves a Star, DeSa, to Asia, *Wall Street Journal:* March 2, 1998.
40 It is, however, most likely an American who first openly acknowledged the implications of such connections for the wider world. In 2001, Harris Miller, President of the Information Technology Association of America (ITAA), noted that an alliance between ITAA and Indian IT industry federation Nasscom was meant "not only to further the trade and business relations between India and U.S.," but "also promote joint marketing of information technology software and services to other countries like Europe, Japan and other parts of Asia, Africa and Latin America." See 'Nasscom and ITAA Sign Information Technology Pact," *Nasscom Press Release:* March 13, 2001.
41 Is This the New Face of Rightwing Deep South Politics?, *Guardian:* November 10, 2003.
42 Democratic Candidates for President Debate in Iowa, *New York Times* (online), November 24, 2003.
43 Gen. Clark's Evolution on H-1B/Offshoring, Online comments by Norm Matloff: December 5, 2003.

Chapter Five

1   Blaming India for Loss of Jobs Is Unfair, Says Prescott, *PTI:* October 6, 2003.
2   Britain Must Get on a Faster Boat to China, Daily Telegraph Online: February 15, 2004.
3   Jobs Migrating Overseas, But It's a Two-Way Street, *Los Angeles Times:* July 20, 2003.
4   For example, "in 2002, India's gross domestic product (GDP) was about $3 trillion." See 'Volatility Hallmark of Single Country Funds,' *Daily Telegraph Online:* November 1, 2003.
5   World Development Indicators Database, World Bank, July 19, 2003.
6   Rice retails in the U.S. at $1.3 per kilo or $1,300 per tonne (Food Marketing and Price Spreads: ERS-USDA Briefing room), compared to $200 in India. The ratio for most other foodgrains is similar. Taking rice as an indicator, India's 210 million tonnes output would be worth $277 billion in terms of prices in the U.S., as against $42 billion in India, a difference of $235 billion, or about 45% of India's $529 billion dollar denominated GDP.
7   A good example of not taking such factors into account is the statement that "the purchasing power of Latin America and the Caribbean is at least 50 percent higher than China's." See 'U.S. Job Anxiety Opens Trade Doors for the Americas,' *washingtonpost.com:* February 26, 2004. This is based on nominal dollars, rather than PPP.
8   If You Get the Ax, Don't Blame India, *Los Angeles Times:* February 6, 2004.
9   The Productivity Advantage in Trade, *Washington Times:* August 27, 2003.
10 This may of course be possible with smaller economies. See 'Singapore's Economy Grows Annualised 17 percent,' *Financial Times:* November 17, 2003.
11 Outsourcing to India, *The Economist:* May 5, 2001.
12 Rs 1 Lakh Car Very Much on Tatas' Radar, *Hindu:* January 17, 2004.
13 A Global Shift to Deflation, *International Herald Tribune:* May 22, 2003.
14 Creating Jobs at Home in a Worldwide Market, *Los Angeles Times:* January 27, 2004.
15 The Bear's Lair: How Low Can Dollars Go?, *Washington Times:* May 27, 2003.

16 See, for example, 'BG burns brightly now, but the future is murky,' *Daily Telegraph*: February 18, 2004; 'Nortel Sees Growth Coming from India, China,' *New York Times*: August 20, 2003; 'Asian Markets Lift Qualcomm Results,' *Los Angeles Times*: July 24, 2003; 'Ericsson Sees Great Potential in Indian Market,' *Reuters:* July 18, 2003; First Data Announces Fourth Quarter Earnings of $0.55 per Share, Up 20%, Press Release: February 3, 2004.

17 L'Europe Défend Son Commerce et Ses Parts de Marché, *Le Monde*, February 13, 2004.

18 The Coca-Cola Company Reports Record Earnings Per Share of $1.77 for the Year, Press Release: February 11, 2004.

19 Motorola $307 m Richer, Thanks to India, *Cyber India Online*: February 20, 2004.

20 India Poised for Construction Boom: Jaitley, *Hindu*: February 12, 2004.

21 Ecclestone Sees 'No Future' For Silverstone, *Guardian*: February 2, 2004.

22 Sun shines down on education, *Cyber India Online*: February 13, 2004.

23 United India Insurance Company Moves 10,000 Users to Sun's Java Desktop System StarOffice Software, Press Release: February 4, 2004.

24 India Fastest Growing Market for Oracle in Asia, *Hindu*: September 18, 2003.

25 U.S. Software Giant Oracle Sees India as Largest Asia Market After China, *AFP*: August 27, 2003.

26 Nine Oracle-Aided E-Gov Projects Under Way, *Hindu*: January 21, 2004.

27 Windows' Malayalam Version in December, *New Indian Express*: October 18, 2003.

28 IBM to Develop IT Applications in Local Languages in India, *Business Standard*: September 6, 2000.

29 Adobe's Hindi Version, Two Months Away, *Cyber India Online*: October 16, 2003.

30 Low-Cost Linux Gaining on Microsoft in India, *Reuters:* August 11, 2003.

31 Red Hat to roll out Linux OS in Hindi, *UPI*: January 22, 2004.

32 Bentley May Shift Mumbai Centre To Hyderabad, *Hindu*, October 20, 2003.

33 Borland Looks East, *Forbes.com*: November 11, 2003.

34 Business in India A Trend, But Not New, *CNBC*: October 20, 2003

35 China and India Likely to Drive Asian Economic Growth: EIU, *AFP*: August 5, 2003.

36 Trap A Dragon, Bush, and Lose An Election, *Guardian*: November 3, 2003.

37 NCAER Raises GDP Forecast to 8 Pc, Hindu: January 21, 2004.

38 L'Information Economique De L'année? Le Décollage De l'Inde, *Le Monde*: December 21, 2003.

39 In 1995, two years before the end of the Southeast Asian 'miracle,' this author noted in an address at a conference in Belgium: "Quite simply, (India) means stability. India has no sheikhs, no politico-business dynasties, no military coups, neither sudden leaps forward nor backwards.... There is no manufactured middle class, only one which has grown over the years and is now not only politically empowered, but organic and structurally seamless—from the lower-middle to the upper-middle.... The contrast with most other developing countries does not need to be further underlined." See 'Investing in India: The Long-Term Choice," *Tijd Academie*, De Jachthoorn, Kontich, 21 November 1995.

40 New Credit Card Trick Invades SE Asia, *UPI*: November 18, 2003.

41 As discussed elsewhere, European business is almost enchantedly out-of-touch with India. In spite of such figures about India's consumer credit, the Chief Executive of Germany's Deutsche Bank said rival "Citigroup's consumer credit franchise saddled it with more risk. 'You'll never come to Deutsche Bank for credit cards in India,' he said." See 'Deutsche Bank Merger Talks Temper Signs of Optimism,' *New York Times*: February 6, 2004.

42 Proposed Interim Budget Presented in India, *Dow Jones*: February 3, 2004.

43 India: No More Aid Please, *The Economist* : June 21, 2003.

44 FM to Return $3.5Bn Debt to ADB, WB, *Financial Express*: January 31, 2004.

45 Import Duty Cut on Inputs for Auto Parts, Others, *Hindu*: January 25, 2004.

46 The Rush to Cash in on India, *BusinessWeek Online*: January 28, 2004.

47 Thus, the (true) stories about Indian-American IT entrepreneurs arriving on U.S. shores with "a few dollars" in their pocket.

48 Globalisation of India Inc, *Financial Express*: January 22, 2004.

49 *Fortune* magazine missed taking note of this fact in its statement: "After years of wondering what all those fiber-optic cables laid around the earth at massive expense in the late 1990s would ever be good for, we finally have an answer: 'They're good for enabling call-center workers in Bangalore or Delhi to sound as if they're next door to everyone. Broadband's killer app, it turns out, is India.'" See 'Where Your Job Is Going,' *Fortune*: November 24, 2003.

50 Corporate India Has New Muscles to Flex, *Asia Times*: January 21, 2004.

51 The Rush To Cash In On India, *BusinessWeek* Online: January 28, 2004.

52 India is Booming, But Not for Everyone, *International Herald Tribune*: January 31, 2004.

53 Boost for India as Debt Rating Upgraded, *Financial Times*: January 22, 2004.

54 India Mutual Funds Drawing the Attention of U.S. Investors, Says S&P, Press Release, February 13, 2004.

55 IMF's Krueger Calls for Full Convertibility, *Financial Express*: January 22, 2004.

56 India Entering Golden Era, Says Deutsche Exec, *Hindu*: October 8, 2003.

57 Sizzling Economy Revitalizes India, *New York Times*: October 20, 2003.

58 India to Meet Phone Targets Much Ahead of Plan, *Reuters*: November 27, 2003.

59 M&M Tractor Sales up 56 pc in Jan, *Hindu*: February 16, 2004.

60 Software Giant India Poised to Become Hardware Hub—IT Minister, *AFP*: February 17, 2004.

61 Nest Building—Will Union Bank's Move Presage Higher Rates, *Financial Express*: December 25, 2003.

62 U.S. Realty Giant Oakwood Eyes Apartment Slot, Times News Network: October 18, 2003.

63 India Poised for Construction Boom: Jaitley, *Hindu*: February 12, 2004.

64 India En Route for Grand Highways, *BBC News*: May 26, 2003.

65 Advani Flags Off MMTS Train In Hyderabad, *PTI*: August 9, 2003.

66 Drive to Link Indian Rivers, *BBC News*: May 23, 2003.

67 India's Largest Hydro-Power Project Kicks Off, *New Indian Express*: October 14, 2003.

68 PM Dedicates 3 Power Projects to Nation, *Hindu*: February 10, 2004.

69 India's Reform of Power Sector Bears Fruit, *Financial Times*: January 27, 2004.

70 India Road-Building Push Fuels Tata Motors, *Bloomberg News*: January 22, 2004.

71 Heavy Duty Trucks Drive Commercial Vehicle Segment, *Hindu*: February 16, 2004.

72 India MRPL May Halt Most Oil Exports To Meet Local Demand, *Dow Jones*, February 4, 2004.

73 What goes around..., *New York Times*: February 26, 2004.

74 Anti-Outsourcing Bills May Be Reintroduced, *United News of India*: September 9, 2003.

75 Outsourcing Backlash, A Political Issue: U.S., *Cyber India Online*: September 15, 2003.

76 Indian Minister Attacks U.S. States for Anti-Outsourcing Moves, *AFP*: June 18, 2003.

77 India Concerned by U.S. Move to Restrict IT Trade, *IANS*: November 21, 2003.

78 India Takes Outsourcing Protest to Washington, *Financial Times*: January 29, 2004.

79 Outsourcing Ban 'would put trade talks at risk', *Financial Times*, February 16, 2004.

80 Sting in The Tail Of U.S. Outsourcing Ban, *Asia Times*: January 30, 2004.

81 Outsourcing Ban Angers U.S. Firms, *Indian Express*: January 31, 2004.

82 Gates Calls for More Innovation, *Guardian*: January 27, 2004.

83 Indian Software Industry Targets U.S. Outsourcing Bill, *Reuters:* January 24, 2004.
84 Outsourcing Row: Zoellick Ticks Off India, Shourie Calls U.S. Poll Bluff, *Financial Express:* March 11, 2004.
85 Silent Lobbying to Counter IT 'Backlash,' *Hindu:* November 23, 2003.
86 3rd Party Surrogates Needed to Dispel Offshoring Doubts, *Hindu:* November 28, 2003.
87 U.S. Congressmen Urge Vajpayee to Authorise Boeing Sale to AI, *PTI:* October 25, 2003.
88 U.S. Seeks Commitment From India Over Outsourcing, *PTI:* February 2, 2004.
89 U.S. Official Allays Fears Over Bill, *Hindu,* February 6, 2004.
90 Zoellick Seeks to Revive Dialogue, *Washington Times:* February 7, 2004.
91 Anxious About Outsourcing, *Washington Post:* January 31, 2004.
92 Information Technology Companies Up in Arms against Western Barriers, *Financial Express:* July 20, 2003.
93 India Readies Services List for WTO Talks, *Financial Express:* October 13, 2003.
94 IT Companies Up in Arms Against Western Barriers, *Financial Express:* July 21, 2003.
95 India Pushes EU on Barriers to Labor, *Bloomberg News:* December 1, 2003.
96 EU Team to Hold Consultations With India on Feb 5-6, *Hindu:* January 26, 2004.
97 Vakbonden Laken Gats-Aanpak Door Lamy, *De Standaard:* July 15, 2003.
98 Hope for Indian Techies in Europe, *Hindustan Times:* July 7, 2003.
99 India, EU Work to Hike Trade and Investment Flows, *Financial Express:* July 20, 2003.
100 Germany to Prolong 'Green Card' Visas for Tech Experts, *AFP:* July 10, 2003
101 India Global Hub for Software, Outsourcing—U.K. Minister, *PTI:* July 1, 2003.
102 U.K. to Continue Outsourcing to India Despite Protests, *IANS:* September 9, 2003
103 U.K. Backs India Outsourcing, *BBC News:* February 4, 2004.
104 No U.K. move to curb outsourcing, says Jack Straw, *Hindu:* February 7, 2004.
105 No EU Backlash Against Outsourcing—Chris Patten, *IANS:* February 17, 2004.
106 Anger Over Indians on Permit Panel, *Daily Telegraph:* August 4, 2003.
107 Companies Asked to Consult Workers Before Layoffs, *Associated Press:* July 8, 2003.
108 Economy to Grow by 8.1 pc in '03-04, *Hindu,* February 10, 2004.
109 Euromoney Asia Poll Reports ICICI Bank as The Best Managed Bank, *Financial Express:* December 18, 2002.
110 India Can Overtake China as Economic Power, *PTI:* July 13, 2003.
111 ibid.
112 The Quest for Asia's Outsourcing Crown, *BusinessWeek* Online: July 30, 2003.
113 Ross Terrill, *The New Chinese Empire and What it Means for the United States,* Basic Books, 2003.
114 The Bear's Lair: How Low Can Dollars Go? *Washington Times:* May 27, 2003.
115 The Rise of India, *Businessweek:* December 8, 2003.
116 Beijing Rejects G-7 Call to Let Its Currency Float, *International Herald Tribune:* September 22, 2003
117 Rupee Surges New 3-Year Peak Against USD, *PTI:* October 1, 2003.
118 Stanchart Predicts Dollar at Rs 43.5 in One Year, *Hindu:* November 4, 2003.
119 "A stronger rupee... is also hurting software companies dependent on exports." See 'Indian software firms to report stronger quarter," Reuters, January 7, 2004.
120 A Gloomy Labor Day for millions of Americans, *Seattle Times:* August 31, 2003.
121 The U.S.'s Blunt Message to China, *International Herald Tribune:* October 29, 2003.
122 Globalisation of India Inc, *Financial Express:* January 22, 2004.
123 Why India Is Singing in The Rain, *Financial Times:* July 15, 2003.
124 Corporates Adopt ERP Technology to Trim Costs, *Indian Express:* April 19, 1998.
125 India Jewelry Catches Global Eye, *UPI:* September 8, 2003.
126 Indians Cash in on Gold's High Price, *BBC News:* February 7, 2003.

127 India's Diamond Trade Reveals Flawed Side, *Asia Times*: February 19, 2004.

128 Indians Unseat Antwerp's Jews as the Biggest Diamond Traders, *Wall Street Journal*: May 27, 2003.

129 Manufacturing Outsourcing to Be The Next Big Wave: Klein, *Financial Express*: November 26, 2003.

130 With a Small Car, India Takes a Big Step, *Wall Street Journal*: February 6-8, 2004.

131 Tata Sons "has a 80-strong dealer network in Italy and, together with another 50 sub-dealers, its network there is very strong. in Spain Tata Engineering has a 160-strong dealership base." Tata.com "The Week That Was": March 29, 2002.

132 Rover Unveils Indian Connection, *BBC News*: July 8, 2003.

133 Romania Hopes to Forge Close Ties with India in Software Sector, *AFP*: January 30, 2004.

134 Swiss Body Woos Indian Businessmen: *Hindu*, February 18, 2004.

135 Mahindra in Talks to Make Scorpio SUVs in China, *PTI*: June 27, 2003.

136 M&M, NIIT Head for Turkey, *Financial Express*: September 19, 2003.

137 MG Rover Signs Up Proton As New Partner, *Guardian*: February 19, 2004.

138 Reinventing Tata Motors, *Financial Express*: November 22, 2003.

139 Tata Eyes Auto, Steel, Telecom & Hospitality Sectors In China, *Financial Express*, February 13, 2004.

140 Bajaj Auto Plans to Capture South East Asian Markets, *PTI*: March 15, 2003.

141 TVS Motors Scouts for Manufacturing Base in SE Asia, *Hindu*: January 12, 2004.

142 Nigerian Province to Buy 250 Tractors From India's Mahindra, *Asia Pulse*: September 8, 2003.

143 Senegal Leader Seeks Indian Cars to Bolster Trade Ties, *AFP*: October 13, 2003.

144 Companies to Watch in 2004, *Business Today*: December 21, 2004.

145 Tatas to Pump in $2 Bn In Telecom, *Financial Express*: February 23, 2004.

146 Auto Components Sector—A Journey From Wilderness to the West, *Hindu*: December 12, 2003.

147 L N Mittal Is World's 2nd Largest Steel Maker, *Rediff.com*, April 11, 2003.

148 Lakshmi Mittal Signs $2 Billion Deal With Polish Government, *Hindustan Times*: October 27, 2003.

149 Enigma of India's Arrival, *Financial Express*: November 27, 2003.

150 Indian Metals Group in £600m U.K. Listing, *Daily Telegraph*: June 8, 2003.

151 Can India Turn Its Prosperity into Power?, *PR Newswire*: January 28, 2004.

152 NTPC Eyes Power Project in UK, Aims to Become MNC, *Hindu*: December 19, 2003.

153 India Offers to Build $1 bn. Liquefaction Plant in Iran, *PTI*: February 25, 2004.

154 India to Sign Agreement for Oil Exploration in Syria, *PTI*: November 15, 2003.

155 Japan and Russia Working Hard to Build Economic Ties, *New York Times*: January 23, 2004.

156 Malaysia Reconsiders Indian Role in Rail Project, *Financial Times*: December 2, 2003.

157 Have Resolve and Pride, *The Week*: January 27, 2002.

158 Tetley Bagged by India's Tata, *BBC News*: February 27, 2000.

159 U.S. and European Union Reach Deal on Farm Goods Trade, *Reuters*: August 13, 2003.

160 India to Resume Wheat, Rice Exports Soon, *Reuters*: August 11, 2003.

161 U.S. Braces for Farm Trade Suits After WTO Failure, *Reuters*: October 1, 2003.

162 Policy Made on the Road to Perdition, *Guardian*: October 13, 2003.

163 Cancun Collapse, *Washington Post*: September 16, 2003.

164 India Forsakes WTO for Trade Deals With Neighbours, *Financial Times*: October 16 2003.

165 Asia Aims for 'Common Market', *BBC News*: October 8, 2003.

166 India to Sign Trade Pact With ASEAN States, *Financial Times*: October 1, 2003.

167 India, S. American Bloc to Ink Trade Pact, *Reuters:* January 25, 2004.

168 G20 Optimistic on Trade, Cautious on 2004, *Reuters:* January 20, 2004.

169 India Eyes Brazil for Military Hardware, and More, *Asia Times:* December 11, 2003.

170 GCC Beckons India, *Indian Express:* October 8, 2003.

171 Role of the European Union in the Gulf Region, Gulf Research Center, 2003.

172 India Ready to Train Oman's Air Force, *PTI:* January 10, 2004.

173 Also see section 'Making Sense of Military Spending With PPP,' which explains that, taken together, India's and China's PPP-adjusted defence spending is in reality higher than that of the U.S.

174 Paul Kennedy, *Preparing for The Twenty-First Century*, Harper Collins, 1993.

175 India Unveils Huge Supercomputer, *BBC News:* April 1, 2003.

176 India Deploys Third Supercomputer in Russia, *Asia Pulse:* August 14, 2003.

177 The LCA is a "fifth-generation combat aircraft," with an "advanced fly-by-wire quadruplex digital flight control system" and "integrated digital avionics in an advanced open architecture." It employs one of the highest ratio of composites ever employed in an airframe (45 percent). See 'India's Indigenous Light Combat Aircraft,' *Air International:* November 2002.

178 Tejas Attains Supersonic Speed, *PTI:* November 27, 2003.

179 ADA in $3 million Deal to Supply Software to U.S. Firm for Airbus, *Economic Times:* July 17, 2001.

180 Russia Mulls New Military Airlifters, *Aviation International News:* Paris 2003.

181 INSAT Search & Rescue System Helps Save 28 Lives, *Spacedaily:* September 1, 2003.

182 Developing With The Aid of An Eye in The Sky, Spacenews: September 20, 1999.

183 India's Spy Satellite Boost, *BBC News:* November 27 2001.

184 Remote Sensing Tutorial Page 3-6, NASA (Rst.Gsfc.Nasa.Gov).

185 Remote Sensing of Forest Fires in Southern Europe Using IRS—WIFS and MODIS Data, Paulo M. Barbosa, Jesús San-Miguel- Ayanz, and Guido Schmuck, European Commission-DG Joint Research Centre: 2001 (JRC Italy).

186 Indian Army Has Been Quick to Learn, *Financial Times:* July 2, 1999.

187 India Sharing With U.S. Data From Spy Satellite, *Space News:* December 4, 2001.

188 Space Imaging Signs with Antrix to Continue Exclusive Access to India's Earth Imaging Satellites, *PR Newswire:* January 27, 2004.

189 India Turns on First Weather Bird, *Space Daily:* September 20, 2002.

190 India's Premier Space Agency to Build A Slew of Satellites, *AFP:* May 1, 2003.

191 India Too is Proud of its Civilian-Led Space Programme, *Financial Times:* October 20, 2003.

192 India to Build Sophisticated Radar Imaging Satellite, *Space Daily:* June 9, 2003

193 Launching Successes, *Hindu:* August 15, 2003.

194 India's Lofty Ambitions in Space Meet Earthly Realities, *New York Times:* January 24, 2004.

195 India Can Build Inter-Continental Ballistic Missile Within 2 Years: U.S., *PTI:* July 16, 2003.

196 India Launches METSAT Into Orbit With Improved PSLV Rocket, Space.Com: September 12, 2002.

197 Second GSLV Rocket Launched, *Spaceflight Now:* May 8, 2003.

198 India Develops Advanced Rocket Engine, *Associated Press:* December 5, 2003.

199 Future Space Missions, *Hindu:* October 25, 2003.

200 Israel's Shavit Launches Spysat Along Retrograde Flight Profile, *Spacenews:* May 28, 2003.

201 Brazil Will Continue Launch System Plans Despite Explosion, *Spacenews:* August 25, 2003.

202 Israel, India to Join Forces on Space Telescope, *AFP:* December 17, 2003.

203 The Space Aspects of The Emerging U.S.-India Alliance, *SpaceEquity:* November 15, 2002.

204 India Revels in New Diplomatic Offensive, *Asia Times:* November 22, 2003.

205 China and India Back EU's Space Race Against U.S., The *Daily Telegraph Online:* October 31, 2003.

206 "India is already self-sufficient in reactor design and construction, as well as uranium supply and fuel production, and China aims to become so." (Nuclear Power in India and China, *UIC Nuclear Issues Briefing Paper # 80:* June 2003).

207 Indian Atomic Scientists Design Novel N-Reactor, *Indian Express* January 4, 2003

208 Indian 'Look East' Policy Set to Succeed, *Stratfor:* January 17, 2001.

209 India to Sell Warships to Vietnam, *PTI:* August 28, 2003.

210 India + Iran = a foundation for stability, *International Herald Tribune:* February 6, 2003.

211 India, Israel to jointly market ALH, *PTI:* January 21, 2003.

212 'Others' Vie for a Place With The Big 5, *Aviation Today:* Rotor & Wing: June 2003.

213 U.S. Customs Likely to Buy Ten HAL Choppers, *PTI:* November 26, 2003.

214 Smart Materials Hold Key to Improved ALH Performance, *Hindu:* January 4, 2004.

215 Such an assessment also applies to the broader field of high technology. For instance, *The Economist* blandly proclaims: "China's "technological prowess (is) arguably greater than that of any other developing country," but offers no arguments. See 'Does China awake?' *The Economist:* October 4, 2003.

216 Jim Rohwer, *Asia Rising,* Simon & Schuster, 1995, pp 313.

217 Benchmarking the size of India's military against other developing country giants is fairly easy. Over the past 15 years, the Indian Air Force has lost more supersonic combat jets in accidents than exist cumulatively in South Africa and the entire continent of Latin America (Brazil, Argentina and Chile included).

218 Richard Bernstein and Ross H. Munro, *The Coming Conflict with China,* Vintage Books, 1998.

219 One of the few public sources for comparative assessment of Indian and Chinese military platforms is the Institute for Defense and Disarmament Studies, whose database is available at www.idds.org.

220 See, for example, U.S., India to Conduct Joint Air Combat Exercise, *Washington Post:* January 28, 2003.

221 India, Russia Sign Defence Deal, *BBC News:* January 20, 2004.

222 Air Defence Ship Facility Inaugurated, *Hindu,* January 24, 2003.

223 Icing on Gorshkov Cake for India: A Nuclear Submarine, *Indian Express:* December 2, 2002.

224 Richard Bernstein and Ross H. Munro, *The Coming Conflict with China,* Vintage Books, 1998.

225 India Challenges China in South China Sea, *Stratfor:* April 26, 2000.

226 Major Acquisitions in 2003 Boost Indian Navy, *Sify News:* December 19, 2003.

227 China Debates the Future Security Environment, Michael Pillsbury, National Defense University Press: January 2000.

228 ibid.

229 ibid.

230 See 'India Earthquake Update' series: January-February 2001, UN Disaster Management Team India. Also see 'Telemedicine: Emergence of The Virtual Doctor,' *Express Computer:* March 10, 2003.

231 Kalam for Creation of World Class Electronic Warfare System, *PTI:* January 19, 2004.

232 India and China Set Sights on Piracy, *International Herald Tribune:* November 23, 1999.

233 The Indian Navy in The Next Millennium, *Rediff on the Net:* December 9, 1999.

234 Tricky Arithmetic of Military Spending, *Financial Times*: February 9-10, 2003.

235 U.S. Opened Cyber-War During Kosovo Fight, *Washington Times*: October 25, 1999.

236 The Japan That Can Say No, Shinto Ishihara, Simon & Schuster: January 1991.

237 Man Admits to Illegal Campaign Donations, *Los Angeles Times*: February 12, 2004.

238 S-Cube CEO Offers Funds, Expertise for Start-Ups, *Hindu*, February 16, 2004.

239 Digit Enterprise Moving State of Montana's Project Management 'Into the Digital Age', Press Release: February 5, 2004.

240 U.S. Firms Lament Cutback in Visas for Foreign Talent, *Los Angeles Times*, February 16, 2004.

241 Inside Outsourcing in India, *CIO Magazine*: June 1, 2003.

242 GE Acquires TCS Engineering Arm, *Cyber India Online*: June 3, 2003.

243 Indian Software COs can tap $44-B U.S. Spend on Security, *Hindu*: February 6, 2004.

244 India Warns Against U.S. Security Software, *TechWeb*: January 15, 1999

245 Indian Company Develops 448-bit Encryption Package', InternetNews.com: November 4, 1998.

246 Outsourcing Our Future, *Los Angeles Times*: February 13, 2004.

247 Nasscom '04 to Focus on Security Concerns, *Hindu*: February 3, 2004.

248 Cyber Forensic Tools to Be Released Today, *Hindu*: February 19, 2004.

249 Police Log in Forensic Tools, *Hindu*: February 21, 2004.

250 SISA Ties Up for Octave, *Hindu*: February 6, 2004.

251 High-Tech Surprises From India, ID-Side: June 1998.

252 India's Nuclear Autonomy, *Washington Post*: July 3, 1998.

253 Confusion Over Supercomputers, Software and Sanctions, *Washington Post*: January 4, 1999.

254 US, India to Conduct Joint Air Combat Exercise, *Washington Post*: January 28, 2003.

255 India Aims High for Arms Exports, *Asia Times*: June 3, 2003.

256 Yes, A Security Council Seat for India, *International Herald Tribune*: February 10, 2003.

257 A Costly Charade at The UN, *Washington Post*: February 28, 2003.

258 Vote France Off The Island, *New York Times*: February 9, 2003.

259 Sweden Backs India's Bid for Permanent UNSC Seat, *AFP*: January 29, 2004.

260 Karzai Gets India Trade Pledge, *BBC News*: March 6, 2003. Both the country's President and its Foreign Minister are educated in Indian universities; other such examples include Myanmar's opposition leader and Nobel Laureate Aung San Suu Kyi and Nigeria's President Olesejun Obasanjo, one of Africa's only military leaders to have peacefully transferred power to a civilian government.

261 India to Help Rebuild Afghanistan's Phone Network, *Reuters*: March 28, 2003.

262 India's Diplomacy Course Wins High Marks Around The World, *Financial Times*: April 28, 2003. The article also mentions the growing popularity of the Indian program with diplomats in the Middle East, Africa as well as the former Soviet Union.

263 Global Security.Org.

264 New Policy on External Assistance Rooted in Nuclear Test Fallout, *Financial Express*: June 6, 2003.

265 India Joins IMF Pool of Lenders, *Associated Press*: June 29, 2003.

266 A Delicate U.S. Dance in S. Asia, *Los Angeles Times*: June 22, 2003. During the month, it was also reported that Russian President Vladimir Putin had proposed such an extension (see Walker's World: Putin's Regal Diplomacy, *UPI*: June 30, 2003).

267 Fool's Gold in Pakistan, *Washington Post*: June 29, 2003. The underlying theme of the difference in India's potential contribution vis-a-vis alternatives has strengthened since, at least in the U.S.

268 Lonely at The Top, *New York Times*: July 17, 2003. More recently, two Brookings Institution scholars separated India from "military middle-weights such as France,

Germany, Russia, Japan, and South Korea." See 'The Heavy Price of the U.S. Going It Alone,' *Financial Times*: August 5, 2003.

269 U.S. Presses India to Supply Iraq Peacekeepers, *Financial Times*: July 28, 2003.

270 Indian Warships to Provide Security for African Union Summit, *AFP*: July 5, 2003.

271 Indian Navy Warship Arrives on Friendly Visit to Nigeria, *AFP*: September 3, 2003.

272 Indian Navy to Guard Mauritian Waters, *Hindustan Times*: July 3, 2003.

273 "So far, the Jewish-Indian alliance in the United States has focused on foreign policy. But the two communities also have combined forces on electoral politics. They worked to defeat former House member Cynthia McKinney (D-Ga.), whom they perceived as antagonistic both to Israel and to India." See 'India, Israel Interests Team Up,' *Washington Post*: July 19, 2003.

274 Moon Mission Is Giant Step for Indian Science, *Financial Times*: August 15, 2003.

275 Space: India Wants The Moon, *UPI*: October 31, 2003.

276 India to Export LCAs Within Next Four to Five Years: George, *PTI*: September 5, 2003.

277 Indian PM: Sharon's Visit Will Raise Relations to 'New Level', *Haaretz*: September 9, 2003.

278 Seek India's Support, *Jerusalem Post*: September 6, 2003.

279 The intriguing possibility of a partnership between India and Israel in information technology was foreseen by this author. As he noted, given the Israelis "superb marketing skills and their ability to consistently leverage know-how at the upper end of the spectrum, one of the most interesting possibilities remains a combination of Indian and Israeli companies. This would be worth watching." See 'Made in India: The Other Country for Software," *ID-Side*: May 1998.

280 India-Israel Phalcon Deal in January, *Times of India*: December 26, 2003.

281 Indigenous AEWACS Being Revived: DRDO, *PTI*: December 3, 2003.

282 VSNL Cable to Land at Asia Netcom Site in Singapore, *Reuters*: February 19, 2004.

283 Pakistan's Electronic Data Becomes Insecure, *News International*: October 26, 2003.

284 Delhi Eyes Olympics Prize, *BBC News*: November 19, 2003.

285 Central Asia's Great Base Race, *Asia Times*: December 19, 2003.

286 India Revels in New Diplomatic Offensive, *Asia Times*: November 22, 2003.

287 Foothold in Central Asia: India Gets Own Military Base, *Indian Express*: November 12, 2003.

288 "Despite weathering the worst drought in living memory, India has granaries overflowing with foodgrain, forcing a worried government to get rid of the surplus.... India has had ever bigger farm harvests every year in the past 12 years." See 'Poverty-Stricken India Suffers Food Glut," *Asia Times*: June 27, 2000.

289 Jan Knappaert, *Malay Myths and Legends*, Heinemann, Singapore, 1980.

290 As 'Das Buch Beyspele' published in 1483, a German translation of the *Panchatantra* was one of the first books to ever be printed.

291 Power Projects of Bhutan, *Bhutan News Online*: February 5, 2001.

292 A Scarred Kingdom, *Rediff.com*, June 20, 2001.

293 Cross-Border Trade Can Raise Per Capita Income, *Hindustan Times*: December 14, 2003.

294 India, a Natural Ally, *Washington Times*: January 23, 2003.

295 India Concerned by U.S. Move to Restrict IT Trade, *IANS*: November 21, 2003.

296 Interview with Tariq Ali, *Progressive*: January 2002.

297 Cold War Thaw Warms Up U.S.-India Relationship, *Associated Press*: January 24, 2004.

298 U.S. Forces Continue Combined Training in India, *AFP*: May 23, 2002.

299 US-India Joint Exercise Begins in Alaska, Press Release, U.S. Embassy, New Delhi,

300 A Partnership of Unequals, *Asia Times*: January 21, 2004.

301 Indians, Americans Continue Wargames, *Associated Press*: September 12, 2003.

302 India, U.S. Hold Biggest Ever Joint Air Exercises, *PTI*: February 16, 2004.

303 India Begins Patrolling Malacca Straits, *Hindu*: April 20, 2002.

304 Engagement on The High Seas, *Frontline*: October 25, 2003.

305 Scientists Discuss Ways to Fight Terror, *Associated Press*: January 13, 2004.

306 Experts Debate Future of U.S.-Israel-India Cooperation, U.S. *Newswire*, February 13, 2004.

307 Bush Seeking Better U.S.-India Relations, *Associated Press*: January 20, 2004.

308 India Says Deeper Nuclear Ties With U.S. Marks Key Milestone in Ties, *AFP*: January 13, 2004.

309 Engagement on The High Seas, *Frontline*: October 25, 2003.

310 Experts Question Logic of Training Indian Troops at American School, *Financial Express*: May 2, 2002.

311 Two Join Missile Defense Program, *Washington Times*: January 14, 2004.

312 Expectations Were Not Realised, *Frontline*: July 4, 2003.

313 France, Germany Seek to Resume China Arms Sales, *Asia Times*, February 12, 2004.

314 Hu Visits France, *International Herald Tribune*: January 31, 2004.

315 Tibet Film Blasts 'Shangri-La Image', *BBC News*: January 8, 2004.

316 India Forced to Bite its Tongue, *Asia Times*: February 7, 2004.

317 Victor M. Gobarev, India as an Emerging World Power, *Cato Institute*: September 11, 2000.

318 Pakistan 'Regrets' 1971 War Excesses, CNN.com: July 29, 2002.

319 Transcript of interview with Noam Chomsky, *washingtonpost.com*, November 26, 2003.

320 For example, "President Clinton set aside part of his Independence Day to persuade Pakistan's Prime Minister, Nawaz Sharif, to back down on Kargil." See 'Kargil: The ongoing conflict,' *BBC News*: July 29, 1999.

321 Pakistan on the Brink, *Nation*: April 17, 2000.

322 Bitter Chill of Winter, *London Review of Books*: April 19, 2001.

323 'Canberra's in the Congo', in Chopra, Pushpindar Singh, William Green and Swanborough, Gordon. Eds. *The Indian Air Force and its Aircraft*. IAF Golden Jubilee. 1932-82. Ducimus Books, London, U.K., 1982.

324 Sir Brian Urquhart Interview: Institute of International Studies, *UC Berkeley*, 1996.

325 Indian Hinds to the Rescue, *Air Forces Monthly*: October 2000.

326 Nepal Seeks Indian Help to Turn Tide Against Rebels, *Reuters*: November 21, 2003.

327 ed. Eric Arnett, *Military Capacity and the Risk of War*, SIPRI 1997, page 264.

328 George Perkovich, *India's Nuclear Bomb*, University of California Press: 1999.

329 Ministry 'In No Hurry' to Put in Force Grain Export Scheme, *Hindu*: February 9, 2004.

330 Paul Krugman, *The Great Unravelling: From Boom to Bust in Three Scandalous Years*, Allen Lane, 2003.

331 Awareness about this huge difference in size is now seeping into the mass media. See 'More Arms Are Not What India and Pakistan Need,' *Los Angeles Times*: February 13, 2004.

332 International Political and Security Risks: What Can We Expect in 2004? *PR Newswire*: November 11, 2003.

333 When Jobs Flee: Cost and Benefit, *New York Times*: February 1, 2004.

334 Pakistan Ought to Concentrate on Pulling Itself Together, *International Herald Tribune*: July 14, 1999.

335 ibid.

336 U.S. Payrolls Change Lives, and Values, in India, *International Herald Tribune*: February 23, 2004.

Chapter Six

1   Living Longer With The Global Economy, *BusinessWeek:* June 27, 2003.
2   China and India: High Stakes for U.S. Interests, *International Herald Tribune:* June 23, 2003.
3   Welcome The Rise of China and India, *Telegraph Online:* October 12, 2003.
4   'Plunder' of Bengal, *Guardian:* February 11, 2004.
5   Mike Davis: *Late Victorian Holocausts: El Nino Famines and the Making of the Third World,* Verso Press, 2001.
6   The New Nationalist Movement in India, *Atlantic Monthly:* October 1908.
7   Captives to The Romance of The Subcontinent, *Los Angeles Times:* July 13, 2003.
8   Fashion from India: Beyond The Bangles, *New York Times:* May 13, 2003.
9   Bangalore—Better by Design, *BBC News:* December 15, 2003.
10 Granting Community Theft, *Guardian:* September 8, 2003.
11 RiceTec Loses in Basmati Battle, International Center for Technology Assessment: September 6, 2001.
12 U.S. Office Cancels Patent on Turmeric, *Hindu:* August 24, 1997.
13 Curry 'may treat radition burns,' *BBC News:* October 8, 2002.
14 Patent Your Heritage, *New York Times:* December 15, 2002.
15 Historical Evidence of Deception by Wireless Inventor Marconi, *Science:* January 23, 1998.
16 The Todays They Gave Have Been Forgotten, *Daily Telegraph,* November 9, 2003.
17 Sushruta was an ancient Indian surgeon (who was possibly born in 7th century BC) and is the author of the book *Sushruta Samhita,* which describes over 120 surgical instruments, 300 surgical procedures and classifies human surgery in 8 categories.
18 Capers Jones, *Psychology, Linguistics, and Physics in Northern India and China from the 6th Century B.C. to the 9th Century A.D,* Capers Jones, June 1997.
19 Denis Guedj, *Numbers: The Universal Language,* Thames and Hudson, New Horizons, 1996.
20 An Overview of Indian Mathematics, J J O'Connor and E F Robertson, University of St Andrews, Scotland: November 2000.
21 Aryabhata The Elder (476-550), J J O'Connor and E F Robertson, University of St Andrews, Scotland: November 2000.
22 Brahmagupta—598-670, J J O'Connor and E F Robertson, University of St Andrews, Scotland: November 2000.
23 Panini, J J O'Connor and E F Robertson, University of St Andrews, Scotland: November 2000.
24 4,000 BC is a "more realistic" date for India's Vedic chants. See 'UN boost for ancient Indian chants,' *BBC News:* February 20, 2004. Critics of India's 'Hindu' revival, closely connected as it to the Vedas, may be intrigued by this statement from American philosopher Henry David Thoreau. With "no touch of sectarianism," the Vedas offer "the royal road for the attainment of the Great Knowledge."
25 MIT Professor Impressed by Akshaya Project, *Hindu,* June 11, 2003.
26 Clinton Champions Information Technology for World's Poor, *Computerworld* Singapore: February 20, 2001.
27 Developing With The Aid of an Eye in The Sky, *Space News:* September 20, 1999.
28 A Blueprint for E-Seva, *Hindu,* July 28, 2002.
29 6,000 Rural E-Seva Kiosks to be Run by Self-Help Groups: *Hindu,* January 8, 2004.
30 Policing Gets A Digital Facelift, *Cyber India Online:* September 4, 2003.
31 Call-Centres to Harvest Indian Farm Woes, *BBC News:* January 24, 2004.
32 Book Rail Tickets on Internet and Sit with Computerised Slips, *PTI:* January 30, 2004.

33 Export/Import Forms go Online, *Cyber India Online*: January 30, 2004.
34 In a commentary in the *Financial Times*, this author noted that India had very different priorities from the U.S. and Russia or even China in terms of its civilian-led space program, which was "clearly the world's only one with an ambitious agenda for empowerment and economic development." See 'India Too Is Proud of Its Civilian-Led Space Programme,' *Financial Times*: October 20, 2003.
35 Polio Vaccine Drive Targets Children in India, *Associated Press*: April 6, 2003.
36 TN to Digitize Land Records This Year, *Cyber India Online*: July 16, 2003.
37 Village Kiosks Bridge India's Digital Divide, *Washington Post*: October 12, 2003.
38 India Leads World in ICT Kiosks, *Cyber India Online*: July 10, 2003.
39 The Telemedicine Revolution, *Hindu*: October 20, 2003.
40 India to Use Satellite for Health Care, *Associated Press*: February 10, 2004.
41 Healing Hearts by Remote Control, *BBC News*: August 14, 2003.
42 ibid.
43 E-Seva to Offer Online Medical Advice, *Hindu*, February 7, 2004.
44 Village Kiosks Bridge India's Digital Divide, *Washington Post*: October 12, 2003.
45 Std. XII Students to Take Exam Online, *New Indian Express*: February 25, 2004.
46 In Pune, Campus Goes Wire-Free to Network Afresh, *Indian Express*, February 16, 2004.
47 Challenges in Rural Connectivity for India, *Bytes for All.org*: May 15, 2002.
48 Information Technology Runs in The Family, *Hindu*: July 16, 2003.
49 A private consortium led by consumer electronics giant BPL is also establishing another (though smaller) fiber-optic national network.
50 India Telecoms 'Set to Invest $12bn in Network', *Financial Times*: December 29, 2003.
51 Reliance Aims to Treble Telecom Market Share, *Reuters*: December 30, 2003.
52 Reliance to Open All WebWorld Stores by End-'03, *Financial Express*: June 19, 2003.
53 Reliance Info Enters Home Phones, Applications Space, *Hindu*: July 13, 2003.
54 Reliance's Massive Rollout Claims A Wired Future at A Fraction, *Financial Express*: December 27, 2002. The network aims to eventually connect all India's 640,000 villages and over 2,000 towns and cities.
55 Trade Deficit Hits $489 Billion, *Washington Post*, February 14, 2004.
56 The Simputer, *New York Times*: December 9, 2001.
57 Transforming Public Health, Bus Travel and More, *Express Computer*: September 15, 2003.
58 Simputer May Be Used for Akshaya Project, *Hindu*: November 11, 2003.
59 corDECT Tech Finds Market in 10 Nations, *Hindu*: November 22, 2003.
60 India Tackles Adult Illiteracy, *BBC News*, January 3, 2004.
61 Open Software in Tamil Planned, *Hindu*: February 2, 2004.
62 C-DAC Makes Multipurpose Indian Language Solution, *Cyber India Online*: February 26, 2001.
63 Village Kiosks Bridge India's Digital Divide, *Washington Post*: October 12, 2003.
64 Clinton Champions Information Technology for World's Poor, *Computerworld* Singapore: February 20, 2001.
65 See, for example, 'Tata Steel Targets Rural Mart, Forms Special Group,' *Financial Express*: July 30, 2003.
66 HLL E-Shakti Going Places; to Cover 100 million in 3 Years, *Hindu*: November 18, 2003.
67 Internet Transforms Farming in India, *New York Times*: January 2, 2004.
68 India Celebrates 2003 as 'Golden Year', *Associated Press*: December 31, 2003.
69 New Credit Card Trick Invades SE Asia, *UPI*: November 18, 2003.
70 India's Manufacturers in Shackles, *BusinessWeek* Online: October 15, 2003.

71 Benefits From Call Centres Start to Trickle Down, *IANS*: December 27, 2003.

72 Le Forum Social á Bombay, de A á Z, *Le Soir*: January 16, 2004.

73 This author noted in 1995: "In just over two decades of independence, the republic of India abolished every single residual privilege of its nearly 550 royal families and several ten thousand feudal lords. Two decades before the term 'affirmative action' became popular in the U.S. in the late 1960s, India had begun reserving 25 percent of government jobs for minorities." See 'Investing in India: The Long-Term Choice,' Presentation to *Tijd Academie*, De Jachthoorn, Kontich: 21 November 1995.

74 India's New Politics of Preference, *Washington Post*: July 14, 2003.

75 Renaissance Man, *Wall Street Journal*, July 18, 2002.

76 Vajpayee's Grand Nephew Killed After Being Thrown Out of Train, *PTI*: January 26, 2004.

77 Indian Untouchable Rockets to Presidential Heights, IPS: July 29, 2002.

78 PM Launches Health Insurance for Senior Citizens, *PTI*: July 14, 2003.

79 Commentary: India Is Raising Its Sights At Last, *BusinessWeek*: December 8, 2003.

80 "Based on limited study, one argument in the relevant literature (about India's 'success as a democracy,' against all odds), suggests that India's democracy is mainly a legacy of British colonialism. This argument immediately runs into the problem of why democracy has not fared as well in some many other former British colonies, including in Pakistan." See Atul Kohli, *The Success of India's Democracy*, Cambridge University Press, 2001.

81 S.P. Sathe, *Judicial Activism in India: Transgressing Borders and Enforcing Limits*, Oxford University Press, 2002.

82 Delhi Bags U.S. Clean City Award, *PTI*: May 22, 2003.

83 Lord Woolf Discards The Sheep's Clothing, *Daily Telegraph Online*: July 10, 2003.

84 Such instances, of openly seeking to learn from India, are growing. For example, the University of Denver Chancellor has modified admissions procedures after he "visited a business school in India." See 'Giving Students Their Say in Admissions,' *Washington Post*: January 13, 2004.

    Another instance occurred after the U.S. blackouts in August 2003. As a British daily reported (U.S. Turns to India for Blackout Advice, *Financial Times*: August 29, 2003), a delegation of American energy regulators "turned to India for help. The country is a world leader in managing blackouts."

85 India's Top Court Backs Fees Cut, BBC News: February 27, 2004.

86 Bofors-India Again, *Frontline*: December 7, 2001.

87 Verdict? Not Guilty, *Tribune*: December 24, 2003.

88 Tehelka Lifts Lid Off Defence Deals, *Rediff.com*, March 13, 2001.

89 Advani Warns Cong Against Using Judeo Tapes, *PTI*: January 13, 2004.

90 India Not Yet IT Super Power: Murthy, *Cyber India Online*: February 5, 2004. The dialectics of such a perpetually self-correcting process also extend elsewhere. One of the only critics of the hallowed Indian Institutes of Technology is none other than the country's Human Resource Development Minister who says "scale spending on the premier technology schools of the country were not paying back ample dividends." See 'Murli Manohar Joshi questions quality of IITs,' *PTI*: January 16, 2004.

91 In Malaysia in the 1990s, says John Buckley, chief operating officer of PA Ventures, "the government threw loads of money at the telecom superhighway, but I have not heard very much about that at all and what it has done for the economy." See 'When governments bank on innovation,' *International Herald Tribune*: February 16, 2004.

92 As the *Wall Street Journal* reported in it post-mortem of L&H: the company was built on "national pride.... Soon Flanders, Belgium's Dutch-speaking region, formed a tax-exempt zone in Ieper—grandly known as the Flanders Language Valley—and showered

L&H with research grants." Stefaan Top, a Belgian venture capitalist, told the *Journal* that the "combination of ambitious entrepreneurs and a government that sorely wanted 'a local tech champion was a combustible mix—it was dangerous.'" See 'How High-Tech Dream Shattered in Scandal at Lernout & Hauspie,' *Wall Street Journal*: December 7, 2000.

93 Indian Women Politicians on Rise, *BBC News*: December 8, 2003.

94 A côté des syndicats directement liés aux différents partis marxistes et socialistes, l'Inde posséde des mouvements de masse d'un poids sans équivalent dans aucun autre pays. See 'A Bombay, les altermondialistes font un saut dans l'inconnu', *Le Monde*: January 16, 2004.

95 India to Reduce Number of Public Holidays, *Financial Times*: August 7, 2003.

96 'Very Rich' in Yes, Calcutta, *Washington Post*: September 24, 2003.

97 Investing in India: The Long-Term Choice, Presentation to *Tijd Academie*, De Jachthoorn, Kontich: 21 November 1995.

98 India Swear in Untouchable as President, CNN Online: July 25, 1997.

99 Where Freedom Reigns, *New York Times*: August 14, 2002. In 2000, Premji's holdings in Wipro made him wealthier than Warren Buffet or the Sultan of Brunei.

100 Miraculous Escape for Bihar Officials in Chopper Crash, *PTI*: February 12, 2004.

101 Stars Share Bollywood Power Crown, *BBC News*: December 2, 2003.

102 India to Reduce Number of Public Holidays, *Financial Times*: August 7, 2003.

103 Guarding Secularism, Religiously, In France, *International Herald Tribune*: February 9, 2004.

104 Gunning for Trouble, *Week*: July 13, 2003.

105 Storm Over Indian Women's Mosque, *BBC News*: January 27, 2004.

106 In India, Rulings for Women, by Women, *Washington Post*: October 5, 2003.

107 Secular Fundamentalism, *New York Times*: November 19, 2003.

108 Dress Code 'Farce' in France, *Globe and Mail*: January 26, 2004.

109 Aiming at Religious Signs, France Eyes Bandanas, Too, *New York Times*: January 21, 2004.

110 "The government should instead...construct a church in a 'very visible' location near the airport to convey the 'Greek Orthodox stamp of the nation,' the church's leader, Archbishop Christodoulos, said." See 'Villagers try to block Athens mosque plan,' *Guardian*, September 16, 2003.

111 Muslim Reinstated as Miss Croatia, *BBC News*, October 28, 1998.

112 The Message of India's Miracle, *International Herald Tribune*: August 15, 2002.

113 Where Your Job Is Going? , *Fortune*: November 24, 2003.

114 Tina Turner Tours India for Film Role, *Associated Press*: February 22, 2004.

115 France's *Le Monde* has understood the key to India's success in implementing reforms is that the program is consensual, step-by-step and 'prudent.' See, for instance, 'L'Inde, apótre d'une libéralisation tempérée,' *Le Monde*: January 16, 2004.

116 Coke to Invest $70 Mn More in India, *Indian Express*: February 17, 2004.

117 Coca-Cola Water Ban 'Unfortunate', *BBC News*: February 18, 2004.

118 Some NGOs still contend that today's poverty rate is actually closer to 35%. Firstly, we must keep in mind the finding of the World Bank (noted in Chapter III) that India's data collection and data analysis techniques "have now become common currency throughout the world." Even should one accept the larger figure as being reality, the number would still be over 500 million.

119 World's Poor Down by 350 million, *Sydney Morning Herald*: May 29, 2002.

120 India and China Fuel Global Recovery, *Asia Times*: January 16, 2004.

121 Cela para't contredire l'observation selon laquelle le fossé entre les pauvres et les riches (non plus par pays, mais par personne) se réduit. C'est exact, mais les chiffres sont

biaisés par le fait que la Chine et l'Inde combinent une population énorme avec une croissance rapide des revenus par personne. See 'Les trois mots-clés de Davos,' *Le Monde*: January 21, 2004.

122 Selected Indicators, Ministry of Finance, *Government of India*, 2002.
123 'Very Rich' in Yes, Calcutta, *Washington Post*: September 24, 2003.
124 GDP Growth Fails to Check Plunge in Jobs, *Hindu*: December 30, 2003.
125 Dalits, femmes et exclus de la société indienne se retrouvent á Bombay, *Le Monde*: January 16, 2004.
126 The Leeward Side, *Outlook*: January 26, 2004.
127 The Job Circus, *Outlook*: February 2, 2004.
128 Strike Hits Banking, Insurance Sectors, *Hindu*: February 25, 2004.
129 BPO Industry Can Create 30 million Jobs in India by 2020, *PTI*: November 18, 2003.
130 Rob Jenkins, *Democratic Politics and Economic Reform in India*, Cambridge University Press, 1999.
131 From The Highlands to Your Grocer, *New York Times*: September 28, 2003.
132 Europe's Subsidy Junkies Stay Hooked, *Observer*: June 29, 2003.
133 India Farm Subsidies Set To Stay, *BBC News*, November 24, 2003.
134 UN Study Finds Global Trade Benefits are Uneven, *New York Times*: February 24, 2004.
135 Global Economy 'Must Adjust to Include Millions it puts in Poverty,' *Guardian*: February 25, 2004.
136 Foreign Activists Hardly Interact With Indian Hosts, *AFP*: January 24, 2004.
137 Persecuted, Suppressed, Abused Roma are Scattered Worldwide, *Guardian*: February 5, 2004.
138 U.S. Urges EU to Eliminate Subsidies on Farm Exports, *Associated Press*: February 21, 2004.
139 India Ready to Shift Stance on Farm Subsidies, *Financial Times*: February 24, 2004.

Chapter Seven

1 Tech Industry's Data Crunch, *Washington Post*: April 20, 1998.
2 Why Tech Companies Have an India Jones, eCompany.com: June 2000.
3 'Curb on U.S. Visas Confronts India's Tech Industry,' *International Herald Tribune*: October 1, 2003.
4 Getting A Job in The Valley Is Easy, If You're Perfect, *New York Times*: November 19, 2003.
5 The picture was remarkably similar in Europe. In May 2001, "two in five European companies cited 'lack of IT talent and manpower' as a hurdle to reaching IT goals." See 'IT spending bucks the trend,' *Network News*: May 23, 2001.
6 Indian IT Will Be Hard Hit by H1-B Visa Cut, *IANS*: September 24, 2003.
7 Brain Curry: American Campuses Crave for IIT of Glory, *Indian Express*: December 7, 1999.
8 The Trend of Vanishing Tech Jobs, *New York Times*: January 29, 2004.
9 Concern Over Outsourcing, But No Solutions, *IANS*: October 24, 2003.
10 Senate Passes Law Against Outsourcing of Government Contracts, *PTI*: January 24, 2004.
11 Asia Should Be Worrying About Its Dollar Reserves, *International Herald Tribune*: February 25, 2004.
12 A Hegemon No More, *Washington Times*, October 19, 2003.
13 "GE, incidentally, now employs more people in India than in America." See 'Outsourcing to India: Back office to the world,' *Economist*: May 5, 2001.

14 California Income Gap Grows Amid Prosperity, *Los Angeles Times*: January 9, 2000.
15 Banishing the 'Sweatshop' Label, *Financial Times*: April 4, 2001.
16 U.S. Relies on Foreign-Born Scientists ñReport, *Reuters*: November 19, 2003.
17 Dot.Com Firms Line Up to Recruit IIM-L Students, *Indian Express*: February 20, 2000.
18 Work Permit Rules Relaxed, *Press Association*: October 31, 2003.
19 Doctor Practicing Patience, *Akron Beacon Journal*: October 28, 2003.
20 Doctors Eying the U.S.: Canada Is Sick About It, *New York Times*: October 17, 2003.
21 *Monthly Labor Review*: December 2001.
22 Nursing Ambitions? The U.S. Beckons, *Hindu*: December 8, 2003.
23 New Visa Ceiling Called Threat to Teacher Recruitment, *Washington Post*: March 8, 2003.
24 L-1 Visas: 'Specialised Knowledge' the Contentious Issue: *Hindu*: February 7, 2004.
25 Second Best May Suffice for Man of the People, *Guardian*: February 9, 2004.
26 Indische Olifanten Krijgen Reflectoren, *De Standaard*, July 22, 2003.
27 Pension Rights for Indian Elephants, *BBC News*: July 24, 2003.
28 Indian Elephants Unwind At Camp, *BBC News*: November 16, 2003.
29 Fast Food, *Forbes*: August 10, 1998.
30 Brain Drain Costs Asia Billions, *BBC News*: July 10, 2001.
31 Techies Wanted, *BusinessWeek*: October 16, 2000.
32 Mihir A. Desai, Devesh Kapur, John McHale, *The Fiscal Impact of the Brain Drain: Indian Emigration to the U.S*, Harvard University, December 2001.
33 Should the Poor Subsidise the IITians? Times News Network, September 9, 2003.
34 IT Professionals Return to India, *BBC News*: July 23, 2003.
35 Farewell My 'H1-Bs': Indian Tech Workers Depart, But Change U.S., *Pacific News Service*: August 18, 2003.
36 Indians Returning Home for Better Jobs, *UPI*: September 6, 2003.
37 Building the New India, *Far Eastern Economic Review*: July 20, 2000.
38 The New Global Job Shift, *BusinessWeek*: February 3, 2003.
39 Silicon Valley: Visas Down, Job Exports Up, *Los Angeles Times*: October 20, 2003.
40 Oracle to Double Its Staff in India, *Financial Times*: July 10, 2003.
41 Tesco Relocates IT to India, *Daily Telegraph*: July 18, 2003
42 BCS Says Regulation Is No Defence Against Offshore Rivals, *CBR* Magazine: November 6, 2003.
43 New Markets: Untapped Almost, *Voice & Data*: September 29, 2003.
44 Business Organization Says Valley Is 'At A Crossroads,' *Mercury News*: September 11, 2003.
45 The Productivity Advantage in Trade, *Washington Times*: August 27, 2003.
46 ibid.
47 Hidden Costs: Travel Time and Expense Add Up Quickly, *TechWeb*: October 21, 2003.
48 Bush Provides Jobs and Reasons to Vote, *Los Angeles Times*: January 25, 2004.
49 Despair of The Jobless, *New York Times*: August 7, 2003.
50 Nike Accused Of Tolerating Sweatshops, *Observer*: May 20, 2001.
51 USA's New Money-Saving Export: White-Collar Jobs, *USA Today*: August 5, 2003.
52 "Offshore delivery, especially from India, has clearly demonstrated the lower cost and increased service delivery advantage. The cliché, they come for cost and stay for quality, has been aptly demonstrated," says Sujay Chohan, Vice President of The Gartner Group. See 'Backlash Can't Harm Offshoring: Gartner,' *Cyber India Online*: June 24, 2003.
53 Manufacturing More Confusion, *Washington Times*: January 16, 2004.

54 India's GDP in PPP in 2002 was $2,694 billion (source: World Bank) while its GDP in U.S. dollars was $529 billion (source: U.S. Department of Commerce). The multiplier would therefore be the ratio between the two, or 5.09.

55 A typical example: Software engineers in India "earn roughly one fifth of what their counterparts earn in the United States". See 'Global Tech Firms Compete to Hire Indian Staff,' *Reuters:* May 28, 2003.

56 Job Exports May Imperil U.S. Programmers, *Associated Press:* July 13, 2003.

57 Those Number Crunchers Need Some Careful Analysis, *Daily Telegraph:* September 1, 2003.

58 Jobs Cut Since 2001 Gone for Good: U.S. Study, *Business Times:* September 29, 2003.

59 "High taxes and property prices mean that even the well-paid in Britain are worse off than their counterparts in some developing countries, according to an international survey published this week." See 'It's Tough at The Top in Britain,' *Daily Telegraph:* July 19, 2003.

60 India—An Emerging IT Superpower, *Business Eye:* September 1998.

61 Indian IT Pros Get a Raw Deal in IT, *Hindustan Times*, January 7, 2002.

62 India Calling, *UPI:* October 23, 2003.

63 The source for all the numbers below consist of population levels in 2002 from the United Nations Economic and Social Affairs Department, and PPP-adjusted gross domestic product (GDP) data from the World Bank's *World Development Indicator Database*, also for the year 2002.

64 Without PPP, the American figure would change to just over 5 days equivalence.

65 Economic Scene: Layoffs Hurt Workers Well Into The Next Job, *International Herald Tribune:* November 3, 2003.

66 Indian Pay Rises Highest in Asia, *BBC News:* November 12, 2003.

67 U.S. Firms Lament Cutback in Visas for Foreign Talent, *Los Angeles Times*, February 16, 2004.

Chapter Eight

1 Two Steps to Protecting Your Job From Offshore Outsourcing, *CNET Networks:* October 16, 2003.

2 First the Jobs, Now Execs are heading for India, *International Herald Tribune:* January 26, 2004.

3 US, British IT Professionals Seek Job Opportunities in India, *IANS:* January 21, 2004.

4 Lure Expat Talent for High-End Work: Panel, *Hindu:* February 14, 2004.

5 Sis Starved for Quality Manpower, *Cyber India Online:* January 19, 2004.

6 Theory vs. Reality, *New York Times:* February 23, 2004.

7 Laid-Off Programmers Sue for Aid, *Associated Press:* January 29, 2004.

8 Concern Over Outsourcing, But No Solutions, *IANS:* October 24, 2003.

9 Indian jobs, U.S. angst, *International Herald Tribune:* February 23, 2004.

10 Outsourcing Remarks by White House Advisor Stir Backlash, *Financial Times:* February 12, 2004.

11 Brown Attacked Over Jobs Exodus, *Guardian:* February 9, 2004.

12 Who Wins in Offshoring, *McKinsey Quarterly:* No. 4, 2003.

13 A step has already been taken in Britain, where financial services giant HSBC has undertaken to provide unions with two years' notice of its 'global resourcing' plans. See 'HSBC in pact with union on Asia jobs,' *Telegraph* Online: February 17, 2004.

14 For example, IBM cut 720 of its 180,000 services employees "as part of an effort to match workers' skills with jobs.... The cuts are part of the company's regular skills rebal-

ancing, the term it uses for efforts to match worker skills to the types of services it is offering." See 'IBM Cuts About 720 U.S. Global Services Positions,' *Reuters:* October 2, 2003.

15 IBM Chief Executive Samuel Palmisano says he foresees the need in 2004 'for approximately 10,000 new positions in key skill areas.' See 'For Many Firms, Jobless Recovery Is a Good Thing,' *Los Angeles Times:* November 12, 2003.

16 One effect would be to prevent another round of translucent disclosures, such as that by PeopleSoft, which seeks to add 1,000 Indian technology staff by the end of 2004, but pads this figure against its employment of "more than 12,000 people worldwide." See 'PeopleSoft to Triple Staff in India,' *CNET News.Com:* February 17, 2004.

17 Bush's Call for Job Training: Cruel Joke on Unemployed, *Los Angeles Times:* January 25, 2004.

18 BT Outlines Exact Offshore Strategy, *CBR Magazine:* December 3, 2003.

19 U.S. Tech Services Giants Shifting Offshore, *Reuters:* November 26, 2003.

20 Indiana State Weighs Response to High-Tech Outsourcing After TCS Row, *Reuters:* November 26, 2003.

21 Watching the Jobs Go By, *New York Times:* February 11, 2004.

22 Giving Students Their Say in Admissions, *Washington Post:* January 13, 2004.

23 U.S. Turns to India for Blackout Advice, *Financial Times:* August 29, 2003.

24 After IIM, IIT Fees May Be Cut Too, *Economic Times:* January 19, 2004.

25 For 2003-2004, MIT's fees were $14,700 per semester and $9,800 for the summer term.

About the Author

Ashutosh Sheshabalaya is a commentator on Indian issues. He has had a varied career: foreign correspondent for the Press Trust of India, consultant with PriceWaterhouse, head of communications at the European pharmaceutical industry federation EFPIA, and guest professor at the Brussels business school ICHEC. He is presently managing director of Allilon, a Belgian IT services firm specialized in modernizing legacy systems.

Sheshabalaya was a National Science Talent Scholar at BITS Pilani, one of India's top engineering schools, but left to study philosophy at Brandeis University in the U.S. after winning a Wien International Scholarship. He graduated in politics and economics from Berhampur University in India.